Contents

PAPER ONE

PAPER TWO

Chapter 1
Arithmetic

Ratio and proportion

Type 1

Divide €5550 in the ratio $\frac{3}{4} : 2\frac{1}{3}$

(i) $\frac{3}{4} : \frac{7}{3}$

(ii) Write both with common denominators $\frac{9}{12} : \frac{28}{12}$

(iii) Drop the common denominators and continue as normal.

$$\Rightarrow \quad 9 : 28$$

$$= \frac{9}{37} : \frac{28}{37} \qquad [9 + 28 = 37]$$

$$\frac{1}{37} = €5550 \div 37 = €150$$

$$\Rightarrow \frac{9}{37} = €150 \times 9 = €1350$$

$$\frac{28}{37} = €150 \times 28 = €4200$$

Type 2

€220 is divided between A, B and C such that B got twice as much as A and C received 4 times B's share. How much did each receive?

With questions such as this...

① Read through very carefully.

② Let the smallest share equal 1.

③ Find the other share(s).

* From the story it's obvious that A received the smallest share.

$$A : B : C$$

$$1 : 2 : 8$$

$$\Rightarrow \frac{1}{11} : \frac{2}{11} : \frac{8}{11}$$

$$\frac{1}{11} = €220 \div 11 = €20$$

⇒ A received €20

B received €40 [€20 × 2]

C received €160 [€20 × 8]

Type 3

€y is divided between John and Mary in the ratio 4 : 7. If John received €128 how much did Mary get?

$$\text{John} : \text{Mary}$$

$$4 : 7$$

$$\Rightarrow \frac{4}{11} : \frac{7}{11}$$

$$€128 = \frac{4}{11}$$

$$\Rightarrow \frac{1}{11} = €128 \div 4 = €32$$

Think about why we divide by 4 and not 11.

$$\Rightarrow \text{Mary received } \frac{7}{11}$$

$$= €224 \; [€32 \times 7]$$

Percentages/VAT

Type 1

A TV costs €1008 which includes 12% VAT. What would the percentage VAT be if the cost was reduced to €972?

€1008 incl. 12% VAT

$$\Rightarrow \quad €1008 = 112\%$$

$$\frac{1008}{112} = €9 = 1\%$$

$$\Rightarrow \text{ Cost without VAT} = 100\%$$

$$= €9 \times 100 = €900$$

$$\% \text{ VAT} = \frac{\text{VAT}}{\text{Cost without VAT}} \times \frac{100}{1}$$

⇒ If cost was €972, €72 was the added VAT

$$\% \text{ VAT} = \frac{72}{900} \times \frac{100}{1} = 8\%$$

Type 2

Denis buys 5 houses in a new development for €240,000 each. He later sells 2 at a 30% profit, 2 at a 40% profit and the last one for a 20% loss. Find his overall profit/loss on the overall transaction.

First 2 houses

Cost price = €480,000

Selling price = €480,000 × 1.30

= €624,000

Second 2 houses

Selling price = €480,000 × 1.40

= €672,000

Final House

Selling price = €240,000 × 0.80

= €192,000

Total cost price = €240,000 × 5

= €1,200,000

Total selling price = €624,000

€672,000

+ €192,000

€1,488,000

$$\% \text{ profit} = \frac{\text{Profit}}{\text{Cost price}} \times \frac{100}{1}$$

$$= \frac{288{,}000}{1{,}200{,}000} \times \frac{100}{1}$$

$$= 24\% \text{ profit}$$

Tax questions

Type 1

Seán earns €30,000. His tax credit is €3500 and his standard rate cut-off point is €12,000. Calculate the total tax paid if his standard tax rate is 28% and he has a higher rate of 42%.

Tax due at standard rate

€12,000 at 28% = €3360

Tax due at higher rate

€30,000 – €12,000 = €18,000

€18,000 at 42% = €7560

Note

Tax due – tax credits = Tax paid

Total tax due = €3360 + €7560

= €10,920

– Tax credit = €3500

€7420

⇒ Total tax paid = €7420

Type 2

Bill pays €7500 in tax. He has a standard rate cut-off of €20,000, a tax credit of €3000, a standard tax rate of 14% and a higher tax rate of 35%. Calculate his total earnings.

Very important

Before starting this question calculate the tax due.

Tax due = tax paid + tax credits

⇒ Tax due = €7500 + €3000

= €10,500

€10,500

14% of €20,000 = €2800

35% of x = €7700

Note

① x = remainder of income

② €7700 = €10500 – €2800

Find x

35% = €7700

1% = €7700 ÷ 35

= €220

⇒ 100% = €22,000

⇒ Total earnings = €20,000 + €22,000

= €42,000

Money in the bank

Note 1

€440 is lodged at x% interest. If there is €506 in the bank after 1 year, find x.

start of year [€440]

↓

end of year [€506]

$$\text{Rate} = \frac{\text{interest}}{\text{a/m at start}} \times \frac{100}{1}$$

$$\Rightarrow \text{Rate} = \frac{€66}{€440} \times \frac{100}{1}$$

$$= \boxed{15\%}$$

Note 2

€x is lodged at 8% interest. Find x if there is €378 in the bank at the end of the year.

start [€x]

↓

end [€378]

Amount at the start of the year is always 100%.

Rate = 8%

$$€378 = 108\%$$

$$€378 \div 108 = 1\%$$

$$\Rightarrow 3.5 = 1\%$$

$$x = 100\% = \boxed{€350}$$

Note 3

How much does €2000 amount to after 3 years at 15% compound interest?

Year 1

$$€2000 \times 0.15 = €300$$

$$\Rightarrow \text{end yr } 1 = €2000 + €300$$

$$= €2300$$

Year 2

$$€2300 \times 0.15 = €345$$

$$\Rightarrow \text{end yr } 2 = €2300 + €345$$

$$= €2645$$

Year 3

$$€2645 \times 0.15 = €396.75$$

$$\Rightarrow \text{end yr } 3 = €2645 + €396.75$$

$$= €3041.75$$

Sample question

Gillian borrows €8000 at a rate of 12% compound interest.

(i) How much is owed after 2 years?

Year 1 $€8000 \times 0.12 = €960$

end yr 1 = €8000 + €960

Year 2 $€8960 \times 0.12 = €1075.20$

end yr 2 = €8960 + €1075.20

= €10,035.20

(ii) If €x is paid back at the end of year 2, find x if there is still €10,350 owed at the end of year 3. The rate for year 3 is 15%.

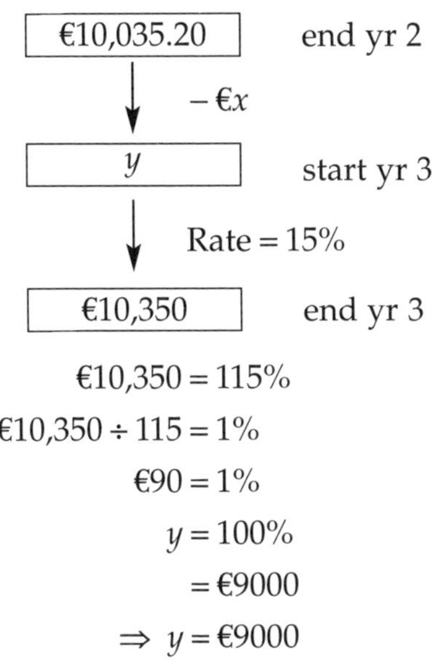

$$€10{,}350 = 115\%$$
$$€10{,}350 \div 115 = 1\%$$
$$€90 = 1\%$$
$$y = 100\%$$
$$= €9000$$
$$\Rightarrow y = €9000$$

So amount paid back (x)

$$= €10{,}035.20 - €9000$$
$$= €1035.20$$

(iii) Find the rate for year 4 if Gillian owes €12,420 at the end of year 4.

start yr 4 | €10,350 |
↓ $r = ?$
end yr 4 | €12,420 |

$$\text{Rate} = \frac{€2070}{€10{,}350} \times \frac{100}{1}$$

$\Rightarrow$ rate for yr 4 = 20%

Chapter 1 Sample questions for you to try

Question 1

(a) John is going on holiday and goes to the bank to change €400 into Japanese yen. The exchange rate is €1 = 85 yen.

(i) Calculate how many yen John receives if the bank charges 1.5% commission

(ii) While in Japan, John purchases a coat for 20,400 yen. He returns to Ireland and sells the coat, making a 12% profit. How much (in euros) did he sell the coat for.

(b) An amount of money is divided between John, Mary and Seán such that Mary got 4 times Seán's share and John received $\frac{1}{2}$ of Seán's share. Mary got €80 more than the other two together. Calculate what each received.

(c) A bike costs €434 which includes 24% VAT.

(i) If the bike is sold for €399 calculate the percentage VAT.

(ii) If the rate of VAT is reduced to 8% what would the bike cost?

Question 2

(a) Tom has a standard rate cut-off of €14,000 and tax credits of €5000. His standard rate of tax is 15% and he has a higher rate of 45%.

Calculate his total earnings if he pays €2050 tax.

(b) €2000 is lodged for 3 years at 5% compound interest.

(i) How much was in the bank at the end of the third year?

(ii) If there is €2407.86 in the bank at the end of year 4, calculate the interest rate for that year.

(c) Divide €1350 in the ratio $\frac{3}{4} : 1\frac{1}{3}$

Question 3

(a) **(i)** €x is lodged at 15% interest. If there is €460 at the end of year 1, find x.

(ii) The money is left in the bank for a second year and earns €55.20 interest. Calculate the rate of interest for year two.

(b) Marian earns €38,000. Her standard rate cut-off is €22,000. She has a standard rate of 22% and a higher rate of 40%. Calculate the total tax paid if her tax credits amount to €3500.

(c) €1000 is divided between A, B and C such that A gets €312.50 and B gets €437.50. If the money was divided in the ratio $x : y : z$, express the ratio in its simplest form.

Solution to question 1

(a)

> **(i)** Calculate how many yen he received if he is charged $1\frac{1}{2}\%$ commission.

$$€400 = (400 \times 85) \text{ yen}$$
$$= 34{,}000 \text{ yen}$$

Find $1\frac{1}{2}\%$

$$\frac{34{,}000 \times 1.5}{100} = 1\frac{1}{2}\% = 510 \text{ yen}$$

$\Rightarrow$ John received

$$34{,}000 - 510 = 33{,}490 \text{ yen}$$

> **(ii)** How much (in euros) did he sell the coat for?

$$\text{Cost price} = 20{,}400 \text{ yen}$$
$$= €(20{,}400 \div 85)$$
$$= €240$$

He makes a 12% profit

$$\Rightarrow \text{Selling price} = €240 \times 1.12$$
$$= €268.80$$

(b)

Having read the question again we find that John received the smallest share. We let the ratio representing John's share be 1.

John	:	Mary	:	Seán
1	:	8	:	2
$\Rightarrow \frac{1}{11}$	:	$\frac{8}{11}$	:	$\frac{2}{11}$

'Mary got €80 more than John and Seán together.'

$$\Rightarrow \frac{8}{11} \text{ is €80 more than } \frac{1}{11} + \frac{2}{11}$$

$$\Rightarrow €80 = \frac{5}{11}$$

Find $\frac{1}{11}$

$$€80 \div 5 = \frac{1}{11}$$

$$\Rightarrow €16 = \frac{1}{11}$$

⇒ John received €16

Mary received €128 (€16 × 8)

Seán received €32 (€16 × 2)

(c)

€434 includes 24% VAT

⇒ €434 = 124%

€434 ÷ 124 = €3.5 = 1%

Cost without VAT = 100% = €350

(i) Find % VAT if cost is €399.

$$\text{VAT} = €399 - €350$$
$$= €49$$

$$\%\text{VAT} = \frac{\text{VAT}}{\text{cost without VAT}} \times \frac{100}{1}$$

$$\Rightarrow \%\text{VAT} = \frac{49}{350} \times \frac{100}{1}$$
$$= 14\%$$

(ii) Find the cost if VAT was 8%.

Cost with 8% VAT = 108%

= €3.5 × 108 = €378

Solution to question 2

(a)

Again it is very important to base this question on tax due and not tax paid.

	€
Tax paid	2050
Tax credit	+ 5000
Tax due	7050

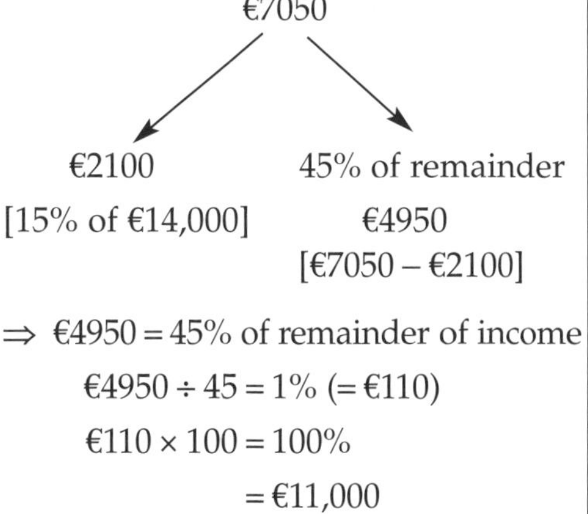

€14,000 is taxed at 15% rate

€11,000 is taxed at 45% rate

⇒ €25,000 = total wage

(b) (i)

Year 1 €2000 × 1.05

= €2100 @ end yr 1

Year 2 €2100 × 1.05

= €2205 @ end yr 2

Year 3 €2205 × 1.05

= €2315.25 @ end yr 3

(ii)

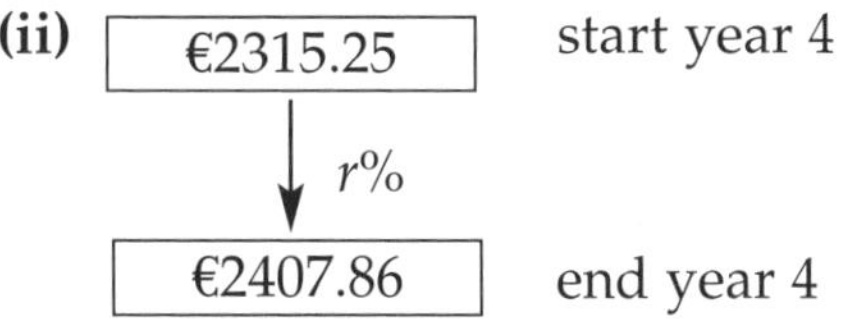

Interest earned = €2407.86 – €2315.25

= €92.61

$$\Rightarrow \text{Interest Rate} = \frac{92.61}{2315.25} \times \frac{100}{1}$$
$$= 4\%$$

(c) Divide €1350 in the ratio

$$\frac{3}{4} : 1\frac{1}{3}$$

$$\frac{3}{4} : \frac{4}{3}$$

① Write each fraction with a common denominator.

$$\frac{9}{12} : \frac{16}{12}$$

② 'Drop' the denominator

9 : 16

③ Carry on as normal.

$$\Rightarrow \frac{9}{25} : \frac{16}{25}$$

④ Find $\frac{1}{25}$

$$€1350 \div 25 = €54$$

$$\Rightarrow \frac{9}{25} = €54 \times 9 = €486$$

$$\Rightarrow \frac{16}{25} = €54 \times 16 = €864$$

Solution to question 3

(a) (i)

€x Start of year (always 100%)

↓ $r = 15\%$

€460 end of year

$$\Rightarrow €460 = 115\%$$

$$\frac{€460}{115} = €4 = 1\%$$

$$\Rightarrow \quad €x = 100\% = €400$$

(ii)

€460 start of yr 2

↓ $r = ?$

€460 + €55.20 = €515.20 end of yr 2

$$\text{Interest Rate} = \frac{55.20}{460} \times \frac{100}{1}$$

$$= 12\%$$

(b)

Tax due

€22,000 at 22% = €4840

€16,000 at 40% = €6400

Total tax due → €11,240

– Tax credits €3500

€7740

⇒ Tax paid = €7740

(c) €1000

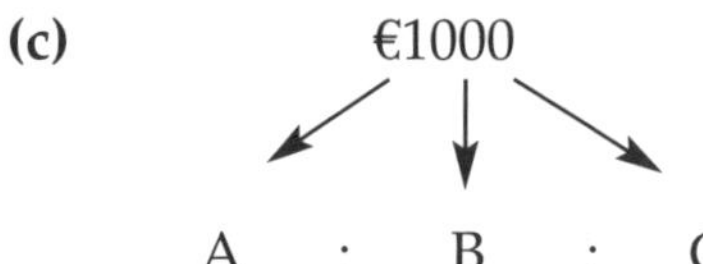

A : B : C

€312.50 : €437.50 : €250

[€1000 – (€312.50 + €437.50) = €250]

= 31,250 : 43,750 : 25,000

[÷ 50] ⇒ 625 : 875 : 500

[÷ 25] ⇒ 25 : 35 : 20

[÷ 5] ⇒ 5 : 7 : 4

Chapter 2

Sets, Indices and Surds

Questions involving sets

Questions with two Venn diagrams

Type 1

30 pupils are in a class. 23 pupils (of course) follow Celtic with 4 following Rangers. If 6 follow neither team, calculate how many follow both.

We are asked to calculate the number who follow both, so we let this amount be x.

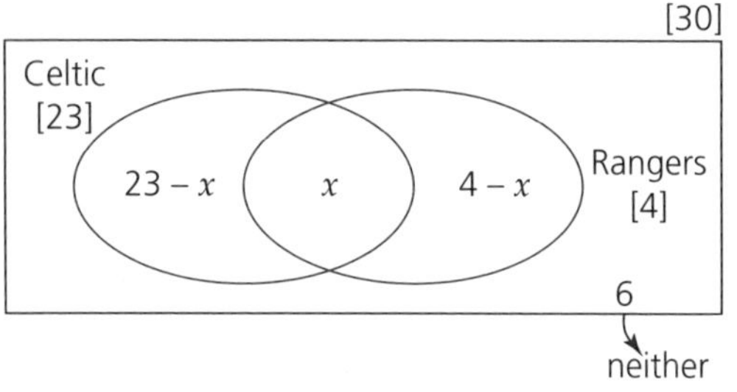

6 follow neither. 30 in total.

$$\Rightarrow (23 - x) + (x) + (4 - x) + 6 = 30$$
$$\Rightarrow 23 - \cancel{x} + \cancel{x} + 4 - x + 6 = 30$$
$$\Rightarrow 23 + 10 - x = 30$$
$$\Rightarrow 33 - x = 30$$
$$\Rightarrow 33 - 30 = x$$
$$\Rightarrow \boxed{3 = x}$$

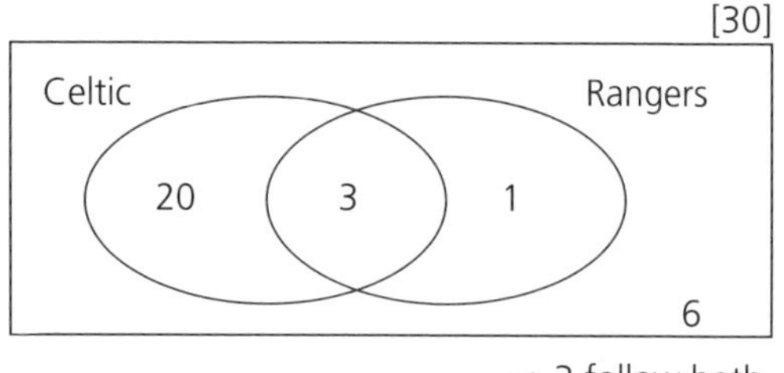

$\Rightarrow$ 3 follow both

To check

$*\ 20 + 3 + 1 + 6 = 30$ ✓

Type 2

Given $\# U = a$ $\quad \# X = b$
$\# Y = c$ $\quad \# X \cap Y = d$
and $\#(X \cup Y)' = e$

(i) Complete the diagram below and express e in terms of a, b, c and d.

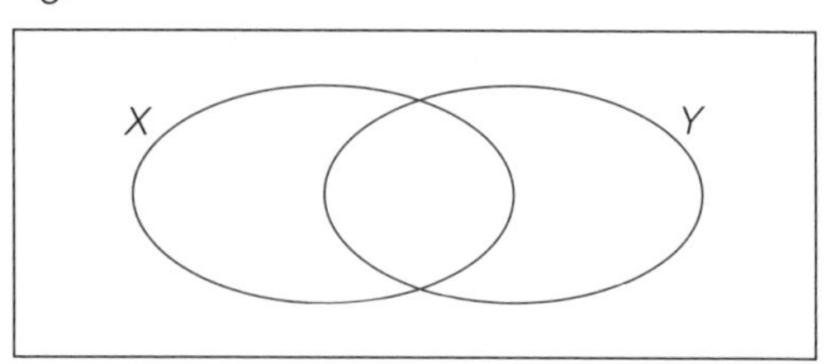

Solution

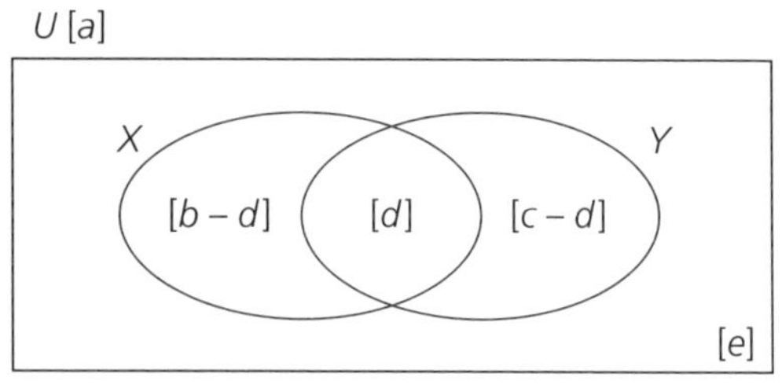

* Please note that the square brackets must be included.

Obviously $a = b - d + d + c - d + e$

$\Rightarrow a - (b - d + d + c - d) = e$

$\Rightarrow a - b + \cancel{d} - \cancel{d} - c + d = e$

$\Rightarrow a - b - c + d = e$

$\Rightarrow e = a - b - c + d$

(ii) If $b > c$, show that the maximum value of e is $a - b$.

U [*a*]

X [*b* – *c*] [*c*] [*c* – *c*] 0 *Y*

e

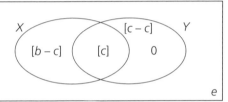

$\Rightarrow e = a - (b - c + c)$

$e = a - b + c - c$

$\Rightarrow e = a - b$

(iii) Show also that if $b = c$

① The maximum value of e is $a - c$.

② The minimum value of e is $a - 2c$.

①

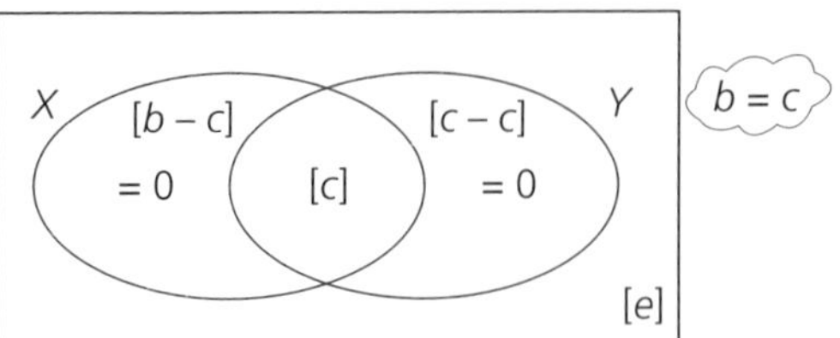

Important to know if e must be as big as possible, $X \cap Y$ must be as big as possible.

Here, # $X = b$ (which is $= c$)

$Y = c$

and $e = a - c$

②

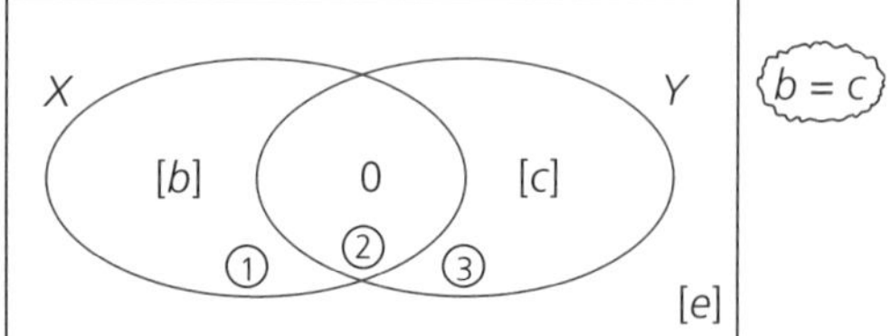

Similarly, if e must be as small as possible, $X \cap Y$ must be as small as possible.

Here

$\#X = b$ $\quad \#Y = c$

and $e = a - (b + c)$

$\Rightarrow e = a - b - c$

(but $b = c$) $\quad \Rightarrow e = a - c - c$

$\Rightarrow e = a - 2c$

Questions involving 3 Venn diagrams

Type 1

$U = \{a, b, c, d, e, f, g, h, i, j, k\}$

$M = \{a, b, c, d\}$

$N = \{b, d, e, f, g\}$

$P = \{b, f, h, i, j\}$

Copy and fill out the Venn diagram below:

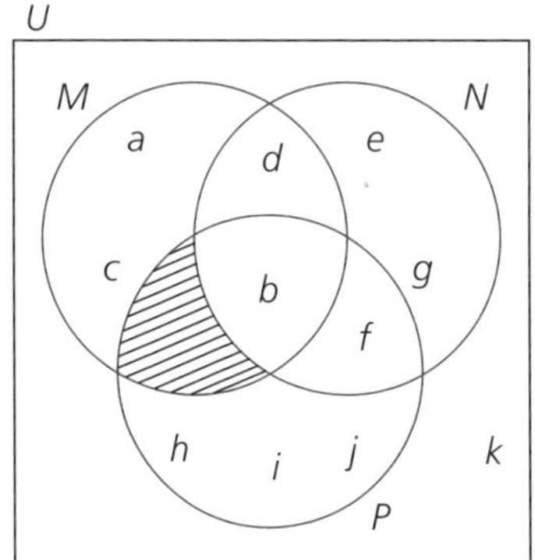

Note

(i) M' (all terms outside M)

$= \{e, f, g, h, i, j, k\}$

(ii) $(N \cup P)'$ (outside N union P)

$= \{a, c, k\}$

(iii) $M/(N \cup P)$ (set M less the terms in N union P)

$= \{a, c, d, b\}/\{d, e, g, b, f, h, i, j\}$

$= \{a, c\}$

(iv) $M \cap (N \cup P)$ (the terms in both set M and $N \cup P$)

$= \{a, c, d, b\} \cap \{d, e, g, b, f, h, i, j\}$

$= \{b, d\}$

Type 2

In a survey 30 people were asked their favourite colour. They were asked to choose from white, brown and red.

2 did not like any of the three
4 liked white only
14 liked brown
15 liked red
4 liked white and brown
7 liked white and red
5 liked brown and red

Draw a Venn diagram to illustrate the data. Hence find how many like all three colours.

In a question of this type, fill out the Venn diagram in this order:

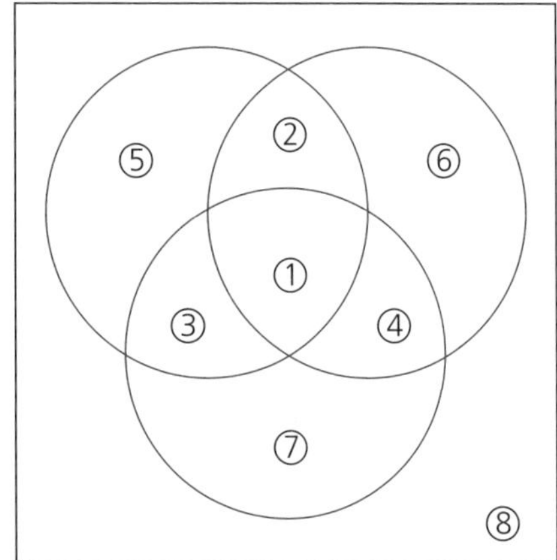

(i) Fill in ①.

(ii) Evaluate ②, ③ and ④ and fill them in.

(iii) Evaluate ⑤, ⑥ and ⑦ and fill them in.

(iv) Fill in ⑧.

(v) Evaluate x.

(i) Fill in ①.

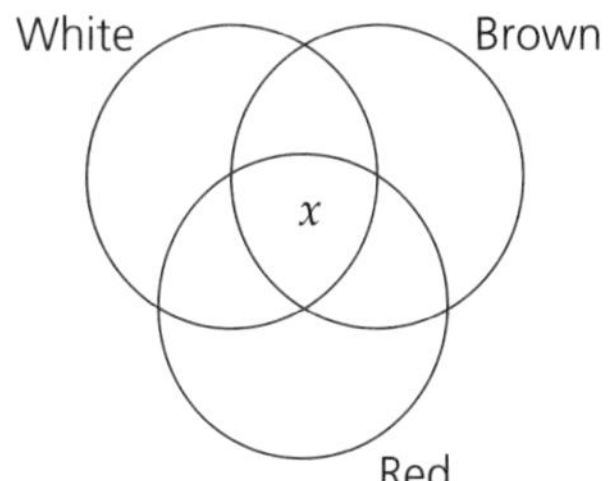

We are not told how many like all 3 colours so we fill in x.

(ii) Evaluate ②, ③ and ④ and fill them in.

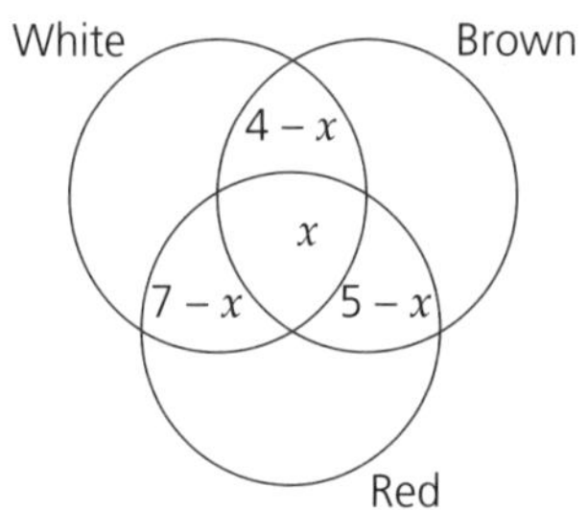

(iii) Evaluate ⑤, ⑥ and ⑦ and fill them in.

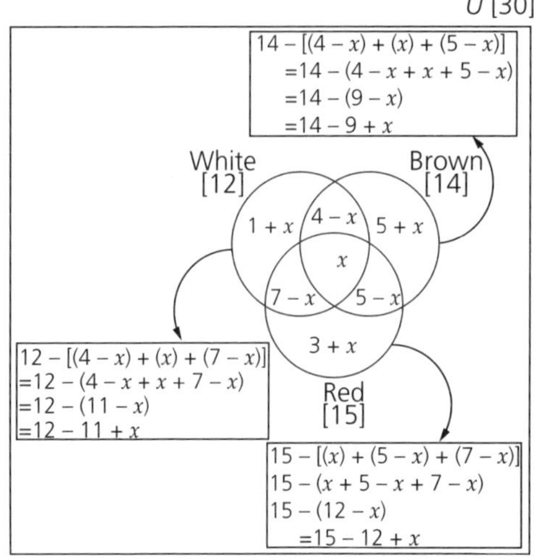

(iv) Fill in ⑧.

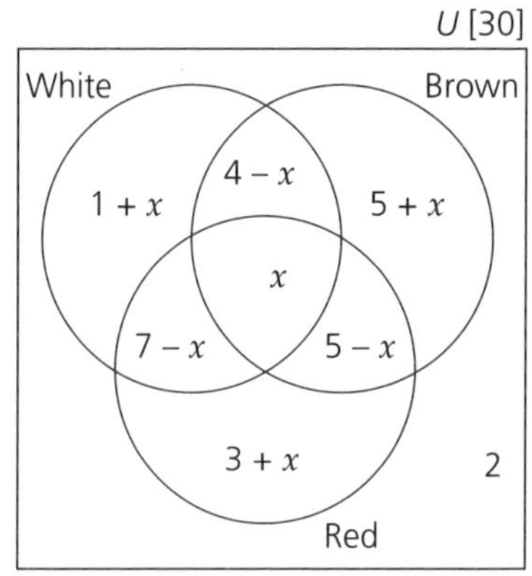

(v) Evaluate x.

$$30 = (1 + x) + (4 - x) + (5 + x) + (7 - x) + (x) + (3 + x) + (5 - x) + 2$$

$$\Rightarrow 30 = 1 + x + 4 - x + 5 + x + 7 - x + x + 3 + x + 5 - x + 2$$

$$\Rightarrow 30 = 27 + x$$

$$\Rightarrow \boxed{3 = x}$$

So three people like all 3 colours.

Indices

Rules for indices.

Rule 1

$$(a^b) \times (a^c) = a^{b+c}$$

So **(i)** $(2^4)(2^3) = 2^7$

(ii) $3^2 \times 3^4 \times 3^{-3} = 3^{2+4-3} = 3^3$

Rule 2

$$\frac{a^b}{a^c} = a^{b-c}$$

So **(i)** $\frac{2^4}{2^6} = 2^{4-6} = 2^{-2}$

(ii) $\frac{3^4}{3^{-2}} = 3^{4-(-2)} = 3^{4+2} = 3^6$

Rule 3

$$(a^b)^c = a^{bc}$$

So **(i)** $(2^3)^4 = 2^{12}$

(ii) $(3^2)^{-3} = 3^{-6}$

Rule 4

$$a^0 = 1$$

So **(i)** $3^0 = 1$

(ii) $\left(\frac{1}{4}\right)^0 = 1$

Rule 5

$$a^{-b} = \left(\frac{1}{a}\right)^b$$

$$\text{or } \left(\frac{1}{a}\right)^{-b} = a^{+b}$$

To change a power from negative to positive, turn the number (never the power) upside down.

So **(i)** $3^{-4} = \left(\frac{1}{3}\right)^4$

(ii) $\left(\frac{2}{3}\right)^{-2} = \left(\frac{3}{2}\right)^{+2}$

(iii) $\left(\frac{1}{3}\right)^{-3} = 3^{+3}$

Rule 6

$$a^{b/c} = \left(a^{1/c}\right)^b$$

So **(i)** $2^{2/3} = \left(2^{1/3}\right)^2$

(ii) $3^{-3/4} = \left(\frac{1}{3}\right)^{+3/4} = \left(\left(\frac{1}{3}\right)^{1/4}\right)^3$

Rule 7

① $\sqrt{a} = a^{1/2}$

② $\sqrt[3]{a} = a^{1/3}$

So, in general $\sqrt[n]{a} = a^{1/n}$

So **(i)** $(27)^{1/3} = \sqrt[3]{27} = 3$

$[3 \times 3 \times 3 = 27]$

(ii) $9^{-1/2} = \left(\frac{1}{9}\right)^{1/2} = \sqrt{\frac{1}{9}} = \frac{1}{3}$

Rule 8

① $(ab)^c = a^c b^c$

② $\left(\frac{a}{b}\right)^c = \frac{a^c}{b^c}$

So **(i)** $\left(\frac{9}{4}\right)^{-1/2} = \left(\frac{4}{9}\right)^{+1/2} = \frac{4^{1/2}}{9^{1/2}}$

$$= \frac{\sqrt{4}}{\sqrt{9}} = \boxed{\frac{2}{3}}$$

(ii) $8^{-1/3} = \left(\frac{1}{8}\right)^{1/3} = \sqrt[3]{\frac{1}{8}} = \boxed{\frac{1}{2}}$

Example 1

Express the following as rational numbers:

(i) $\left(\frac{1}{9}\right)^{-3/2}$ **(ii)** $\left(\frac{64}{125}\right)^{-2/3}$

(i) $\left(\frac{1}{9}\right)^{-3/2}$

Note
A 'rational number' is a number which can be expressed in the form of a fraction.

Make the index positive by turning the number upside down.

$$\left(\frac{1}{9}\right)^{-3/2} = 9^{+3/2}$$

$$= \left(9^{1/2}\right)^3 \qquad \boxed{a^{b/c} = (a^{1/c})^b \text{ .... rule 6}}$$

$$= \left(\sqrt{9}\right)^3 = 3^3 = \boxed{27}$$

(ii) $\left(\frac{64}{125}\right)^{-2/3}$

$$= \left(\frac{125}{64}\right)^{+2/3} = \left(\left(\frac{125}{64}\right)^{1/3}\right)^2$$

$$= \left(\frac{125^{1/3}}{64^{1/3}}\right)^2 = \left(\frac{\sqrt[3]{125}}{\sqrt[3]{64}}\right)^2$$

$$= \left(\frac{5}{4}\right)^2 = \boxed{\frac{25}{16}}$$

Example 2

Simplify the following, giving your answer in the form 3^n where $n \in Z$.

$$\frac{81 \times \frac{1}{9}}{\sqrt[3]{\frac{1}{27}} \times 9^{-3/2}}$$

First we write each term in the form 3^n.

① $81 = 3^4$

② $\frac{1}{9} = \frac{1}{3^2} = \left(\frac{1}{3}\right)^2 = 3^{-2}$

③ $\sqrt[3]{\frac{1}{27}} = \frac{\sqrt[3]{1}}{\sqrt[3]{27}} = \frac{1}{3} = \left(\frac{1}{3}\right)^1 = 3^{-1}$

④ $9^{-3/2} = \left(\frac{1}{9}\right)^{3/2} = \left(\left(\frac{1}{9}\right)^{1/2}\right)^3$

$$= \left(\frac{1^{1/2}}{9^{1/2}}\right)^3 = \left(\frac{\sqrt{1}}{\sqrt{9}}\right)^3 = \left(\frac{1}{3}\right)^3 = 3^{-3}$$

Therefore $\frac{3^4 \times 3^{-2}}{3^{-1} \times 3^{-3}}$

$$\boxed{a^b \times a^c = a^{b+c}} \Rightarrow \frac{3^{4-2}}{3^{-1-3}} = \frac{3^2}{3^{-4}}$$

$$\boxed{\frac{a^b}{a^c} = a^{b-c}} = 3^{2-(-4)} = 3^{2+4} = \boxed{3^6}$$

Exponential equations

An 'exponential equation' is an equation in which the variable is contained in an index.

Example

$$8 = 2^{3x-1}$$

We solve these equations as follows:

① Write all numbers as powers of the same number.

② Write both sides with one single power.

③ Let both powers be equal to each other and solve for x.

Example 1

Solve for x given:

$$\frac{\sqrt{8}}{16} = \left(\frac{1}{4}\right)^{2x-1}$$

① Write all numbers as powers of the same number.

- $\sqrt{8} = (8)^{1/2} = (2^3)^{1/2} = 2^{1.5}$
- $16 = 2^4$
- $\frac{1}{4} = \frac{1}{2^2} = 2^{-2}$

② Write both sides with a single power.

$$\Rightarrow \frac{2^{1.5}}{2^4} = (2^{-2})^{2x-1}$$

$$\Rightarrow 2^{1.5-4} = 2^{-4x+2}$$

$$\Rightarrow 2^{-2.5} = 2^{-4x+2}$$

③ Let both powers be equal to each other and solve for x.

So $-2.5 = -4x + 2$

$$-2.5 - 2 = -4x$$

$$-4.5 = -4x$$

$$\frac{-4.5}{-4} = x \quad \Rightarrow \quad \boxed{1.125 = x}$$

Example 2

Solve for x given:

$$\left(\sqrt{125}\right)\left(\frac{1}{5}\right) = \left(\sqrt{\frac{1}{25}}\right)^{4x}$$

① • $\sqrt{125} = (125)^{1/2} = (5^3)^{1/2} = 5^{1.5}$

- $\frac{1}{5} = \left(\frac{1}{5}\right)^1 = 5^{-1}$
- $\sqrt{\frac{1}{25}} = \left(\frac{1}{25}\right)^{1/2} = \left(\frac{1}{5^2}\right)^{1/2} = (5^{-2})^{1/2} = 5^{-1}$

② $(5^{1.5})(5^{-1}) = (5^{-1})^{4x}$

$$\Rightarrow \quad 5^{1.5-1} = (5^{-1})^{4x}$$

$$5^{0.5} = 5^{-4x}$$

③ $5^{0.5} = 5^{-4x}$

$$\Rightarrow \quad 0.5 = -4x$$

$$\frac{0.5}{-4} = x \quad \Rightarrow \quad \boxed{-0.125 = x}$$

Index notation

'Index notation' expresses very large or very small numbers in the following manner:

A number between 1 and 10 (but not 10)	×	a power of 10

This is normally written as:

$a \times 10^n$ where $1 \leqslant a < 10$ and $n \in Z$

Note 1

$2.3 \times 10^4 = 23000$

⇓

Increase 2.3 by moving the decimal point 4 places to the right.

Note 2

$2.3 \times 10^{-4} = 0.00023$

⇓

Decrease 2.3 by moving the decimal point 4 places to the left.

Note 3 Using the calculator

① 8.6×10^4

⇓

8.6 [Exp] 4

[=] 86000

1.7×10^{-3}

⇓

1.7 [Exp] [+−] 3

[=] 0.0017

Example 1

Express the following in the form $a \times 10^n$ where $1 \leqslant a < 10$ and $n \in Z$:

(i) $\dfrac{32{,}000}{0.04}$ **(ii)** $\left(\dfrac{8}{125}\right)^{4/3}$

(i) $\dfrac{32{,}000}{0.04}$

$\dfrac{32{,}000}{0.04} = 800{,}000$

$= 8 \times 10^5$

(ii) $\left(\dfrac{8}{125}\right)^{4/3}$

⇒ 8 [$a^{b/c}$] 125 [y^x] 4 [$a^{b/c}$] 3

$= 0.0256$

$= 2.56 \times 10^{-2}$

Example 2

Express **(i)** $(2.4 \times 10^5) + (7.1 \times 10^4)$

(ii) $\dfrac{4.8 \times 10^3}{9.6 \times 10^7}$

(i) $(2.4 \times 10^5) + (7.1 \times 10^4)$

2.4 [Exp] 5 + 7.1 [Exp] 4

$= 311{,}000 = 3.11 \times 10^5$

(ii) $\dfrac{4.8 \times 10^3}{9.6 \times 10^7}$

4.8 [Exp] 3 ÷ 9.6 [Exp] 7

$= 0.00005$

$= 5 \times 10^{-5}$

Questions involving surds

Type 1

Example 1

Write the following in the form $a\sqrt{b}$ where b is a prime number:

$$\sqrt{27} + \sqrt{48} - 2\sqrt{3}$$

Important

① Write out the factors of 27 and 48.

Choose the pair which includes a prime number and a perfect square.

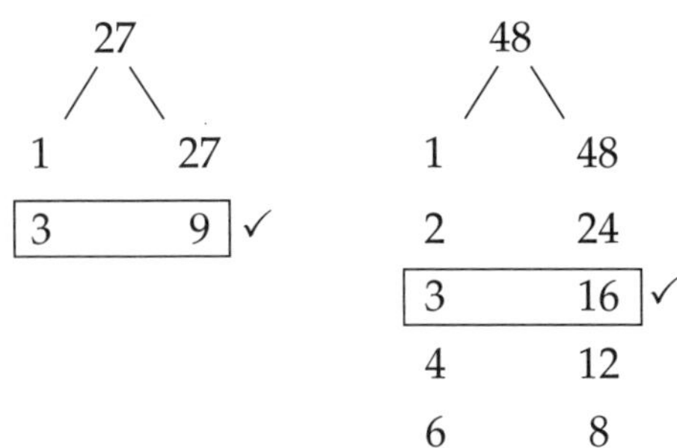

② $\sqrt{27} = \sqrt{3 \times 9} = \sqrt{3}\,\sqrt{9}$

$= (\sqrt{3})3 = 3\sqrt{3}$

$\sqrt{48} = \sqrt{3 \times 16} = \sqrt{3}\sqrt{16}$

$= (\sqrt{3})4 = 4\sqrt{3}$

$\Rightarrow \sqrt{27} + \sqrt{48} - 2\sqrt{3} = 3\sqrt{3} + 4\sqrt{3} - 2\sqrt{3}$

$= 7\sqrt{3} - 2\sqrt{3} = \boxed{5\sqrt{3}}$

Example 2

Write the following in the form $c\sqrt{6}$ where $c \in Z$:

$$\sqrt{54} - \sqrt{24} + 5\sqrt{6}$$

① Write out the factors of 54 and 24.

Choose the pair which includes a perfect square and 6.

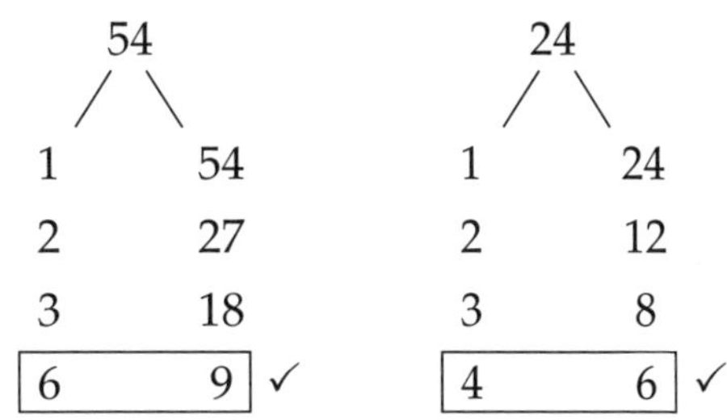

② $\sqrt{54} = \sqrt{6 \times 9} = \sqrt{6}\,\sqrt{9}$

$= (\sqrt{6})3 = 3\sqrt{6}$

$\sqrt{24} = \sqrt{4 \times 6} = \sqrt{4}\,\sqrt{6}$

$= 2\sqrt{6}$

$\Rightarrow \sqrt{54} - \sqrt{24} + 5\sqrt{6}$

$= 3\sqrt{6} - 2\sqrt{6} + 5\sqrt{6}$

$= 6\sqrt{6}$

Type 2

Multiply out the following, leaving your answer in surd form:

$$(2 - \sqrt{5})\,(3 + \sqrt{5})$$

Note	$a(\sqrt{b}) = a\sqrt{b}$ $\sqrt{c}\,(-\sqrt{c}) = -c$

$\underline{(2 - \sqrt{5})}\,(3 + \sqrt{5})$

$\underline{2}(3 + \sqrt{5}) \underline{- \sqrt{5}}\,(3 + \sqrt{5})$

$6 + 2\sqrt{5} - 3\sqrt{5} - 5$

$\Rightarrow 6 - 5 + 2\sqrt{5} - 3\sqrt{5}$

$= 1 - 1\sqrt{5}$

Chapter 2
Sample questions for you to try

Question 1

(a) In a class of 30 pupils, 14 like Snickers, 17 like Mars and 12 like Twix. All pupils like at least one bar. 3 like all 3 bars, 5 like Snickers and Twix, 7 like Mars and Snickers.

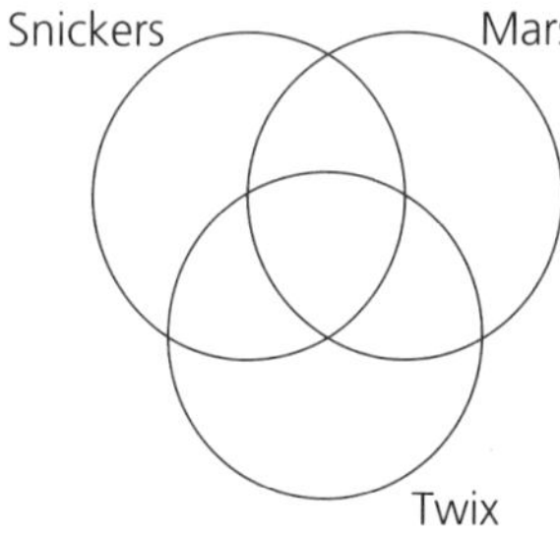

Complete the Venn diagram to illustrate the above information. Hence find the number of pupils who like Twix and Mars but not Snickers.

(b) Multiply out $(4 - \sqrt{7})\,(6 + \sqrt{7})$ fully giving your answer in surd form.

(c) Evaluate the following giving your answer in the form $a \times 10^b$ where $1 \leqslant a < 10$ and $b \in \mathrm{Z}$.

$$\frac{32^{-1/5} \times \left(\frac{2}{5}\right)^4}{\left(\frac{1}{2}\right)^{-3}}$$

Question 2

(a) A class of 20 pupils were asked whether they liked Mars or Twix. 2 pupils liked neither bar with 6 liking both.

Twice as many liked Mars only as liked Twix only.

Express the information given on a Venn diagram and use it to find how many like Twix.

(b) (i) Evaluate the following expressing your answer in the form 2^n:

$$\frac{\sqrt{8} \times \frac{1}{32}}{16 \times \frac{1}{4}}$$

(ii) Evaluate the following using your calculator. Hence write the list in descending order:

$$\left(\frac{1}{25}\right)^{-1/2},\ 300^0,\ 125^{-1/3},\ 25^{-3/2},\ \frac{\pi}{2}$$

(c) Given

$U = \{1, 2, 3, 4, 5, 6, 7, 8\}$

$A = \{2, 4, 1, 5\}$

$B = \{4, 5, 6, 7\}$

$C = \{8, 4, 7\}$

draw a Venn diagram to illustrate the above sets.

Hence find:

(i) $A/(B \cup C)$

(ii) $B/(A \cap C)$

(iii) $(A \cup B)'$

(iv) $A' \cap B'$

(v) $\#(B \cap C)'$

Question 3

(a)

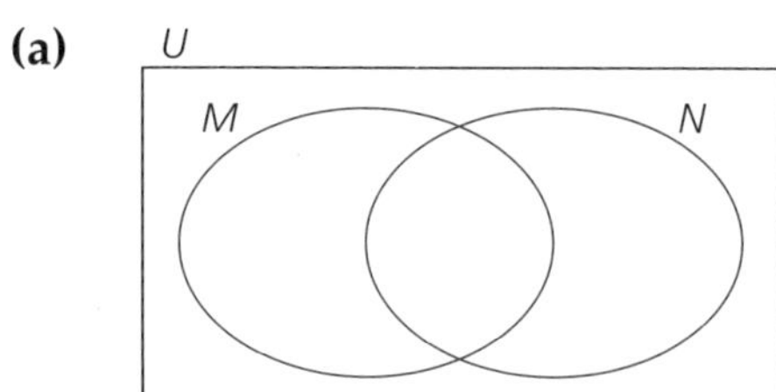

Complete the diagram above given

$\# M = m \quad \# N = n \quad \# U = u$

$M \cap N = x$ and $\# (M \cup N)' = p$

(i) Express p in terms of u, m, x and n.

(ii) If $n < m$ prove that the maximum value of p is $u - m$.

(iii) If $n = m$ prove that the minimum value of p is $u - 2m$.

(b) Evaluate x in each of the following:

(i) $\frac{1}{32} = 2^x$

(ii) $\sqrt{27} = 3^x$

(iii) $125^3 = 5^x$

(c) Evaluate the following and express your answer in the form $a \times 10^b$ where $1 \leqslant a < 10$ and $b \in Z$:

(i) $\frac{241.3 \times 84.2}{\frac{3}{5}}$

(ii) Evaluate the following, writing your answer in the form $c\sqrt{d}$ where d is a prime number:

$$\sqrt{28} - 3\sqrt{63}$$

Solution to question 1

(a)

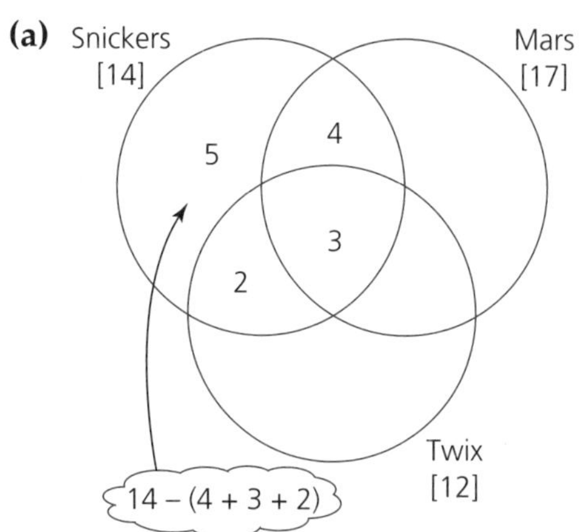

Find how many like Mars and Twix but not Snickers.

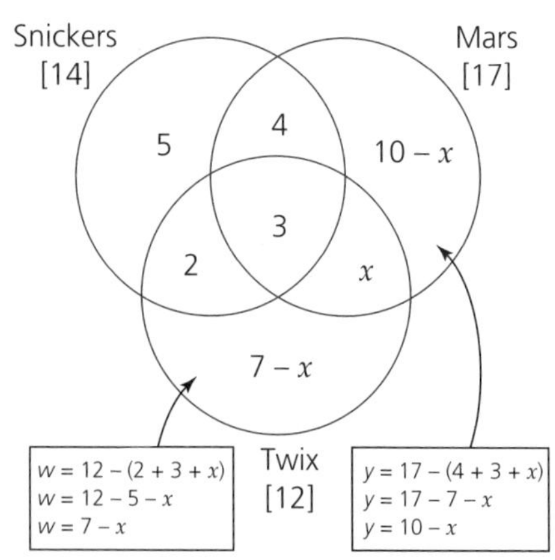

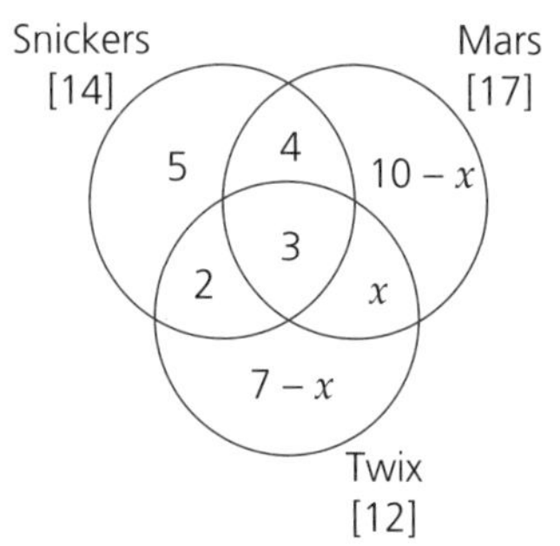

$*$ 30 pupils in total $*$

$\Rightarrow\ 30 = 5 + 4 + 3 + 2 + (10 - x) + x + (7 - x)$

$\Rightarrow\ 30 = 31 - x$

$\Rightarrow\ x = 1$

So one pupil likes Mars and Twix but not Snickers.

(b) Multiply $(4 - \sqrt{7})(6 + \sqrt{7})$

$$(4 - \sqrt{7})(6 + \sqrt{7})$$

$$4(6 + \sqrt{7}) - \sqrt{7}(6 + \sqrt{7})$$

$$= 24 + 4\sqrt{7} - 6\sqrt{7} - 7$$

$$= 24 - 7 + 4\sqrt{7} - 6\sqrt{7}$$

$$\boxed{= 17 - 2\sqrt{7}}$$

(c) Evaluate $\dfrac{32^{-1/5} \times \left(\dfrac{2}{5}\right)^4}{\left(\dfrac{1}{2}\right)^{-3}}$

$$= \frac{0.5 \times 0.0256}{8} = 0.0016$$

$$= 1.6 \times 10^{-3}$$

Solution to question 2

(a) [20]

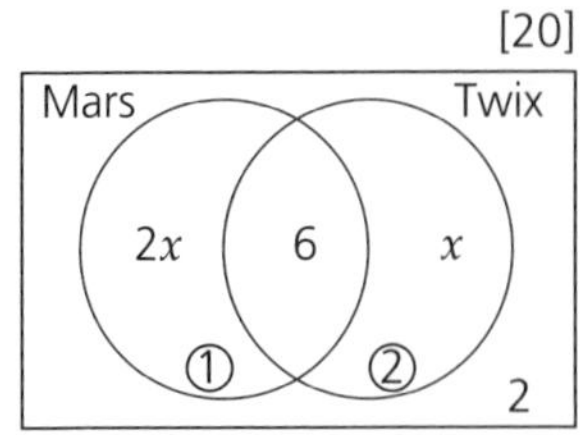

Note

$$① + ② = 20 - (6 + 2)$$
$$= 12$$

$\Rightarrow\ 12 = 2x + x$

$12 = 3x \qquad \Rightarrow\ 4 = x$

How many like Twix ?

$(6 + x)$ like Twix

$\Rightarrow$ 10 like Twix

(b)

(i) Evaluate the following giving your answer in the form 2^n:

$$\frac{\sqrt{8} \times \dfrac{1}{32}}{16 \times \dfrac{1}{4}}$$

$\rightarrow\ \sqrt{8} = 8^{1/2} = (2^3)^{0.5} = \boxed{2^{1.5}}$

$\rightarrow\ \dfrac{1}{32} = \dfrac{1}{2^5} = \boxed{2^{-5}}$

$\rightarrow\ 16 = \boxed{2^4}$

$\rightarrow\ \dfrac{1}{4} = \dfrac{1}{2^2} = \boxed{2^{-2}}$

$\Rightarrow\ \dfrac{2^{1.5} \times 2^{-5}}{2^4 \times 2^{-2}} = \dfrac{2^{1.5-5}}{2^{4-2}}$

$\Rightarrow\ \dfrac{2^{-3.5}}{2^2} = 2^{-3.5-2} = \boxed{2^{-5.5}}$

> **(ii)** Write in descending order:
> $\left(\frac{1}{25}\right)^{-1/2}$, 300^0, $125^{-1/3}$, $25^{-3/2}$, $\frac{\pi}{2}$

$\left(\frac{1}{25}\right)^{-1/2}$

(1 [$a^{b/c}$] 25 [y^x] [+_] 1 [$a^{b/c}$] 2)

= [5]

$300^0 =$ [1]

$125^{-1/3} =$ [0.2]

$25^{-3/2}$

(25 [y^x] [+_] 3 [$a^{b/c}$] 2) = [0.008]

$\frac{\pi}{2} =$ [1.57]

⇒ 5, 1.57, 1, 0.2, 0.008

⇒ $\left(\frac{1}{25}\right)^{-1/3}$, $\frac{\pi}{2}$, 300^0, $125^{-1/3}$, $25^{-3/2}$

(c)

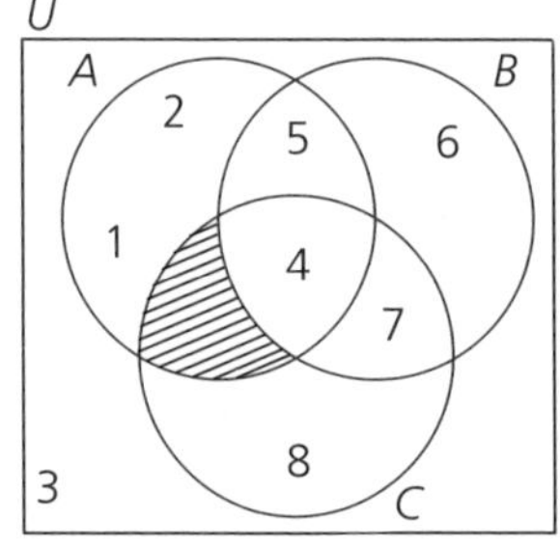

(i) $A/(B \cup C)$

= {1, 2, 4, 5} 'less' {4, 5, 6, 7, 8}

= {1, 2}

(ii) $B/(A \cap C)$

= {4, 5, 6, 7} 'less' {4}

= {5, 6, 7}

(iii) $(A \cup B)'$

'All terms outside $A \cup B$'

= {3, 8}

(iv) $A' \cap B'$

= {3, 6, 7, 8} ∩ {1, 2, 3, 8}

= {3, 8}

(v) $\#(B \cap C)'$

'The amount of elements outside $(B \cap C)$'

= 6

> This is an amount of elements so it's never written in a bracket.

Solution to question 3

(a)

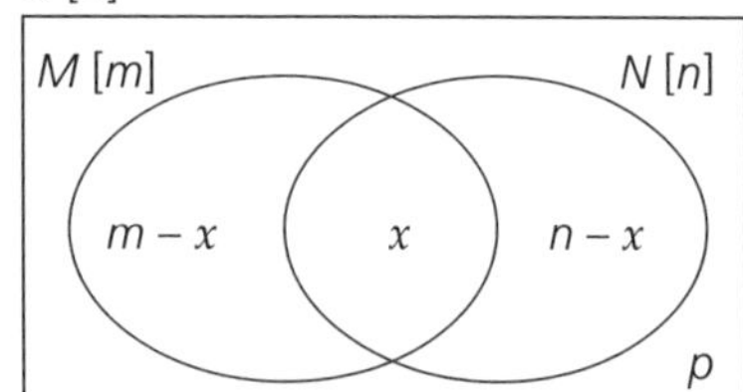

> **(i)** Express p in terms of m, n, x, and u.

$p = u - [(m - x) + (x) + (n - x)]$

$p = u - (m - x + x + n - x)$

$p = u - m + x - x - n + x$

⇒ $p = u - m - n + x$

(ii) If $n < m$ show that the maximum value of p is $u - m$.

* Again, because p must be as big as possible, M∩N must be as big as possible.

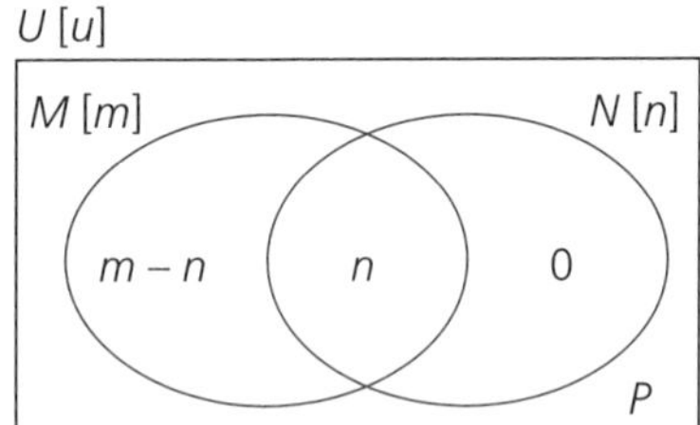

$\Rightarrow p = u - [(m - n) + (n)]$

$p = u - (m - n + n)$

$\Rightarrow p = u - m$

(iii) If $n = m$ show that the minimum value of p is $u - 2m$.

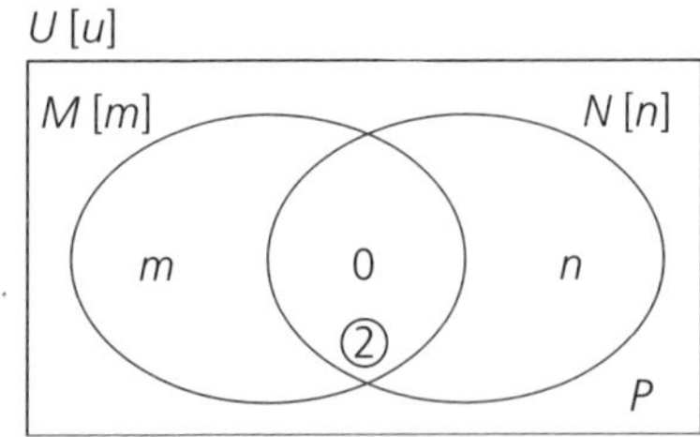

* If the value of p must be as small as possible, ② must be as small as possible.

$\Rightarrow p = u - (m + n)$

$p = u - m - n$

$\Rightarrow p = u - 2m \qquad (as\ m = n)$

(b) **(i)** $\frac{1}{32} = 2^x$

$$\frac{1}{32} = \frac{1}{2^5} = 2^{-5}$$

$\Rightarrow \qquad x = -5$

(ii) $\sqrt{27} = 3^x$

$$\sqrt{27} = (27)^{1/2} = (3^3)^{0.5}$$

$$= 3^{1.5} \qquad \Rightarrow x = 1.5$$

(iii) $125^3 = 5^x$

$$125^3 = (5^3)^3 = 5^9$$

$\Rightarrow \qquad x = 9$

(c) Evaluate the following and express in the form $a \times 10^b$:

(i) $\dfrac{241.3 \times 84.2}{\frac{3}{5}} = 33{,}862.43$

$$33{,}862.43 = 3.386 \times 10^4$$

(ii) Evaluate $\sqrt{28} - 3\sqrt{63}$ in the form $a\sqrt{b}$ where b is a prime number.

28	
1	28
2	14
4	7

63	
1	63
3	21
7	9

We find the pair of factors:

① Each with a perfect square.

② Containing the same prime number.

$\Rightarrow \quad \sqrt{28} - 3\sqrt{63}$

$\Rightarrow \quad \sqrt{4 \times 7} - 3\sqrt{9 \times 7}$

$= (\sqrt{4} \times \sqrt{7}) - 3(\sqrt{9} \times \sqrt{7})$

$= 2\sqrt{7} - 3(3\sqrt{7})$

$= 2\sqrt{7} - 9\sqrt{7}$

$= \boxed{-7\sqrt{7}}$

Chapter 3
Algebra One

Solving for x

Equations containing only x terms and numbers.

Solve $4x - 2 = 8x + 10$

Note 1 When an equation contains only x terms and numbers we must rearrange as follows before solving:

x terms = numbers

$$\Rightarrow 4x - 8x = 10 + 2$$
$$\Rightarrow -4x = 12 \qquad \Rightarrow x = \frac{12}{-4}$$
$$\boxed{x = -3}$$

Quadratic Equations
Equations containing at least one x^2 term.

Type 1

Solve $-5 - 4x = -9 + 4x - 3x^2$

Note 2 When an equation contains an x^2 term, we <u>must</u> rearrange as follows before solving:

x^2 terms | x terms | number | = 0

$$\Rightarrow 3x^2 - 4x - 4x + 9 - 5 = 0$$
$$\Rightarrow \qquad 3x^2 - 8x + 4 = 0$$

Only now can we use the '$-b$ formula' to solve for x.

$3x^2 - 8x + 4 = 0$

$$\frac{-b \pm \sqrt{b^2 - 4ac}}{2a}$$

$a = 3 \qquad b = -8 \qquad c = 4$

$$\Rightarrow \frac{-(-8) \pm \sqrt{(-8)^2 - 4(3)(4)}}{2(3)}$$

$$\Rightarrow \frac{8 \pm \sqrt{64 - 48}}{6}$$

$$\Rightarrow \frac{8 \pm \sqrt{16}}{6}$$

① $x = \dfrac{8+4}{6} = \dfrac{12}{6} = \boxed{2}$

② $x = \dfrac{8-4}{6} = \dfrac{4}{6} = \boxed{\dfrac{2}{3}}$

Type 2

Solve for x given

$x(4-3x)-4=2(x-2)+x$

(a) Multiply out

$4x-3x^2-4=2x-4+x$

(b) Rearrange correctly

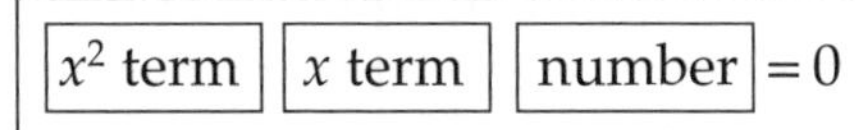

$\Rightarrow -3x^2+4x-2x-x-4+4=0$

$-3x^2+1x+0=0$

(c) Solve using the '$-b$ formula'.

$$\frac{-b \pm \sqrt{b^2-4ac}}{2a}$$

$a=-3 \qquad b=1 \qquad c=0$

$$\Rightarrow \frac{-(1) \pm \sqrt{(1)^2-4(-3)(0)}}{2(-3)}$$

$$\Rightarrow \frac{-1 \pm \sqrt{1}}{-6}$$

(Please understand that $-4(-3)(0)=0$.)

$$\Rightarrow \frac{-1 \pm 1}{6}$$

$\Rightarrow$ ① $x=\dfrac{-1+1}{6} \quad \Rightarrow \boxed{x=0}$

② $x=\dfrac{-1-1}{6} \quad \Rightarrow x=-\dfrac{2}{6}$

$=\boxed{-\dfrac{1}{3}}$

Type 3

Solve for x given

$-4(-x^2+2)-2x=2x(x-1)-4$

(a) Multiply out

$4x^2-8-2x=2x^2-2x-4$

(b) Rearrange correctly

x^2 term	x term	number	= 0

$\Rightarrow 4x^2-2x^2-2x+2x-8+4=0$

$\Rightarrow 2x^2-4=0$

$\Rightarrow 2x^2+0x-4=0$

(c) Solve using the '$-b$ formula'.

$$\frac{-b \pm \sqrt{b^2-4ac}}{2a}$$

$a=2 \qquad b=0 \qquad c=-4$

$$\Rightarrow \frac{-(0) \pm \sqrt{(0)^2-4(2)(-4)}}{2(2)}$$

$\Rightarrow \dfrac{0 \pm \sqrt{32}}{4} \quad \Rightarrow \dfrac{0 \pm 5.65}{4}$

$\Rightarrow$ ① $x=\dfrac{+5.65}{4} \quad \Rightarrow \boxed{x=1.41}$

② $x=-\dfrac{5.65}{4} \quad \Rightarrow \boxed{x=-1.41}$

Type 4

Example 1

Solve $3x^2-7x=3$ correct to one decimal place.

Hence, or otherwise, solve for t correct to one decimal place given

$3(4t-2)^2-7(4t-2)-3=0$

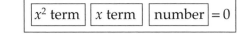

(i) Solve $3x^2 - 7x = 3$

As usual we must rearrange the quadratic equation thus:

$$\boxed{x^2}\boxed{x}\boxed{\text{number}} = 0$$

$\Rightarrow 3x^2 - 7x = 3 \quad \rightarrow 3x^2 - 7x - 3 = 0$

$$\frac{-b \pm \sqrt{b^2 - 4ac}}{2a}$$

$a = 3 \qquad b = -7 \qquad c = -3$

$$\Rightarrow \frac{-(-7) \pm \sqrt{(-7)^2 - 4(3)(-3)}}{2(3)}$$

$$\Rightarrow \frac{7 \pm \sqrt{49 + 36}}{6}$$

$$\Rightarrow \frac{7 \pm \sqrt{85}}{6} \quad \Rightarrow \frac{7 \pm 9.22}{6}$$

① $x = \dfrac{7 + 9.22}{6} = \dfrac{16.22}{6} = \boxed{2.7}$

② $x = \dfrac{7 - 9.22}{6} = \dfrac{-2.22}{6} = \boxed{-0.4}$

(ii) Evaluate t

Compare both equations:

$$3x^2 - 7x - 3 = 0$$

$$3(4t - 2)^2 - 7(4t - 2) - 3 = 0$$

$$\Rightarrow \boxed{x = 4t - 2}$$

(important to make this statement)

$x = 2.7$	$x = 0.4$
$\Rightarrow \quad 2.7 = 4t - 2$	$\Rightarrow \quad -0.4 = 4t - 2$
$\Rightarrow 2.7 + 2 = 4t$	$\Rightarrow 2 - 0.4 = 4t$
$4.7 = 4t$	$1.6 = 4t$
$\dfrac{4.7}{4} = t$	$\dfrac{1.6}{4} = t$
$\Rightarrow \quad \underline{\underline{1.2 = t}}$	$\Rightarrow \quad \underline{\underline{0.4 = t}}$

Example 2

Solve $3x^2 - 4x - 4 = 0$

Hence, or otherwise, solve for a given

$$3\left(a - \frac{3}{a}\right)^2 - 4\left(a - \frac{3}{a}\right) - 4 = 0$$

(i) Solve $3x^2 - 4x - 4 = 0$

$$\frac{-b \pm \sqrt{b^2 - 4ac}}{2a}$$

$a = 3 \qquad b = -4 \qquad c = -4$

$$\Rightarrow \frac{-(-4) \pm \sqrt{(-4)^2 - 4(3)(-4)}}{2(3)}$$

$$\Rightarrow \frac{4 \pm \sqrt{16 + 48}}{6}$$

$$\Rightarrow \frac{4 \pm \sqrt{64}}{6}$$

$\Rightarrow$ ① $x = \dfrac{4 + 8}{6} \quad \Rightarrow \boxed{x = 2}$

② $x = \dfrac{4 - 8}{6} \quad \Rightarrow \boxed{x = \dfrac{-2}{3}}$

(ii) Evaluate a

Comparing the two equations:

$$3x^2 - 4x - 4 = 0$$

$$3\left(a - \frac{3}{a}\right)^2 - 4\left(a - \frac{3}{a}\right) - 4 = 0$$

$$\Rightarrow \boxed{x = a - \frac{3}{a}}$$

$x = 2$

$$\Rightarrow 2 = a - \frac{3}{a}$$

Multiply across by a

$\Rightarrow 2a = a^2 - 3$

Rearranging

a^2 term	a term	number	$= 0$

$\Rightarrow -1a^2 + 2a + 3 = 0$

Solving using the '$-b$ formula'.

$$\frac{-b \pm \sqrt{b^2 - 4ac}}{2a}$$

$a = -1 \qquad b = 2 \qquad c = 3$

$$\Rightarrow \frac{-(2) \pm \sqrt{(2)^2 - 4(-1)(3)}}{2(-1)}$$

$$\Rightarrow \frac{-2 \pm \sqrt{16}}{-2} = \frac{-2 \pm 4}{-2}$$

① $a = \dfrac{-2+4}{-2} \Rightarrow \boxed{a = -1}$

② $a = \dfrac{-2-4}{-2} \Rightarrow \boxed{a = 3}$

$x = -\dfrac{2}{3}$

$$\Rightarrow -\frac{2}{3} = a - \frac{3}{a}$$

(i) Multiply across by 3

$\Rightarrow \quad -2 = 3a - \dfrac{9}{a}$

Multiply across by a

$\Rightarrow \quad -2a = 3a^2 - 9$

(ii) Rearranging correctly

$\Rightarrow \quad -3a^2 - 2a + 9 = 0$

(iii) Solving

$$\frac{-b \pm \sqrt{b^2 - 4ac}}{2a}$$

$a = -3 \qquad b = -2 \qquad c = 9$

$$\Rightarrow \frac{-(-2) \pm \sqrt{(-2)^2 - 4(-3)(9)}}{2(-3)}$$

$$\Rightarrow \frac{2 \pm \sqrt{112}}{-6}$$

① $a = \dfrac{2 \pm 10.583}{-6} \qquad \Rightarrow \boxed{a = -2.1}$

② $a = \dfrac{2 - 10.583}{-6} \qquad \Rightarrow \boxed{a = 1.43}$

Questions involving fractions

Type 1

Solve for x

$$\frac{5}{6}(x-1) = \frac{3}{4}(2x+1) - 1\frac{1}{2}$$

(a) Multiply into each bracket.

$$\frac{5x-5}{6} = \frac{6x+3}{4} - \frac{3}{2}$$

Common denominator = 12

(b) Multiply each fraction by the common denominator.

$$\frac{12(5x-5)}{6} = \frac{12(6x+3)}{4} - \frac{12(3)}{2}$$

$\Rightarrow 2(5x-5) = 3(6x+3) - 6(3)$

(c) Multiply out as usual

$\Rightarrow\ 10x - 10 = 18x + 9 - 18$

Note

As this equation does not contain an x^2 term, we rearrange the terms as normal.

x terms = numbers

$\Rightarrow\ 10x - 18x = 9 - 18 + 10$

(d) Solve for x

$\Rightarrow\ -8x = 1 \qquad \Rightarrow\ \boxed{x = -\frac{1}{8}}$

Type 2

Solve for x correct to two decimal places given $\frac{1}{x+1} + \frac{2}{x-3} = 4$

(a) Ensure that all terms are written as a fraction.

$$\frac{1}{x+1} + \frac{2}{x-3} = \frac{4}{1}$$

(b) Find the common denominator and multiply all terms by it.

Common denom. $= (x+1)(x-3)$

$$\Rightarrow\ \frac{1(x+1)(x-3)}{x+1} + \frac{2(x+1)(x-3)}{x-3}$$

$$= \frac{4(x+1)(x-3)}{1}$$

$\Rightarrow\ 1(x-3) + 2(x+1) = 4(x+1)(x-3)$

$\Rightarrow\ 1(x-3) + 2(x+1) = 4(x^2 - 2x - 3)$

$\Rightarrow\ 1x - 3 + 2x + 2 = 4x^2 - 8x - 12$

$(x+1)(x-3)$
$x(x-3) + 1(x-3)$
$x^2 - 3x + 1x - 3$
$x^2 - 2x - 3$

Note

As this equation does contain an x^2 term, we rearrange the terms as before.

x^2 term	x term	number	$= 0$

$\Rightarrow\ -4x^2 + 1x + 2x + 8x + 12 - 3 + 2 = 0$

$\Rightarrow\ -4x^2 + 11x + 11 = 0$

(c) Solve using the '$-b$ formula'.

$$\frac{-b \pm \sqrt{b^2 - 4ac}}{2a}$$

$a = -4 \qquad b = 11 \qquad c = 11$

$$\Rightarrow\ \frac{-11 \pm \sqrt{(11)^2 - 4(-4)(11)}}{2(-4)}$$

$$\Rightarrow\ \frac{-11 \pm \sqrt{121 + 176}}{-8}$$

$$\Rightarrow\ \frac{-11 \pm \sqrt{297}}{-8}$$

① $x = \dfrac{-11 + 17.23368}{-8}$

$\Rightarrow x = -0.7792$

$\Rightarrow \boxed{x = -0.78}$ correct to 2 dec. places

② $x = \dfrac{-11 - 17.23368}{-8}$

$\Rightarrow x = 3.52921$

$\Rightarrow \boxed{x = 3.53}$ correct to 2 dec. places

Factorising

Difference of 2 squares

Type 1

$36x^2 - 49y^4$

$= (6x)^2 - (7y^2)^2$

(1st bkt – 2nd bkt)(1st bkt + 2nd bkt)

$\Rightarrow (6x - 7y^2)(6x + 7y^2)$

Type 2

$27a^2 - 12b^2c^4$

> 27 and 12 are not perfect squares ⇒ divide each by either 2, 3 or 5 so that the result gives us perfect squares.

$\Rightarrow 3(9a^2 - 4b^2c^4)$

$\Rightarrow 3[(3a)^2 - (2bc^2)^2]$

$\Rightarrow 3(3a - 2bc^2)(3a + 2bc^2)$

Type 3

$25t^2 - (2n - 4t)^2$

$\Rightarrow (5t)^2 - (2n - 4t)^2$

$\Rightarrow [5t - (2n - 4t)]\ [5t + 2n - 4t]$

↓

> Important to leave the 2nd bracket after the minus sign.

$\Rightarrow (5t - 2n + 4t)(5t + 2n - 4t)$

$\Rightarrow (9t - 2n)(1t + 2n)$

Factorising by grouping

Type 1

$6tm - 9nt - 8nm + 12n^2$

$3t(2m - 3n) - 4n(2m - 3n)$

$(3t - 4n)(2m - 3n)$

> It is important to always check that the brackets are the same. Here they are so we know we are correct.

Type 2

$15ac - 8b^2 - 6bc + 20ab$

Because this will not factorise correctly, we rearrange the terms.

$15ac + 20ab - 6bc - 8b^2$

$\Rightarrow 5a(3c + 4b) - 2b(3c + 4b)$

$(5a - 2b)(3c + 4b)$

Type 3

$6ac - 9bc + 4a^2 - 9b^2$

Here we have a 'hidden' difference of 2 squares.

Factorise accordingly:

$\underline{3c}(2a - 3b) + (2a - 3b)\underline{(2a + 3b)}$

$\Rightarrow (2a - 3b)\ \underline{(2a + 3b + 3c)}$

Factorising quadratic type questions

Type 1

Factorise $3x^2 + 7x - 6$

As there isn't an 'equal to' sign, we can't use the '$-b$ formula'.

We can therefore use the following technique to factorise:

① Multiply the first number by the last number $(3)(-6) = -18$.

② List the factors of -18.

Very important

* The sign before the middle term (+) goes before the large factors.

* The small factors will have to be (−) because each pair must multiply to get −18.

-18

−1	+18
−2	+9
−3	+6

③ Pick out the pair which adds up to the middle number $[-2 + 9 = +7]$.

④ Rewrite the question, substituting the middle term $(+7x)$ with $-2x + 9x$.

$\Rightarrow 3x^2 + 7x - 6$

becomes $3x^2 - 2x + 9x - 6$

⑤ Factorising $3x^2 - 2x + 9x - 6$.

$1x(3x - 2) + 3(3x - 2)$

$\Rightarrow \boxed{(1x + 3)(3x - 2)}$

Type 2

Factorise $8a^2 - 18ab + 4b^2$

When 3 terms are in the form m^2, mn, n^2 or t^2, tw, w^2 etc., factorise using the same technique that was used in the quadratic equation in Type 1.

$+32 \leftarrow (8)(4)$

−1	−32
−2	−16 ✓
−4	−8

$8a^2 - 2ab - 16ab + 4b^2$

$2a(4a - 1b) - 4b(4a - 1b)$

$\Rightarrow (2a - 4b)(4a - 1b)$

Important

The technique given here is an alternative to the more common 'back-to-back brackets' method. Both methods are valid.

<u>'Back-to-back brackets'</u>

$3x^2 + 7x - 6 = (3x - 2)(1x + 3)$

<u>To check</u>

$(3x-2)(1x+3)$ $\quad (3x)(1x) = 3x^2$ ✓

$\quad (-2)(+3) = -6$ ✓

$(3x-2)(1x+3)$ $\quad (3x)(3) = 9x$

$\quad (-2)(1x) = \underline{-2x}$ ✓

$\quad +7x$

Combining the different types of factorising

(i) Simplify $\dfrac{3a^2+2a-8}{9a^2-16}$

Factorise each part separately.

$$\boxed{3a^2+2a-8}$$

This is a 'Type 3' question.

$(3)(-8) = -24$

-24	
-1	$+24$
-2	$+12$
-3	$+8$
-4	$+6$ ✓

$3a^2-4a+6a-8$

$1a(3a-4)+2(3a-4)$

$(1a+2)(3a-4)$

$$\boxed{9a^2-16}$$

This is a difference of 2 squares question (Type 1).

$$9a^2-16=(3a)^2-(4)^2=(3a-4)(3a+4)$$

$$\Rightarrow \frac{3a^2+2a-8}{9a^2-16}=\frac{(1a+2)(3a-4)}{(3a-4)(3a+4)}$$

$$=\boxed{\frac{1a+2}{3a+4}}$$

(ii) Simplify $\dfrac{4t^2-9m^2}{2t^2-3tm-9m^2}$

Factorise $\underline{4t^2-9m^2}$

$$4t^2-9m^2=(2t)^2-(3m)^2$$
$$=(2t-3m)(2t+3m)$$

Factorise $\underline{2t^2-3tm-9m^2}$

$(2)(-9) = -18$

-18	
$+1$	-18
$+2$	-9
$+3$	-6 ✓

$2t^2+3tm-6tm-9m^2$

$1t(2t+3m)-3m(2t+3m)$

$(1t-3m)(2t+3m)$

$$\Rightarrow \frac{4t^2-9m^2}{2t^2-3tm-9m^2}$$

$$=\frac{(2t-3m)(2t+3m)}{(1t-3m)(2t+3m)}=\boxed{\frac{2t-3m}{1t-3m}}$$

Changing the subject of a formula

Type 1

Express w in terms of m and v

$$\frac{3}{w}-\frac{5}{v}=\frac{4}{m}$$

(i) Multiply across by each of the terms under the line.

Note 1

$$\left(\frac{a}{b}\right)c=\frac{ac}{b} \quad \text{not} \quad \frac{ac}{bc}$$

Note 2

$$\left(\frac{a}{b}\right)b=\frac{ab}{b}=a$$

$$\Rightarrow \left(\frac{m}{y}\right)(y)=m \quad \text{etc.}$$

$$\frac{3}{w} - \frac{5}{v} = \frac{4}{m}$$

$$[\times w] \quad 3 - \frac{5w}{v} = \frac{4w}{m}$$

$$[\times v] \quad 3v - 5w = \frac{4vw}{m}$$

$$[\times m] \quad 3mv - 5mw = 4vw$$

(ii) Bring all the terms containing a 'w' term to the same side.

$$\Rightarrow 3mv = 5mw + 4vw$$

(iii) Divide those terms by w.

$$\Rightarrow 3mv = w(5m + 4v)$$

(iv) Divide each side by $(5m + 4v)$.

$$\Rightarrow \boxed{\frac{3mv}{5m + 4v} = w}$$

Type 2

Express x in terms of y and z.

$$\sqrt{\frac{3x - 2y}{4x}} = 2z$$

(i) Square both sides to eliminate the square root sign.

$$\Rightarrow \left(\sqrt{\frac{3x - 2y}{4x}}\right)^2 = (2z)^2$$

$$\Rightarrow \frac{3x - 2y}{4x} = 4z^2 \qquad [\text{not } 2z^2]$$

(ii) Cross multiplying

$$\frac{3x - 2y}{4x} = \frac{4z^2}{1}$$

$$\Rightarrow (3x - 2y)(1) = (4z^2)(4x)$$

$$\Rightarrow 3x - 2y = 16xz^2$$

(iii) Isolate the x terms and proceed as in Type 1.

$$3x - 16xz^2 = 2y$$

$$x(3 - 16z^2) = 2y$$

$$\boxed{x = \frac{2y}{3 - 16z^2}}$$

Simultaneous equations

Type 1

Solve for x and y

$$4x = -5y + 2$$

$$7y - 1 = -5x$$

Note

Before starting it's very important that you rearrange both equations as follows:

$\boxed{x \text{ term}}\ \boxed{y \text{ term}} = \boxed{\text{number}}$

$$\Rightarrow \quad 4x + 5y = 2$$

$$5x + 7y = 1$$

Eliminating the x term

$$\begin{array}{lll} \boxed{4}x + 5y = 2 & (\times -5) & -20x - 25y = -10 \\ \boxed{5}x + 7y = 1 & (\times\ 4) & 20x + 28y = 4 \\ & & 3y = -6 \\ & & \Rightarrow \boxed{y = -2} \end{array}$$

Solving for x

$$\boxed{4x + 5y = 2}$$

$$y = -2 \quad \Rightarrow 4x + 5(-2) = 2$$

$$\Rightarrow 4x - 10 = 2 \quad \Rightarrow 4x = 12 \quad \Rightarrow \boxed{x = 3}$$

Type 2

Solve for a and b

$$4a + b = 17$$

$$\frac{a-3}{4} + \frac{b}{2} = 2\frac{1}{2}$$

$$\boxed{\frac{a-3}{4} + \frac{b}{2} = \frac{5}{2}}$$

$\Downarrow$

$\Rightarrow$ Common denom. = 4

$\Downarrow$

$$\Rightarrow \quad \frac{4(a-3)}{4} + \frac{4(b)}{2} = \frac{4(5)}{2}$$

$\Downarrow$

$\Rightarrow \quad 1(a-3) + 2(b) = 2(5)$

$\Rightarrow \quad 1a - 3 + 2b = 10 \quad \Rightarrow 1a + 2b = 13$

Solving

$4a + b = 17 \qquad\qquad 4a + b = 17$

$1a + 2b = 13 \quad (\times -4) \quad -4a - 8b = -52$

$-7b = -35$

$\boxed{b = 5}$

Solve for a

$4a + b = 17$

$b = 5 \qquad \Rightarrow 4a + 5 = 17$

$\Rightarrow 4a = 12 \quad \Rightarrow \boxed{a = 3}$

Simplifying fractions

Express as a single fraction

$$\frac{3}{4x-1} - \frac{2}{3x+2}$$

Common denom. = $(4x-1)(3x+2)$

Multiply each fraction by the common denominator.

$$\frac{\cancel{(4x-1)}(3x+2)(3)}{\cancel{4x-1}} - \frac{2(4x-1)\cancel{(3x+2)}}{\cancel{3x+2}}$$

Important note

When a fractions question does not have an equal to sign, multiply out on top but leave the common denominator under the line.

$$\Rightarrow \frac{9x + 6 - 8x + 2}{(4x-1)(3x+2)}$$

$$\Rightarrow \boxed{\frac{1x + 8}{(4x-1)(3x+2)}}$$

Division

Divide $6x^3 + 17x^2 + 6x - 8$ by $3x + 4$

$$3x + 4\overline{)6x^3 + 17x^2 + 6x - 8}$$

Step 1 – Divide $3x$ into $6x^3$. Put the answer on top.

$$\begin{array}{r} 2x^2 \\ 3x + 4\overline{)6x^3 + 17x^2 + 6x - 8} \end{array}$$

Step 2 – Multiply $2x^2$ by $3x + 4$. Put the answer underneath the first two terms.

$$\begin{array}{r} 2x^2 \\ 3x + 4\overline{)6x^3 + 17x^2 + 6x - 8} \\ 6x^3 + 8x^2 \end{array}$$

Step 3 – Change both signs and add.

$$\begin{array}{r} 2x^2 \\ 3x + 4\overline{)6x^3 + 17x^2 + 6x - 8} \\ \ominus 6x^3 \overset{\ominus}{+} 8x^2 \\ \hline + 9x^2 \end{array}$$

Step 4 – Bring down the next term ($6x$) and start the steps again.

$$\begin{array}{r} 2x^2+3x-2 \\ 3x+4\,\overline{)\,6x^3+17x^2+6x-8} \\ \ominus 6x^3 + 8x^2 \\ \hline 9x^2+6x \\ \ominus 9x^2 \ominus 12x \\ \hline -6x-8 \\ \oplus -6x \oplus -8 \\ \hline \end{array}$$

- $3x$ into $9x^2$
- $+3x$ on top
- $3x(3x+4)$
- $9x^2+12x$ underneath
- Change signs and add.
- Bring down -8 and repeat.
- $3x$ into $-6x$
  Put -2 on top.
- $-2(3x+4)$
  Put $-6x-8$ underneath.
- Change signs and add.
  $\Rightarrow 6x^3+17x^2+6x-8 \div 3x+4$
  $= 2x^2+3x-2$

Chapter 3 Sample questions for you to try

Question 1

(a) Solve for x
$-3(2x-1)-4=2(-4x+3)-5x$

(b) Divide $2x^3+x^2-25x+12$ by $2x-1$

(c) Express a in terms of b and c given $\frac{3}{b}=\frac{4}{a}-\frac{2}{c}$

(d) Solve $5x^2-13x=6$ correct to 1 decimal place.

Hence, or otherwise, solve for t correct to one decimal place given

$$5\left(\frac{3}{t}-5\right)^2-13\left(\frac{3}{t}-5\right)-6=0$$

Question 2

(a) Write $\frac{4}{3x-1}-\frac{2}{4x-3}$ as a single fraction.

Hence, or otherwise, evaluate when $x=\frac{1}{2}$

(b) Solve for x and y

$$x+\frac{y+3}{4}=5$$

$$\frac{x-3}{4}+\frac{y}{2}=2\frac{1}{2}$$

(c) Simplify

$(2m+p)(4m-2p)-(3n+a)(6n-2a)$

(d) Simplify

$$\frac{10m^2-11mn-6n^2}{4m^2-9n^2}$$

Question 3

(a) Solve for x

$\frac{2}{3}(3x-1)-\frac{1}{2}(2x-5)=2\frac{1}{4}$

(b) Factorise

(i) $12a^2+6ct-8at-9ac$

(ii) $25t^2-(4t-3w)^2$

(c) Divide $6x^3 + 7x^2 - 14x - 8$ by $3x - 4$

(d)

(i) Solve $x^2 = 6x - 3$ correct to two decimal places.

(ii) Hence, or otherwise, solve for t correct to two decimal places given $(2t^2 - 4)^2 - 6(2t^2 - 4) + 3 = 0$

Solution to question 1

(a) $-3(2x - 1) - 4 = 2(-4x + 3) - 5x$

$$-6x + 3 - 4 = -8x + 6 - 5x$$

* $\boxed{x \text{ terms} = \text{numbers}}$ *

$$-6x + 8x + 5x = 6 - 3 + 4$$

$$7x = 7$$

$$\Rightarrow \boxed{x = 1}$$

(b) Divide $2x^3 + x^2 - 25x + 12$ by $2x - 1$

$$\begin{array}{r} 1x^2 + 1x - 12 \\ 2x - 1 \overline{)\, 2x^3 + 1x^2 - 25x + 12} \\ \ominus 2x^3 \overset{\oplus}{-} 1x^2 \qquad\qquad \\ \hline 2x^2 - 25x \qquad \\ \ominus 2x^2 \overset{\oplus}{-} 1x \qquad \\ \hline -24x + 12 \\ \overset{\oplus}{-}24x \overset{\ominus}{+} 12 \\ \hline \end{array}$$

$\Rightarrow 1x^2 + 1x - 12$

(c) Express a in terms of b and c given $\frac{3}{b} = \frac{4}{a} - \frac{2}{c}$

(i) Multiply across by each of the denominators.

$$\frac{3}{b} = \frac{4}{a} - \frac{2}{c}$$

$$[\times b] \quad 3 = \frac{4b}{a} - \frac{2b}{c}$$

$$[\times a] \quad 3a = 4b - \frac{2ab}{c}$$

$$[\times c] \quad 3ac = 4bc - 2ab$$

(ii) Bring the terms containing 'a' together.

$$3ac + 2ab = 4bc$$

$$\Rightarrow \quad a(3c + 2b) = 4bc$$

$$\Rightarrow \quad a = \boxed{\frac{4bc}{3c + 2b}}$$

(d) Solve $5x^2 - 13x = 6$ correct to 1 decimal place.

Rewrite in the form:

$\boxed{x^2 \text{ term}}\ \boxed{x \text{ term}}\ \boxed{\text{number}} = 0$

$\Rightarrow 5x^2 - 13x - 6 = 0$

$$\frac{-b \pm \sqrt{b^2 - 4ac}}{2a}$$

$a = 5 \qquad b = -13 \qquad c = -6$

$$\frac{-(-13) \pm \sqrt{(-13)^2 - 4(5)(-6)}}{2(5)}$$

$$\Rightarrow \frac{13 \pm \sqrt{169 + 120}}{10} \qquad \Rightarrow \frac{13 \pm \sqrt{289}}{10}$$

$$\frac{13 \pm 17}{10}$$

$\frac{13+17}{10}$	$\frac{13-17}{10}$
$\Rightarrow \frac{30}{10}$	$\Rightarrow \frac{-4}{10}$
$\Rightarrow x = 3$	$\Rightarrow x = -0.4$

> Hence, or otherwise, solve for t given $5\left(\frac{3}{t}-5\right)^2 - 13\left(\frac{3}{t}-5\right) - 6 = 0$

* Write both equations underneath each other.

$5x^2 - 13x - 6 = 0$

$5\left(\frac{3}{t}-5\right)^2 - 13\left(\frac{3}{t}-5\right) - 6 = 0$

* It is very important that you make the following statement:

$$\boxed{\Rightarrow x = \frac{3}{t} - 5}$$

$x = 3$ (from above)	$x = -0.4$ (from above)
$3 = \frac{3}{t} - 5$	$-0.4 = \frac{3}{t} - 5$
$\Rightarrow 8 = \frac{3}{t}$	$\Rightarrow 5 - 0.4 = \frac{3}{t}$
	$4.6 = \frac{3}{t}$

* Write both sides as a fraction and cross multiply.

$\frac{8}{1} = \frac{3}{t}$	$\frac{4.6}{1} = \frac{3}{t}$
$\Rightarrow 8t = 3$	$(4.6)t = 3$
$\Rightarrow t = \frac{3}{8}$	$\Rightarrow t = \frac{3}{4.6}$
$\boxed{t = 0.4}$	$\boxed{t = 0.7}$

Solution to question 2

> **(a)** Write $\frac{4}{3x-1} - \frac{2}{4x-3}$ as a single fraction.

$$\frac{4}{3x-1} - \frac{2}{4x-3}$$

> Common denom. $= (3x-1)(4x-3)$

Multiplying both fractions by the common denominator:

$$\frac{4\cancel{(3x-1)}(4x-3)}{\cancel{3x-1}} - \frac{2(3x-1)\cancel{(4x-3)}}{\cancel{4x-3}}$$

$$\Rightarrow \frac{4(4x-3) - 2(3x-1)}{(3x-1)(4x-3)}$$

(again, we leave the common denominator under the line because there is no 'equal to' sign)

$$\Rightarrow \frac{16x - 12 - 6x + 2}{(3x-1)(4x-3)}$$

$$= \boxed{\frac{10x - 10}{(3x-1)(4x-3)}}$$

Evaluate when $x = \frac{1}{2}$

$$\Rightarrow \frac{10(0.5) - 10}{[3(0.5) - 1][4(0.5) - 3]}$$

$$\Rightarrow \frac{5 - 10}{(1.5 - 1)(2 - 3)}$$

$$\Rightarrow \frac{-5}{(0.5)(-1)} \quad \Rightarrow \frac{-5}{-0.5} = \boxed{10}$$

(b) Solve for x and y

$$x + \frac{y+3}{4} = 5$$

$$\frac{x-3}{4} + \frac{y}{2} = 2\frac{1}{2}$$

Line 1: $\frac{x}{1} + \frac{y+3}{4} = \frac{5}{1}$

Common denom. = 4

$$\frac{4x}{1} + \frac{4(y+3)}{4} = \frac{4(5)}{1}$$

$\Rightarrow \quad 4x + 1(y+3) = 20$

$\Rightarrow \quad 4x + 1y = 17$

Line 2: $\frac{x-3}{4} + \frac{y}{2} = \frac{5}{2}$

CD = 4

$\Rightarrow \quad \frac{4(x-3)}{4} + \frac{4(y)}{2} = \frac{4(5)}{2}$

$\Rightarrow \quad 1(x-3) + 2y = 2(5)$

$\Rightarrow \quad 1x - 3 + 2y = 10$

$\Rightarrow \quad 1x + 2y = 13$

* Solving simultaneously:

$4x + 1y = 17 \qquad\qquad 4x + 1y = 17$

$1x + 2y = 13 \quad (\times -4) \quad -4x - 8y = -52$

$-7y = -35$

$\Rightarrow y = 5$

Solve for x

$4x + 1y = 17$

$y = 5 \Rightarrow 4x + 1(5) = 17$

$4x = 17 - 5$

$\Rightarrow 4x = 12 \qquad x = 3$

(c) Simplify

$(2m+p)(4m-2p) - (3n+a)(6n-2a)$

$(2m+p)(4m-2p)$

$2m(4m-2p) + p(4m-2p)$

$8m^2 - 4mp + 4mp - 2p^2$

$= 8m^2 - 2p^2$

$* = 2(4m^2 - 1p^2)$

$= 2(2m - 1p)(2m + 1p)$

$(3n+a)(6n-2a)$

$3n(6n-2a) + a(6n-2a)$

$18n^2 - 6an + 6an - 2a^2$

$18n^2 - 2a^2 = 2(9n^2 - 1a^2)$

$\Rightarrow 2(3n-a)(3n+a)$

$\Rightarrow (2m+p)(4m-2p) - (3n+a)(6n-2a)$

$= 2(2m-1p)(2m+1p) - 2(3n-a)(3n+a)$

(d) Simplify

$$\frac{10m^2 - 11mn - 6n^2}{4m^2 - 9n^2}$$

(i) $10m^2 - 11mn - 6n^2$

$(10)(-6) = -60$

+1	−60
+2	−30
+3	−20
+4	−15 ✓
+5	−12
+6	−10

$10m^2 - 11mn - 6n^2$

$10m^2 + 4mn - 15mn - 6n^2$

$2m(5m + 2n) - 3n(5m + 2n)$

$(2m - 3n)(5m + 2n)$

(ii) $4m^2 - 9n^2$

$= (2m)^2 - (3n)^2$

$= (2m - 3n)(2m + 3n)$

$$\Rightarrow \frac{\cancel{(2m-3n)}(5m + 2n)}{\cancel{(2m-3n)}(2m + 3n)}$$

$$= \boxed{\frac{5m + 2n}{2m + 3n}}$$

Solution to question 3

> **(a)** Solve for x
>
> $$\frac{2}{3}(3x - 1) - \frac{1}{2}(2x - 5) = 2\frac{1}{4}$$

$$= \frac{2(3x-1)}{3} - \frac{1(2x-5)}{2} = \frac{9}{4}$$

$$= \frac{6x-2}{3} - \frac{2x-5}{2} = \frac{9}{4}$$

Common denom. = 12

$$\Rightarrow \frac{12(6x-2)}{3} - \frac{12(2x-5)}{2} = \frac{12(9)}{4}$$

$\Rightarrow \quad 4(6x - 2) - 6(2x - 5) = 3(9)$

$\Rightarrow \quad 24x - 8 - 12x + 30 = 27$

$\Rightarrow \quad 24x - 12x = 8 - 30 + 27$

$\Rightarrow \quad 12x = 5 \qquad x = \boxed{\frac{5}{12}}$

(b)

> **(i)** Factorise
>
> $12a^2 + 6ct - 8at - 9ac$

* If we attempt to factorise this as it is written, it will not work (the brackets will not be the same).

Therefore we must rearrange:

$12a^2 - 8at - 9ac + 6ct$

$4a(3a - 2t) - 3c(3a - 2t)$

$(4a - 3c)(3a - 2t)$

> **(ii)** Factorise $25t^2 - (4t - 3w)^2$

$\Rightarrow \quad (5t)^2 - (4t - 3w)^2$

$[(5t) - (4t - 3w)][5t + 4t - 3w]$

* Again we see that if there is more than one term in the second bracket we <u>must</u> leave that bracket intact after the minus sign.

$\Rightarrow (5t - 4t + 3w)(5t + 4t - 3w)$

$= (1t + 3w)(9t - 3w)$

> **(c)** Divide
>
> $6x^3 + 7x^2 - 14x - 8$ by $3x - 4$

$$
\begin{array}{r}
2x^2 + 5x + 2 \\
3x - 4 \overline{)\,6x^3 + 7x^2 - 14x - 8} \\
\ominus 6x^3 \overset{\oplus}{-} 8x^2 \qquad\qquad \\
\hline
15x^2 - 14x \quad\; \\
\ominus 15x^2 \overset{\oplus}{-} 20x \quad\; \\
\hline
6x + 8 \\
\ominus 6x \overset{\oplus}{-} 8 \\
\hline
\end{array}
$$

$\Rightarrow 2x^2 + 5x + 2$

(d)

(i) Solve $x^2 = 6x - 3$ correct to two decimal places.

Rearranging $1x^2 - 6x + 3 = 0$

$$\frac{-b \pm \sqrt{b^2 - 4ac}}{2a}$$

$a = 1 \qquad b = -6 \qquad c = 3$

$$\Rightarrow \frac{-(-6) \pm \sqrt{(-6)^2 - 4(1)(3)}}{2(1)}$$

$$\Rightarrow \frac{6 \pm \sqrt{36 - 12}}{2} \Rightarrow \frac{6 \pm \sqrt{24}}{2}$$

$$\frac{6 \pm 4.89}{2}$$

① $x = \dfrac{6 + 4.89}{2} = \dfrac{10.89}{2} = 5.45$

$\left(\dfrac{10.89}{2} = 5.445 \Rightarrow 5.45\right.$ correct to 2 decimal places$\left.\right)$

② $x = \dfrac{6 - 4.89}{2} = \dfrac{1.11}{2} = 0.55$

(ii) Hence, or otherwise, solve for t given

$$(2t^2 - 4)^2 - 6(2t^2 - 4) + 3 = 0$$

$$x^2 - 6x + 3 = 0$$

$$(2t^2 - 4)^2 - 6(2t^2 - 4) + 3 = 0$$

$$\boxed{\Rightarrow x = 2t^2 - 4}$$

$x = 5.45$	$x = 0.55$
$5.45 = 2t^2 - 4$	$0.55 = 2t^2 - 4$

* Again, isolate the t term

$9.45 = 2t^2$	$4.55 = 2t^2$
$\Rightarrow 4.73 = t^2$	$\Rightarrow 2.275 = t^2$
$\sqrt{4.73} = t$	$\sqrt{2.275} = t$
$\Rightarrow 2.18 = t$	$\Rightarrow 1.51 = t$

Chapter 4

Algebra Two

Inequalities

Graphing inequalities

(i) Natural numbers (N)

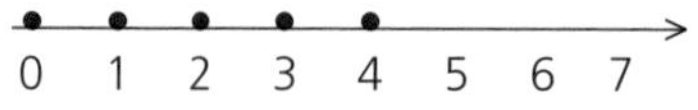

0 1 2 3 4 5 6 7

$x < 5, \quad x \in N$

* Positive, whole numbers only.

* 5 is not indicated because x is not equal to 5.

(ii) Integers (Z)

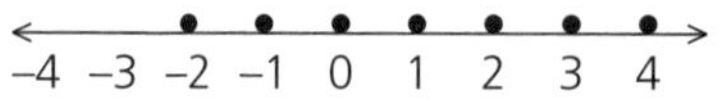

−4 −3 −2 −1 0 1 2 3 4

$x \geqslant -2, \quad x \in Z$

* Positive and negative whole numbers.
* −2 is indicated because x is equal to −2.

(iii) Real numbers (R)

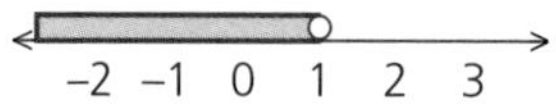

−2 −1 0 1 2 3

$x < 1 \quad x \in R$

* All positive and negative numbers (incl. fractions and decimals).
* Because x is not equal to 1, draw a hollow circle at 1 to indicate same.

(iv) Two inequalities

When both inequalities are 'less than', indicate between the numbers.

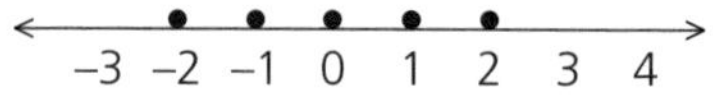

−3 −2 −1 0 1 2 3 4

$-2 \leqslant x < 3 \quad x \in Z$

When both inequalities are 'greater than' we indicate outside the numbers.

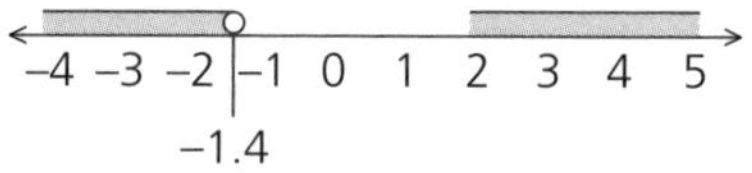

−4 −3 −2 −1 0 1 2 3 4 5

−1.4

$-1.4 > x \geqslant 2 \quad x \in R$

Solving for x

Type 1

Solve the following inequality and graph on the appropriate number line.

$$\frac{2x-1}{4} < \frac{3x+5}{3} - 2 \quad x \in R$$

Common denom. = 12

$$\frac{12(2x-1)}{4} < \frac{12(3x+5)}{3} - \frac{12(2)}{1}$$

$$3(2x-1) < 4(3x+5) - 24$$

$$6x - 3 < 12x + 20 - 24$$

x terms < numbers

$$6x - 12x < 3 + 20 - 24$$

$$-6x < -1$$

> **Very important**
>
> When the x term is negative:
>
> ① Change the sign on both sides of the inequality.
>
> ② Change the direction of the inequality.

$$-6x < -1$$

$$\Rightarrow \quad 6x > +1 \quad \Rightarrow \quad \boxed{x > \frac{1}{6}}, \quad x \in R$$

-1 0 1 2 3 4 5 6
$\frac{1}{6}$

Type 2

Solve for x and graph on the appropriate number line.

$$2(x-2) \leqslant 2(2x-1) < 6, \quad x \in Z$$

(i) Multiply out fully.

$$\Rightarrow 2x - 4 \leqslant 4x - 2 < 6$$

(ii) Deal with both inequalities individually.

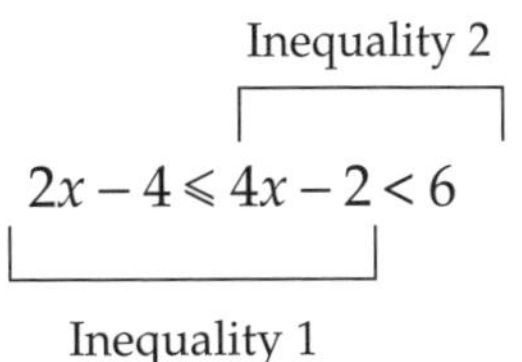

① $2x - 4 \leqslant 4x - 2$

$\Rightarrow 2x - 4x \leqslant 4 - 2$

$-2x \leqslant 2$

> Again, because the x term is negative:
>
> **(a)** Change the sign on both sides of the inequality.
>
> **(b)** Change the direction of the inequality.

$\Rightarrow 2x \geqslant -2$

$\boxed{x \geqslant -1}$

② $4x - 2 < 6 \quad \Rightarrow \quad 4x < 8$

$\boxed{x < 2}$

> **Important**
>
> Always write your final answer thus:
>
> | small number | x | big number |

$$\Rightarrow \quad -1 \leqslant x < 2, \quad x \in Z$$

-2 -1 0 1 2 3 4 5

Written Problems

Very important

When we are told the difference between two things:

① Let one equal the other.

② Add the difference to the smaller side.

Example

'2 pencils cost 15c more than 3 pens.'

Let $x =$ cost of a pencil
$y =$ cost of a pen

cost of 3 pens

① $\Rightarrow$ $2x = 3y$ [let one equal the other]

cost of 2 pencils

② Add the difference to the small side

$$2x = 3y + 15$$

Type 1

A racehorse costs €15,000 with x people each purchasing an equal share. If 25 fewer people had bought a share in the horse, each would have had to pay an extra €20. Express the above information in a single equation and hence evaluate x.

$\frac{15{,}000}{x}$ is the cost per person when x people invest.

Cost when fewer people invest is $\frac{15{,}000}{x-25}$

Again, let both equal to each other and add the difference to the smaller side.

* When there were $(x - 25)$ people the cost was more.

$$\Rightarrow \frac{15{,}000}{x} < \frac{15{,}000}{x-25}$$

* Easy to make a mistake here. *

$\Rightarrow$ Add the difference to the small side.

$$\frac{15{,}000}{x} + 20 = \frac{15{,}000}{x-25}$$

Now solve $\frac{15{,}000}{x} + \frac{20}{1} = \frac{15{,}000}{x-25}$

Common denominator $= (x)(x - 25)$

$$\frac{15{,}000(x)(x-25)}{x} + \frac{20(x)(x-25)}{1}$$

$$= \frac{15{,}000(x)(x-25)}{x-25}$$

$\Rightarrow 15{,}000(x - 25) + 20x(x - 25) = 15{,}000(x)$

$\Rightarrow 15{,}000x - 375{,}000 + 20x^2 - 500x$
$= 15{,}000x$

Rearrange:

x^2 term | x term | number | $= 0$.

$20x^2 + 15{,}000x - 15{,}000x$
$- 500x - 375{,}000 = 0$

$\Rightarrow 20x^2 - 500x - 375{,}000 = 0$

Dividing across by 20

$$1x^2 - 25x - 18{,}750 = 0$$

Solve using the '$-b$ formula'.

$$\frac{-b \pm \sqrt{b^2 - 4ac}}{2a}$$

$a = 1 \qquad b = -25 \qquad c = -18{,}750$

$$\Rightarrow \frac{-(-25) \pm \sqrt{(-25)^2 - 4(1)(-18{,}750)}}{2(1)}$$

$$\Rightarrow \frac{25 \pm \sqrt{625 + 75{,}000}}{2} = \frac{25 \pm \sqrt{75{,}625}}{2}$$

① $x = \dfrac{25 + 275}{2} \quad \Rightarrow x = \dfrac{300}{2}$

$\Rightarrow \quad \boxed{x = 150}$

② $x = \dfrac{25 - 275}{2} \quad \Rightarrow x = \dfrac{-250}{2}$

$\Rightarrow \quad \boxed{x = -125}$

As x is a number of people, we can disregard the negative value.

$\Rightarrow \quad \boxed{x = 150}$

Type 2

A rectangular field has a perimeter of 36 m and an area of 80 m². Letting the length equal to x, write an expression in x to illustrate the above information. Hence find the length and width.

Perimeter = 36

$\Rightarrow$ Length + width = 18

$\Rightarrow$ If length = x,
width = $18 - x$

x

$18 - x$

Area = Length × Width

$= (x)(18 - x)$

$= 18x - x^2$

$18 - x$

x

$\Rightarrow 18x - x^2 = 80$

Rearranging correctly

$x^2 - 18x + 80 = 0$

Solve using the '$-b$ formula'.

$$\frac{-b \pm \sqrt{b^2 - 4ac}}{2a}$$

$a = 1 \qquad b = -18 \qquad c = 80$

$$\Rightarrow \frac{-(-18) \pm \sqrt{(-18)^2 - 4(1)(80)}}{2(1)}$$

$$\Rightarrow \frac{18 \pm \sqrt{324 - 320}}{2} \Rightarrow \frac{18 \pm \sqrt{4}}{2}$$

$\Rightarrow$ ① $x = \dfrac{18 + 2}{2} \quad \Rightarrow \boxed{x = 10}$

② $x = \dfrac{18 - 2}{2} \quad \Rightarrow \boxed{x = 8}$

Important

x represents the length.

Therefore length has two valid values:

① Length = 10 m and width = 8 m (as we know length + width = 18 m).

② Length = 8 m and width = 10 m.

Type 3

Five CDs and 4 tapes cost €64. 2 CDs cost €2 less than 3 tapes. Write two equations in x and y to find the cost of each.

x = cost of a CD
y = cost of a tape

Equation 1

'5 CDs and 4 tapes cost €64.'

$$\boxed{5x + 4y = 64}$$

Equation 2

'2 CDs cost €2 less than 3 tapes.'

> Let $2x$ equal to $3y$ and add €2 to the small side.
>
> $$2x + 2 = 3y$$
> $$\Rightarrow 2x - 3y = -2$$

Solve for x and y

$$\begin{array}{lll} 5x + 4y = 64 & [\times 2] & 10x + 8y = 128 \\ 2x - 3y = -2 & [\times -5] & -10x + 15y = 10 \\ & & 23y = 138 \\ & & \Rightarrow \boxed{y = 6} \end{array}$$

Solve for y

$$2x - 3y = -2$$
$$\boxed{y = 6} \Rightarrow \quad 2x - 3(6) = -2$$
$$2x = -2 + 18 \Rightarrow x = 16$$
$$\boxed{x = 8}$$

$\Rightarrow$ A CD costs €8 while a tape costs €6.

Type 4

Questions involving age

> **Golden rule**
>
> If we are told how much older one person is than the other person is <u>at present</u>, express their ages in terms of the same letter.
>
> **Example**
>
> John is 5 years older than Sheila...
> John's age $x + 5$
> Sheila's age x

Example 1

Richard is 3 years younger than Philip. The product of their ages is 70.

* We are told that Richard is 3 years younger at present.

$\Rightarrow$ Richard age $= x - 3$

Philip's age $= x$

The product of their ages is 70

$$\Rightarrow \quad (x)(x - 3) = 70$$
$$\Rightarrow \quad x^2 - 3x = 70$$

Now solve $x^2 - 3x - 70 = 0$

Example 2

The sum of John and Aine's ages is 45. In 6 years' time John will be 4 times Aine's age. Write 2 expressions in x and y and hence evaluate John's age and Aine's age.

> Are we told the difference in ages at present?
>
> No! – so we represent the ages using different letters.

	Now	6 years' time
John's age	x	$x + 6$
Aine's age	y	$y + 6$

① 'Sum of the ages is 45.'

$$\boxed{x + y = 45}$$

② 'In 6 years' time John will be 4 times Aine's age.'

$\Rightarrow$ $(x + 6)$ is 4 times $(y + 6)$

$$\Rightarrow \quad x + 6 = 4(y + 6)$$
$$x + 6 = 4y + 24$$

Rearranging $\boxed{x - 4y = 18}$

Now solve simultaneously

$$x + y = 45$$
$$x - 4y = 18$$

Chapter 4
Sample questions for you to try

Question 1

(a) Given $A: 7 - 4x \geqslant 2x + 1, \quad x \in Z$ and $B: 8x - 1 > 5(x - 2), \quad x \in Z$ illustrate $A \cap B$ on the number line.

(b)

(i) Given $a = 4 - 2b$ and $c = 2a - 3b^2$ express c in terms of b.

(ii) Hence evaluate b if $c = 4$.

(c) A prize of €5000 is shared between x people. If there had been an extra 5 winners, each would have won €50 less. Write an expression in x to illustrate the above information. Hence evaluate x.

Question 2

(a) Solve the inequality

$\frac{2x-1}{2} > \frac{4x-3}{3} - 1$ and hence graph

$\frac{2x-1}{2} > \frac{4x-3}{3} - 1, \quad x \in R$ on the number line

(b) Mary ran the New York marathon (a distance of 42 km) at x km/hr. Her friend Martin ran the same race but was, on average, 1 km/hr faster than Mary. If he finished 45 minutes ahead of Mary, write an equation, in x, to represent the above information. Hence find x.

(c) The sum of a father's and a son's ages is 54. In 3 years' time, the father will be 3 times as old as his son will be then. Write two equations in x and y and hence evaluate the age of each.

Question 3

(a) Solve the inequality

$$2x - 1 < x - 2 \leqslant 3x + 10, \quad x \in Z$$

and illustrate your answer on the number line.

(b) If $n = \frac{3}{m}$ and $a = 2nm^2$ express a in terms of n.

(c) If the area of a rectangle is 60 cm^2 and the perimeter is 34 cm, let the length be x and write an equation in x to represent the above information. Hence solve the equation and find the dimensions of the rectangle.

Solution to question 1

(a) $A: 7 - 4x \geqslant 2x + 1, \quad x \in Z$

$B: 8x - 1 > 5(x - 2), \quad x \in Z$

Illustrate $A \cap B$.

① $7 - 4x \geqslant 2x + 1$

$-4x - 2x \geqslant 1 - 7$

$-6x \geqslant -6 \quad \Rightarrow 6x \leqslant 6$

$\boxed{x \leqslant 1}$

② $8x - 1 > 5x - 10$

$8x - 5x > -10 + 1$

$3x > -9 \quad \boxed{x > -3}$

small number	x	big number

$-3 < x \leqslant 1, \quad x \in Z$

(b) $A \cap B$ 

(i) Given $a = 4 - 2b$ and $c = 2a - 3b^2$ express c in terms of b.

If $a = 4 - 2b$ and $c = 2a - 3b^2$

$\Rightarrow \quad c = 2(4 - 2b) - 3b^2$

$= 8 - 4b - 3b^2$

$\Rightarrow \quad c = 8 - 4b - 3b^2$

(ii) Hence evaluate b when $c = 4$.

$\Rightarrow 4 = 8 - 4b - 3b^2$

$\Rightarrow -3b^2 - 4b + 4 = 0$

Using the '$-b$ formula':

$$\frac{-b \pm \sqrt{b^2 - 4ac}}{2a}$$

$a = -3 \qquad b = -4 \qquad c = 4$

$$\frac{-(-4) \pm \sqrt{(-4)^2 - 4(-3)(4)}}{2(-3)}$$

$$\frac{4 \pm \sqrt{16 + 48}}{-6} = \frac{4 \pm \sqrt{64}}{-6} = \boxed{\frac{4 \pm 8}{-6}}$$

① $b = \dfrac{4 + 8}{-6} = \dfrac{12}{-6} = \boxed{-2}$

② $b = \dfrac{4 - 8}{-6} = \dfrac{-4}{-6} = \boxed{\dfrac{2}{3}}$

(c) €5000 is shared between x people. If there were 5 extra winners, each would have received €50 less.

$\dfrac{5000}{x} \rightarrow$ The amount of money each person received when there were x winners.

$\dfrac{5000}{x + 5} \rightarrow$ The amount of money each person received when there were $(x + 5)$ winners.

* This is €50 less than $\dfrac{5000}{x}$ *

$$\Rightarrow \frac{5000}{x} = \frac{5000}{x + 5} + 50$$

Solving for x

$$\frac{5000}{x} = \frac{5000}{x + 5} + \frac{50}{1}$$

Common denom. $= (x)(x + 5)(1)$

$5000(x + 5)(1) = 5000(x)(1) + 50(x)(x + 5)$

$\Rightarrow 5000x + 25{,}000 = 5000x + 50x^2 + 250x$

Rearranging correctly

$\Rightarrow 50x^2 + 250x - 5000x + 5000x - 25{,}000 = 0$

$50x^2 + 250x - 25{,}000 = 0$

$\Rightarrow [\div 50] \quad 1x^2 + 5x - 500 = 0$

Solving for x

We can use the '$-b$ formula' or:

$(x + 25)(x - 20)$

$\Rightarrow x + 25 = 0 \qquad x - 20 = 0$

$\boxed{x = -25} \qquad \boxed{x = 20}$

* As x is a number of people, we can eliminate $x = -25$ as a possible answer.

$\Rightarrow \boxed{x = 20}$

Solution to question 2

> **(a)** Solve and graph
>
> $$\frac{2x-1}{2} > \frac{4x-3}{3} - 1, \quad x \in R$$

$$\frac{2x-1}{2} > \frac{4x-3}{3} - \frac{1}{1}$$

$$\boxed{CD = 6}$$

$$\frac{6(2x-1)}{2} > \frac{6(4x-3)}{3} - \frac{6(1)}{1}$$

$\Rightarrow \quad 3(2x-1) > 2(4x-3) - 6$

$\quad 6x - 3 > 8x - 6 - 6$

$\Rightarrow \quad 6x - 8x > -6 - 6 + 3$

$\Rightarrow \quad -2x > -9 \qquad$ (x term is (−))

$\Rightarrow \quad 2x < 9$

$$\boxed{x < 4.5, \quad x \in R}$$

−2 −1 0 1 2 3 4 5 6

4.5

(b) 'Mary ran 42 km at a speed of x km/hr.'

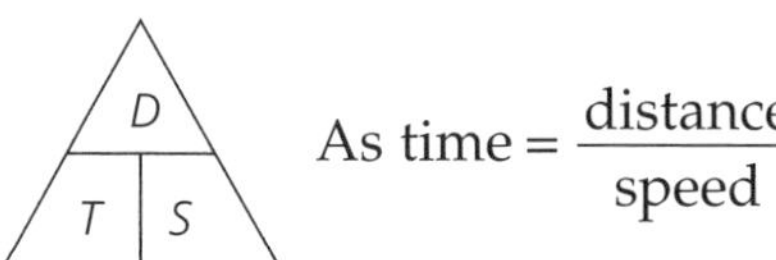

As time $= \dfrac{\text{distance}}{\text{speed}}$

$$\boxed{\text{Mary's time} = \frac{42}{x}}$$

'Martin ran 42 km at 1 km/hr faster than Mary.'

$\Rightarrow$ Martin's speed was $x + 1$ km/hr

$$\boxed{\text{So Martin's time} = \frac{42}{x+1}}$$

'Martin was 45 minutes quicker.'

> **Very important**
>
> Because the speed is given in km per hour, any time difference must be given as a fraction of an hour.
>
> And 45 minutes = $\frac{3}{4}$ of an hour.

⇓

$\Rightarrow$ Martin was $\dfrac{3}{4}$ of an hour quicker.

⇓

$\Rightarrow \dfrac{42}{x+1}$ is $\dfrac{3}{4}$ of an hour less than $\dfrac{42}{x}$

$$\Rightarrow \boxed{\frac{42}{x+1} + \frac{3}{4} = \frac{42}{x}}$$

Solving for x

Common denom. $= (x+1)(4)(x)$

$$\frac{42(x+1)(4)(x)}{x+1} + \frac{3(x+1)(4)(x)}{4}$$

$$= \frac{42(x+1)(4)(x)}{x}$$

$$42(4)(x) + 3(x+1)(x) = 42(x+1)(4)$$

$\Rightarrow \quad 168(x) + 3x(x+1) = 168(x+1)$

$\quad 168x + 3x^2 + 3x = 168x + 168$

Rearranging

$$3x^2 + 168x - 168x + 3x - 168 = 0$$

$$3x^2 + 3x - 168 = 0$$

Solve using the '$-b$ formula'.

$$\frac{-b \pm \sqrt{b^2 - 4ac}}{2a}$$

$a = 3 \qquad b = 3 \qquad c = -168$

$$\frac{-(3) \pm \sqrt{(3)^2-4(3)(-168)}}{2(3)}$$

$$\frac{-3 \pm \sqrt{2025}}{6} = \frac{-3 \pm 45}{6}$$

$\Rightarrow$ ① $x = \dfrac{-3+45}{6}$ $\Rightarrow$ $\boxed{x = 7}$

$\Rightarrow$ ② $x = \dfrac{-3-45}{6}$ $\Rightarrow$ $\boxed{x = -8}$

As x represents speed, we can discard the negative value.

$\Rightarrow$ $x = 7$ so Mary ran the race at a speed of 7 km/hr

> **(c)** Sum of a father's and a son's age is 54. In 3 years' time, the father will be 3 times as old his son.

Were we told the difference in the ages at present? $\rightarrow$ No

Therefore we represent their ages using **different** letters.

	Age now	Age in 3 years
Father's age	x	$x+3$
Son's age	y	$y+3$

① Sum of the ages is 54

$\Rightarrow$ $\boxed{x + y = 54}$

② In 3 years' time the father will be 3 times as old as his son.

$x + 3 = 3(y+3)$ ← [we multiply the smaller age by 3]

$x + 3 = 3y + 9$

$\Rightarrow$ $\boxed{x - 3y = 6}$

Now solve for x and y.

$x + y = 54$ $\qquad$ $x + y = 54$

$x - 3y = 6$ $\quad [\times -1]$ $\qquad$ $-x + 3y = -6$

$4y = 48$

$y = 12$

$x + y = 54$

$y = 12 \quad \Rightarrow x + 12 = 54 \quad \Rightarrow x = 42$

$\Rightarrow$ The son's age is 12. The father's age is 42.

Solution to question 3

> **(a)** Solve and illustrate.
> $2x - 1 < x - 2 \leqslant 3x + 10, \quad x \in Z$

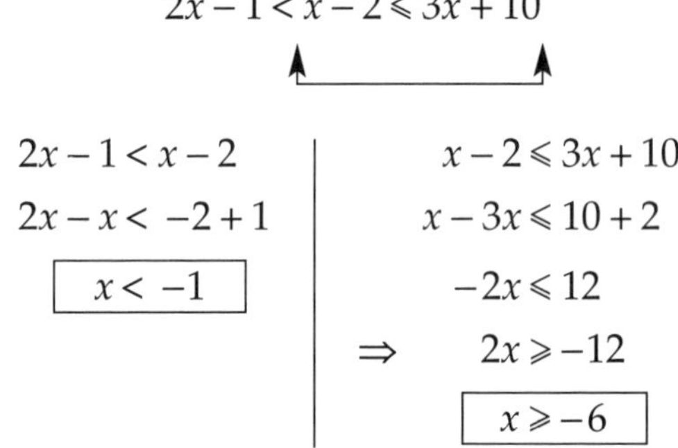

$2x - 1 < x - 2$

$2x - x < -2 + 1$

$\boxed{x < -1}$

$x - 2 \leqslant 3x + 10$

$x - 3x \leqslant 10 + 2$

$-2x \leqslant 12$

$\Rightarrow \quad 2x \geqslant -12$

$\boxed{x \geqslant -6}$

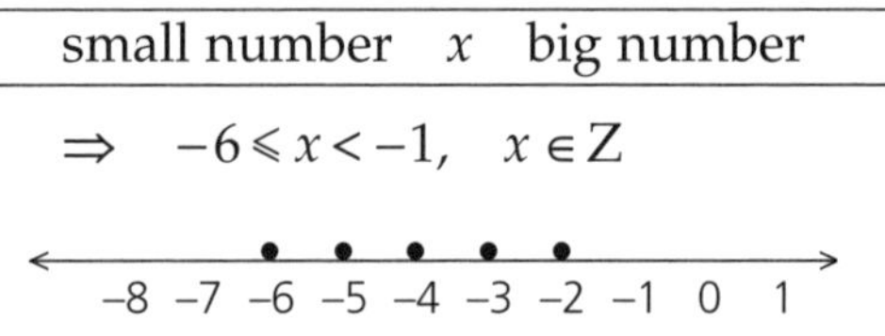

(b) If $n = \frac{3}{m}$ and $a = 2nm^2$

express a in terms of n.

Very important

This can be perceived as a difficult question. However, if we follow these two steps it is very easy:

① If we wish to express 'a' in terms of n, we must first of all express 'm' in terms of n.

② Substitute the result into the second equation.

① Write m in terms of n

$$\frac{n}{1} = \frac{3}{m}$$

Cross multiply: $nm = 3 \Rightarrow \boxed{m = \frac{3}{n}}$

② Substitute the result into eqn. 2

$$a = 2nm^2$$

Let $m = \frac{3}{n}$ $\quad \Rightarrow a = 2n\left(\frac{3}{n}\right)^2$

$$\Rightarrow a = 2n\left(\frac{9}{n^2}\right)$$

$$\Rightarrow a = \frac{2n(9)}{n^2}$$

$\Rightarrow a = \frac{18n}{n^2} \quad \Rightarrow \boxed{a = \frac{18}{n}}$

(c) Area of rectangle = 60 cm^2
Perimeter = 34 cm

Let the length = x and express using two equations.

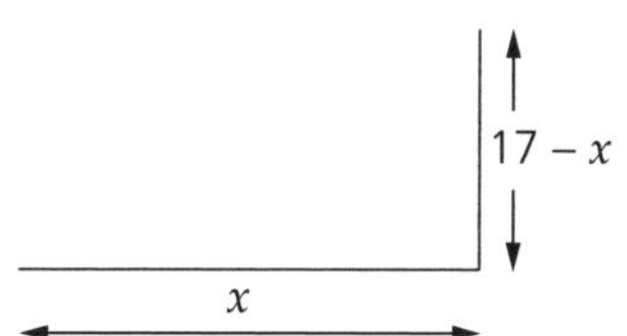

* Perimeter = 34

$\Rightarrow$ Length + Width = 17

* But length = x

$\Rightarrow$ Width = $17 - x$

Area = (length) × (width)

$= (x)(17 - x)$

$\Rightarrow \quad 60 = 17x - x^2$

$\Rightarrow$ Solve $x^2 - 17x + 60 = 0$

We can use the '$-b$ formula' or alternatively:

$$(x - 12)(x - 5)$$

$x - 12 = 0 \qquad x - 5 = 0$

$\Rightarrow \boxed{x = 12} \qquad \boxed{x = 5}$

① Length + Width = 17

$\boxed{x = 12} \Rightarrow$ length = 12 cm, width = 5 cm

Important

The length of a rectangle does not have to be longer than the width. Therefore we must consider a length equal to 5 cm.

② Length + Width = 17

$\boxed{x = 5} \Rightarrow$ length = 5 cm, width = 12 cm

Both pairs of answers are correct.

Chapter 5

Quadratic Graph One

Question type 1

(a) A rectangle has a perimeter of 16 m. If its length is x metres, show that its area is $(8x - x^2)$ m^2.

① Total perimeter
$= 16$ m

② $\Rightarrow$ Length + Width = 8 m

③ If length $= x$
width $= 8 - x$

④ Area of a rectangle = Length × Width
$= (x)(8 - x)$
$= 8x - x^2$

This is an extremely popular question type. Please get into the habit of laying the solution out in point format as above.

(b) Hence graph $f: x \to 8x - x^2$ in the domain $1 \leqslant x \leqslant 7$. Use your graph to find:

(i) The area of the rectangle when its length is 2.3 m.

(ii) The length and width of the rectangle when the area is 10 m^2.

(iii) The area of the rectangle when the width is 6.5 m.

(iv) **(a)** The maximum area.

(b) The length and width corresponding to maximum area.

Things to remember when graphing in a question of this type:

① There will never be a negative x or y value.

② It is important to clearly state what each axis represents.

- The x-axis will always represent either length or width (the question will tell you).
- The y-axis will always represent area.

(b) Hence graph $f: x \to 8x - x^2$ for $x = 1, 2, 3, 4, 5, 6, 7$.

x	1	2	3	4	5	6	7
$8x$ $-x^2$	8 -1	16 -4	24 -9	32 -16	40 -25	48 -36	56 -49
y	7	12	15	16	15	12	7

Points (1, 7)(2, 12)(3, 15)(4, 16)(5, 15)(6, 12)(7, 7)

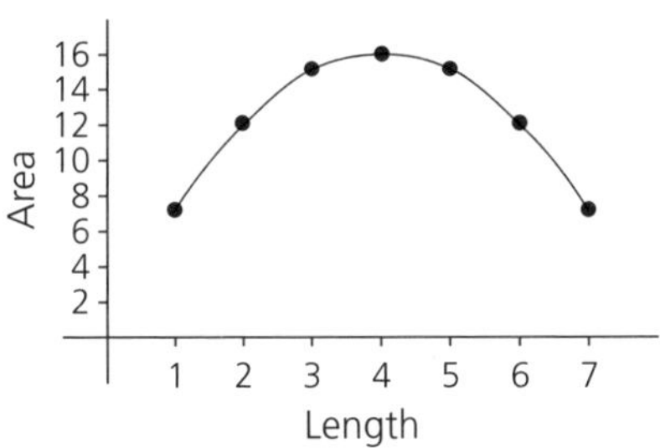

From the graph find:

(i) The area of the rectangle when its length is 2.3 m.

Go to 2.3 on the x-axis.

Find the corresponding y value.

$\Rightarrow$ Area = 12.4 m^2

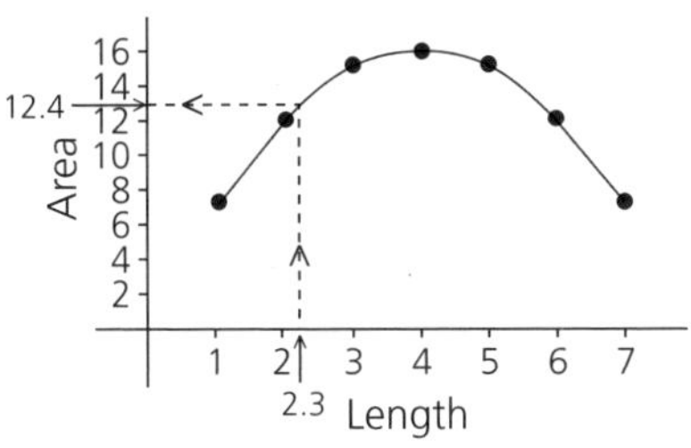

(ii) The length and width of the rectangle when the area is equal to 10 m^2.

Go to 10 on the y-axis.

Find the corresponding x values.

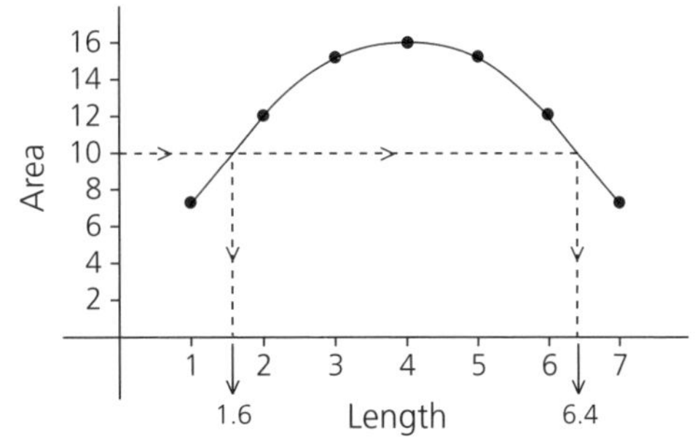

Note 1

We know 'length + width = 8 m'. In the same way, when we find two x values corresponding to a specific area, they will also have to add up to 8.

Note 2

Both values of x are valid and must be given in the final answer. Remembering that: ① x represents length, ② length + width = 8; our answers are: **(a)** length = 1.6 m and width = 6.4 m, and **(b)** length = 6.4 m and width = 1.6 m.

(iii) The area of the rectangle when its width is 6.5 m.

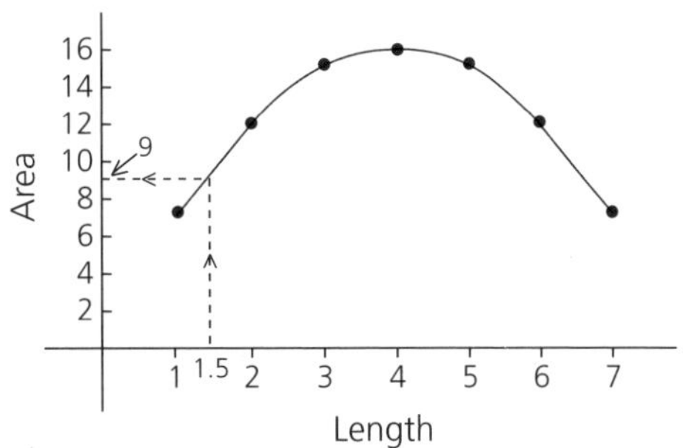

'Length + Width = 8 m'

$\Rightarrow$ If width = 6.5 m, length = 1.5 m

So, we go to 1.5 on the x-axis.

> Please don't make the mistake of going to 6.5 on the x-axis. Understand why this would be wrong.

Therefore when the width is 6.5 m, the area is 9 m^2.

> **(iv)** Calculate:
>
> **(a)** The maximum area.
>
> **(b)** The length and width corresponding to maximum area.

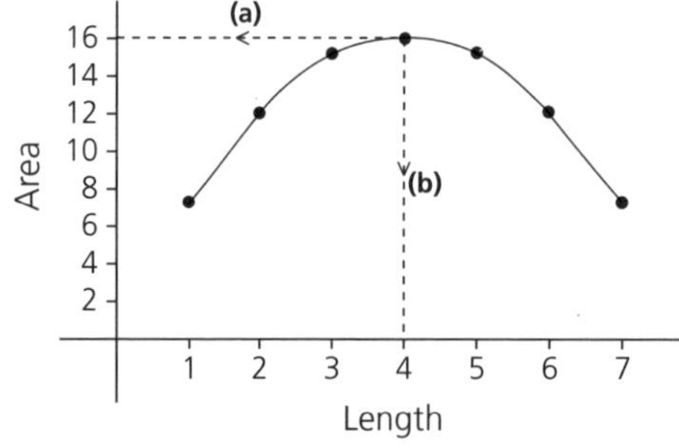

(a) From the diagram we see that the maximum area is 16 m^2.

(b) The length corresponding to the maximum area is 4 m.

As 'length + width = 8 m', width is 4 m also.

> **Important**
>
> In all questions of this type, when the area is maximum, the length and width will always be equal.

Question type 2

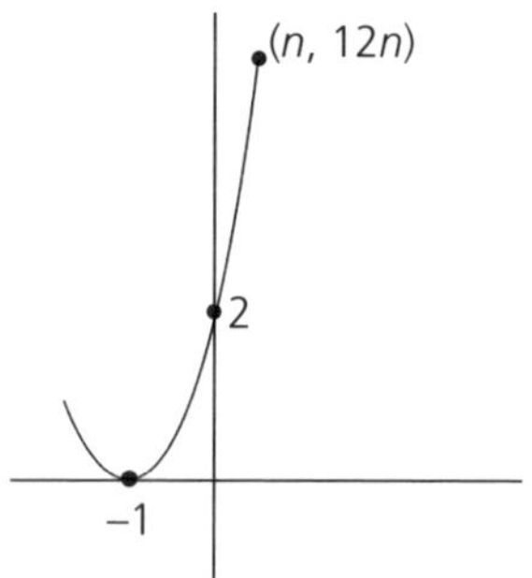

> The equation of the graph shown above is
>
> $$f: x \rightarrow ax^2 + 5x + b$$

(i) Calculate a and b.

> **Important**
>
> If a graph contains a point.
>
> ① Fill the x value in for x in the eqn. of the graph.
>
> ② Let the eqn. of the graph equal to the y value.
>
> **Example**
>
> If $(2, -4)$ is on $ax^2 + bx - 2$...
>
> $$a(2)^2 + b(2) - 2 = -4$$
> $$4a + 2b - 2 = -4$$
> $$\Rightarrow 4a + 2b = -2$$

In this example, the graph contains $(-1, 0)$ and $(0, 2)$.

① $ax^2 + 5x + b$

$$(-1, 0) \Rightarrow \begin{bmatrix} x = -1 \\ \text{Equation} = 0 \end{bmatrix}$$

$\Rightarrow a(-1)^2 + 5(-1) + b = 0$

$\Rightarrow 1a - 5 + b = 0$

$\Rightarrow 1a + b = 5$

② $ax^2 + 5x + b$

$(0, 2) \Rightarrow a(0)^2 + 5(0) + b = 2$

$\Rightarrow \quad b = 2$

Now use both outcomes to solve for a and b.

$1a + b = 5$

$\boxed{b = 2} \quad \Rightarrow a + 2 = 5$

$\Rightarrow \quad a = 3$

Substitute both values back into the given equation.

Eqn. of graph $\rightarrow 3x^2 + 5x + 2$

> **(ii)** The graph also contains $(n, 12n)$. Calculate n if $n > 1$.

$f: x \rightarrow 3x^2 + 5x + 2$

$(n, 12n)$

$\Rightarrow$ Let $x = n$

Let eqn. of the graph $= 12n$

$\Rightarrow 3(n)^2 + 5(n) + 2 = 12n$

$3n^2 + 5n + 2 = 12n$

$3n^2 - 7n + 2 = 0$

Solve using the '$-b$ formula'.

$$\frac{-b \pm \sqrt{b^2 - 4ac}}{2a}$$

$a = 3 \qquad b = -7 \qquad c = 2$

$$= \frac{-(-7) \pm \sqrt{(-7)^2 - 4(3)(2)}}{2(3)}$$

$$= \frac{7 \pm \sqrt{49 - 24}}{6} = \frac{7 \pm \sqrt{25}}{6}$$

$\Rightarrow$ ① $x = \dfrac{7+5}{6} \quad \Rightarrow x = 2$

② $x = \dfrac{7-5}{6} \quad \Rightarrow x = \dfrac{1}{3}$

But we are told that $n > 1$.

$\Rightarrow \quad \boxed{n = 2}$

Question type 3

> **(i)** Using simultaneous equations, find the point of intersection of $x + 3y - 9 = 0$ and $4x - y - 10 = 0$

$1x + 3y = 9 \quad [\times -4] \quad -4x - 12y = -36$

$4x - 1y = 10 \qquad\qquad\quad 4x - 1y = 10$

$-13y = -26$

$\boxed{y = 2}$

$1x + 3y = 9$

$y = 2 \quad \Rightarrow 1x + 3(2) = 9$

$x = 9 - 6 \Rightarrow \boxed{x = 3}$

$\Rightarrow$ Point of intersection $= (3, 2)$

> **(ii)** Confirm your answer by graphing both lines and showing the point of intersection.

To graph a line, let $x = 0$ and let $y = 0$.

$1x + 3y = 9$

$x = 0 \quad \Rightarrow 3y = 9 \quad \Rightarrow y = 3$

$y = 0 \quad \Rightarrow x = 9$

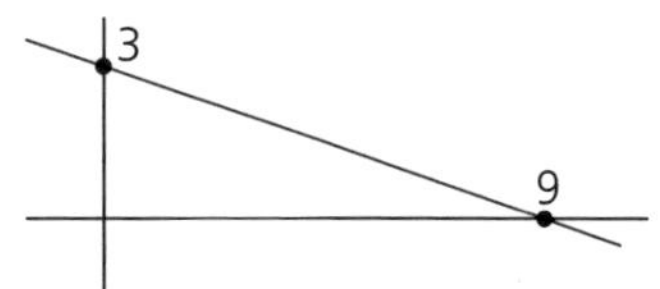

$$4x - y - 10 = 0$$

$$x = 0 \quad \Rightarrow -y = 10 \quad \Rightarrow y = -10$$

$$y = 0 \quad \Rightarrow 4x = 10 \quad \Rightarrow x = 2\frac{1}{2}$$

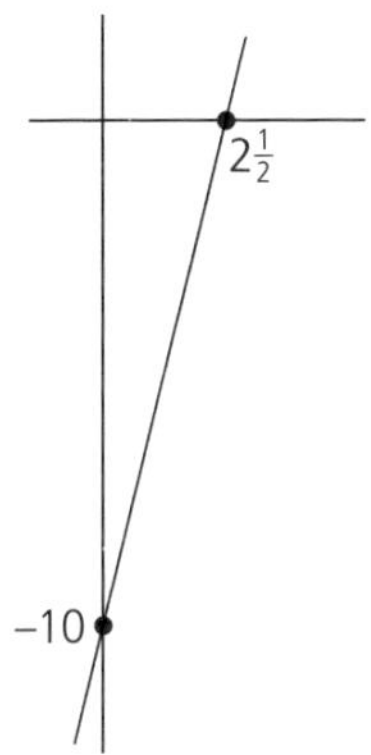

Now use graph paper to graph both lines together.

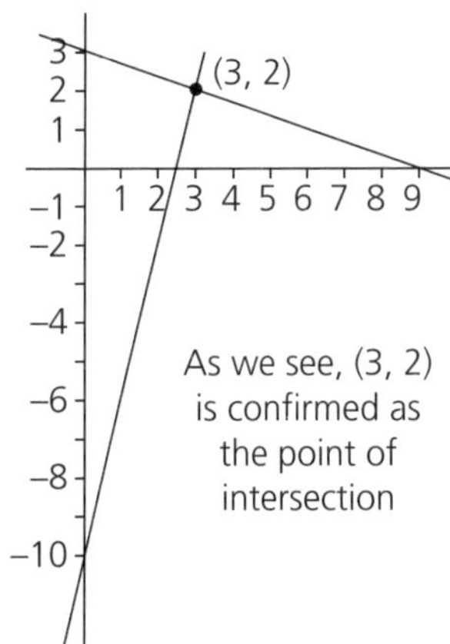

Chapter 5
Sample questions for you to try

Question 1

A farmer wishes to make a rectangular enclosure. He has 20 m of fencing and four posts. The length of the enclosure is x metres.

x metres

(a) Show that the enclosure has an area of $10x - x^2$ square metres.

(b) Let f be the function f: $x \rightarrow 10x - x^2$. Evaluate $f(x)$ when $x = 1, 2, 3, 4, 5, 6, 7$. Draw $f(x)$ in the domain $1 \leqslant x \leqslant 7$.

(c) Use your graph to estimate:

(i) The area of the enclosure when the length = 5.5 metres.

(ii) Two possible lengths for which the area is 23 m^2.

(iii) The maximum area.

(iv) The length and width of the enclosure corresponding to maximum area.

Question 2

(a) **(i)** Using graph paper, draw the following lines on a single diagram:

$$x - 4y = 11$$

$$2x - 3y = 12$$

(ii) From your diagram, estimate the point of intersection of the lines.

(iii) Check your answer to part **(ii)** by solving the simultaneous equations:

$$x - 4y = 11$$

$$2x - 3y = 12$$

(b) The graph shows the function

$$f: x \rightarrow 2x^2 + ax + b$$

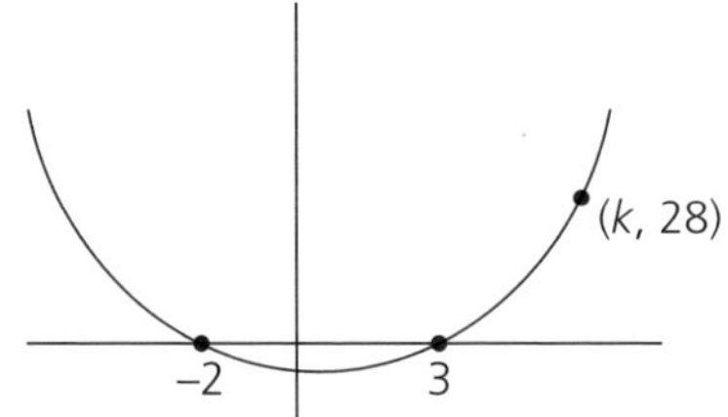

(i) Evaluate a and b.

(ii) Evaluate k.

(iii) If the graph also contains $(t, 3t)$ evaluate t if $t > 0$.

Question 3

(a) This is a diagram of $f: x \rightarrow ax + b$. Find a and b.

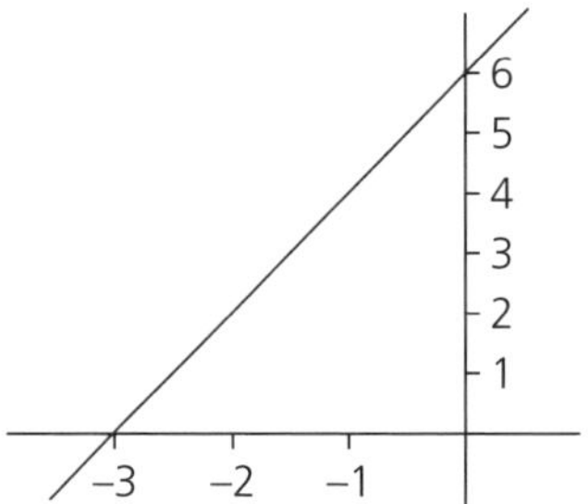

(b) The graph here shows the function

$$f: x \rightarrow cx^2 + dx + 5$$

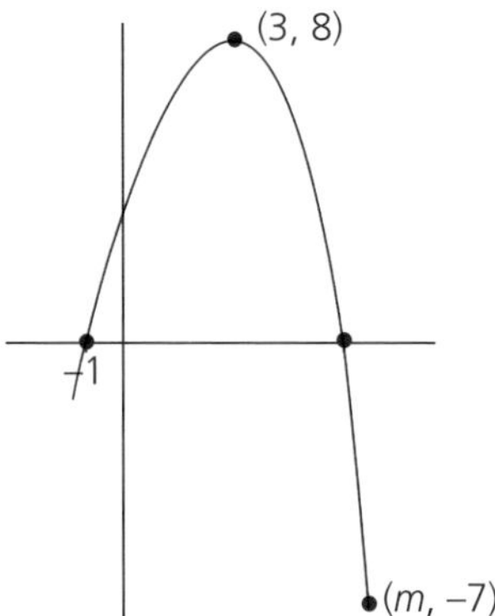

(i) Evaluate c and d.

(ii) We see that $(m, -7)$ is a point on the graph. Find m.

(iii) If the graph also contains the point $(2t, 7t)$ evaluate t if $t < 0$.

Solution to question 1

(a)

This fence is 20 m in total.

If the length $= x$, prove that the area of the rectangle is $10x - x^2$.

$\Rightarrow$ length + width = 10 m

The length $= x$.

$\Rightarrow$ width $= 10 - x$

Area = (length) × (width)

$= x(10 - x)$

$= (10x - x^2)$ square metres

(b) Draw $f: x \rightarrow 10x - x^2$ in the domain $1 \leqslant x \leqslant 7$.

x	1	2	3	4	5	6	7
$10x$	10	20	30	40	50	60	70
$-x^2$	−1	−4	−9	−16	−25	−36	−49
y	9	16	21	24	25	24	21

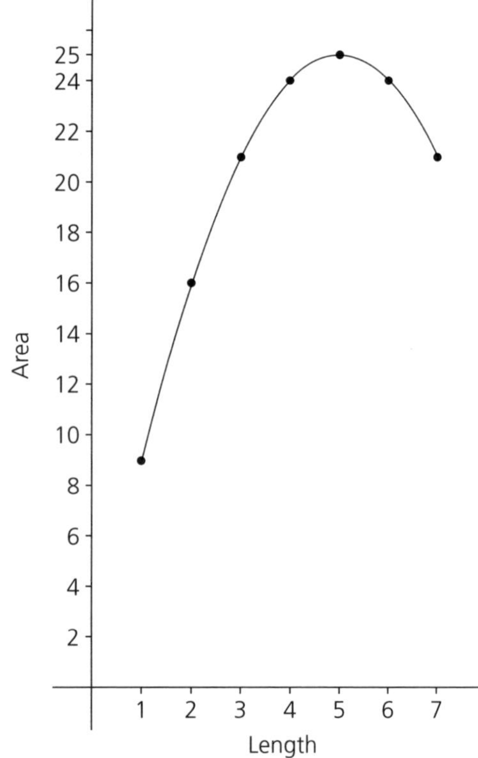

Again, it is very important to show you understand that the x-axis represents the length of the enclosure and the y-axis represents its area.

(c)

(i) Find the area when the length is 5.5 m.

Length is shown on the x-axis.

$\Rightarrow$ if length is 5.5 m, $x = 5.5$

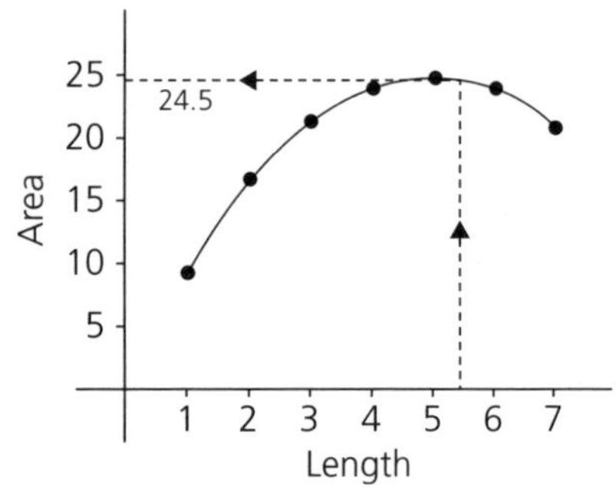

$\Rightarrow$ when length is 5.5 m, area $= 24.5\ m^2$

(ii) Two possible lengths when the area is 23 m^2.

Area is shown on the y-axis.

$\Rightarrow$ if area is 23 m^2, $y = 23$

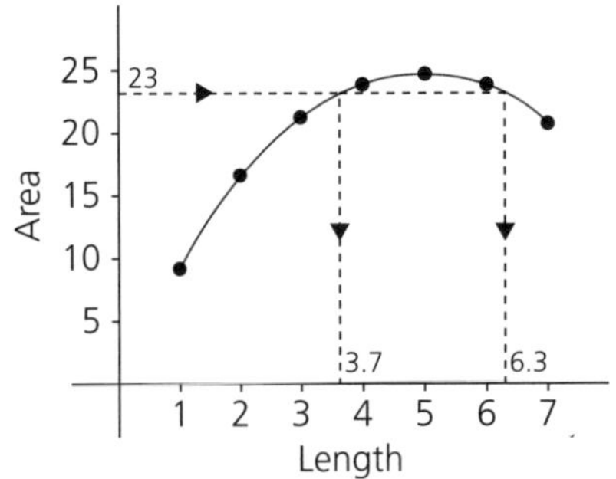

$\Rightarrow$ When area is 23 m^2, the length is 3.7 m or 6.3 m.

(iii) Find the maximum area.

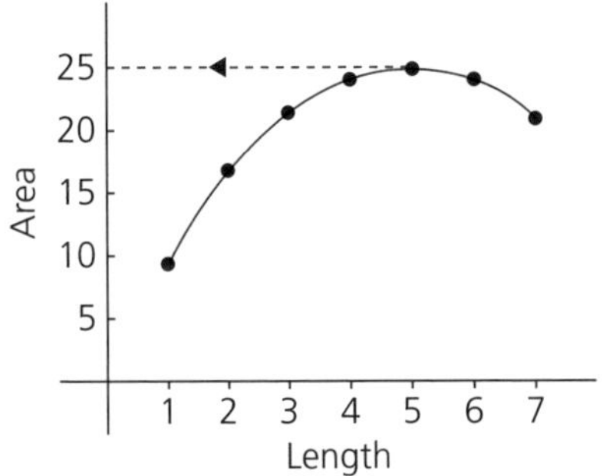

Maximum area = 25 m^2

(iv) Find the length and width corresponding to maximum area.

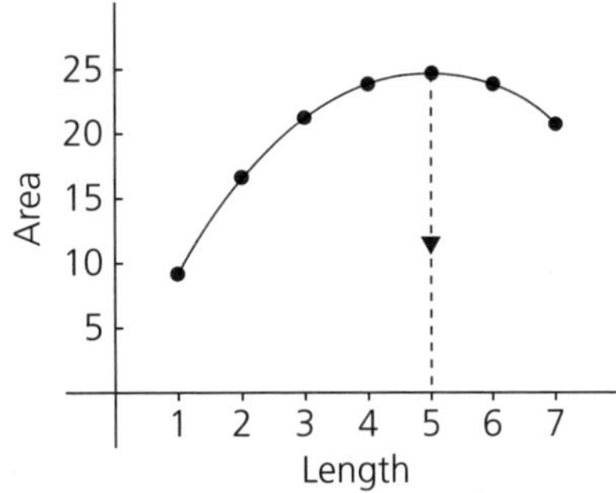

$*$ The length corresponding to the maximum area is 5 m.

At the start of this question we found that length + width = 10 m.

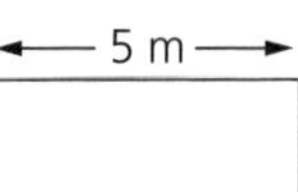

$\Rightarrow$ If the length is 5 m, the width is also 5 m.

Therefore, for maximum area
length = 5 m
width = 5 m.

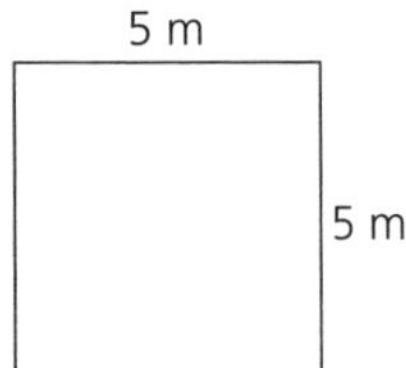

Important

Please remember that it will always be the case that for maximum area the 'rectangle' will be a square.

Solution to question 2

(a)

(i) Draw $x - 4y = 11$ and $2x - 3y = 12$ on a single diagram.

$x - 4y = 11$

$x = 0 \quad \Rightarrow \quad -4y = 11 \quad \Rightarrow y = -2.75$

$y = 0 \quad \Rightarrow \quad x = 11$

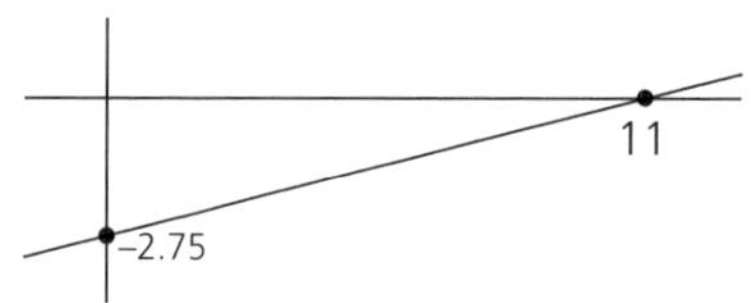

$2x - 3y = 12$

$x = 0 \quad \Rightarrow -3y = 12 \quad \Rightarrow y = -4$

$y = 0 \quad \Rightarrow \quad 2x = 12 \quad \Rightarrow x = 6$

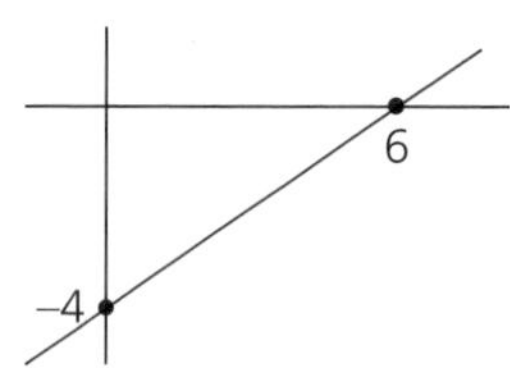

(ii) From the diagram we see that the point of intersection is (3, −2).

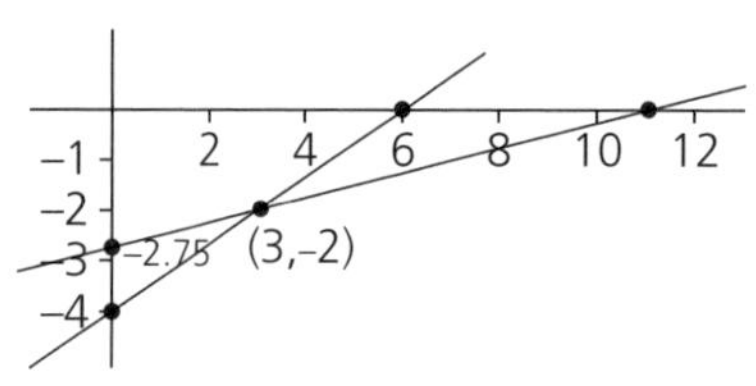

> **(iii)** Verify your answer by solving
> $x - 4y = 11$
> $2x - 3y = 12$ simultaneously

$x - 4y = 11 \quad (\times -2) \quad -2x + 8y = -22$

$2x - 3y = 12 \qquad\qquad\quad 2x - 3y = 12$

$5y = -10$

$\boxed{y = -2}$

Solve for x

$x - 4y = 11$

$y = -2 \quad \Rightarrow x - 4(-2) = 11$

$x + 8 = 11 \quad \Rightarrow x = 3$

⇒ The point of intersection has been verified as (3, − 2).

(b)

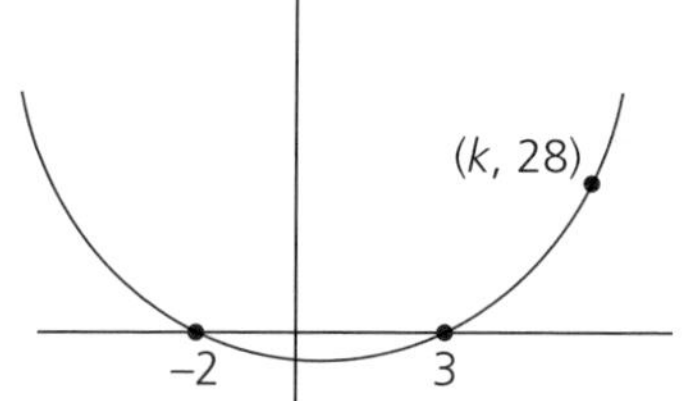

$f: x \to 2x^2 + ax + b$

> **(i)** Evaluate a and b.

$2x^2 + ax + b$

$(-2, 0) \quad \Rightarrow$ Let $x = -2$

Let the eqn. of the graph = 0

$2(-2)^2 + a(-2) + b = 0$

$8 - 2a + b = 0 \quad \Rightarrow -2a + 1b = -8$

(3, 0)

$\Rightarrow 2(3)^2 + a(3) + b = 0$

$18 + 3a + b = 0$

$\Rightarrow \quad 3a + b = -18$

Solving for a and b

$-2a + 1b = -8 \quad [\times -1] \quad 2a - 1b = 8$

$3a + 1b = -18 \qquad\qquad 3a + 1b = -18$

$5a = -10$

$\Rightarrow a = -2$

Solve for b

$3a + 1b = -18$

$\boxed{a = -2}$

$\Rightarrow 3(-2) + b = -18$

$b = -18 + 6$

$\Rightarrow \quad \boxed{b = -12}$

(ii) Evaluate k if the graph contains $(k, 28)$.

As $a = -2$ and $b = -12$

$$f: x \rightarrow 2x^2 - 2x - 12$$

$(k, 28) \Rightarrow$ let k be equal to x

let 28 be equal to the equation of the graph

$$\Rightarrow 2(k)^2 - 2(k) - 12 = 28$$

$$\Rightarrow 2k^2 - 2k - 40 = 0$$

$$\frac{-b \pm \sqrt{b^2 - 4ac}}{2a}$$

$a = 2 \qquad b = -2 \qquad c = -40$

$$\Rightarrow \frac{-(-2) \pm \sqrt{(-2)^2 - 4(2)(-40)}}{2(2)}$$

$$\Rightarrow \frac{2 \pm \sqrt{4 + 320}}{4} = \frac{2 \pm \sqrt{324}}{4}$$

$$\Rightarrow ① \; k = \frac{2 + 18}{4} \qquad \Rightarrow k = 5$$

$$\Rightarrow ② \; k = \frac{2 - 18}{4} \qquad \Rightarrow k = -4$$

Important

From the graph we can see: ① k is the x coordinate, ② k is positive. We can therefore discard the negative k value above $\Rightarrow$ $\boxed{k = 5}$

(iii) Evaluate $t > 0$ if the graph contains $(t, 3t)$.

$$f: x \rightarrow 2x^2 - 2x - 12$$

$$(t, 3t)$$

$$\Rightarrow \quad 2(t)^2 - 2(t) - 12 = 3t$$

$$\Rightarrow \quad 2t^2 - 2t - 12 = 3t$$

$$2t^2 - 5t - 12 = 0$$

Using the '$-b$ formula'

$t = -1.5 \qquad t = 4$

As $t > 0$, $t = 4$

Solution to question 3

(a)

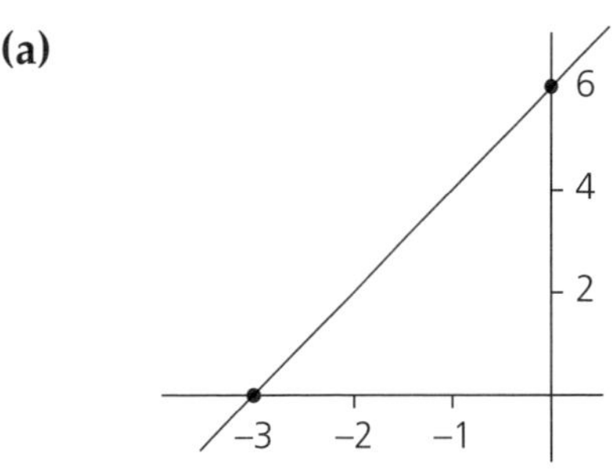

$$f: x \rightarrow ax + b$$

The graph contains $(0, 6)$ and $(-3, 0)$.

$(0, 6) \Rightarrow$ let $0 = x$

let $6 =$ the eqn. of the graph

$\Rightarrow a(0) + b = 6 \qquad \Rightarrow b = 6$

$(-3, 0)$

$$\Rightarrow a(-3) + b = 0$$

$$\Rightarrow \quad -3a + b = 0$$

$\boxed{b = 6}$

$$\Rightarrow \quad -3a + 6 = 0$$

$$-3a = -6$$

$$\boxed{a = 2}$$

(b)

(i) Evaluate c and d.

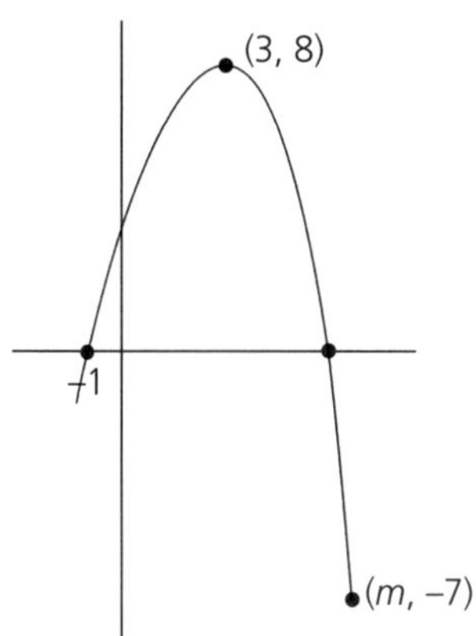

$f: x \to cx^2 + dx + 5$

$(-1, 0)$

$\Rightarrow c(-1)^2 + d(-1) + 5 = 0$

$\boxed{1c - 1d = -5}$

$(3, 8)$

$\Rightarrow c(3)^2 + d(3) + 5 = 8$

$\boxed{9c + 3d = 3}$

Solving for c and d

$9c + 3d = 3 \qquad\qquad 9c + 3d = 3$

$1c - 1d = -5 \quad [\times -9] \quad -9c + 9d = 45$

$12d = 48$

$d = 4$

$9c + 3d = 3$

$\boxed{d = 4} \Rightarrow 9c + 3(4) = 3$

$9c + 12 = 3$

$\Rightarrow 9c = -9 \qquad \boxed{c = -1}$

(ii) Evaluate m.

$c = -1, \qquad d = 4$

$\Rightarrow f: x \to -1x^2 + 4x + 5$

$(m, -7)$

$\Rightarrow -1(m)^2 + 4(m) + 5 = -7$

$-1m^2 + 4m + 12 = 0$

Using the '$-b$ formula'

$m = 6$ and $m = -2$

Important

From the diagram, however, we can see that m is positive.

$\Rightarrow m = 6$

(iii) If the graph also contains $(2t, 7t)$, find t given $t < 0$.

$f: x \to -1x^2 + 4x + 5$

$(2t, 7t)$

$\Rightarrow \quad -1(2t)^2 + 4(2t) + 5 = 7t$

$-4t^2 + 8t + 5 = 7t$

$-4t^2 + 1t + 5 = 0$

Using the '$-b$ formula'

$t = -1$ and $t = 1.25$

But $t < 0 \quad \Rightarrow t = -1$

Chapter 6

Quadratic Graph Two

Functions

Type 1

Given $f: x \rightarrow 3x^2 - 4x - 2$

(i) Evaluate $f(-3)$

> In any functions question to evaluate $f(a)$, substitute a in the function instead of x.

$\Rightarrow f(-3) = 3(-3)^2 - 4(-3) - 2$

$= 27 + 12 - 2 = \boxed{37}$

(ii) Evaluate $f(2t)$

$\Rightarrow 3(2t)^2 - 4(2t) - 2$

$= 3(4t^2) - 8t - 2$

$= 12t^2 - 8t - 2$

(iii) Solve for $f(3t) = -4$

$\Rightarrow 3(3t)^2 - 4(3t) - 2 = -4$

$\Rightarrow 27t^2 - 12t - 2 + 4 = 0$

$27t^2 - 12t + 2 = 0$

and solve using the '$-b$ formula'.

Type 2

Given $f: x \rightarrow \dfrac{2x^2 - 3}{4x}$

(i) Evaluate $f(-2)$

$$= \frac{2(-2)^2 - 3}{4(-2)} = \frac{2(4) - 3}{-8} = \boxed{-\frac{5}{8}}$$

(ii) Solve for $f(x) = -5$

$\Rightarrow \dfrac{2x^2 - 3}{4x} = -5 \qquad \Rightarrow \dfrac{2x^2 - 3}{4x} = \dfrac{-5}{1}$

Cross-multiplying

$(2x^2 - 3)(1) = (-5)(4x)$

$\Rightarrow \quad 2x^2 - 3 = -20x$

$\Rightarrow 2x^2 + 20x - 3 = 0$

and again, solve using the '$-b$ formula'.

Type 3

(i) Given $f: x \rightarrow ax - 4$

Find a, if $f(-3) = 2$.

Again we substitute -3 for x

$\Rightarrow a(-3) - 4 = 2 \quad \Rightarrow -3a = 6$

$\Rightarrow a = -2$

(ii) Given $f: x \rightarrow ax^2 + bx - 4$

$f(-2) = 12$ and $f(4) = 36$

evaluate a and b

$f(-2) = 12$

$\Rightarrow a(-2)^2 + b(-2) - 4 = 12$

$4a - 2b = 16$

$f(4) = 36$

$\Rightarrow a(4)^2 + b(4) - 4 = 36$

$16a + 4b = 40$

Now solve $4a - 2b = 16$

$16a + 4b = 40$ simultaneously

Quadratic graph questions

Type 1

> Graph $f{:}x \rightarrow 8 + 8x - 2x^2$ and $g{:}x \rightarrow 4x + 2$ on the same axes and scales in the domain $-1 \leqslant x \leqslant 5$.

$f{:}x \rightarrow 8 + 8x - 2x^2$

x	-1	0	1	2	3	4	5
$-2x^2$	-2	0	-2	-8	-18	-32	-50
$+8x$	-8	0	8	16	24	32	40
$+8$	8	8	8	8	8	8	8
y	-2	8	14	16	14	8	-2

$(-1, -2)$ $(0, 8)$ $(1, 14)$ $(2, 16)$ $(3, 14)$ $(4, 8)$ $(5, -2)$

$g{:}x \rightarrow 4x + 2$

x	-1	0	1	2	3	4	5
$4x$	-4	0	4	8	12	16	20
$+2$	$+2$	2	2	2	2	2	2
y	-2	2	6	10	14	18	22

$(-1, -2)$ $(0, 2)$ $(1, 6)$ $(2, 10)$ $(3, 14)$ $(4, 18)$ $(5, 22)$

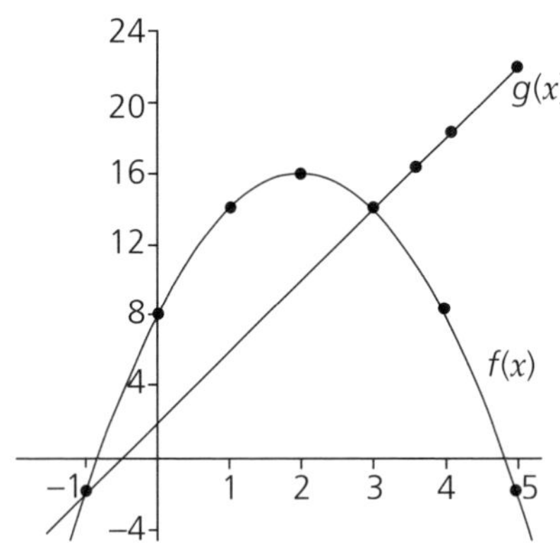

There are 6 frequently asked questions on the graph.

> ① From the graph find:
>
> **(i)** $f(3\frac{1}{2})$
>
> **(ii)** $f(0)$

* To solve $f(t)$ from the graph go to t on the x-axis. Find the corresponding y value.

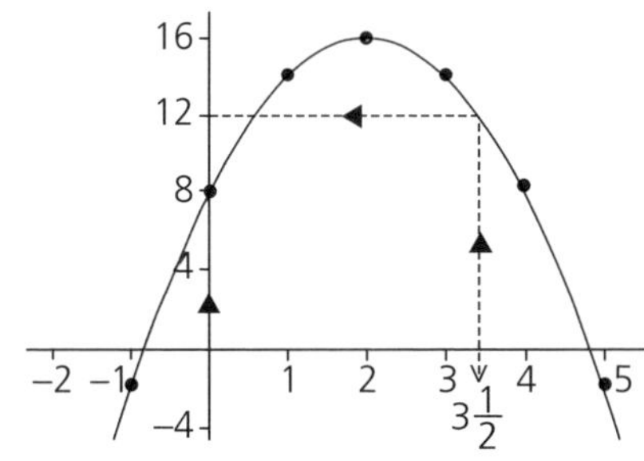

$\Rightarrow f(0) = 8$ $\Rightarrow f(3\frac{1}{2}) = 12$

② From the graph find:

(i) $f(x) = 0$

(ii) $f(x) - 10 = 0$

* '$f(x)$' means y

① $\Rightarrow f(x) = 0$ means $y = 0$

So, go to 0 on the y-axis and find the corresponding x values.

② $f(x) - 10 = 0$

$\Downarrow$

$f(x) = 10$, so go to 10 on the y-axis etc.

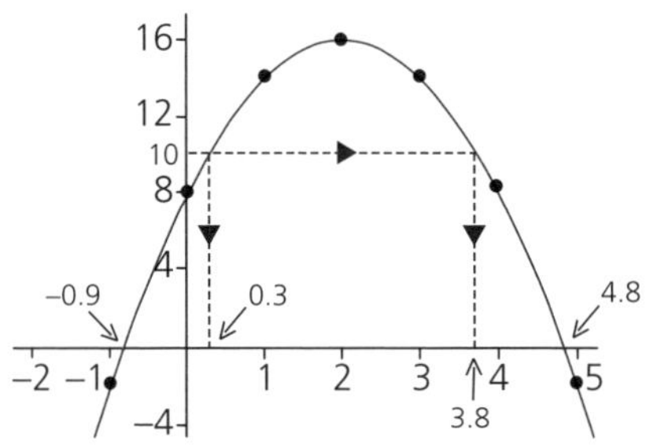

$\Rightarrow$ For $f(x) = 0$ $\boxed{x = -0.9}$ and $\boxed{x = 4.8}$

For $f(x) = 10$ $\boxed{x = 0.3}$ and $\boxed{x = 3.8}$

③ Use the graph to solve for

$$-2x^2 + 8x + 4 = 0$$

* Rewrite the question putting the equation of the $f(x)$ graph before the 'equal to' sign.

$$-2x^2 + 8x + 4 = 0$$

$$\Downarrow$$

$$-2x^2 + 8x + 8 = 4$$

$$\Rightarrow f(x) = 4$$

$\Rightarrow$ Go to 4 on the y-axis.

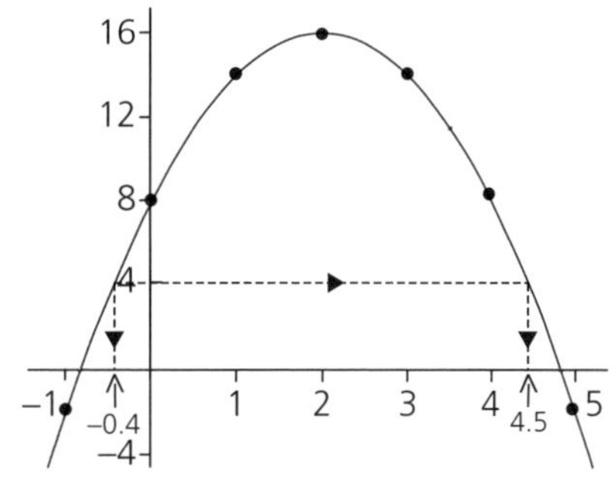

$\Rightarrow$ For $-2x^2 + 8x + 4 = 0$, $\boxed{x = 4.5}$ and $\boxed{x = -0.4}$

④ Use your graph to solve:

(i) $f(x) \leqslant 12$

(ii) $-2x^2 + 8x - 4 \leqslant 0$

(i) $f(x) \leqslant 12$

Solve for $f(x) = 12$

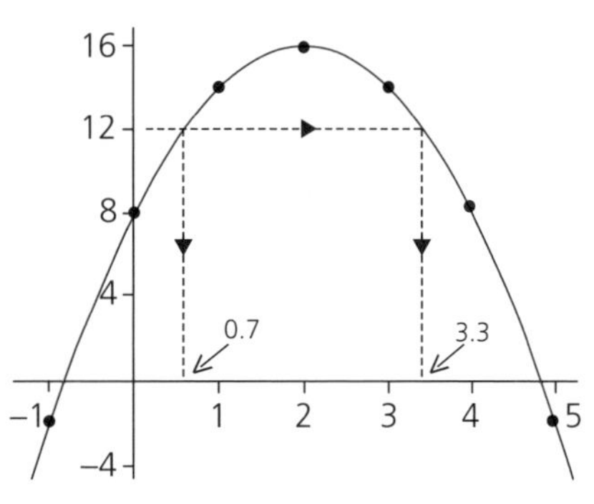

$\Rightarrow x = 0.7 \qquad x = 3.3$

$\Downarrow$

Small number	x	Big number
$\Rightarrow$ 0.7	x	3.3

Important

– If the graph is ⋃ shaped keep the inequality given in the question.

– If the graph is ⋂ shaped, change the inequality given in the question.

∗ Here, the inequality in the question is '$\leqslant$'. As the graph is ⋂ shaped, we change it.

$\Rightarrow 0.7 \geqslant x \geqslant 3.3$

(ii) $-2x^2 + 8x - 4 \leqslant 0$

Again, rewrite the question by putting the equation of the graph before the inequality.

$$-2x^2 + 8x - 4 \leqslant 0$$

$$\Downarrow$$

$$-2x^2 + 8x + 8 \leqslant 12$$

$\Rightarrow f(x) \leqslant 12$

As we see $-2x^2 + 8x - 4 \leqslant 0$ is the same question as $f(x) \leqslant 12$.

⑤ Use your graph to solve

$$2x^2 - 8x - 10 < 0$$

∗ Because the x^2 term is a different sign to the one in the $f(x)$ equation.

(i) Change all the signs across $-2x^2 + 8x + 10$

(ii) Change the direction of the inequality $\Rightarrow -2x^2 + 8x + 10 > 0$

$$-2x^2 + 8x + 10 > 0$$

$$\Downarrow$$

$$-2x^2 + 8x + 8 > -2$$

$\Rightarrow f(x) > -2$ and solve in the normal way.

⑥ Use the graph to solve:

(i) $f(x) - g(x) \geqslant 0$

(ii) $-2x^2 + 4x + 6 \geqslant 0$

(i) $f(x) - g(x) \geqslant 0$

$\Rightarrow f(x) \geqslant g(x)$

Again solve for $f(x) = g(x)$. This occurs where the $f(x)$ graph intersects the $g(x)$ graph.

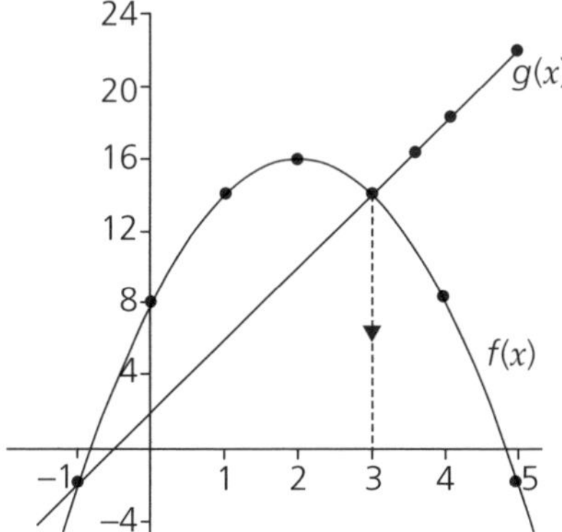

$\Rightarrow f(x) = g(x)$ at $x = -1$ and $x = 3$

$\Rightarrow$ For $f(x) \geqslant g(x) \quad -1 \leqslant x \leqslant 3$

(Again the inequality was changed because the $f(x)$ graph is ⋂ shaped.)

(ii) $-2x^2 + 4x + 6 \geqslant 0$

$$-2x^2 + 4x + 6 \geqslant 0$$

$$\Downarrow$$

$$-2x^2 + 8x + 8 \geqslant 4x + 2$$

$$\Rightarrow \quad f(x) \geqslant g(x)$$

(Which is solved above.)

Quadratic graph questions

Type 2

Graph $f: x \to -x^2 + 4x + 6$ in the domain $-1 \leqslant x \leqslant 5$.

Let the graph represent the height of a stone in metres.

The stone is in the air for 12 seconds.

x	-1	0	1	2	3	4	5
$-x^2$	-1	0	-1	-4	-9	-16	-25
$+4x$	-4	0	4	8	12	16	20
$+6$	6	6	6	6	6	6	6
y	1	6	9	10	9	6	1

$(-1, 1)$ $(0, 6)$ $(1, 9)$ $(2, 10)$ $(3, 9)$ $(4, 6)$ $(5, 1)$

In all questions such as this, be clear about what the x-axis (seconds in the air) and the y-axis (height in metres) represent.

As the stone is in the air for 12 seconds, each gap along the x-axis represents 2 seconds. Important to mark this information on the graph.

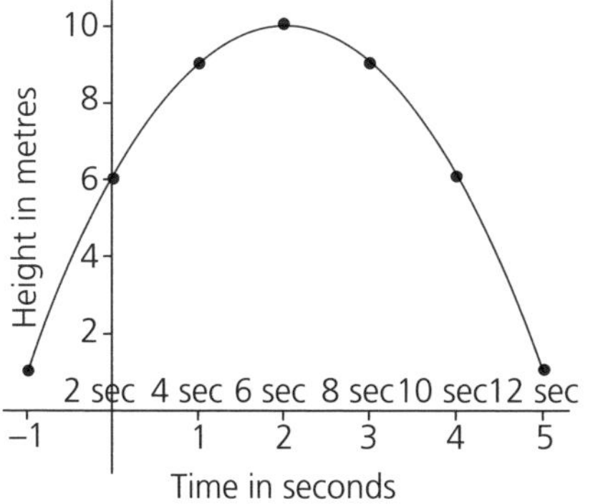

(i) For how long was the height of the stone greater than 7 metres?

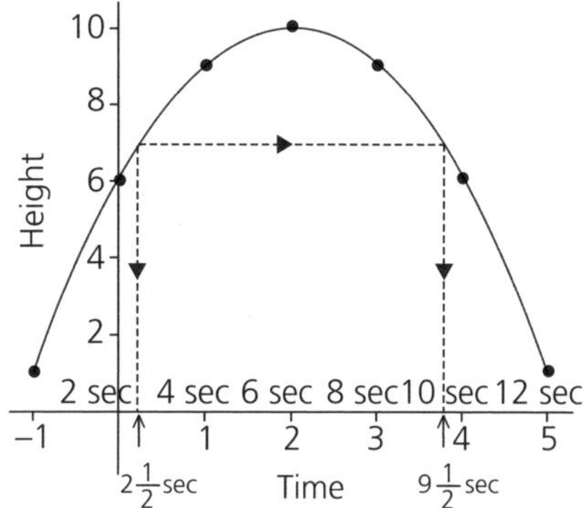

From the diag. we see that the height was above 7 metres for $(9\frac{1}{2} - 2\frac{1}{2})$ sec.

$\Rightarrow$ 7 seconds

(ii) What was the speed in m/s of the stone in the final six seconds?

After 6 secs $\to$ 10 m high.

After 12 secs $\to$ 1 m high.

$\Rightarrow$ It travelled 9 m in 6 secs.

$\Rightarrow$ Speed $= 9$ m/6 sec

$= 1.5$ m/sec

If you state:

① What each axis represents.

② What each unit on the x-axis represents.

You will find the questions on these types of problems quite easy to answer.

Final Type

The graph shows the function

$f: x \rightarrow x^2 - 4x - 5$

Find a, b, c, d.

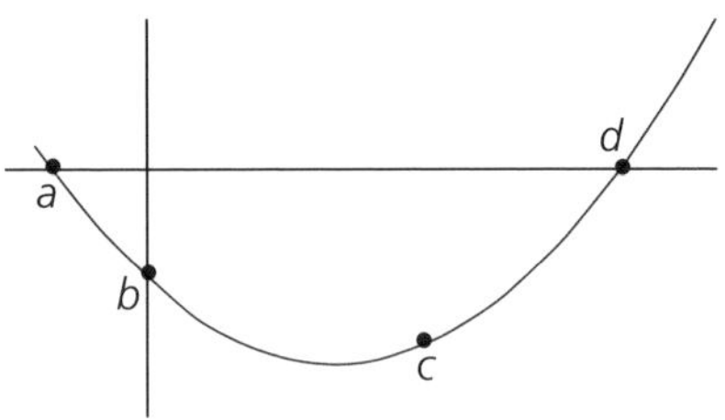

Find a and d.

At pt. a and pt. d, $y = 0$. $[f(x) = 0]$

$$f(x) = x^2 - 4x - 5$$

$\Rightarrow$ At pt. a and pt. d, $x^2 - 4x - 5 = 0$

Solve $x^2 - 4x - 5 = 0$ using '$-b$ formula'.

$x = -1 \qquad x = 5$

$\Rightarrow \underline{\underline{a(-1, 0)}} \qquad \underline{\underline{d(5, 0)}}$

Find b.

At pt. b, $x = 0$

$$f(x) = x^2 - 4x - 5$$

$\Rightarrow y = (0)^2 - 4(0) - 5 \qquad \Rightarrow y = -5$

$\Rightarrow \underline{\underline{b(0, -5)}}$

Find c.

Point c is the minimum point on the graph.

> * Look at where the graph cuts the x-axis. ($x = -1$ and $x = 5$)
>
> The x value of any minimum or maximum point is halfway between those two values.

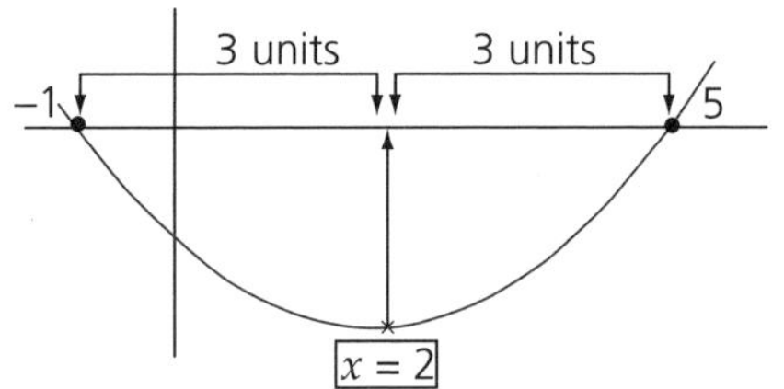

$\Rightarrow$ At pt. $c \qquad x = 2$

$f(x) = x^2 - 4x - 5$

$f(x) = (2)^2 - 4(2) - 5$

$= 4 - 8 - 5 = -9$

$\Rightarrow \underline{\underline{c(2, -9)}}$

Chapter 6 Sample questions for you to try

Question 1

(a) The diagram shows the graph of $f: x \rightarrow -x^2 + 2x + 8$. Find a, b, c, d.

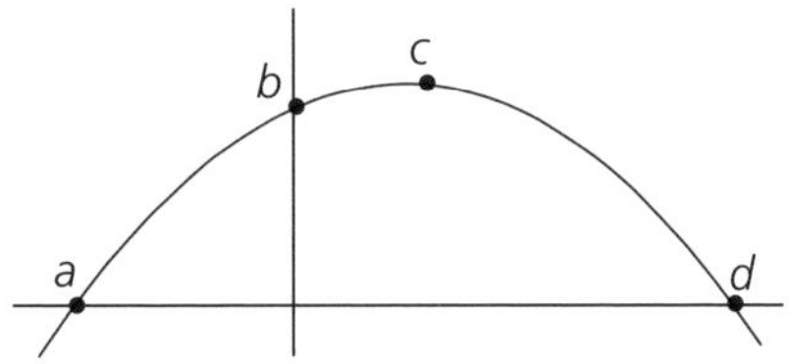

(b) Graph $f: x \to 2x^2 - 4x - 5$ in the domain $-2 \leqslant x \leqslant 4$. From the graph find:

(i) The values for which $f(x) - 6 = 0$.

(ii) The values for which $2x^2 - 4x - 2 = 0$.

(iii) $f(x) > 3$

(iv) $2x^2 - 4x - 14 \leqslant 0$

(v) $-2x^2 + 4x - 1 < 0$

Question 2

(a) Given $f: x \to 3x^2 - 4x$

(i) Solve for $f(x) = 4$

(ii) Find k if $f(4) = kf(2)$

(b) Graph $f: x \to 7 + 5x - 2x^2$ in the domain $-1 \leqslant x \leqslant 4$. The graph shows the height in metres of a missile fired from ground level. The missile is in flight for 1 hr 40 minutes.

Use the graph to find:

(i) How long did it take for the missile to reach maximum height?

(ii) What was the maximum height?

(iii) For how long was the missile over 5 m from the ground?

Question 3

(a) Given $f: x \to \dfrac{3x^2 - 2}{-2x}$

(i) If the domain of f is $\{-2, -1, 1, 2, 3\}$, find the range of f.

(ii) Solve for $f(x) = 2\frac{1}{2}$

(b) Graph $f: x \to 8 + 8x - 2x^2$ and $g: x \to 2x + 1$ in the domain $-1 \leqslant x \leqslant 5$.

From the graph find:

(i) The values for which $f(x) - g(x) = 0$

(ii) The values of x for which $-2x^2 + 6x + 7 = 0$

(iii) Solve for $f(x) < g(x)$

(iv) The range of values of x for which $-2x^2 + 6x + 7 \geqslant 0$

Solution to question 1

(a) $f: x \to -x^2 + 2x + 8$

Find pts. a, b, c and d.

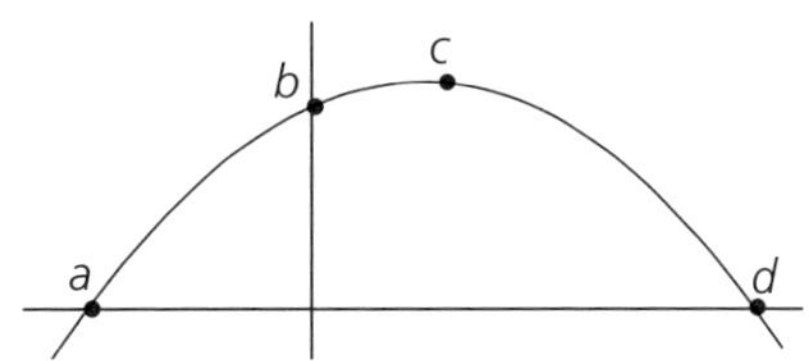

Find pt. a and pt. d.

At pt. a and pt. d $y = 0$ $[f(x) = 0]$

$\Rightarrow -1x^2 + 2x + 8 = 0$

$a = -1 \quad b = 2 \quad c = 8$

$$\frac{-2 \pm \sqrt{(2)^2 - 4(-1)(8)}}{2(-1)} = \frac{-2 \pm \sqrt{36}}{-2}$$

① $x = \dfrac{-2 + 6}{-2} = \dfrac{4}{-2} = -2 \quad \Rightarrow a(-2, 0)$

② $x = \dfrac{-2 - 6}{-2} = \dfrac{-8}{-2} = 4 \quad \Rightarrow d(4, 0)$

Find point b.

At point b, $x = 0$

$f(x) = -1x^2 + 2x + 8$

$\Rightarrow f(x) = -1(0)^2 + 2(0) + 8 = 8$

$\Rightarrow b(0, 8)$

Find point c.

The x value at pt. c is halfway between pt. a and pt. d.

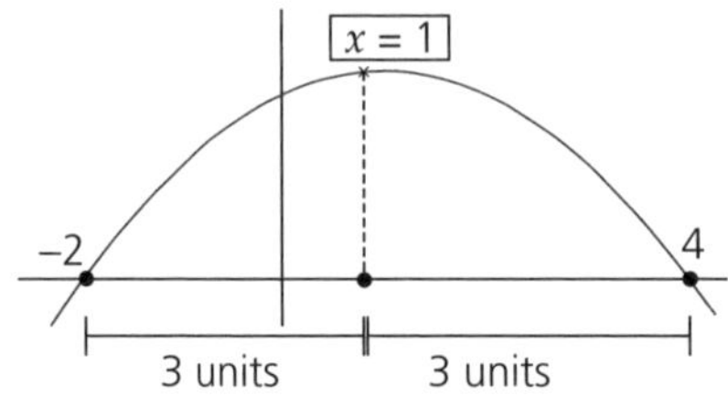

$\Rightarrow$ At pt. c, $x = 1$

$f(x) = -1x^2 + 2x + 8$

$x = 1 \quad \Rightarrow \quad -1(1)^2 + 2(1) + 8 = 9$

$\Rightarrow c(1, 9)$

(b) Graph $f: x \to 2x^2 - 4x - 5$ in the domain $-2 \leqslant x \leqslant 4$.

x	−2	−1	0	1	2	3	4
$2x^2$	8	2	0	2	8	18	32
$-4x$	8	4	0	−4	−8	−12	−16
-5	−5	−5	−5	−5	−5	−5	−5
y	11	1	−5	−7	−5	1	11

(−2, 11) (−1, 1) (0, −5) (1, −7) (2, −5) (3, 1) (4, 11)

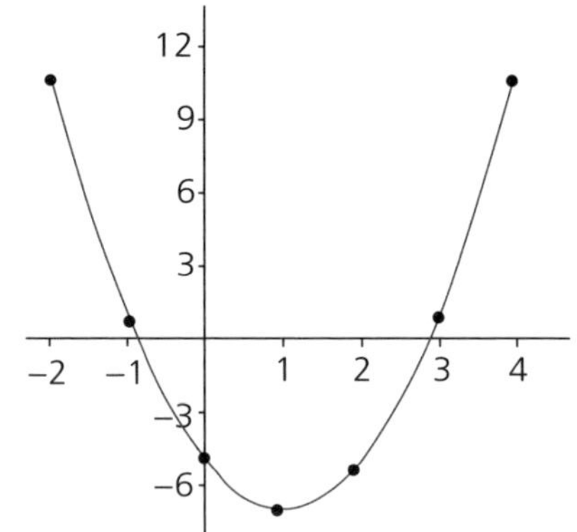

From the graph find:

(i) $f(x) - 6 = 0$

(ii) $2x^2 - 4x - 2 = 0$

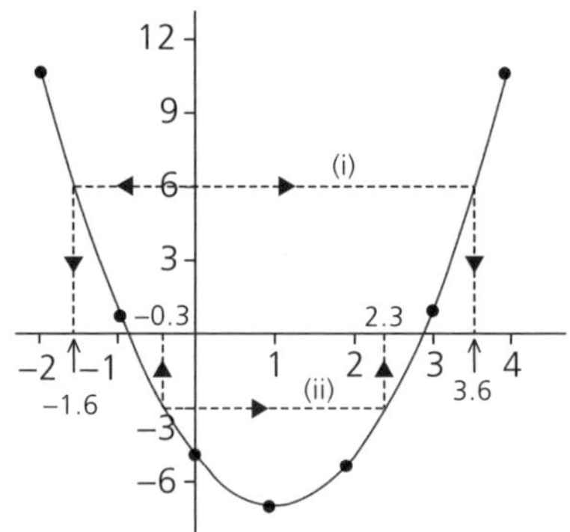

(i) $f(x) - 6 = 0$

$\Rightarrow \quad f(x) = 6$

Go to 6 on the y-axis. Find the corresponding x values.

$\Rightarrow$ $\underline{x = -1.6}$ and $\underline{x = 3.6}$

(ii) $2x^2 - 4x - 2 = 0$

$\Rightarrow 2x^2 - 4x - 5 = -3$

$\Rightarrow \quad f(x) = -3$

$\Rightarrow$ $\underline{x = -0.3}$ and $\underline{x = 2.3}$

From the graph find:

(iii) $f(x) > 3$

(iv) $2x^2 - 4x - 14 \leqslant 0$

(v) $-2x^2 + 4x - 1 < 0$

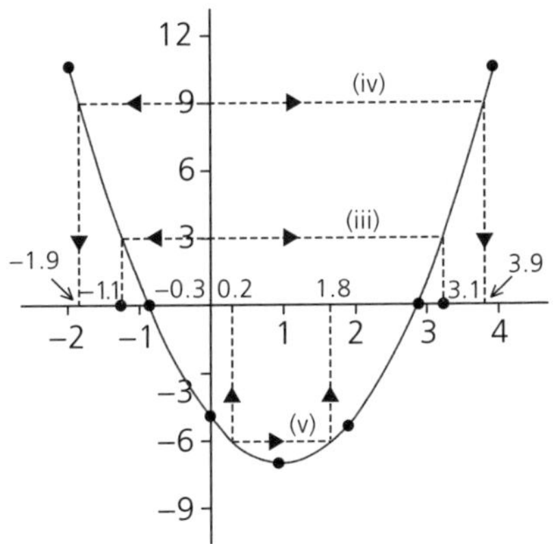

(iii) $f(x) > 3$

Solve for $f(x) = 3$

$x = -1.1 \qquad x = 3.1$

Solve for $f(x) > 2$

Small no. x Big no.

$-1.1 > x > 3.1$

* Because the graph is '⋃' shaped we leave the inequality in the question (>) as it is.

(iv) $2x^2 - 4x - 14 \leqslant 0$

$\Rightarrow 2x^2 - 4x - 5 \leqslant 9$

$\Rightarrow f(x) \leqslant 9$

$\Rightarrow$ (from graph) $-1.9 \leqslant x \leqslant 3.9$

(v) $-2x^2 + 4x - 1 < 0$

Again, because the x^2 term is a different sign compared to the one in the equation of the graph change the signs of each term.

$$-2x^2 + 4x - 1 < 0$$
$$\Downarrow$$
$$2x^2 - 4x + 1 > 0$$

(inequality must also change)

$\Rightarrow 2x^2 - 4x - 5 > -6$

$\Rightarrow f(x) > -6$

(From graph) $0.2 > x > 1.8$

Solution to question 2

(a) $f: x \to 3x^2 - 4x$

(i) Solve for $f(x) = 4$

(ii) Find k if $f(4) = kf(2)$

(i) Solve for $f(x) = 4$

$\Rightarrow \quad 3x^2 - 4x = 4$

$\Rightarrow 3x^2 - 4x - 4 = 0$

Solving using the '$-b$ formula'

$x = -\dfrac{2}{3}$ and $x = 2$

(ii) $f(4) = kf(2)$

$\Rightarrow 3(4)^2 - 4(4) = k[3(2)^2 - 4(2)]$

$\Rightarrow \quad 48 - 16 = k(12 - 8)$

$\Rightarrow \quad 32 = 4k$

$k = 8$

(b) Graph $f: x \rightarrow 7 + 5x - 2x^2$ in the domain $-1 \leqslant x \leqslant 4$.

x	-1	0	1	2	3	4
$-2x^2$	-2	0	-2	-8	-18	-32
$+5x$	-5	0	5	10	15	20
$+7$	7	7	7	7	7	7
y	0	7	10	9	4	-5

$(-1, 0)$ $(0, 7)$ $(1, 10)$ $(2, 9)$ $(3, 4)(4, -5)$

The graph shows the height, in metres, of a missile fired from ground level. The missile is in flight for 1 hr 40 minutes.

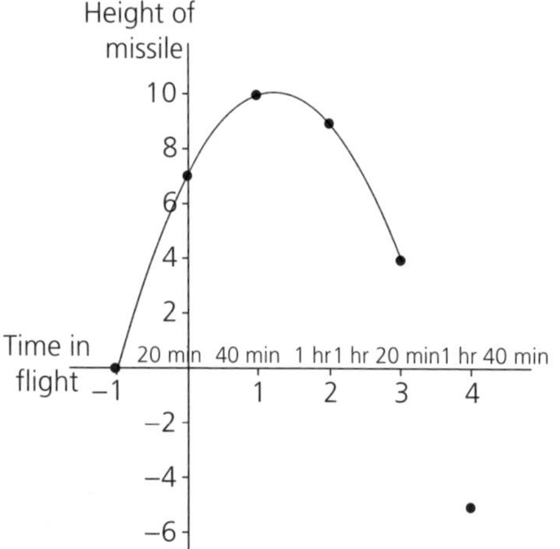

From the graph find:

(i) How long did it take to reach maximum height?

(ii) What was the maximum height?

(iii) For how long was the missile over 5 m above ground level?

Notice from the graph:

① You must state what each axis represents.

② You must state what each x value represents.

* 1 hr 40 min = 100 min.

There are 5 units along the x-axis.

⇒ Each unit represents 20 min.

(i) How long did it take to reach maximum height?

* From the graph we see that the missile reached maximum height after 40 minutes.

(ii) What was the maximum height?

* Again, from the graph, we see that maximum height was 10 metres.

(iii) For how long was the height of the missile over 5 metres?

* From the graph, the missile was exactly 5 m above the ground after 16 minutes and after 1 hr 16 min.

* Between these times it was above 5 metres.

⇒ It was above 5 metres for 60 minutes.

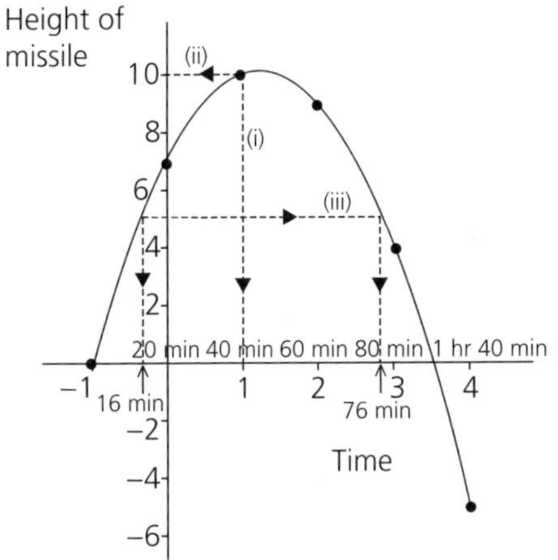

Solution to question 3

(a) $f: x \to \dfrac{3x^2 - 2}{-2x}$

> **(i)** The domain is $\{-2, -1, 0, 1, 2, 3\}$. Find the range of f.

$$f: x \to \frac{3x^2 - 2}{-2x}$$

Domain				Range
$-2 \to$	$\dfrac{3(-2)^2 - 2}{-2(-2)}$	$\to$	$\dfrac{10}{4}$	$2\dfrac{1}{2}$
$-1 \to$	$\dfrac{3(-1)^2 - 2}{-2(-1)}$	$\to$	$\dfrac{1}{2}$	$\dfrac{1}{2}$
$1 \to$	$\dfrac{3(1)^2 - 2}{-2(1)}$	$\to$	$\dfrac{1}{-2}$	$-\dfrac{1}{2}$
$2 \to$	$\dfrac{3(2)^2 - 2}{-2(2)}$	$\to$	$\dfrac{10}{-4}$	$-2\dfrac{1}{2}$
$3 \to$	$\dfrac{3(3)^2 - 2}{-2(3)}$	$\to$	$\dfrac{25}{-6}$	$-4\dfrac{1}{6}$

> **(ii)** Solve for $f(x) = 2\frac{1}{2}$

$$\Rightarrow \frac{3x^2 - 2}{-2x} = 2\frac{1}{2}$$

$$\Rightarrow \frac{3x^2 - 2}{-2x} = \frac{2.5}{1}$$

$$\Rightarrow (3x^2 - 2)(1) = (2.5)(-2x)$$

$$\Rightarrow 3x^2 - 2 = -5x$$

$$\Rightarrow 3x^2 + 5x - 2 = 0$$

Solving using the '$-b$ formula'

$\boxed{x = -2}$ $\boxed{x = \frac{1}{3}}$

> **(b)** Graph $f: x \to 8 + 8x - 2x^2$ and $g: x \to 2x + 1$ in the domain $-1 \leqslant x \leqslant 5$.

$$f: x \to -2x^2 + 8x + 8$$

x	-1	0	1	2	3	4	5
$-2x^2$	-2	0	-2	-8	-18	-32	-50
$+8x$	-8	0	8	16	24	32	40
$+8$	8	8	8	8	8	8	8
y	-2	8	14	16	14	8	-2

$(-1, -2)$ $(0, 8)$ $(1, 14)$ $(2, 16)$ $(3, 14)$ $(4, 8)$ $(5, -2)$

$$g: x \to 2x + 1$$

x	-1	2	5
$2x$	-2	4	10
$+1$	1	1	1
y	-1	5	11

$(-1, -1)$ $(2, 5)$ $(5, 11)$

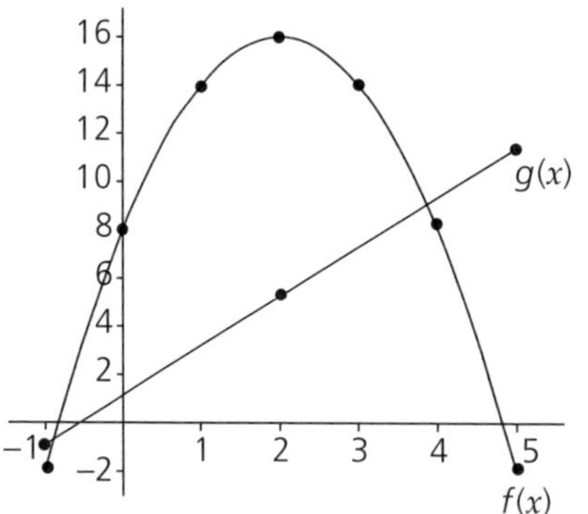

<u>Note on the $g(x)$ graph:</u>

It is only necessary to plot the first and last points and one other point on the line. You will know you are correct if the three points are in a straight line.

(i) From the graph find the values for which $f(x) - g(x) = 0$.

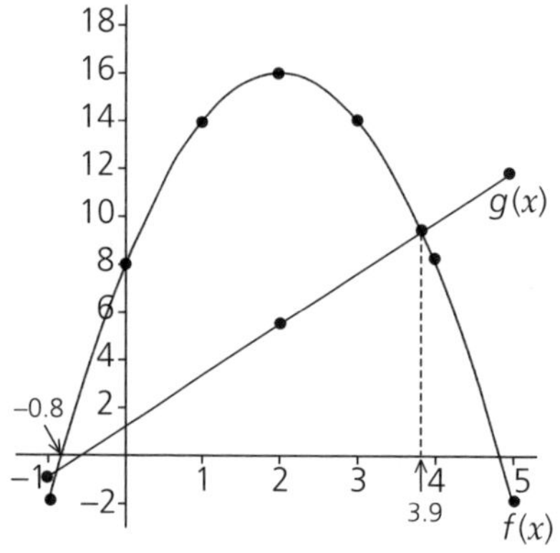

$$f(x) - g(x) = 0$$
$$\Downarrow$$
$$f(x) = g(x)$$

$*$ From the graph, find where the $f(x)$ graph intersects the $g(x)$ graph.

This occurs at $x = -0.8$ and at $x = 3.9$

(ii) Find the values of x for which $-2x^2 + 6x + 7 = 0$.

$$-2x^2 + 6x + 7 = 0$$
$$\Downarrow$$
$$-2x^2 + 8x + 8 = 2x + 1$$
$$\Downarrow$$
$$f(x) = g(x)$$

From part **(i)** $x = -0.8$ and $x = 3.9$

(iii) Solve for $f(x) < g(x)$

Solve for $f(x) = g(x)$

$x = -0.8$ $\quad$ $x = 3.9$

small no.	x	big no.

-0.8 $\quad$ x $\quad$ 3.9

$*$ The $f(x)$ curve is $\cap$ shaped so we change the inequality in the question.

$\Rightarrow$ For $f(x) < g(x)$

$-0.8 > x > 3.9$

(iv) Find the range of values of x for which $-2x^2 + 6x + 7 \geqslant 0$.

$$-2x^2 + 6x + 7 \geqslant 0$$
$$\Downarrow$$
$$-2x^2 + 8x + 8 \geqslant 2x + 1$$
$$\Downarrow$$
$$f(x) \geqslant g(x)$$

$\Rightarrow$ $-0.8 \leqslant x \leqslant 3.9$

Chapter 7

Sample Paper One with Solutions

Question 1

(a) Sheila buys 20 coats for €40 each and later sells them all for Stg£600.

(i) Find her percentage profit when the exchange rate is €1.6 = Stg£1.

(ii) Find, correct to one decimal place, the percentage profit when the exchange rate is €1 = 70p sterling.

(b) **(i)** Evaluate the following, writing your answer in the form $a\sqrt{b}$ where b is a prime number:

$$\sqrt{20} + \sqrt{45} - 7\sqrt{5}$$

(ii) Simplify $(2 - \sqrt{3})(4 + \sqrt{3})$ writing your answer in the form:

$$c + d\sqrt{3}$$

(c) **(i)** By rounding off appropriately, estimate:

$$(3.52)^2 + \frac{1}{4.11} \times \sqrt{48.1}$$

Then evaluate correct to 2 decimal places.

(ii) Divide €1560 in the ratio

$$\frac{1}{2} : 1\frac{2}{3}$$

Question 2

(a)

[30]

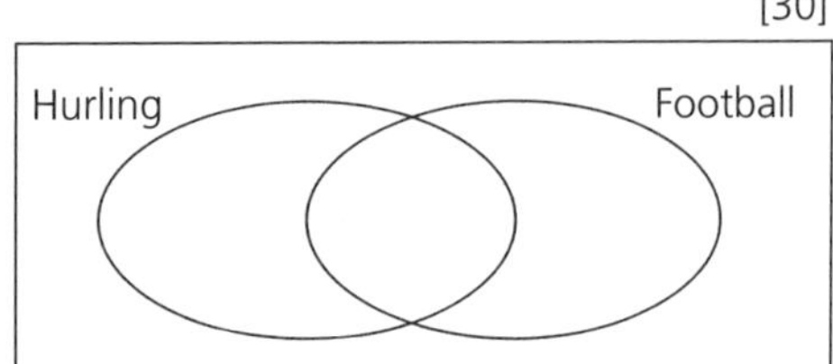

In a class of 30 pupils, 10 like hurling and 18 like football. Calculate:

(i) The maximum number that could have liked neither sport.

(ii) The minimum number that could have liked neither sport.

(b) **(i)** Evaluate the following, expressing your answer in the form 3^n:

$$\frac{\sqrt{3} \times \frac{1}{81}}{\sqrt{27} \times 9}$$

(ii) Solve for x given

$$\left(\frac{1}{8}\right)^{2x-4} = \sqrt{32}$$

Question 3

(a) Solve for x $\quad \frac{3}{x-2} - \frac{1}{2} = \frac{1}{x+3}$

(b) Factorise

(i) $9a^2b^2 - 16c^4$

(ii) $6g^2 + 7hg - 20h^2$

(iii) $12ch - 9gc + 16h^2 - 9g^2$

(c) Solve for x and y

$2x = 24 + 3y$

$12 = \frac{5x}{3} - \frac{1}{2}y$

(d) Express w in terms of t and f.

$$\sqrt{\frac{3w-2t}{5w}} = 3f$$

Question 4

(a)

(i) On a single diagram, draw the two lines whose equations are:

$3x - 2y = -7$

$2x + 5y = 8$

(ii) Write down, from the graph, the point of intersection of the lines.

(iii) Check your answer from part **(ii)** by solving the equations simultaneously.

(b) Seán gets planning permission to build an extension to his house. The extension must have a perimeter of 14 metres. The width of the extension is x metres as shown.

Prove that the extension has an area of $(7x - x^2)$ metres^2.

(c) Let f be the function $f: x \to 7x - x^2$.

Graph $f(x)$ in the domain $1 \leqslant x \leqslant 7$.

Use your graph to estimate:

(i) What was the area when the width = 1.5 metres?

(ii) What was the area when the length = 3.2 metres?

(iii) Two possible widths when the area = 7 m^2.

(iv) The maximum area.

(v) The length and width of the enclosure of maximum area.

Question 5

(a) Mary is 5 years older than Patrick. The product of their ages is 126. Write an equation in x and hence calculate both Mary's and Patrick's ages.

(b) Solve the inequality $-5 \leqslant 1 - 3x < 10, \quad x \in R$ and illustrate your answer on the number line.

(c) Three apples and two oranges cost €1.35. Five oranges cost 50 cents more than four apples. Write two equations in x and y to illustrate the above information. Hence evaluate the cost of an apple and the cost of an orange.

Question 6

(a) Given $h: x \to ax^2 + bx + 1$, evaluate a and b if $h(1) = 2$ and $h(2) = 9$.

Hence evaluate $h(-2)$.

(b) Graph $f: x \to -2x^2 + 7x - 3$ in the domain $-1 \leqslant x \leqslant 4$.

From the graph find:

(i) The value of $f(0)$.

(ii) The values for which $f(x) = 0$.

(iii) The value of $f(3.7)$.

(iv) The values for which $f(x) + 7 = 0$.

(v) Solve for $-2x^2 + 7x = 0$.

(vi) Solve for $2x^2 - 7x + 4 = 0$.

(vii) The maximum value of $f(x)$.

(viii) The maximum coordinate.

(ix) The equation of the axis of symmetry.

Detailed Solutions to Paper One

Solution to question 1

(a) 20 coats @ €40 each

$\Rightarrow$ Cost price = €800

(i) €1.6 = Stg£1

Selling price = Stg£600

$= €(600 \times 1.6)$

$= €960$

$$\Rightarrow \ \% \text{ profit} = \frac{160}{800} \times \frac{100}{1} = 20\%$$

(ii) €1 = 70p Stg

Selling price = Stg£600

$$\frac{£600}{70} \times 100 = €857.14$$

$$\Rightarrow \ \% \text{ profit} = \frac{€57.14}{€800} \times \frac{100}{1}$$

$$= 7.1\%$$

(b) **(i)** Express in the form $a\sqrt{b}$ where b is a prime number.

$$\sqrt{20} + \sqrt{45} - 7\sqrt{5}$$

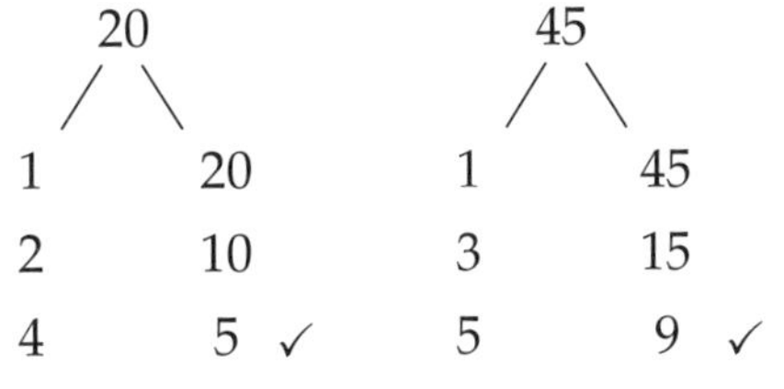
Again, list the factors of
20 and 45.
Find the pair, in each case, which
includes a prime number and a
perfect square.

20		45	
1	20	1	45
2	10	3	15
4	5 ✓	5	9 ✓

$\Rightarrow \sqrt{20} = \sqrt{4 \times 5} = \sqrt{4}\sqrt{5} = 2\sqrt{5}$

$\sqrt{45} = \sqrt{9 \times 5} = \sqrt{9}\sqrt{5} = 3\sqrt{5}$

$\Rightarrow \sqrt{20} + \sqrt{45} - 7\sqrt{5}$

$= 2\sqrt{5} + 3\sqrt{5} - 7\sqrt{5}$

$= -2\sqrt{5}$

(ii) Simplify $(2-\sqrt{3})(4+\sqrt{3})$

$$(2-\sqrt{3})(4+\sqrt{3})$$
$$2(4+\sqrt{3})-\sqrt{3}(4+\sqrt{3})$$
$$=8+2\sqrt{3}-4\sqrt{3}-3$$
$$=5-2\sqrt{3}$$

(c) **(i)** Estimate
$$(3.52)^2+\frac{1}{4.11}\times\sqrt{48.1}$$
Then evaluate correct to 2 dec. pl.

Estimation.

① $(3.52)^2 \approx (3.5)^2$

So $(3.52)^2 \approx \underline{\underline{12.25}}$

$$\begin{array}{r} 3.5 \\ \times\, 3.5 \\ \hline 175 \\ +\,1050 \\ \hline 12.25 \end{array}$$

② $\dfrac{1}{4.11} \approx \dfrac{1}{4}$

$$4\,\underline{|1.00}$$
$$0.25$$

So $\dfrac{1}{4.11} \approx \underline{\underline{0.25}}$

③ $\sqrt{48.1} \approx \sqrt{49}$

So $\sqrt{48.1} \approx \underline{\underline{7}}$

$\Rightarrow\ 12.25+0.25\times 7$

$=12.25+1.75$

$=\boxed{14}$

So $(3.52)^2+\dfrac{1}{4.11}\times\sqrt{48.1}\approx 14$

Remember to do the multiplication part before the addition.

$$\begin{array}{r} 0.25 \\ \times\, 7 \\ \hline 1.75 \end{array}$$

Evaluation.

$$(3.52)^2+\frac{1}{4.11}\times\sqrt{48.1}$$
$$=14.08$$

(be sure to check a few times)

(ii) Divide €1560 in the ratio
$$\frac{1}{2}:1\frac{2}{3}$$

$$\frac{1}{2}:\frac{5}{3}$$

$=\dfrac{3}{6}:\dfrac{10}{6}$ (write both with common denominators)

$=\ 3:10$ (drop the denominators)

$=\dfrac{3}{13}:\dfrac{10}{13}$

[* $\dfrac{1}{13}$ = €120] $\Rightarrow$ €360 : €1200

Solution to question 2

(a) [30]

H F
8 10 0
12

(i) Max. possible number who liked neither sport is 12.

(ii)

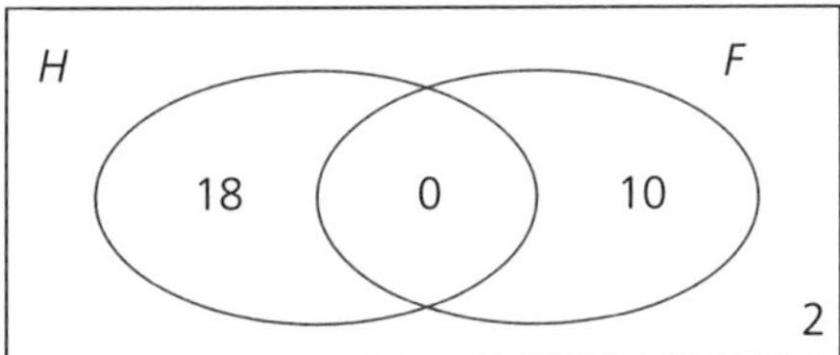

Minimum possible number who liked neither sport is 2.

(b)

> **(i)**
>
> Express $\dfrac{\sqrt{3} \times \dfrac{1}{81}}{\sqrt{27} \times 9}$ in the form 3^n.

- $\sqrt{3} = 3^{1/2}$
- $\dfrac{1}{81} = \dfrac{1}{3^4} = \boxed{3^{-4}}$
- $\sqrt{27} = (27)^{1/2} = (3^3)^{0.5} = \boxed{3^{1.5}}$
- $9 = \boxed{3^2}$

$$\Rightarrow \frac{3^{0.5} \times 3^{-4}}{3^{1.5} \times 3^2} = \frac{3^{0.5-4}}{3^{1.5+2}}$$

$$= \frac{3^{-3.5}}{3^{3.5}} = 3^{-3.5-3.5}$$

$$= \boxed{3^{-7}}$$

> **(ii)** Solve for x given
>
> $$\left(\frac{1}{8}\right)^{2x-4} = \sqrt{32}$$

- $\dfrac{1}{8} = \dfrac{1}{2^3} = \boxed{2^{-3}}$
- $\sqrt{32} = \sqrt{(2^5)} = (2^5)^{1/2} = \boxed{2^{2.5}}$

$$\text{So } (2^{-3})^{2x-4} = 2^{2.5}$$

$$2^{-6x+12} = 2^{2.5}$$

Let the powers be equal to each other.

$$-6x + 12 = 2.5$$

$$\Rightarrow \quad -6x = 2.5 - 12$$

$$-6x = -9.5$$

$$x = \frac{-9.5}{-6}$$

$$\Rightarrow \quad \boxed{x = 1.58}$$

Solution to question 3

> **(a)** Solve for x
>
> $$\frac{3}{x-2} - \frac{1}{2} = \frac{1}{x+3}$$

$$\frac{3}{x-2} - \frac{1}{2} = \frac{1}{x+3}$$

$$\boxed{\text{CD} = (x-2)(2)(x+3)}$$

$$\frac{3\cancel{(x-2)}(2)(x+3)}{\cancel{x-2}} - \frac{1(x-2)\cancel{(2)}(x+3)}{\cancel{2}}$$

$$= \frac{1(x-2)(2)\cancel{(x+3)}}{\cancel{x+3}}$$

$$\Rightarrow 3(2)(x+3) - 1(x-2)(x+3)$$

$$= 1(x-2)(2)$$

$$(x-2)(x+3) = x(x+3) - 2(x+3)$$
$$x^2 + 3x - 2x - 6 \quad \Rightarrow x^2 + 1x - 6$$

$$\Rightarrow 6x + 18 - 1(x^2 + 1x - 6) = 2x - 4$$
$$6x + 18 - 1x^2 - 1x + 6 = 2x - 4$$

* Rearranging correctly

$$-1x^2 + 6x - 1x - 2x + 6 + 4 + 18 = 0$$
$$\Rightarrow \quad -1x^2 + 3x + 28 = 0$$

$a = -1 \qquad b = 3 \qquad c = 28$

$$\Rightarrow \frac{-3 \pm \sqrt{(3)^2 - 4(-1)(28)}}{2(-1)}$$

$$\Rightarrow \frac{-3 \pm \sqrt{9 + 112}}{-2} \quad \Rightarrow \frac{-3 \pm \sqrt{121}}{-2}$$

$$\Rightarrow \frac{-3 \pm 11}{-2}$$

① $x = \dfrac{-3 + 11}{-2} = \dfrac{8}{-2} = \boxed{-4}$

② $x = \dfrac{-3 - 11}{-2} = \dfrac{-14}{-2} = \boxed{7}$

(b)

(i) Factorise $9a^2b^2 - 16c^4$

$9a^2b^2 - 16c^4$
$= (3ab)^2 - (4c^2)^2$
$= (3ab - 4c^2)(3ab + 4c^2)$

* **(ii)** Factorise $6g^2 + 7hg - 20h^2$

Again, because the terms are in the form g^2, gh, h^2, we treat it like a basic quadratic equation.

$(6)(-20) = -120$

-1	$+120$
-2	$+60$
-3	$+40$
-4	$+30$
-5	$+24$
-6	$+20$
-8	$+15$ ✓
-10	$+12$

$6g^2 + 7hg - 20h^2$
$6g^2 - 8hg + 15hg - 20h^2$
$2g(3g - 4h) + 5h(3g - 4h)$
$(2g + 5h)(3g - 4h)$

(iii) Factorise
$12ch - 9gc + 16h^2 - 9g^2$

* Here we must deal with the 'hidden' difference of 2 squares sum.

$16h^2 - 9g^2 = (4h)^2 - (3g)^2$
$= (4h - 3g)(4h + 3g)$

$\Rightarrow 12ch - 9gc + 16h^2 - 9g^2$
$3c(4h - 3g) + (4h - 3g)(4h + 3g)$
$\Rightarrow (3c + 4h + 3g)(4h - 3g)$

> **(c)** Solve for x and y
> $$2x = 24 + 3y$$
> $$12 = \frac{5x}{3} - \frac{1}{2}y$$

① $2x - 3y = 24$

② $12 = \frac{5x}{3} - \frac{y}{2} \quad \Rightarrow \quad \frac{12}{1} = \frac{5x}{3} - \frac{y}{2}$

Common denom. = 6

$$\frac{6(12)}{1} = \frac{6(5x)}{3} - \frac{6(y)}{2}$$

$\Rightarrow \quad 6(12) = 2(5x) - 3y$

$\Rightarrow \quad 72 = 10x - 3y$

$\Rightarrow \quad 10x - 3y = 72$

$2x - 3y = 24 \quad [\times -5] \quad -10x + 15y = -120$

$10x - 3y = 72 \qquad\qquad 10x - 3y = 72$

$12y = -48$

$\boxed{y = -4}$

$2x - 3y = 24$

$y = -4 \quad \Rightarrow 2x - 3(-4) = 24$

$2x = 24 - 12 \quad \Rightarrow 2x = 12$

$\Rightarrow \boxed{x = 6}$

> **(d)** Express w in terms of t and f.
> $$\sqrt{\frac{3w - 2t}{5w}} = 3f$$

$$\sqrt{\frac{3w - 2t}{5w}} = \frac{3f}{1}$$

$$\left(\sqrt{\frac{3w - 2t}{5w}}\right)^2 = \left(\frac{3f}{1}\right)^2$$

$$\Rightarrow \quad \frac{3w - 2t}{5w} = \frac{9f^2}{1}$$

Cross-multiply

$(3w - 2t)(1) = (9f^2)(5w)$

$\Rightarrow \quad 3w - 2t = 45wf^2$

Isolating the w terms

$3w - 45wf^2 = 2t$

$w(3 - 45f^2) = 2t$

$\Rightarrow \quad \boxed{w = \frac{2t}{3 - 45f^2}}$

Solution to question 4

(a)

> **(i)** Sketch $3x - 2y = -7$ and $2x + 5y = 8$ on a single diagram.

$3x - 2y = -7$

$x = 0 \quad \Rightarrow \; -2y = -7 \quad \Rightarrow \; y = 3.5$

$y = 0 \quad \Rightarrow \; 3x = -7 \quad \Rightarrow \; x = -2\frac{1}{3}$

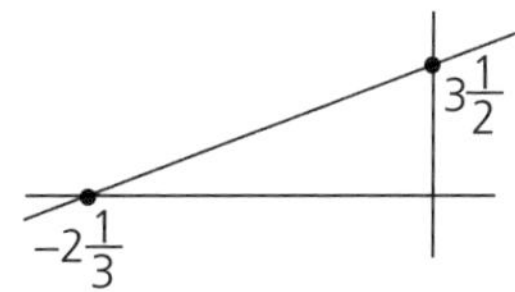

$2x + 5y = 8$

$x = 0 \quad \Rightarrow \; 5y = 8 \quad \Rightarrow \; y = 1.6$

$y = 0 \quad \Rightarrow \; 2x = 8 \quad \Rightarrow \; x = 4$

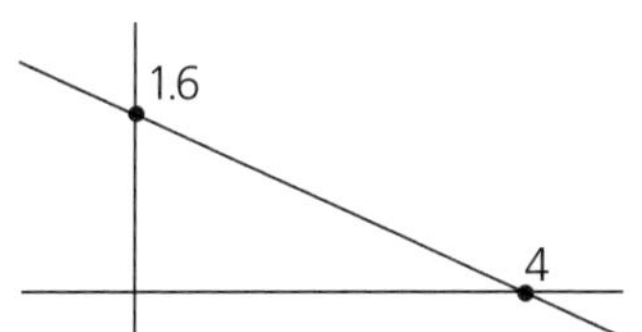

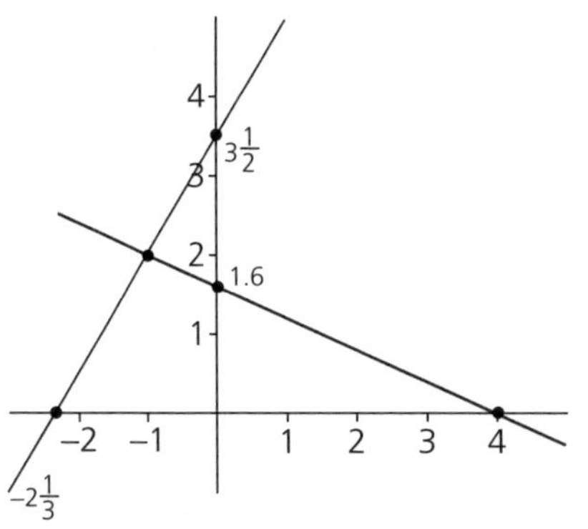

(ii) From the graph, we find the point of intersection is (–1, 2).

> **(iii)** Verify the answer by solving simultaneously.

$$
\begin{aligned}
3x - 2y &= -7 \quad (\times 2) & 6x - 4y &= -14 \\
2x + 5y &= 8 \quad (\times -3) & -6x - 15y &= -24 \\
& & -19y &= -38 \\
& & y &= 2
\end{aligned}
$$

Solve for x

$3x - 2y = -7$

$$
\begin{aligned}
y = 2 \quad \Rightarrow \quad 3x - 2(2) &= -7 \\
3x &= -7 + 4 \\
3x &= -3 \\
\Rightarrow \quad x &= -1
\end{aligned}
$$

$\Rightarrow$ The point of intersection is verified as (–1, 2).

(b) Perimeter $= 14$

Width $= x$

$\Rightarrow$ Length + Width $= 7$

Width $= x$

$\Rightarrow$ Length $= 7 - x$

* Area = (length) × (width)

$= (7 - x)(x) = 7x - x^2$

> **(c)** Graph $7x - x^2$ in the domain $1 \leqslant x \leqslant 7$.

x	1	2	3	4	5	6	7
$7x$	7	14	21	28	35	42	49
$-x^2$	−1	−4	−9	−16	−25	−36	−49
y	6	10	12	12	10	6	0

(1, 6)(2, 10)(3, 12)(4, 12)(5, 10)(6, 6)
(7, 0)

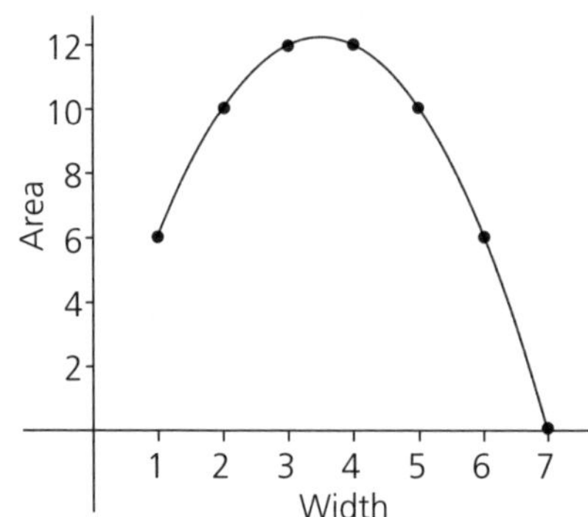

* Again we clearly state what each axis represents.

It is important to understand that in this question, the x-axis represents width.

(i) Find the area when the width = 1.5 metres.

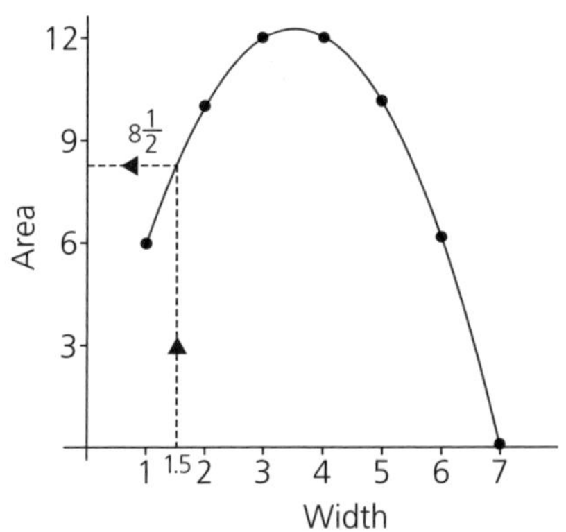

Area = $8\frac{1}{2}$ m^2 when width = 1.5 m.

(ii) Find the area when the length = 3.2 m.

* At the start of part **(b)** we saw that length + width = 7.

Length = 3.2 m $\Rightarrow$ Width = 3.8 m

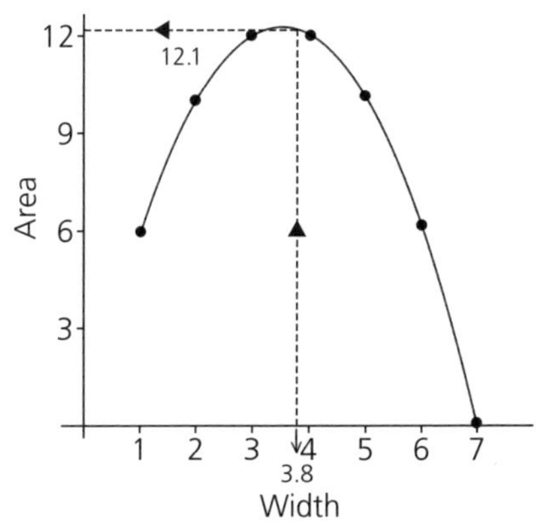

$\Rightarrow$ When length = 3.2 m (width = 3.8 m) the area = 12.1 m^2.

(iii) Find two possible widths when the area is 7 m^2.

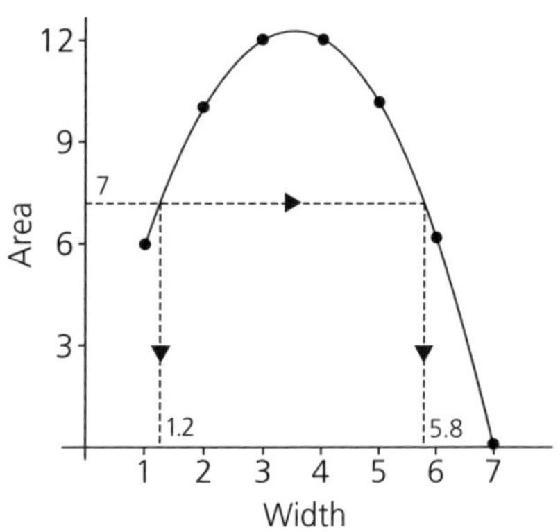

Therefore when the area = 7 m^2, the width is either 1.2 m or 5.8 m.

(iv) Calculate the maximum area.

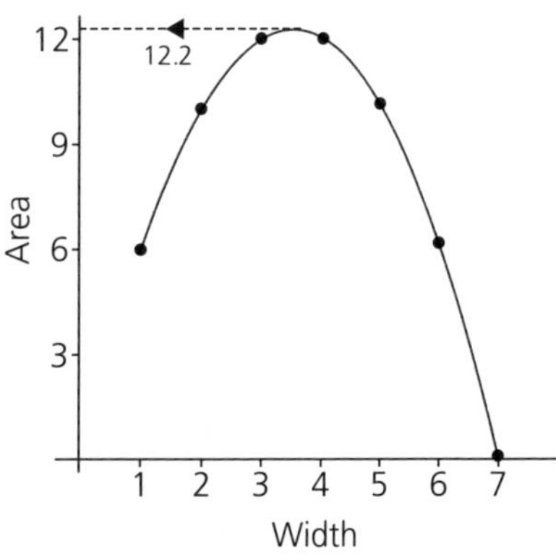

Therefore the maximum area is 12.2 m^2.

> **(v)** Calculate the length and width of the enclosure of maximum area.

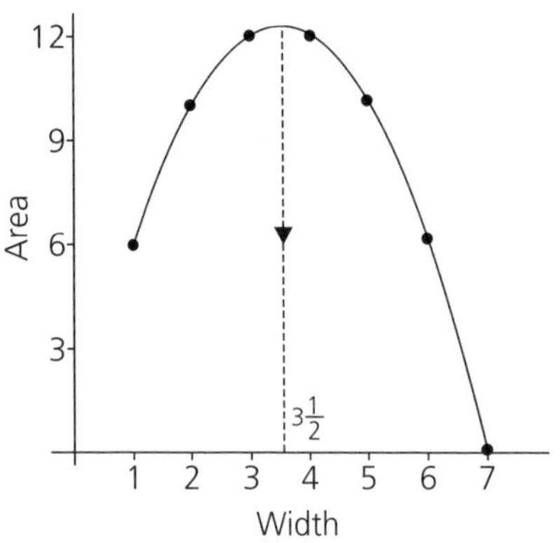

$\Rightarrow$ In the enclosure of maximum area, the width is $3\frac{1}{2}$ m.

$*$ Length + Width = 7 m

$\Rightarrow$ length is $3\frac{1}{2}$ m also.

$3\frac{1}{2}$m

$3\frac{1}{2}$m

The enclosure of maximum area is a 'rectangle' with both length and width $3\frac{1}{2}$ m.

Solution to question 5

> **(a)** Mary is 5 years older than Patrick. The product of their ages is 126. Write an equation in x to find their ages.

Are we told the difference in their ages at present? $\rightarrow$ Yes

Therefore we represent their ages using the same letter.

Mary's age $\quad x+5$

Patrick's age $\quad x$

Product = 126 $\quad \Rightarrow (x)(x+5)=126$

$\Rightarrow$ Solve $x^2+5x-126=0$

$a=1 \qquad b=5 \qquad c=-126$

$$\frac{-b \pm \sqrt{b^2-4ac}}{2a}$$

$$\Rightarrow \frac{-5 \pm \sqrt{(5)^2-4(1)(-126)}}{2(1)}$$

$$\frac{-5 \pm \sqrt{25+504}}{2}$$

$$\Rightarrow \frac{-5 \pm \sqrt{529}}{2}$$

$$\frac{-5 \pm 23}{2}$$

① $x = \dfrac{-5-23}{2} = \dfrac{-28}{2}$ $\quad \boxed{x=-14}$

② $x = \dfrac{-5+23}{2} = \dfrac{18}{2}$ $\quad \boxed{x=9}$

Therefore, Patrick is 9 years old and Mary is 14 years old.

> **(b)** Solve and illustrate the inequality $-5 \leqslant 1-3x < 10, \quad x \in R$.

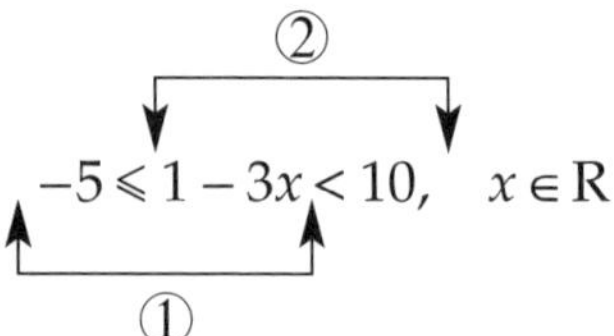

① $-5 \leqslant 1 - 3x$

$-5 - 1 \leqslant -3x \quad \Rightarrow \quad -6 \leqslant -3x$

[x term is negative] $\Rightarrow \quad 6 \geqslant 3x$

$\boxed{2 \geqslant x}$

② $1 - 3x < 10$

$-3x < 10 - 1 \quad \Rightarrow \quad -3x < 9$

[x term is negative] $\Rightarrow \quad 3x > -9$

$\boxed{x > -3}$

small no.	x	big no.

$-3 \quad < \quad x \quad \leqslant \quad 2 \qquad x \in R$

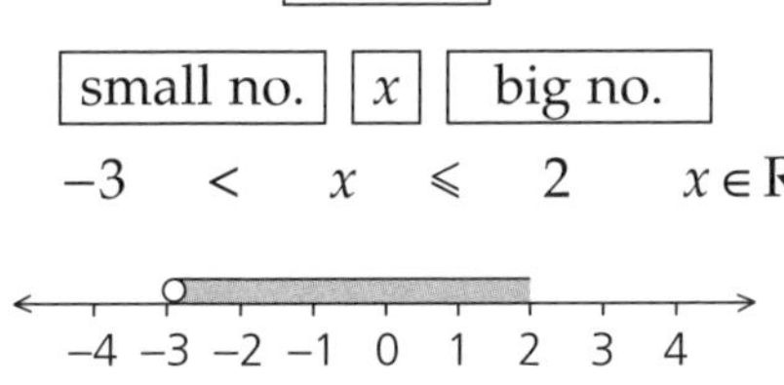

(c) 3 apples and 2 oranges cost €1.35. 5 oranges cost 50 cents more than 4 apples. Write 2 equations in x and y.

x = The cost of an apple.

y = The cost of an orange.

① 3 apples and 2 oranges cost €1.35

$\boxed{3x + 2y = 135}$

② 5 oranges cost 50 cents more than 4 apples

$5y = 4x + 50$

* We add 50 to $4x$ because the cost of the 4 apples was smaller.

$\boxed{4x - 5y = -50}$

Now solve

$$\begin{array}{lll} 3x + 2y = 135 & [\times 4] & 12x + 8y = 540 \\ 4x - 5y = -50 & [\times -3] & -12x + 15y = 150 \\ \hline & & 23y = 690 \\ & & \Rightarrow y = 30 \end{array}$$

$3x + 2y = 135$

$\boxed{y = 30}$

$\Rightarrow 3x + 2(30) = 135$

$3x = 135 - 60 \quad \Rightarrow \quad 3x = 75$

$x = 25$

Therefore an apple costs 25c and an orange costs 30c.

Solution to question 6

(a) Given $h: x \to ax^2 + bx + 1$ evaluate a and b if $h(1) = 2$ and $h(2) = 9$.

$$h: x \to ax^2 + bx + 1$$

$h(1) = 2$

Therefore let $x = 1$ and let the equation = 2.

$\Rightarrow a(1)^2 + b(1) + 1 = 2$

$1a + 1b + 1 = 2$

$\Rightarrow \quad 1a + 1b = 1$

$h(2) = 9$

$\Rightarrow a(2)^2 + b(2) + 1 = 9$

$4a + 2b = 8$

Solving for a and b

$$\begin{array}{lll} 1a + 1b = 1 & [\times -4] & -4a - 4b = -4 \\ 4a + 2b = 8 & & 4a + 2b = 8 \\ \hline & & -2b = 4 \\ & & b = -2 \end{array}$$

$1a + 1b = 1$

$b = -2 \quad \Rightarrow \quad 1a + 1(-2) = 1$

$1a = 3$

Hence evalute $h(-2)$

$h: x \to ax^2 + bx + 1$

$a = 3$ and $b = -2$

$\Rightarrow \quad h(x) = 3x^2 - 2x + 1$

$\Rightarrow h(-2) = 3(-2)^2 - 2(-2) + 1$

$= 12 + 4 + 1$

$= \boxed{17}$

(b) Graph $f: x \to -2x^2 + 7x - 3$ in the domain $-1 \leqslant x \leqslant 4$.

x	-1	0	1	2	3	4
$-2x^2$	-2	0	-2	-8	-18	-32
$+7x$	-7	0	7	14	21	28
-3	-3	-3	-3	-3	-3	-3
y	-12	-3	2	3	0	-7

$(-1, -12)(0, -3)(1, 2)(2, 3)(3, 0)(4, -7)$

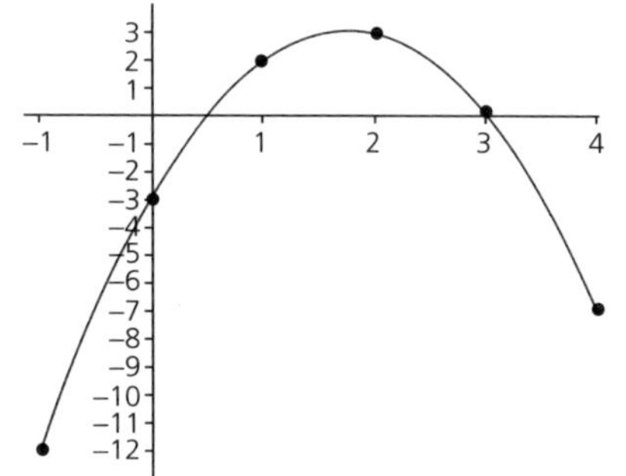

From the graph find:

(i) $f(0)$

(ii) $f(x) = 0$

(iii) $f(3.7)$

(iv) $f(x) + 7 = 0$

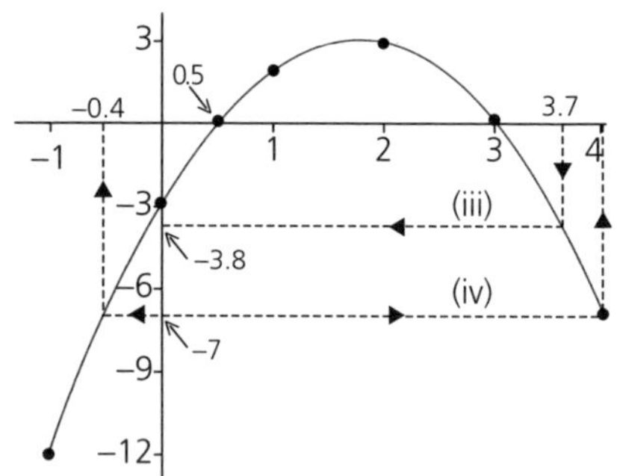

(i) $f(0)$

Because the number is in the bracket, go to zero on the x-axis. The corresponding y value is -3.

$\Rightarrow$ For $f(0)$, $y = -3$

(ii) $f(x) = 0$

Go to zero on the y-axis. The corresponding x values are $x = 0.5$ and $x = 3$.

$\Rightarrow$ For $f(x) = 0 \; x = 0.5$ and $x = 3$

(iii) $f(3.7)$

Go to 3.7 on the x-axis. From the graph $y = -3.8$

(iv) $f(x) + 7 = 0$

$f(x) + 7 = 0$

$\Downarrow$

$f(x) = -7$

$\Rightarrow$ go to -7 on the y-axis from the graph

$x = -0.4$ and $x = 4$

From the graph find:

(v) The values for which $-2x^2 + 7x = 0$.

(vi) The range of values for which $2x^2 - 7x + 4 \leqslant 0$.

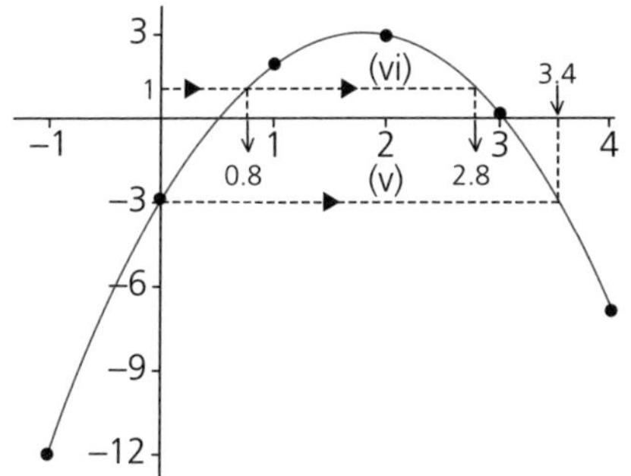

(v) Solve for $-2x^2+7x=0$

$$-2x^2+7x=0$$
$$\Downarrow$$
$$-2x^2+7x-3=-3$$
$$\Downarrow$$
$$f(x)=-3$$

Go to -3 on the y-axis.

From the graph $x=0$ and $x=3.4$

(vi) Solve for $2x^2-7x+4\leqslant 0$

∗ Because the sign of the x^2 term is different to the corresponding term in the equation of the graph.

① Change the signs all the way across.

$\Rightarrow\ -2x^2+7x-4$

② Change the inequality

$$\Rightarrow\ -2x^2+7x-4\geqslant 0$$
$$\Downarrow$$
$$-2x^2-7x-4\geqslant 0$$
$$\Downarrow$$
$$-2x^2-7x-3\geqslant 1$$
$$\Downarrow$$
$$f(x)\geqslant 1$$

For $f(x)=1$ (from graph) $x=0.8$
$x=2.8$

$\Rightarrow\ 0.8\leqslant x\leqslant 2.8$

∗ The inequality was changed because the graph is ∩ shaped.

> **(vii)** The maximum value of $f(x)$.
>
> **(viii)** The maximum coordinate.
>
> **(ix)** The equation of the axis of symmetry.

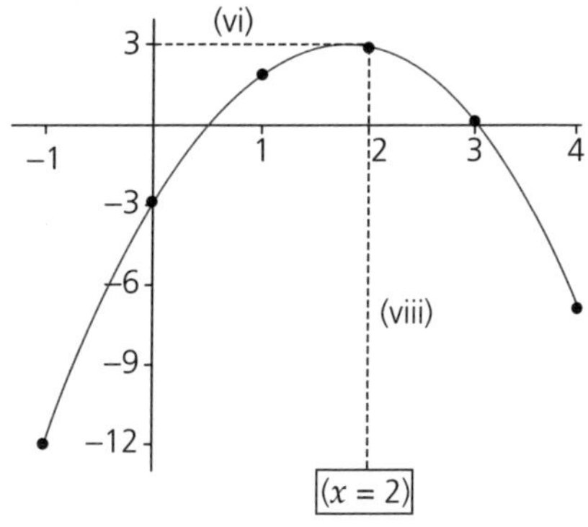

(vii) The maximum value of $f(x)$.

Basically the maximum (largest) value of y.

From the graph $\boxed{y=3}$

(viii) The maximum coordinate.

The highest point on the graph (x value and y value)

$\Rightarrow$ (2, 3)

(ix) The equation of the axis of symmetry is $x=2$ because the line cuts the x-axis at 2.

Chapter 8

Area and Volume

Perimeter and area

Relevant formulas

Circle

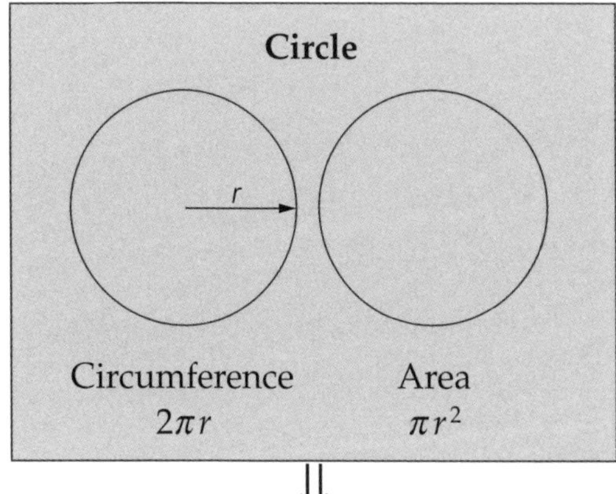

Circumference $2\pi r$ | Area πr^2

⇓

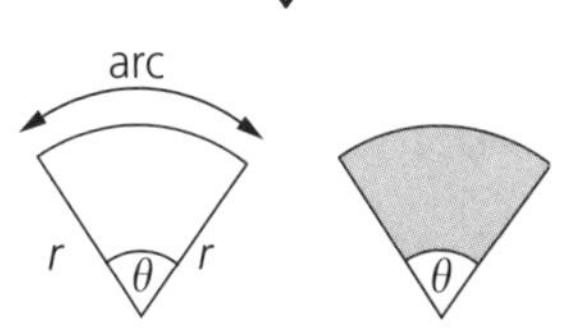

Length of arc $\frac{\theta}{360} \times 2\pi r$

Area of sector $\frac{\theta}{360} \times \pi r^2$

Parallelogram

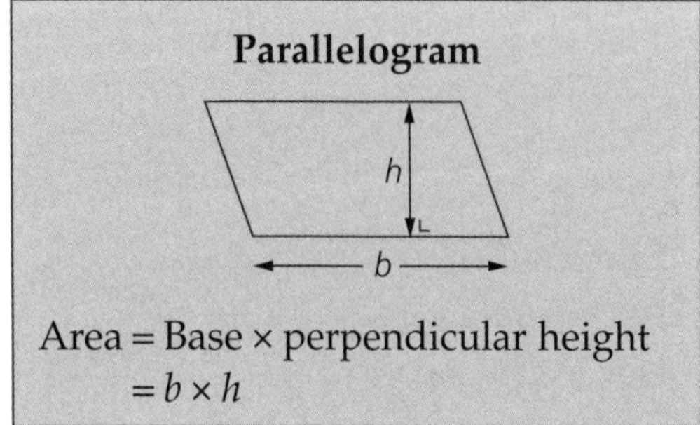

Area = Base × perpendicular height $= b \times h$

Triangle

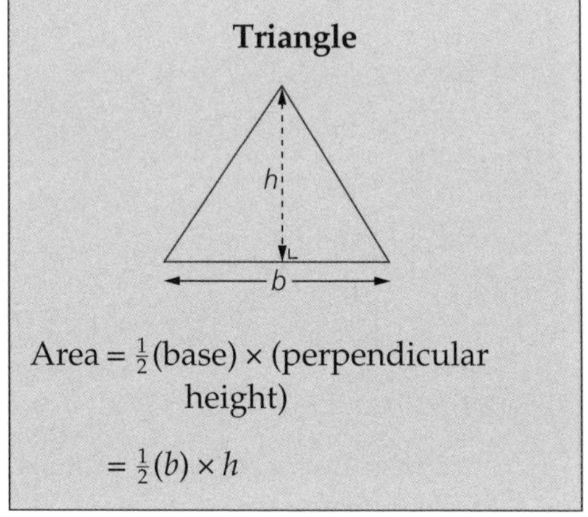

Area = $\frac{1}{2}$(base) × (perpendicular height)

$= \frac{1}{2}(b) \times h$

Question 1

A circle has a diameter of 10 cm. Find its area in terms of π.

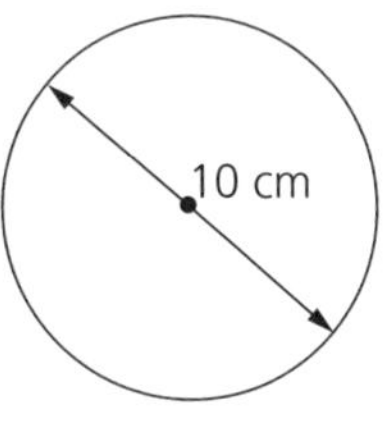

* If diameter = 10 cm, radius = 5 cm

Area = πr^2

Important – We are asked to find the area in terms of π. Therefore leave π as it is.

$\Rightarrow$ Area = $\pi \times 5 \times 5$

$= \boxed{25\pi}$

Question 2

Here we have a triangle surmounted by a semicircle.
Find the area.

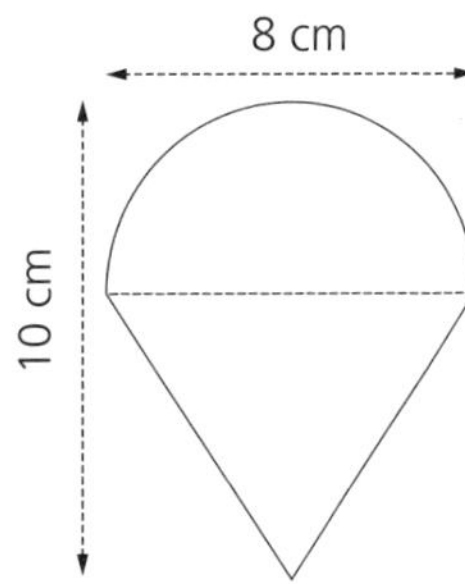

Important

4 cm
4 cm
4 cm
6 cm

$\Rightarrow$ Height of the triangle = 6 cm

We could now easily find the area of each.

Area of semicircle

$$\tfrac{1}{2}(2\pi r) = \left(\tfrac{1}{2}\right)(2)(3.14)(4)$$

$$= 12.56 \text{ cm}^2$$

Area of triangle

$$\tfrac{1}{2}(\text{base}) \times \text{perp. height}$$

$$\tfrac{1}{2}(8)(6) = 24 \text{ cm}^2$$

Area of shape

$$12.56 \text{ cm}^2 + 24 \text{ cm}^2$$

$$= 36.56 \text{ cm}^2$$

Question 3

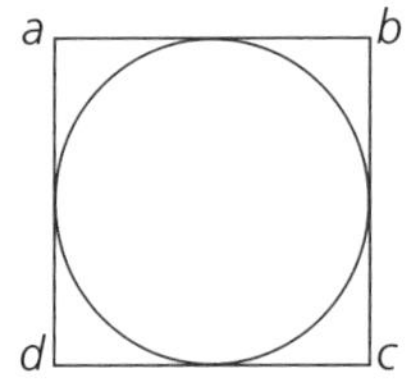

$|ac| = 12$ cm. Find the area of the circle.

Theory of Pythagorus is necessary in many Area + Volume solutions – please be very aware of it.

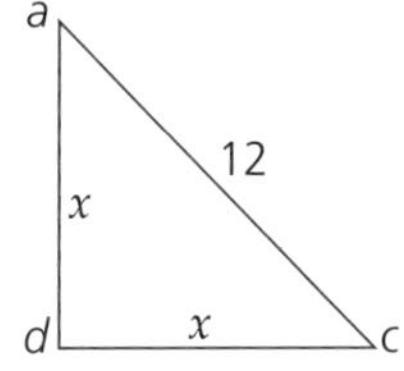

$$12^2 = x^2 + x^2$$

$$144 = 2x^2$$

$$\Rightarrow \quad 72 = x^2$$

$$\Rightarrow \quad 8.48 = x$$

$\Rightarrow$ Radius = 4.24 cm

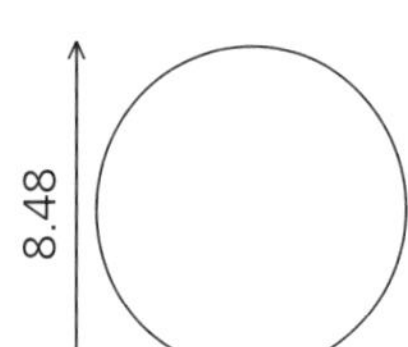

$$\text{Area} = \pi r^2$$

$$= (3.14)(4.24)^2$$

$$= 56.45 \text{ cm}^2$$

Question 4

(a)

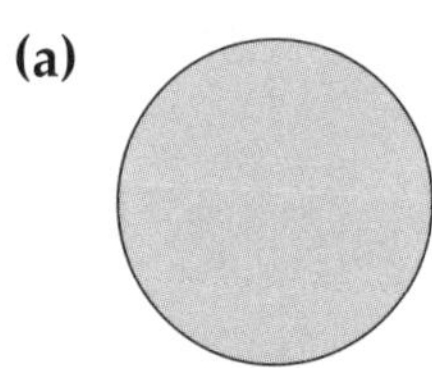

The circle has an area of 78.57 cm^2. Calculate its radius.

$$\pi = \frac{22}{7}$$

Important
Let the area = the area formula.
Hence calculate r.

$\Rightarrow \quad 78.57 = \pi r^2$

$\Rightarrow \quad 78.57 = \dfrac{22}{7} \times r^2$

$\Rightarrow \quad \dfrac{78.57}{\left(\dfrac{22}{7}\right)} = r^2 \qquad \Rightarrow$ Radius = 5 cm

↓

$78.57 \div (22 \div 7)$

Question 5

John finds a piece of wire 50.24 cm in length. He makes it into a wheel.

Calculate:

(i) The radius of the wheel.

(ii) How many times would the wheel have to turn on the road in order to travel a distance of 1.256 km.

(i)

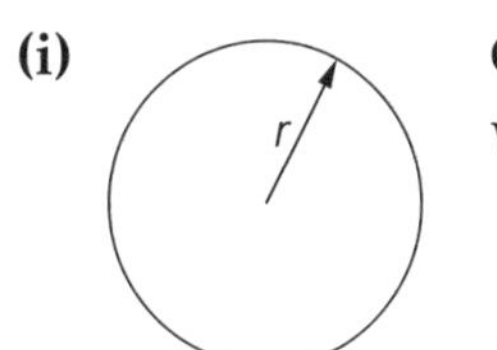

Circumference of wheel = 50.24 cm

Let the relevant formula = 50.24

$\Rightarrow \quad 2\pi r = 50.24$

$\Rightarrow \quad (2)(3.14)r = 50.24$

$\Rightarrow \quad (6.28)r = 50.24$

$r = \dfrac{50.24}{6.28} \qquad \Rightarrow$ Radius = 8 cm

(ii)

The circumference of the wheel is 50.24 cm.
Therefore if it turns once along the road, it would travel 50.24 cm.

1.256 km = 1256 m = 125,600 cm

$\Rightarrow$ To travel 125,600 cm, this wheel would have to turn $\left(\dfrac{125{,}600}{50.24}\right)$ times

$= 2500$ times

Area + Volume

Relevant formulas

Note 1
'Area' is always measured in cm^2 or m^2.

Note 2
'Volume' is always measured in cm^3 or m^3.

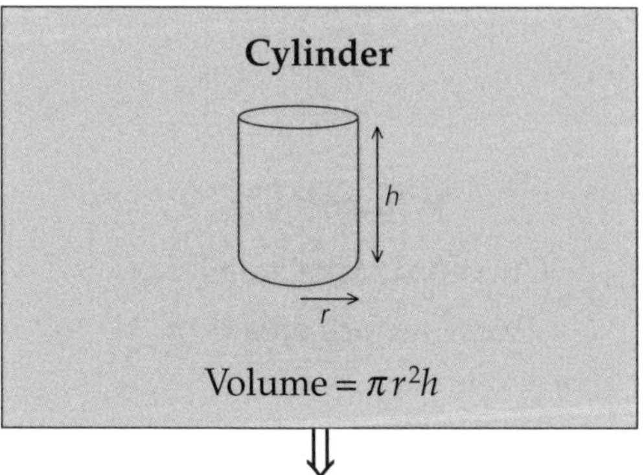

⇓

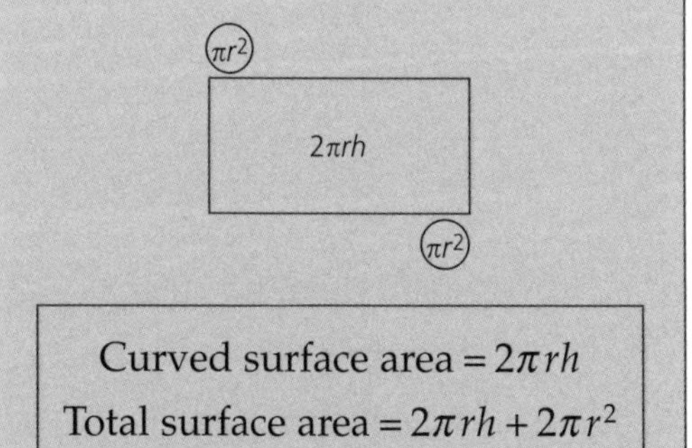

Curved surface area = $2\pi rh$

Total surface area = $2\pi rh + 2\pi r^2$

Sphere

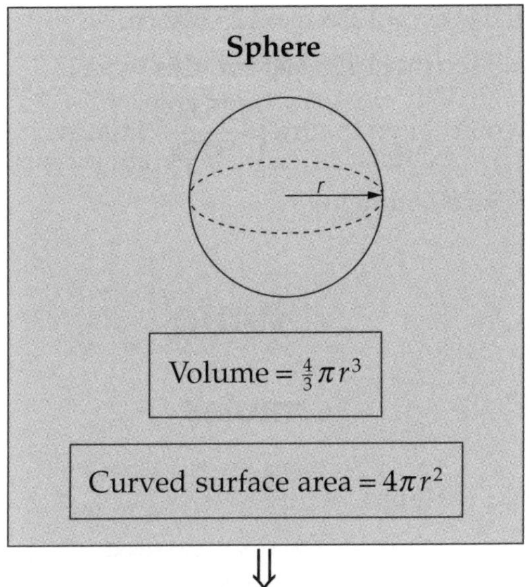

Volume $= \frac{4}{3}\pi r^3$

Curved surface area $= 4\pi r^2$

⇓

Hemisphere

(not in log tables)

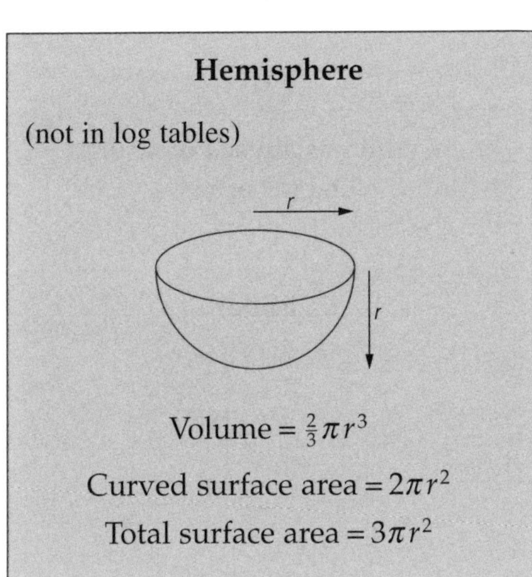

Volume $= \frac{2}{3}\pi r^3$

Curved surface area $= 2\pi r^2$

Total surface area $= 3\pi r^2$

Cone

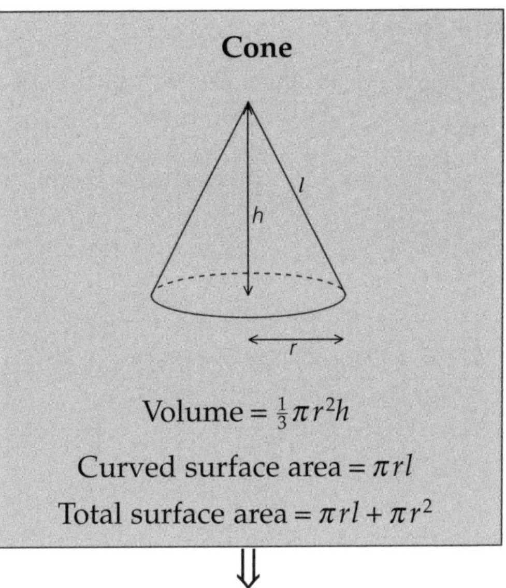

Volume $= \frac{1}{3}\pi r^2 h$

Curved surface area $= \pi r l$

Total surface area $= \pi r l + \pi r^2$

⇓

Important

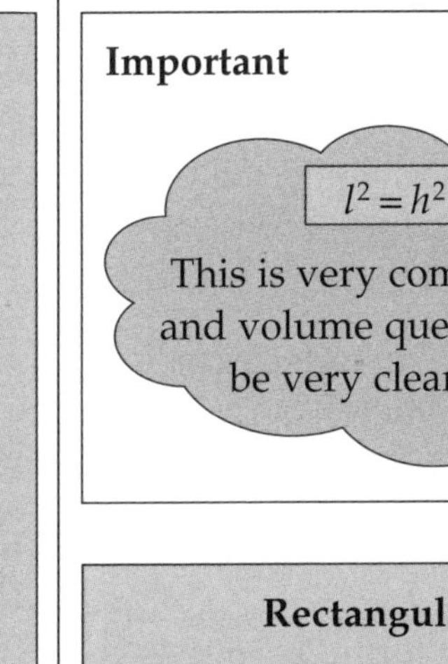

$l^2 = h^2 + r^2$

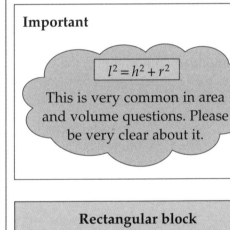

This is very common in area and volume questions. Please be very clear about it.

Rectangular block

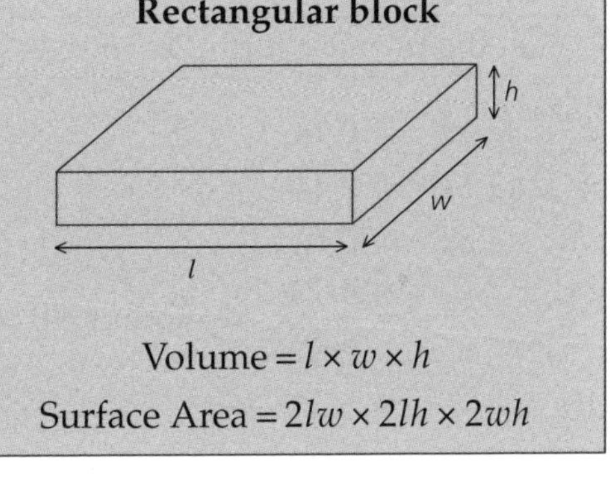

Volume $= l \times w \times h$

Surface Area $= 2lw \times 2lh \times 2wh$

Example 1

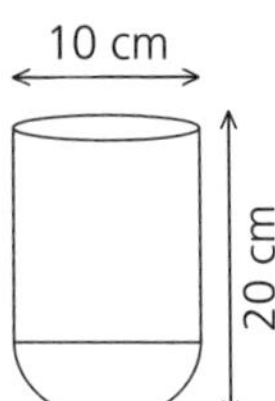

Calculate the volume of this container consisting of a cylinder surmounted by a hemisphere.

> If the radius of the hemisphere is 5 cm, its 'height' is 5 cm.

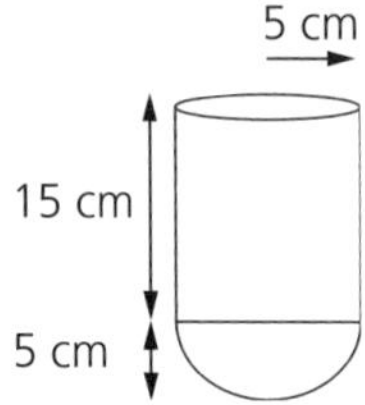

Volume of cylinder

$\pi r^2 h = (3.14)(5)(5)(15)$

$= 1177.5 \text{ cm}^3$

Volume of hemisphere

$\frac{2}{3}\pi r^3 = \frac{2}{3}(3.14)(5)(5)(5)$

$= 261.67 \text{ cm}^3$

$\Rightarrow$ Volume of container $= 1177.5 + 261.67$

$= 1439.17 \text{ cm}^3$

Example 2

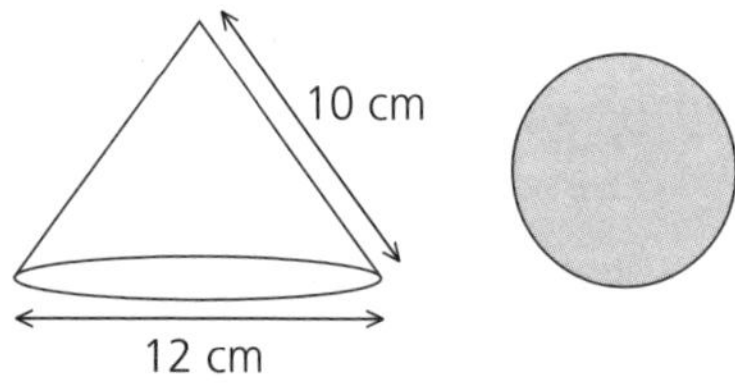

(i) Calculate the volume of the cone in terms of π.

(ii) The volume of the sphere is four times the volume of the cone. Calculate the radius of the cone.

(i) Calculate the vertical height of the cone.

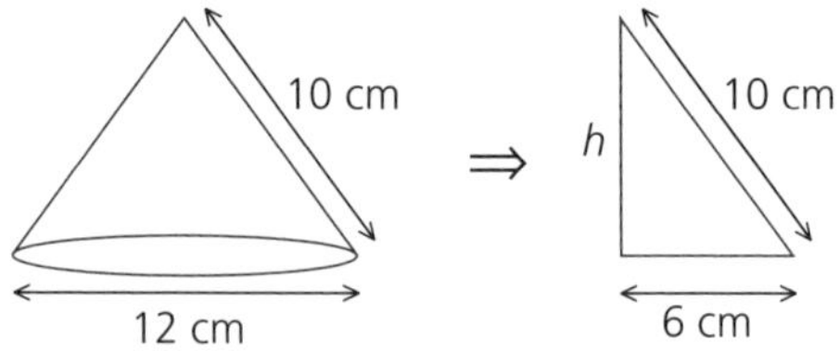

$\Rightarrow 10^2 = h^2 + 6^2 \qquad \Rightarrow 100 = 36 + h^2$

$\Rightarrow 100 - 36 = h^2 \qquad \Rightarrow 64 = h^2$

$\Rightarrow$ Vertical height $= 8$ cm

Volume $= \frac{1}{3}\pi r^2 h$

> Again, when we are asked to express a volume 'in terms of π' leave π as it is in the formula. Do not substitute $\frac{22}{7}$ or 3.14 for it.

$= \left(\frac{1}{3}\right)(\pi)(6)(6)(8)$

$= 96\pi \text{ cm}^3$

(ii) Vol. of sphere = 4(vol. of cone)

$\Rightarrow \quad \frac{4}{3}\pi r^3 = 4\left(\frac{1}{3}\pi r^2 h\right)$

$\Rightarrow \left(\frac{4}{3}\right)\cancel{(\pi)}(r^3) = (4)\left(\frac{1}{3}\right)\cancel{(\pi)}(6)(6)(8)$

$\Rightarrow (1.33)(r^3) = 384$

$r^3 = \frac{384}{1.33}$

$r^3 = 288$

$r = \sqrt[3]{288} = 6.6$ cm

> Please follow the layout of this solution for all questions of this type.

Example 3

A solid metal block of height 10 cm, width 8 cm and length 20 cm is melted down.

It is recast into 3 solid cylinders of height 5 cm. Calculate (to the nearest cm) the radius of the cylinders.

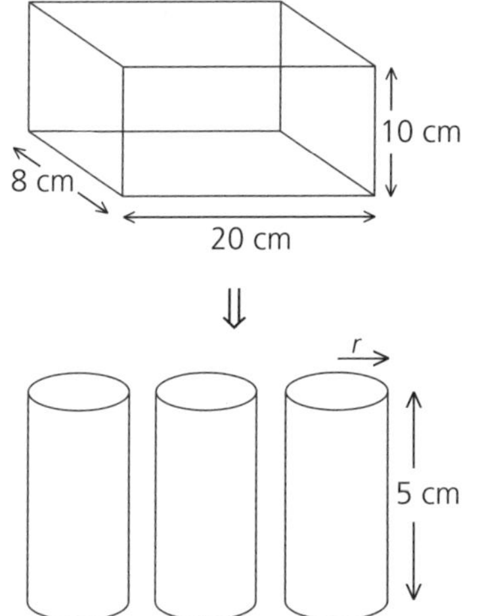

Volume of block = Volume of three cylinders

$\Rightarrow \quad l \times w \times h = 3(\pi r^2 h)$

$\Rightarrow \quad 20 \times 8 \times 10 = 3(3.14)(r^2)(5)$

$\Rightarrow \quad 1600 = (47.1)(r^2)$

$\Rightarrow \quad \frac{1600}{47.1} = r^2 \quad \Rightarrow 5.83 = r$

$\Rightarrow$ The radius of the cylinders (to the nearest cm) is 6 cm.

Liquid in a container

It is very common to be given the volume of liquid in a container and asked to find the height of the liquid.

To find the height in such a question:

① Let the volume of liquid equal to the formula of the container.

② Hence find the height (h).

Question 1

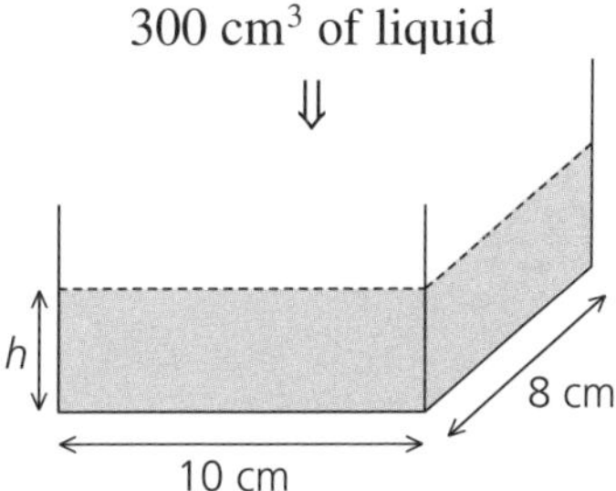

Let the volume of liquid = formula for the tank.

$\Rightarrow \quad 300 = l \times w \times h$

$\Rightarrow \quad 300 = 10 \times 8 \times h$

$\Rightarrow \quad \frac{300}{80} = h$

Question 2

Let the volume of liquid = the formula for the tank (cylinder).

600 cm^3 of liquid

⇓

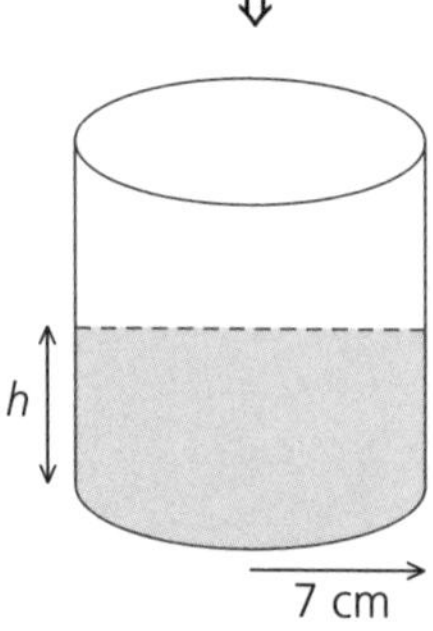

$$\Rightarrow \quad 600 = \pi r^2 h$$
$$600 = 3.14 \times 7 \times 7 \times h$$
$$\Rightarrow \quad 600 = 153.86 \times h$$
$$\Rightarrow \quad \frac{600}{153.86} = h$$

Objects put in/taken out of water

Example 1

3 solid cylinders of height 6 cm are submerged in a rectangular tank of length 10 cm and width 5 cm. If the water level in the tank rose by 2 cm calculate the radius of the cylinders.

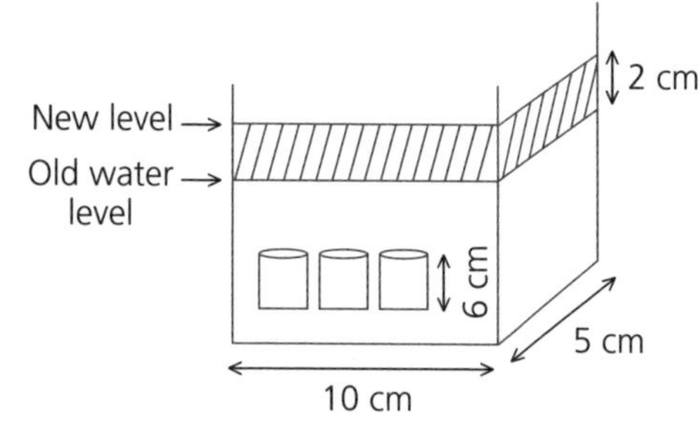

For your own benefit, draw a diagram to illustrate the question.

Important

① Show the difference in water level clearly.

② Always let the volume of what is put in/taken out of the water = volume of the difference in water level.

From the diagram we see that in this question the 'difference in water level' is a rectangular block of height 2 cm.

Volume of what is put in/taken out of the water.	=	Volume of the 'difference in water level'.

$$3(\pi r^2 h) = l \times w \times h$$
$$3 \times 3.14 \times r^2 \times 6 = 10 \times 5 \times 2$$
$$\Rightarrow \quad 56.52 \times r^2 = 100$$
$$r^2 = \frac{100}{56.52}$$
$$\Rightarrow \quad \text{Radius} = 1.33 \text{ cm}$$

Example 2

2 spheres of radius 6 cm are submerged in a cylindrical tank of radius 14 cm. Calculate by how much the water level drops when the spheres are taken out.

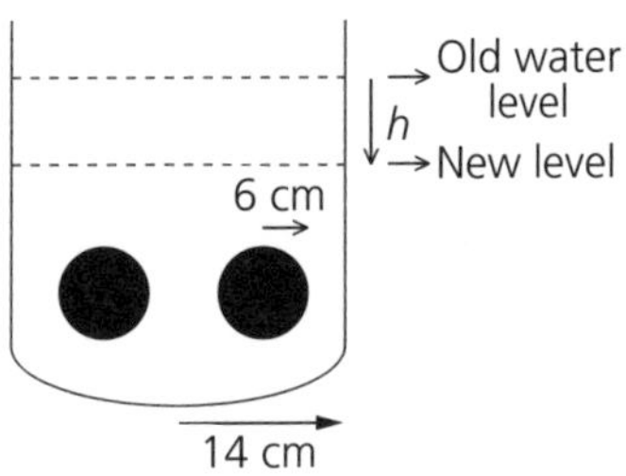

Vol. of the 2 spheres = Difference in water level

In this question we see that the 'difference in water level' is a cylinder of height 'h'.

$$2\left(\tfrac{4}{3}\pi r^3\right) = \pi r^2 h$$

$$\Rightarrow\ 2 \times \frac{4}{3} \times 6^3 = 14^2 \times h$$

$$\Rightarrow\ 576 = 196 \times h$$

$$\Rightarrow\ \frac{576}{196} = h$$

$\Rightarrow$ Water level fell by 2.9 cm

Items being packed

There are three main questions which are frequently asked.

Example 1

6 spheres of radius 4 cm packed into a rectangular box. Find the volume of the box.

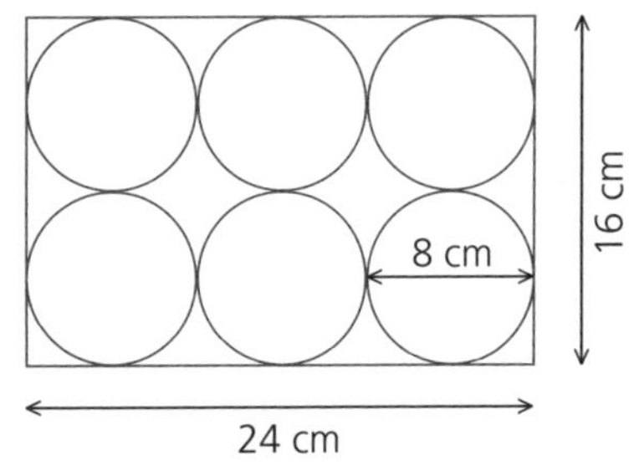

* Height of box = 'Height' of a sphere

Volume = length × width × height

Volume = 24 × 16 × 8

Example 2

6 cylinders of radius 5 cm and height 7 cm packed into a rectangular box. Find the volume of the box.

* Here think of a packet of cigarettes. Height of the box = Height of the cigarette.

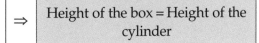

$\Rightarrow$ Height of the box = Height of the cylinder

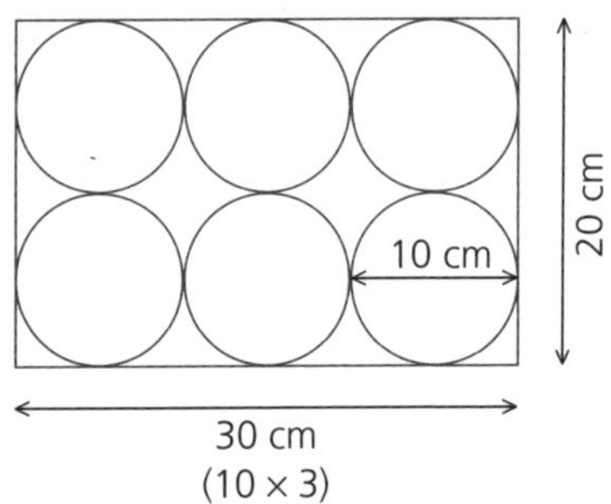

$$\begin{aligned}\text{Volume} &= \text{length} \times \text{width} \times \text{height}\\ &= 30 \times 20 \times 7\\ &= 4200\ \text{cm}^3\end{aligned}$$

Example 3

4 spheres of radius 3 cm packed into a cylinder. Find the volume of the cylinder.

Volume of cylinder $= \pi r^2 h$

$= \dfrac{22}{7} \times 3 \times 3 \times 24$

$= 678.8 \text{ cm}^3$

Chapter 8 Sample questions for you to try

Question 1

(a) The figure shown consists of a triangle and a semicircle.

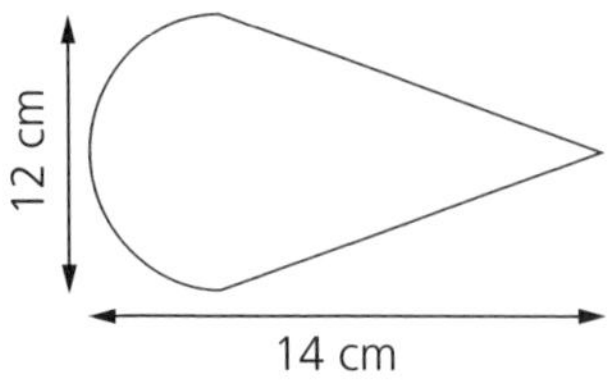

(i) Calculate its area.

(ii) Calculate the perimeter of the figure.

(b) A rectangular tank of length 45 cm and width 10 cm is half-filled with water. Three solid spheres of radius 5 cm are fully submerged in the tank. Calculate (to the nearest cm) the rise in water in the tank.

(c) **(i)** Find, in terms of π, the volume of a cylinder of radius 4 cm and height 9 cm.

(ii) Eight such cylinders are packed into a rectangular box. Calculate the volume of the box.

(iii) Calculate the % of empty space in the box.

Question 2

(a)

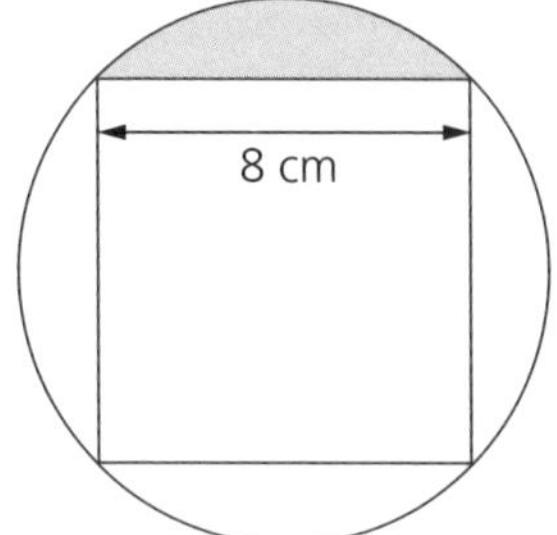

The inscribed square has sides 8 cm in length. Calculate:

(i) The radius of the circle.

(ii) The circumference of the circle.

(iii) The area of the shaded area.

(b) The diagram shows a cylinder surmounted by a cone.

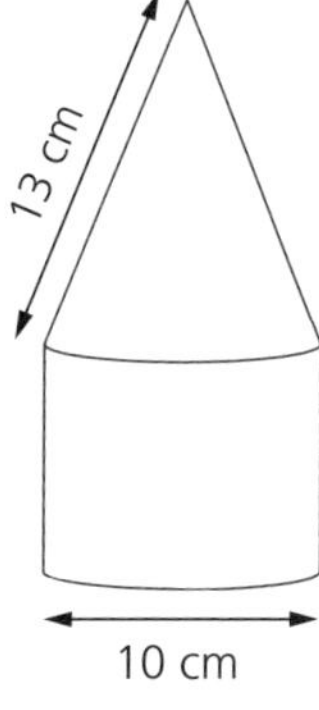

Calculate:

(i) The height of the cone.

(ii) The volume of the cone in terms of π.

(iii) The height of the cylinder if the volume of the cylinder is eight times the volume of the cone.

(c) The shape shown in part **(b)** is melted down and recast as 6 solid spheres. Calculate (to the nearest cm) the radius of the spheres.

Question 3

(a) Given $|\angle acb| = 50^\circ$ and the length of the arc $ab = 8.73$ cm, find:

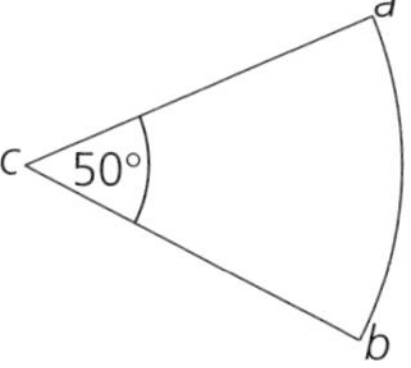

(i) The radius of the sector.

(ii) The area of the sector.

(b) **(i)** Water flows through a cylindrical pipe of radius 4 cm at a speed of 8 cm/sec. Calculate the rate of flow of water from the pipe, in terms of π.

(ii) The water flows into a cylindrical container of radius 15 cm. Calculate the height of water in the container after 20 sec.

(c) The volume of a cone is 45π. If the height of the cone is five times its radius. Calculate the radius of the cone.

Solution to question 1

(a)

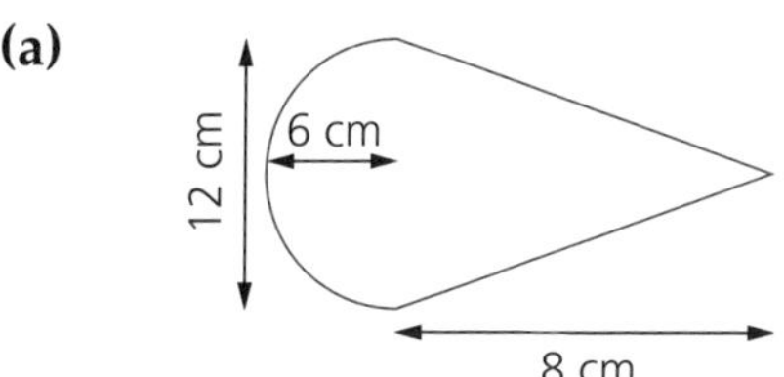

(i) Calculate the area:

① Semicircle

$$\text{Area} = \tfrac{1}{2}(\pi r^2)$$

$$= (0.5)(3.14)(6)(6)$$

$$= 56.52\ \text{cm}^2$$

② Triangle

$$= \tfrac{1}{2}(\text{base}) \times (\text{perp. height})$$

$$= \tfrac{1}{2}(12) \times (8)$$

$$= 48\ \text{cm}^2$$

$$\Rightarrow \text{Total area} = 56.52 + 48$$

$$= 104.52\ \text{cm}^2$$

(ii) Calculate its perimeter:

① Semicircle

$$\text{Perimeter} = \tfrac{1}{2}(2\pi r)$$
$$= (0.5)(2)(3.14)(6)$$
$$= 18.84 \text{ cm}$$

② Triangle

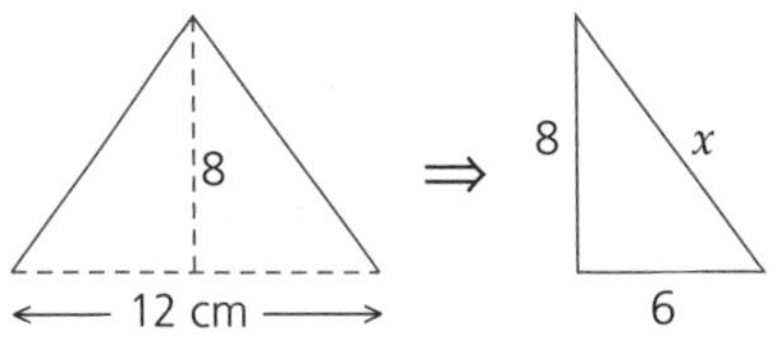

$x^2 = 8^2 + 6^2 \quad \Rightarrow x^2 = 64 + 36$

$\Rightarrow x^2 = 100 \quad \Rightarrow x = 10$

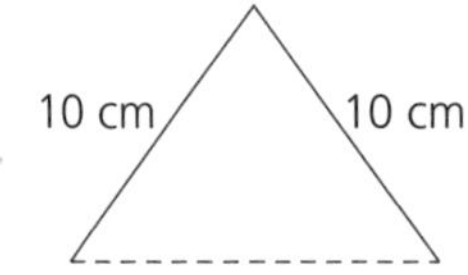

'Perimeter' = 20 cm

$\Rightarrow$ Total perimeter

$= 20 \text{ cm} + 18.84 \text{ cm}$

$=$ **38.84 cm**

(b)

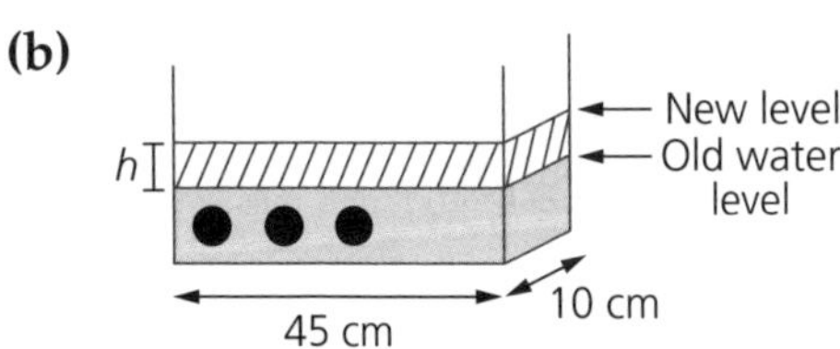

Volume of rise in water level = Volume of the three spheres

> **Note**
> The rise in water level here is shown clearly to be a rectangular block of length 45 cm, width 10 cm and height h.

$$\Rightarrow \quad l \times w \times h = 3\left(\tfrac{4}{3}\pi r^3\right)$$
$$\Rightarrow \quad 45 \times 10 \times h = (3)\left(\tfrac{4}{3}\right)(3.14)(5^3)$$
$$\Rightarrow \quad 450 \times h = 1570$$
$$\Rightarrow \quad h = \frac{1570}{450}$$

Therefore the water rose by 3.49 cm.

(c) (i) Vol. of cylinder $= \pi r^2 h$

$\Rightarrow \quad \pi(4^2)(9)$

$= 144\pi$

(ii)

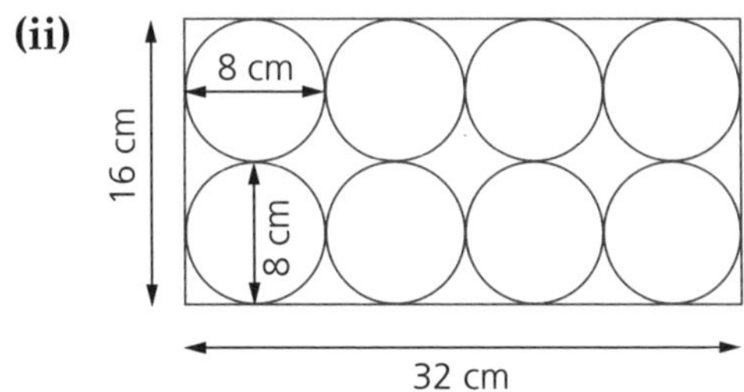

> Again, think of this as a box of 8 cigarettes. The height of each cylinder is the same as the height of the box.

$\Rightarrow$ Volume of the box

$= \text{length} \times \text{width} \times \text{height}$

$= 32 \times 16 \times 9$

$= 4608 \text{ cm}^3$

(iii) Calculate the % of empty space in the box.

Volume of the box = 4608 cm^3

Volume of the 8 cylinders

$= 8 \times 144\pi = 1152\pi$

$\Rightarrow$ Volume of empty space

$= 4608 \text{ cm}^3 - 1152\pi$

$= 989 \text{ cm}^3$

% of empty space

$$= \frac{\text{Vol. of empty space}}{\text{Vol. of box}} \times \frac{100}{1}$$

$$= \frac{989}{4608} \times \frac{100}{1} = 21.46\%$$

Solution to question 2

(a) (i)

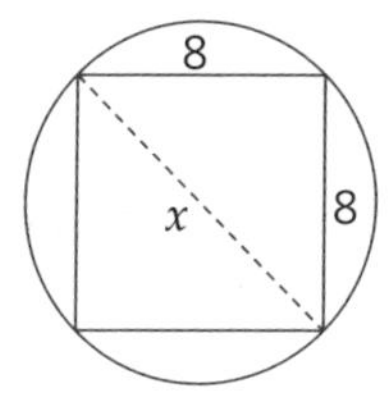

Calculate radius:

$x^2 = 8^2 + 8^2$

$\Rightarrow \quad x^2 = 64 + 64$

$\Rightarrow \quad x^2 = 128$

$\Rightarrow \quad x = 11.31$

$\Rightarrow$ diameter = 11.31 cm

So radius = 5.66 cm

(ii) Circumference $= 2\pi r$

$= 2 \times 3.14 \times 5.66$

$= 35.53 \text{ cm}$

(iii) ① Area of square $= 8 \times 8$

$= 64 \text{ cm}^2$

② Area of circle

$= \pi r^2$

$= 3.14 \times 5.66 \times 5.66$

$= 100.6 \text{ cm}^2$

Difference $= 100.6 - 64$

$= 36.6 \text{ cm}^2$

$\Rightarrow$ Shaded area $= 36.6 \div 4$

$= 9.15 \text{ cm}^2$

(b)

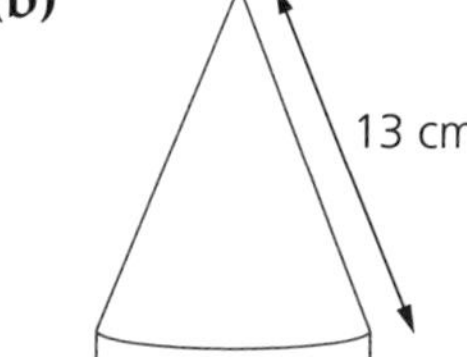

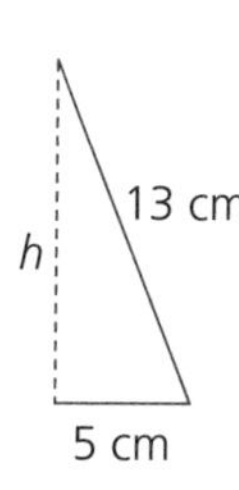

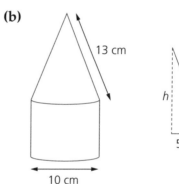

(i)

$13^2 = 5^2 + h^2$

$169 - 25 = h^2$

$12 = h$

$\Rightarrow$ Height of cylinder = 12 cm

(ii) Vol. of cone $= \frac{1}{3}\pi r^2 h$

$= \frac{1}{3} \times \pi \times 5^2 \times 12$

$\Rightarrow$ Volume in terms of $\pi = 100\pi$

(iii) Vol. of cylinder

$$= 8(\text{Vol. of cone})$$

$$\pi r^2 h = 8(100\pi)$$

$$\cancel{\pi} \times 5 \times 5 \times h = 800\cancel{\pi}$$

$$\Rightarrow \quad 25h = 800 \text{ ... cancelling } \pi$$

$$\Rightarrow \quad h = \frac{800}{25}$$

$\Rightarrow$ Height of cylinder = 32 cm

(c) Shape is melted down and recast as 6 solid spheres.

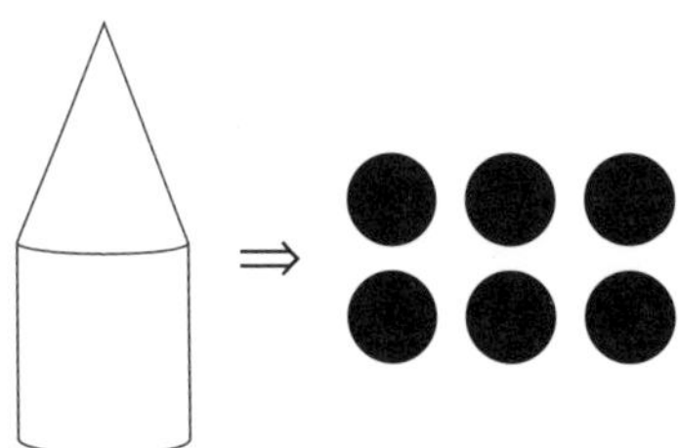

$\Rightarrow$ Volume of shape

= Volume of the 6 spheres

$$\Rightarrow \quad 100\pi + 800\pi = 6\left(\tfrac{4}{3}\pi r^3\right)$$

$$\Rightarrow \quad 900\pi = 6\left(\tfrac{4}{3}\right)(\pi)(r^3)$$

$$\Rightarrow \quad 900\cancel{\pi} = 8\cancel{\pi}(r^3)$$

$$\Rightarrow \quad 112.5 = r^3$$

$$\Rightarrow \quad \sqrt[3]{112.5} = r$$

$\Rightarrow$ Radius of sphere = 5 cm (to nearest cm)

Solution to question 3

(a)

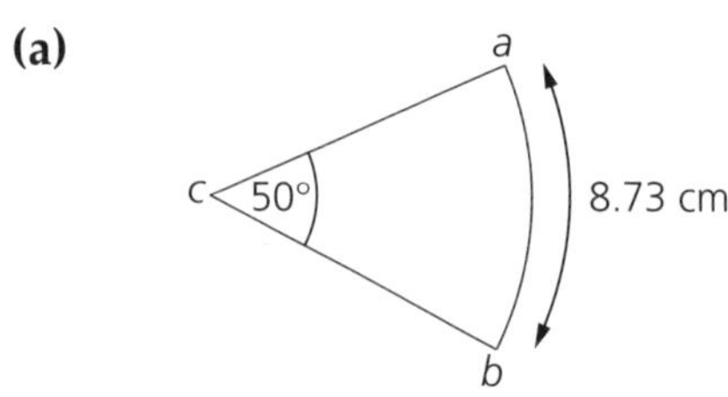

(i) $\frac{50°}{360°} \times 2\pi r = 8.73$

$$\Rightarrow \quad 0.138 \times 2 \times \frac{22}{7} \times r = 8.73$$

$$\Rightarrow \quad 0.873r = 8.73$$

$$\Rightarrow \quad \text{Radius} = 10 \text{ cm}$$

(ii) Area of sector $= \frac{50°}{360°} \times \pi r^2$

$$= \frac{50°}{360°} \times \frac{22}{7} \times 10^2$$

$\Rightarrow$ Area = 43.65 cm^2

(b)

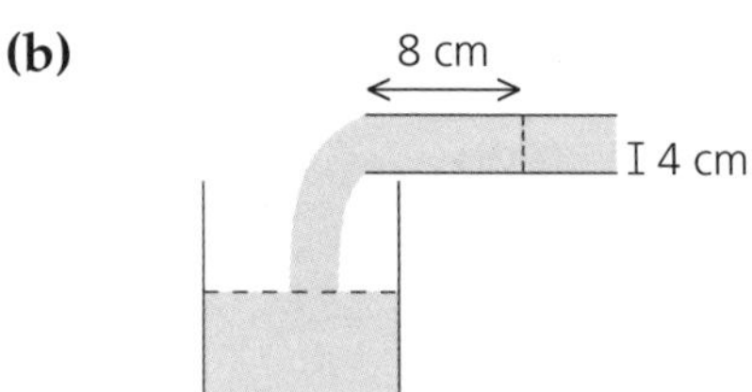

(i) Rate of flow from the pipe in terms of π.

4 cm

8 cm

Rate of flow = 8 cm/sec

$\Rightarrow$ The water in this section of pipe would flow into the tank in one second.

$$\Rightarrow \quad \text{Rate of flow} = \pi r^2 h$$

$$= \pi \times 4^2 \times 8$$

$$= (128\pi) \text{ cm}^3/\text{sec}$$

(ii)

In 20 sec, 2560π $(128\pi \times 20)$ flows into the tank.

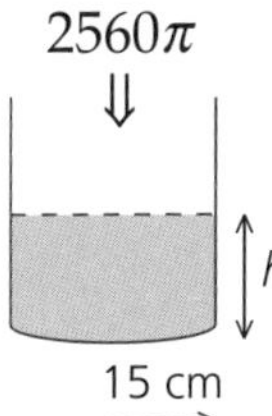

Let 2560π = Vol. of container

$\Rightarrow \quad 2560\pi = \pi r^2 h$

$\Rightarrow \quad 2560\pi = \pi(15^2)(h)$

$\Rightarrow \quad \dfrac{2560}{225} = h$

$\Rightarrow$ Height of water in tank = 11.38 cm

(c) Height = 5(Radius)

$\Rightarrow \quad \boxed{h = 5r}$

Volume of cone = $\frac{1}{3}\pi r^2 h$

$\Rightarrow \quad 45\cancel{\pi} = \frac{1}{3}\cancel{\pi}(r^2)(5r)$

$\Rightarrow \quad 45 = \left(\frac{1}{3}\right) \times 5r^3$

$\Rightarrow \quad 45 = 1.6 \times r^3$

$\Rightarrow \quad 27 = r^3$

$\Rightarrow \quad$ Radius = 3 cm

Chapter 9
Coordinate Geometry

Slope of a line

Type 1

Given $a(-1, 4)$ $b(3, -2)$ find the slope of $[ab]$.

Slope between two points $= \dfrac{y_2 - y_1}{x_2 - x_1}$

$$a(\underset{x_1}{-1},\ \underset{y_1}{4}) \qquad b(\underset{x_2}{3},\ \underset{y_2}{-2})$$

$$\Rightarrow \frac{-2-4}{3-(-1)} = \frac{-2-4}{3+1} = \frac{-6}{4} = \boxed{\frac{-3}{2}}$$

Type 2

Find the slope of

$$2x - 3y - 1 = 0$$

$2x - 3y - 1 = 0$

① Isolate the y term on the left.

$$-3y = -2x + 1$$

② Divide across by the number before the y term.

$$y = \frac{-2}{-3}x\ \frac{+1}{-3}$$

③ The slope is the number before the x term.

$$\Rightarrow \qquad \text{Slope} = \frac{-2}{-3} = \boxed{+\frac{2}{3}}$$

Type 3

Prove $[cd]$ is parallel to $8x - y + 2 = 0$ given

$$c(-2, -5) \quad d(-1, 3)$$

Important
If two lines are parallel, (//) they have the same slope.

① Slope of $[cd]$

$$c(\underset{x_1}{-2},\ \underset{y_1}{-5}) \qquad d(\underset{x_2}{-1},\ \underset{y_2}{3})$$

$$= \frac{3-(-5)}{-1-(-2)} = \frac{3+5}{-1+2} = \boxed{8}$$

② Slope of $8x - y + 2 = 0$

$$-1y = -8x - 2$$

$$y = \frac{-8}{-1}x\ \frac{-2}{-1}$$

$$\Rightarrow \text{Slope} = \frac{-8}{-1} = \boxed{8}$$

Because the lines have the same slope, they are parallel.

Type 4

Prove $[ef]$ is perpendicular to $6x-2y+1=0$ given

$e(-4,-3) \quad f(2,-5)$

Important

To show two lines are perpendicular ($\perp$):

① Find both slopes.

② Multiply the slopes.

③ If the lines are perpendicular, the answer will be –1.

① Slope of $[ef]$

$$\begin{matrix} e(-4, & -3) & \quad f(2, & -5) \\ x_1 & y_1 & \quad x_2 & y_2 \end{matrix}$$

$$\text{Slope} = \frac{-5-(-3)}{2-(-4)} = \frac{-5+3}{2+4} = \frac{-2}{6} = \boxed{\frac{-1}{3}}$$

② Slope of $6x-2y+1=0$

$$-2y=-6x-1$$

$$y=\frac{-6}{-2}x\,\frac{-1}{-2}$$

$$\Rightarrow \text{Slope} = \frac{-6}{-2} = +\frac{6}{2} = \boxed{3}$$

③ Multiply the slopes

$$\left(\frac{-1}{3}\right)(3) = -1$$

'Because the product of their slopes is -1, $[ef]$ is perpendicular to $6x-2y+1=0$.'

Type 5

Calculate t if $4x-5y+1=0$ is perpendicular to $tx+2y-3=0$.

Important

If line $A \perp$ line B and slope of line

$$A=\frac{c}{d} \text{ slope of line } B=\frac{-d}{c}$$

(turn the slope of line A upside down and change its sign).

① Slope of $4x-5y+1=0$

$$-5y=-4x-1$$

$$y=\frac{-4}{-5}x\,\frac{-1}{-5}$$

$$\Rightarrow \text{Slope} = \frac{-4}{-5} = \boxed{+\frac{4}{5}}$$

② Slope of $tx+2y-3=0$

$$2y=-tx+3 \qquad y=\frac{-t}{2}x+\frac{3}{2}$$

$$\Rightarrow \text{Slope} = \boxed{\frac{-t}{2}}$$

But $4x-5y+1=0 \perp tx+2y-3=0$

Slope of $4x-5y+1=0$ is $\frac{4}{5}$

$\Rightarrow$ Slope of $tx+2y-3=0$ <u>must</u> be $\frac{-5}{4}$

$$\Rightarrow \frac{-5}{4} = \frac{-t}{2}$$

Cross-multiplying: $(-5)(2)=(4)(-t)$

$$\Rightarrow -10=-4t \Rightarrow \frac{-10}{-4}=t \quad \boxed{t=\frac{5}{2}}$$

Equation of a line

Type 1

Find the equation of $[ab]$ given
$a(3, -9)$ $b(-1, -3)$

Important
To find the equation of a line we need:
① A point on the line $(x_1\ y_1)$.
② The slope of the line (m).

① Point on line $[ab]$ $(3, -9)$
$(x_1 \quad y_1)$

② Slope of $[ab]$

$a(3, -9)$ $b(-1, -3)$
$x_1 \quad y_1 \qquad x_2 \quad y_2$

$$\text{Slope} = \frac{-3-(-9)}{-1-3} = \frac{-3+9}{-4} = \frac{6}{-4}$$

$$= \boxed{\frac{-3}{2}} \ m$$

Equation $y - y_1 = m(x - x_1)$

$$\Rightarrow \quad y + 9 = \frac{-3}{2}(x-3)$$

$$\Rightarrow \quad 2(y+9) = -3(x-3)$$

$$\Rightarrow \quad 2y + 18 = -3x + 9$$

$$\Rightarrow 3x + 2y + 9 = 0$$

Type 2

Find the equation of line P which contains $(-2, 3)$ if $P \parallel [ab]$ given $a(2, -5)$ $b(-3, 1)$.

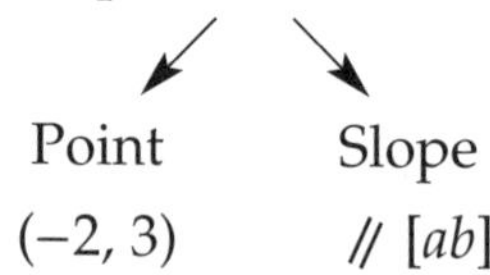

Point $(-2, 3)$ Slope $\parallel [ab]$

(i) Find the slope of $[ab]$.

$a(2, -5)$ $b(-3, 1)$
$x_1 \quad y_1 \qquad x_2 \quad y_2$

$$\text{Slope} = \frac{y_2 - y_1}{x_2 - x_1} = \frac{1-(-5)}{-3-2} = \frac{1+5}{-5}$$

$$= \boxed{-\frac{6}{5}}$$

(ii) Find the slope of P.

As $P \parallel [ab]$, they have the same slope.

$\Rightarrow$ Slope of P is $\frac{-6}{5}$ also

(iii) Find the equation of P.

$(-2, 3)$ $m = \frac{-6}{5}$
$x_1 \quad y_1$

$$y - y_1 = m(x - x_1)$$

$$\Rightarrow \quad y - 3 = \frac{-6}{5}(x+2)$$

$$\Rightarrow \quad 5(y-3) = -6(x+2)$$

$$\Rightarrow \quad 5y - 15 = -6x - 12$$

$$\Rightarrow 6x + 5y - 3 = 0$$

Type 3

> Find the equation of line A which contains $(3, -4)$, if
>
> $$A \perp 2x - 3y + 1 = 0$$

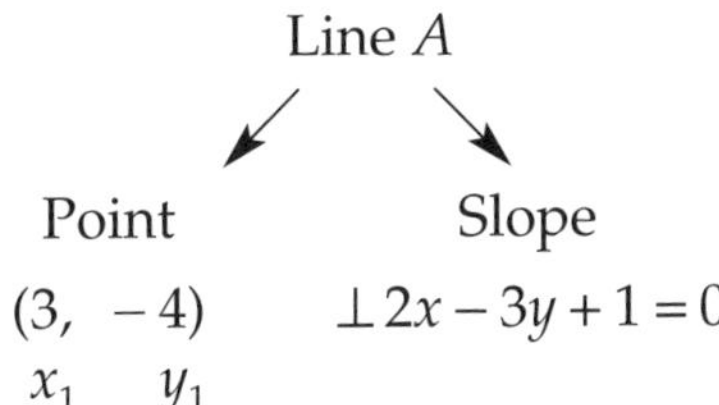

$(3, \; -4)$ $\qquad \perp 2x - 3y + 1 = 0$

$x_1 \quad y_1$

① Find slope of $2x - 3y + 1 = 0$.

$$-3y = -2x - 1$$

$$y = \frac{-2}{-3}x \; \frac{-1}{-3}$$

$\Rightarrow$ Slope of $2x - 3y + 1 = 0 = \boxed{\frac{2}{3}}$

② Find slope of line A.

As line $A \perp 2x - 3y + 1 = 0$, slope of line $A = \frac{-3}{2}$

③ Find the equation of line A.

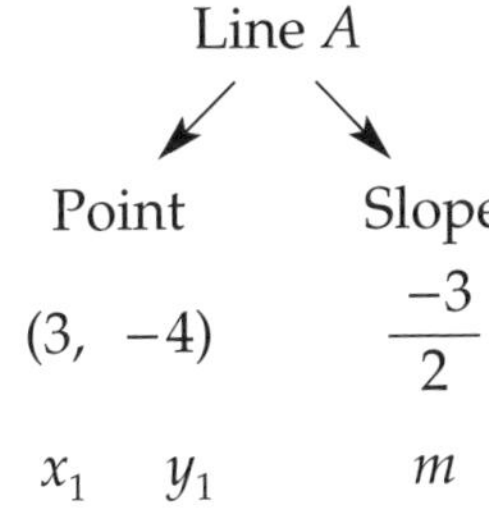

$(3, \; -4)$ $\qquad \frac{-3}{2}$

$x_1 \quad y_1 \qquad m$

$$y - y_1 = m(x - x_1)$$

$$\Rightarrow \quad y + 4 = \frac{-3}{2}(x - 3)$$

$$2(y + 4) = -3(x - 3)$$

$$2y + 8 = -3x + 9$$

$$\Rightarrow A: 3x + 2y - 1 = 0$$

Type 4

Prove that $a(3, -4)$ $\; b(-3, -1)$ and $c(-9, 2)$ are collinear.

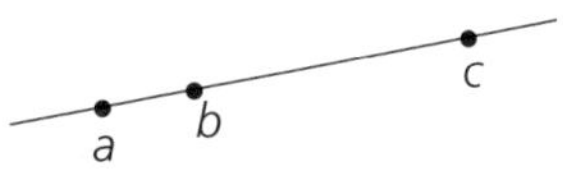

> If three points are collinear, they lie on the same straight line.

(i) Find the equation of $[ab]$.

$a(3, \; -4) \qquad b(-3, \; -1)$

$x_1 \quad y_1 \qquad\quad x_2 \quad y_2$

$$\text{Slope} = \frac{y_2 - y_1}{x_2 - x_1} = \frac{-1 + 4}{-3 - 3} = \frac{3}{-6}$$

$$= \boxed{\frac{-1}{2}}$$

Equation $\Rightarrow y - y_1 = m(x - x_1)$

Point $(3, \; -4)$ $\qquad$ Slope $= -\frac{1}{2}$

$x_1 \quad y_1 \qquad\qquad m$

$$y + 4 = \frac{-1}{2}(x - 3)$$

$$\Rightarrow \quad 2(y + 4) = -1(x - 3)$$

$$\Rightarrow \quad 2y + 8 = -1x + 3$$

$$\Rightarrow 1x + 2y + 5 = 0$$

(ii) Show that $c(-9, 2)$ lies on $[ab]$.
Fill $(-9, 2)$ into the equation of $[ab]$.

$$1(-9) + 2(2) + 5 = 0$$

$$\Rightarrow \quad -9 + 4 + 5 = 0 \; ✓$$

As $(-9, 2)$ satisfies the equation of $[ab]$, it must be on the line $[ab]$. Therefore the 3 points are collinear.

Area of a triangle

Type 1

Find the area of the triangle enclosed by $2x - 3y + 12 = 0$, the x-axis and the y-axis.

Find where $2x - 3y + 12 = 0$ cuts both axes.

① Where $2x - 3y + 12 = 0$ cuts the x-axis:

Let $y = 0$

$\Rightarrow\ 2x - 3(0) + 12 = 0 \quad \Rightarrow\ 2x = -12$

$\Rightarrow\ \quad x = -6 \quad \Rightarrow\ (-6, 0)$

② Where $2x - 3y + 12 = 0$ cuts the y-axis:

Let $x = 0$

$\Rightarrow\ 2(0) - 3y + 12 = 0 \quad \Rightarrow\ -3y = -12$

$\Rightarrow\ \quad y = 4 \quad \Rightarrow\ (0, 4)$

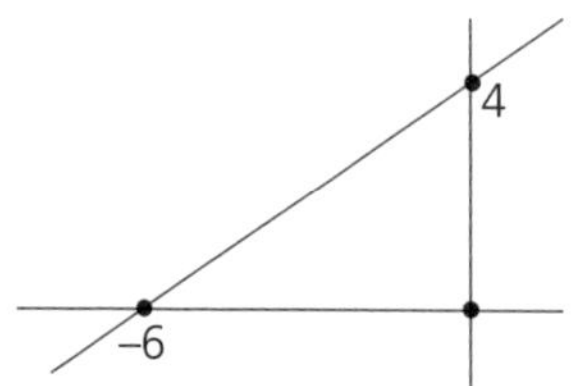

Area of a right-angled triangle

$= \frac{1}{2}(\text{base}) \times (\text{perpendicular height})$

$\Rightarrow$ Area $= \frac{1}{2}(6)(4) = \boxed{12}$

Type 2

Given L: $2x - y + 2 = 0$ and W: $4x + 3y - 16 = 0$, find the area of the triangle enclosed by L, W and the x-axis.

(i) Draw a rough diagram of what the triangle could look like.

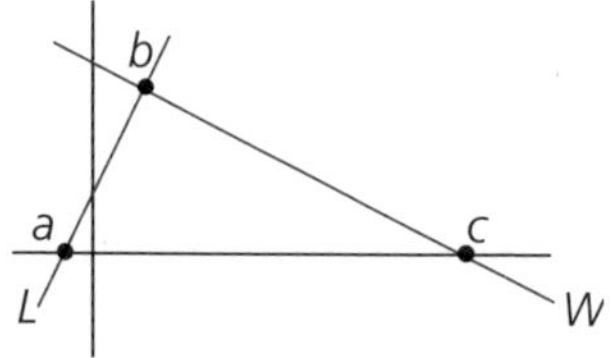

(ii) Find each of the three vertices.

$\boxed{\text{Pt. } a}$ $\rightarrow$ Where $2x - y + 2 = 0$ cuts the x-axis.

Let $y = 0 \quad \Rightarrow\ 2x - 0 + 2 = 0$

$\Rightarrow\ 2x = -2 \quad \Rightarrow\ a(-1, 0)$

$\boxed{\text{Pt. } c}$ $\rightarrow$ Where $4x + 3y - 16 = 0$ cuts the x-axis.

Let $y = 0 \quad \Rightarrow\ 4x + 3(0) - 16 = 0$

$\Rightarrow\ 4x = 16 \quad \Rightarrow\ c(4, 0)$

$\boxed{\text{Pt. } b}$ $\rightarrow$ Where the lines intersect each other.

To find where two lines intersect, we solve them using simultaneous equations.

$2x - 1y = -2 \quad [\times -2] \quad -4x + 2y = 4$

$4x + 3y = 16 \qquad\qquad\qquad 4x + 3y = 16$

$5y = 20$

$\Rightarrow\ \boxed{y = 4}$

$2x - 1y = -2$

$\boxed{y = 4} \quad \Rightarrow\ 2x - 1(4) = -2$

$2x = 2 \quad \Rightarrow\ \boxed{x = 1}$

$\Rightarrow\ b(1, 4)$

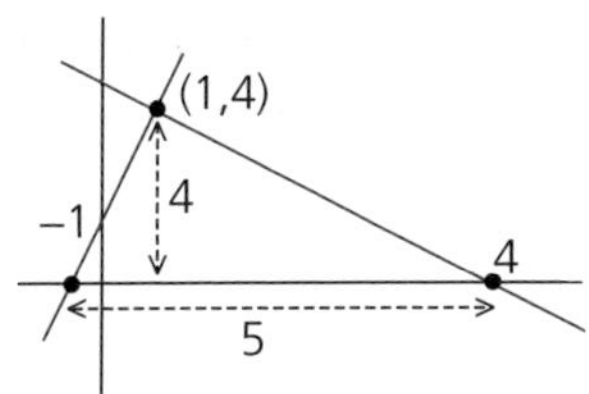

Area = $\frac{1}{2}$(base) × (perp. height)

$= \frac{1}{2}(5) \times (4)$

$\Rightarrow$ Area = 10

Midpoint

Type 1

> Given $p(2, -7)$ and $r(-6, -3)$. Find the midpoint of $[pr]$.

$$\text{Midpoint} = \left(\frac{x_1 + x_2}{2}, \frac{y_1 + y_2}{2}\right)$$

$p(2, -7)$ $r(-6, -3)$

x_1 y_1 x_2 y_2

$$\text{Midpoint} = \left(\frac{2-6}{2}, \frac{-7-3}{2}\right)$$

$$= \left(\frac{-4}{2}, \frac{-10}{2}\right) = (-2, -5)$$

Type 2

> Find point c if $a(-1, 3)$ is the midpoint of $[bc]$ given $b(3, -5)$.

$b(3, -5)$ $a(-1, 3)$ Pt. c

∗ Obviously pt. c is the image of pt. b under a central symmetry in pt. a.

$(3, -5) \rightarrow (-1, 3) \rightarrow c(-5, 11)$

$\begin{bmatrix} x \text{ down } 4 \\ y \text{ up } 8 \end{bmatrix}$ each time

Distance between two points

> Given $m(2, -2)$ $n(1, 6)$ $p(-3, -1)$ prove that $\triangle mnp$ is isosceles.

$$\text{Distance} = \sqrt{(x_2 - x_1)^2 + (y_2 - y_1)^2}$$

$|mn|$ $m(2, -2)$ $n(1, 6)$

x_1 y_1 x_2 y_2

$= \sqrt{(1-2)^2 + (6+2)^2}$

$= \sqrt{(-1)^2 + (8)^2} = \sqrt{65}$

$|mp|$ $m(2, -2)$ $p(-3, -1)$

x_1 y_1 x_2 y_2

$= \sqrt{(-3-2)^2 + (-1+2)^2}$

$= \sqrt{(-5)^2 + (1)^2} = \sqrt{26}$

$|np|$ $n(1, 6)$ $p(-3, -1)$

x_1 y_1 x_2 y_2

$= \sqrt{(-3-1)^2 + (-1-6)^2}$

$= \sqrt{(-4)^2 + (-7)^2} = \sqrt{65}$

As $|mn| = |np|$, $\triangle mnp$ is isosceles.

> An isosceles triangle is one which has two sides equal in length.

Image of a point

Find the image of (−3, 4) under:

(i) The translation $(-1, 2) \rightarrow (3, -1)$.

(ii) A central symmetry through (4, 2).

(iii) Sx, axial symmetry in the x-axis.

(vi) Sy, axial symmetry in the y-axis.

(v) Axial symmetry in the line $x = 2$.

(vi) Axial symmetry in the line $y = 1$.

(i) Image of (−3, 4) under
$(-1, 2) \rightarrow (3, -1)$.

$$(-1, 2) \rightarrow (3, -1) \quad \left[\begin{matrix} x \text{ up } 4 \\ y \text{ down } 3 \end{matrix}\right] \text{ each time}$$

$\Rightarrow (-3, 4) \rightarrow (1, 1)$

$\Rightarrow$ Image = (1, 1)

(ii) Image of (−3, 4) under a central symmetry through (4, 2).

y down 2 each time

$(-3, 4) \rightarrow (4, 2) \rightarrow (11, 0)$

x up 7 each time

$\Rightarrow$ Image = (11, 0)

(iii) Image of (−3, 4) under Sx.

* Simply change the sign of the y term.

$\Rightarrow$ Image = (−3, −4)

(iv) Image of (−3, 4) under Sy.

* Simply change the sign of x term.

$\Rightarrow$ Image = (3, 4)

(v) Image of (−3, 4) under an axial symmetry in the line $x = 2$.
Easiest method:

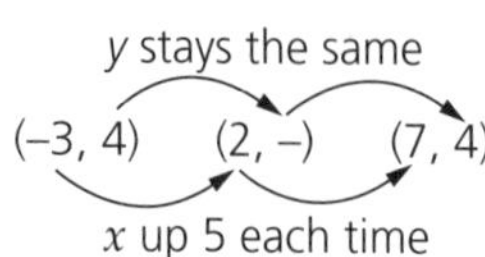

$\Rightarrow$ Image = (7, 4)

(vi) Image of (−3, 4) under an axial symmetry in the line $y = 1$.

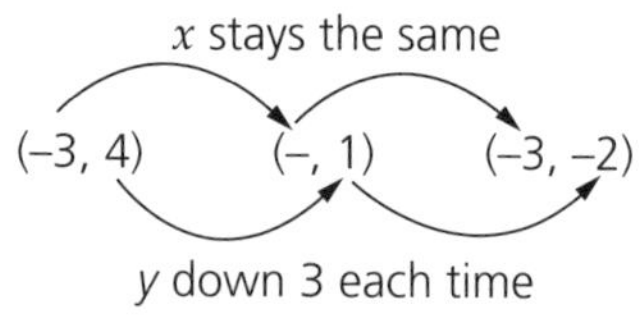

$\Rightarrow$ Image = (−3, −2)

Image of a line

Find the image of $2x - 3y + 1 = 0$ under:

(i) Sx, axial sym. in the x-axis.

(ii) Sy, axial sym. in the y-axis.

(iii) So, central sym. in the origin.

(i) Image of $2x - 3y + 1 = 0$ under Sx.

* Simply change the sign of the y term.

$\Rightarrow$ Image is $2x + 3y + 1 = 0$

(ii) Image of $2x - 3y + 1 = 0$ under Sy.

* Simply change the sign of the x term.

$\Rightarrow$ Image is $-2x - 3y + 1 = 0$

$\Rightarrow 2x + 3y - 1 = 0$

(iii) Image of $2x - 3y + 1 = 0$ under So.

* Simply change both the x and y signs.

$\Rightarrow$ Image is $-2x + 3y + 1 = 0$

$\Rightarrow 2x - 3y - 1 = 0$

Other important questions

Question 1

Prove (−2, 3) is on $4x + 3y - 1 = 0$.

Substitute −2 for x and 3 for y into the equation:

$$4(-2)+3(3)-1=0$$
$$-8+9-1=0 \quad \Rightarrow \; 0=0 \checkmark$$

As (−2, 3) satisfies the equation, the point is on the line.

Question 2

If $(1, t)$ is on $4x+3y-1=0$, find t.

As $(1, t)$ is on $4x+3y-1=0$, it must satisfy the equation.

$$4(1)+3(t)-1=0$$
$$4+3t-1=0 \quad \Rightarrow \; 3t=-3$$
$$\Rightarrow \; t=-1$$

Question 3

$a(-3, 3)$ $b(-5,-2)$ $c(1,-1)$ are three points of the parallelogram $abcd$. Find point d.

* Draw a rough diagram joining pt. a to pt. b to pt. c.

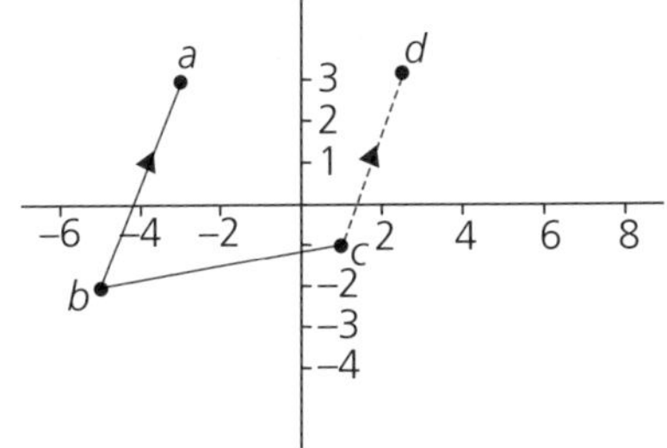

From the diagram we see that point d is the image of point c under $\vec{ba}$.

$b(-5,-2) \rightarrow a(-3, 3)$
$c(1,-1) \rightarrow d(3, 4)$
$\begin{bmatrix} x \text{ up } 2 \\ y \text{ up } 5 \end{bmatrix}$

Question 4

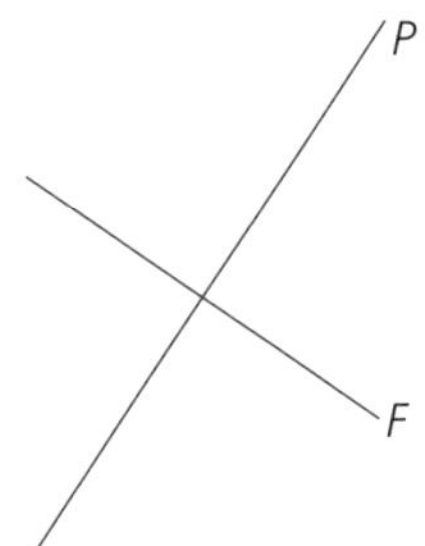

$F: 2x+3y-21=0$ and
$P: 3x-2y+1=0$ are two lines as shown.

(i) Prove P is perpendicular to F.

slope of P is $\frac{3}{2}$

slope of F is $\frac{-2}{3}$

The product of their slopes is:

$$\left(\frac{3}{2}\right)\left(\frac{-2}{3}\right)=\frac{-6}{6}=\boxed{-1}$$

$\Rightarrow$ P is perpendicular to W

(ii) Prove $c(-3,-4)$ is on line P.

$$3x-2y+1=0$$
$$c(-3,-4) \Rightarrow 3(-3)-2(-4)+1=0$$
$$\Rightarrow \quad -9+8+1=0 \checkmark$$

As (−3, −4) satisfies the equation, it must be on the line.

(iii) Find the image of pt. c under axial symmetry in line F.

First find the pt. where the lines intersect.

$$2x+3y-21=0 \quad [\times 3] \quad 6x+9y=63$$
$$3x-2y+1=0 \quad [\times -2] \quad -6x+4y=2$$
$$13y=65$$
$$\Rightarrow \boxed{y=5}$$

$2x + 3y - 21 = 0$

$y = 5 \quad \Rightarrow \quad 2x + 3(5) - 21 = 0$

$\Rightarrow \quad 2x = 21 - 15$

$\Rightarrow \quad 2x = 6$

$\boxed{x = 3}$

$\Rightarrow \quad (3, 5)$

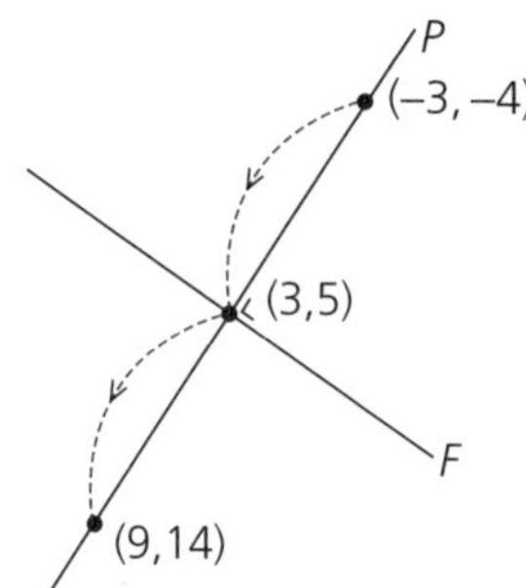

The image of $(-3, -4)$ under axial symmetry in F can be found thus:

$(-3, -4) \rightarrow (3, 5) \rightarrow (9, 14)$

$\begin{bmatrix} x \text{ up } 6 \\ y \text{ up } 9 \end{bmatrix}$ each time

$\Rightarrow$ Image is $(9, 14)$

Chapter 9
Sample questions for you to try

Question 1

(a) Given $c(-2, 3)$ and $d(-5, -6)$:

(i) Find the equation of line L which contains $(2, -3)$ if L is parallel to $[cd]$.

(ii) $2x + ty - 5 = 0$ is perpendicular to line L. Find t.

(b) **(i)** $n(3, 2)$ $p(-4, -1)$ $r(1, -3)$ are three points of the parallelogram $nprt$. Find t.

(ii) Find the image of pt. t under an axial symmetry in the line $y = 1$.

(c) P: $3x - 4y - 24 = 0$ cuts the x-axis at pt. a and the y-axis at pt. b.

(i) Draw a rough sketch of P.

(ii) Hence find the area enclosed by P, the x-axis and the y-axis.

Question 2

(a) **(i)** Find pt. y if x is the midpoint of $[yz]$ given $x(3, -5)$ and $z(-2, 1)$.

(ii) Find the equation of line T which contains pt. y if T is perpendicular to $4x + 5y - 3 = 0$.

(b) **(i)** Given $a(1, 1)$ $b(5, 1)$ $c(3, 6)$ prove that $\triangle abc$ is isosceles.

(ii) Find t if $2x - 5y + 1 = 0$ is parallel to $tx + 4y - 1 = 0$.

(c) Find the image of $(8, -5)$ under an axial symmetry in the line $x = 2$.

Question 3

(a) Given $a(-1, 4)$ and $b(3, -7)$.

(i) Find the equation of $[ab]$.

(ii) Find w if $c(w, 15)$ is on $[ab]$.

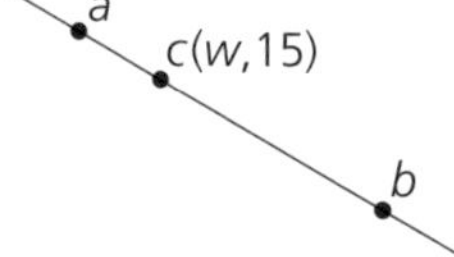

(iii) Find the equation of line E which contains pt. b if E is perpendicular to $[ab]$.

(iv) Hence find the image of point c under an axial symmetry in line E.

(b) Prove $2x - 5y + 1 = 0$ is perpendicular to $10x + 4y - 3 = 0$.

Solution to question 1

(a)

> **(i)** Given $c(-2, 3)$ $d(-5, -6)$, find the equation of line L which contains $(2, -3)$ if $L \parallel [cd]$.

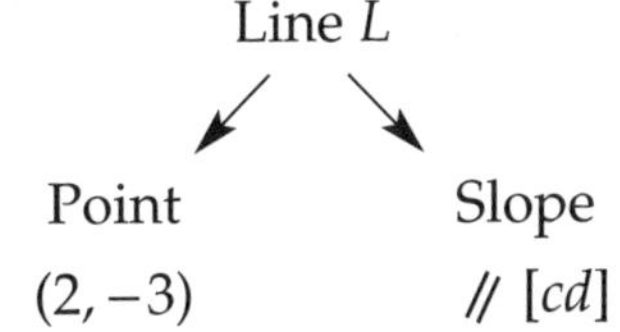

① Find slope of $[cd]$.

$c(-2,\ 3)$ $d(-5,\ -6)$

$x_1\ y_1$ $x_2\ y_2$

$$\text{slope} = \frac{y_2 - y_1}{x_2 - x_1} = \frac{-6-3}{-5+2} = \frac{-9}{-3} = \boxed{3}$$

② Find slope of line L.
As $L \parallel [cd]$, slope of L is also 3.

③ Find the equation of L.

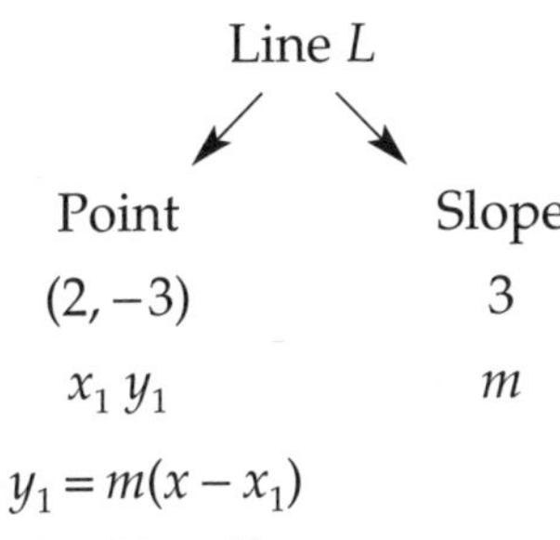

$y - y_1 = m(x - x_1)$

$y + 3 = 3(x - 2)$

$y + 3 = 3x - 6$

$\Rightarrow L: 3x - 1y - 9 = 0$

> **(ii)** $2x + ty - 5 = 0 \perp$ line L. Find t.

$2x + ty - 5 = 0 \perp 3x - 1y - 9 = 0$

① Find slope of $2x + ty - 5 = 0$.

$ty = -2x + 5$

$$y = \frac{-2}{t}x \frac{+5}{t}$$

$$\Rightarrow \text{Slope} = \boxed{\frac{-2}{t}}$$

② Find slope of $3x - 1y - 9 = 0$.
Slope $= 3$

* Slope of $L = +3$
As $L \perp 2x + ty - 5 = 0$,
slope of $2x + ty - 5 = 0$ must be $-\frac{1}{3}$

$$\Rightarrow \frac{-2}{t} = -\frac{1}{3}$$

Cross-multiplying: $(-2)(3) = (-1)(t)$

$-6 = -1t \quad \Rightarrow \underline{\underline{t = 6}}$

(b)

> **(i)** $n(3, 2)$ $p(-4, -1)$ $r(1, -3)$.
> Find pt. t, the fourth point of the parallelogram $nprt$.

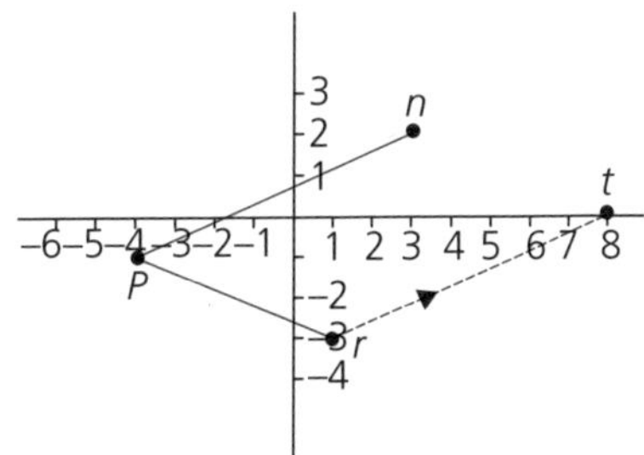

* The important thing here, is to join the points in the order in which they are written.

'$\square nprt$' $\Rightarrow$ join n to p to r...

From the diagram, point t is the image of pt. r under $\vec{pn}$.

$$p(-4,-1) \rightarrow n(3,2) \quad \begin{bmatrix} x \text{ up } 7 \\ y \text{ up } 3 \end{bmatrix} \text{ each time}$$
$$\Rightarrow r(1,-3) \rightarrow t(8,0)$$
$$\Rightarrow \underline{\underline{t(8,0)}}$$

(ii) Find the image of pt. t under an axial symmetry in the line $y = 1$.

$t(8, 0)$
$\downarrow$
$(-, 1)$ $\begin{bmatrix} x \text{ stays the same} \\ y \text{ goes up } 1 \end{bmatrix}$ each time
$\downarrow$
$(8, 2)$

$\Rightarrow$ Image of t under an axial symmetry in $y = 1$ is $(8, 2)$.

(c)

(i) P: $3x - 4y - 24 = 0$ cuts the x-axis at pt. a and pt. b. Draw a rough sketch of P.

P cuts the x-axis at pt. a

$\Rightarrow$ Let $y = 0$

$\Rightarrow 3x - 4(0) - 24 = 0$

$\Rightarrow 3x = 24 \qquad \Rightarrow x = 8$

$a(8, 0)$

P cuts the y-axis at pt. b

$\Rightarrow$ Let $x = 0$

$\Rightarrow 3(0) - 4y - 24 = 0$

$\Rightarrow -4y = 24$

$\Rightarrow y = -6$

$b(0, -6)$

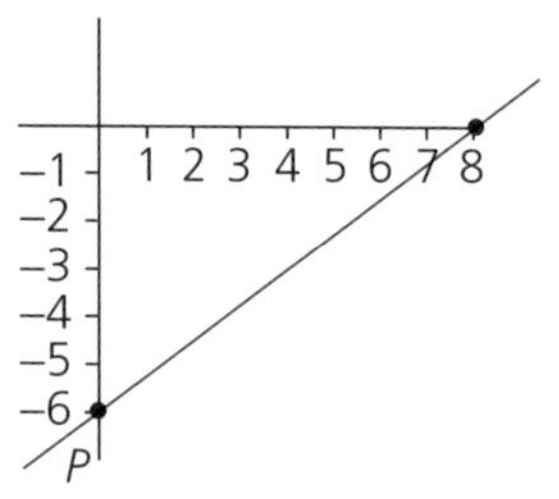

(ii) Find the area enclosed by P, the x-axis and the y-axis.

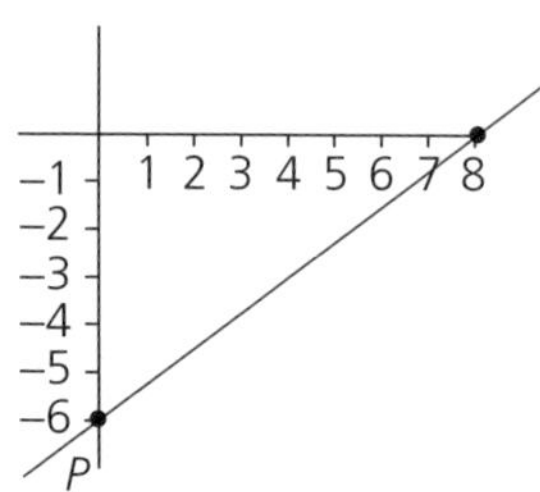

Area $= \frac{1}{2}(\text{base}) \times (\text{perp. height})$

$= \frac{1}{2}(8)(6)$

$= \boxed{24}$

Solution to question 2

(a)

(i) Find pt. y if x is the midpoint of $[yz]$ given $x(3, -5)$ and $z(-2, 1)$.

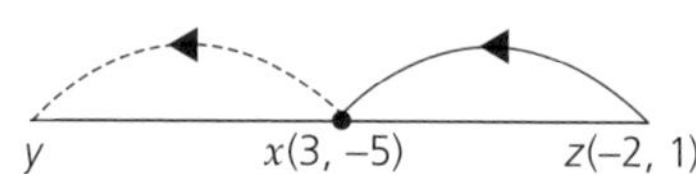

Therefore, y is the image of z under a central symmetry in pt. x.

y(8, −11) x(3, −5) z(−2, 1)

$\begin{bmatrix} x \text{ up } 5 \\ y \text{ down } 6 \end{bmatrix}$ each time $\Rightarrow y(8, -11)$

(ii) Find the equation of line T which contains pt. y if

$$T \perp 4x + 5y - 3 = 0$$

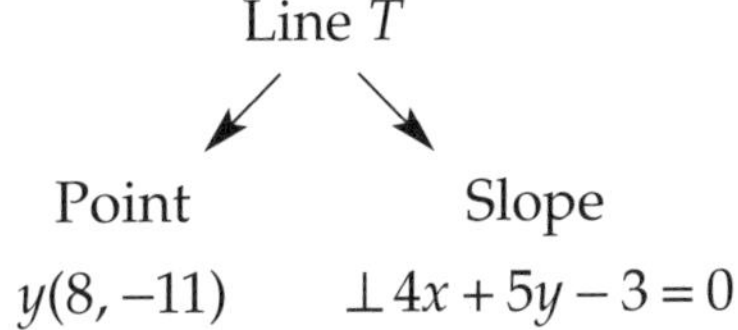

$y(8, -11)$ $\quad\quad$ $\perp 4x + 5y - 3 = 0$

① Find the slope of $4x + 5y - 3 = 0$.

$$4x + 5y - 3 = 0$$

$$5y = -4x + 3$$

$$y = \frac{-4}{5}x + \frac{3}{5}$$

$$\Rightarrow \text{Slope} = \frac{-4}{5}$$

② Find the slope of line T.

Slope of $4x + 5y - 3 = 0$ is $\frac{-4}{5}$

But $T \perp 4x + 5y - 3 = 0$

$$\Rightarrow \text{Slope of } T = \boxed{\frac{+5}{4}}$$

③ Find the equation of line T.

Line T

Point $\quad\quad$ Slope

$(8, -11)$ $\quad\quad$ $\frac{5}{4}$

$x_1 \quad y_1$ $\quad\quad$ m

$$y - y_1 = m(x - x_1)$$

$$y + 11 = \frac{5}{4}(x - 8)$$

$$\Rightarrow \quad 4(y + 11) = 5(x - 8)$$

$$4y + 44 = 5x - 40$$

$$\Rightarrow T: 5x - 4y - 84 = 0$$

(b)

(i) $a(1, 1)$ $b(5, 1)$ $c(3, 6)$.
Prove $\triangle abc$ is isosceles.

$$\text{Distance} = \sqrt{(x_2 - x_1)^2 + (y_2 - y_1)^2}$$

$|ab|$ $\quad a(1,\ 1)$ $\quad b(5,\ 1)$

$\quad\quad x_1\ y_1 \quad\quad x_2\ y_2$

$$= \sqrt{(5-1)^2 + (1-1)^2} = \sqrt{16} = \boxed{4}$$

$|bc|$ $\quad b(5,\ 1)$ $\quad c(3,\ 6)$

$\quad\quad x_1\ y_1 \quad\quad x_2\ y_2$

$$= \sqrt{(3-5)^2 + (6-1)^2} = \sqrt{29}$$

$|ac|$ $\quad a(1,\ 1)$ $\quad c(3,\ 6)$

$\quad\quad x_1\ y_1 \quad\quad x_2\ y_2$

$$= \sqrt{(3-1)^2 + (6-1)^2} = \sqrt{29}$$

As $|bc| = |ac|$, $\triangle abc$ is isosceles

(ii) Find t given
$2x - 5y + 1 = 0$ // $tx + 4y - 1 = 0$.

① Slope of $2x - 5y + 1 = 0$

$$-5y = -2x - 1$$

$$y = \frac{-2}{-5}x \frac{-1}{-5}$$

$$\text{Slope} = \boxed{\frac{2}{5}}$$

② Slope of $tx + 4y - 1 = 0$

$$4y = -tx + 1$$

$$y = \frac{-t}{4}x + \frac{1}{4}$$

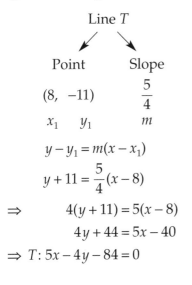

$$\text{Slope} = \boxed{\frac{-t}{4}}$$

Because the lines are parallel the slopes must be equal.

$\Rightarrow \frac{2}{5} = \frac{-t}{4}$

Cross-multiplying: $-5t = 8$

$\Rightarrow t = \boxed{\frac{8}{-5}}$

> **(c)** Find the image of $(8, -5)$ under an axial symmetry in the line $x = 2$.

$(8, -5)$
$\downarrow$
$(2, -)$
$\downarrow$
$(-4, -5)$

$\begin{bmatrix} x \text{ down } 6 \\ y \text{ unchanged} \end{bmatrix}$ each time

$\Rightarrow$ Image $= (-4, -5)$

Solution to question 3

(a)

> **(i)** Given $a(-1, 4)$ $b(3, -7)$. Find the equation of $[ab]$.

① Find slope of $[ab]$.

$a(\underset{x_1}{-1}, \underset{y_1}{4})$ $\quad b(\underset{x_2}{3}, \underset{y_2}{-7})$

$$\text{Slope} = \frac{y_2 - y_1}{x_2 - x_1} = \frac{-7-4}{3+1} = \boxed{\frac{-11}{4}}$$

② Find the equation of $[ab]$.

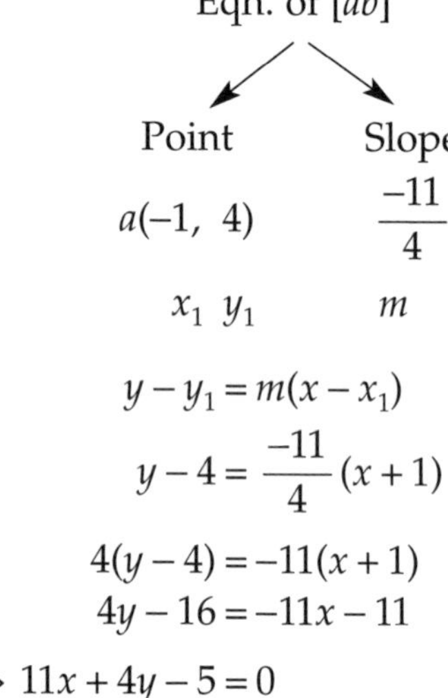

$$y - y_1 = m(x - x_1)$$

$$y - 4 = \frac{-11}{4}(x + 1)$$

$$4(y - 4) = -11(x + 1)$$

$$4y - 16 = -11x - 11$$

$\Rightarrow 11x + 4y - 5 = 0$

> **(ii)** Find w if $c(w, 15)$ is on $[ab]$.

$$11x + 4y - 5 = 0$$

$(w, 15)$

$11(w) + 4(15) - 5 = 0$

$\Rightarrow 11w = 5 - 60$

$11w = -55 \quad \Rightarrow w = -5$

> **(iii)** Find the equation of line E which contains pt. b if $E \perp [ab]$.

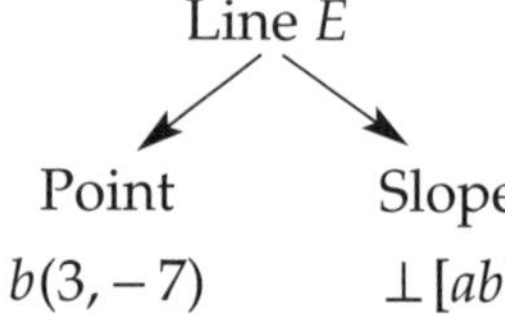

Point: $b(3, -7)$ $\qquad$ Slope: $\perp [ab]$

① Find the slope of $[ab]$.

Slope of $[ab] = \frac{-11}{4}$

② Find slope of line E.

$$[ab] \perp E$$

Slope of $[ab] = \dfrac{-11}{4}$

$\Rightarrow$ Slope of line $E = \dfrac{+4}{11}$

③ Find the equation of line E.

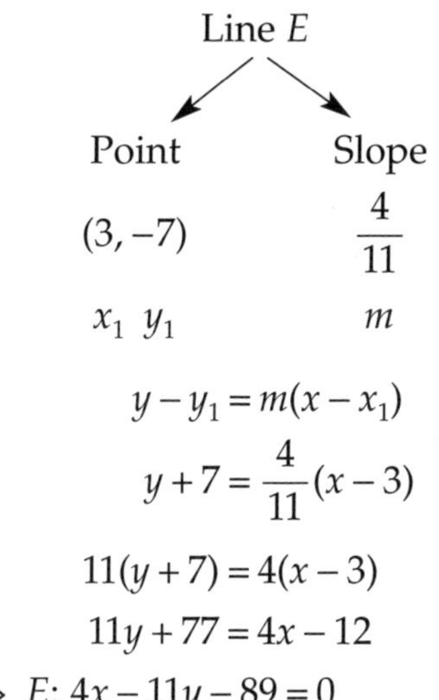

Line E

Point	Slope
$(3, -7)$	$\dfrac{4}{11}$
$x_1 \ y_1$	m

$$y - y_1 = m(x - x_1)$$

$$y + 7 = \frac{4}{11}(x - 3)$$

$$11(y + 7) = 4(x - 3)$$

$$11y + 77 = 4x - 12$$

$\Rightarrow$ E: $4x - 11y - 89 = 0$

> **(iv)** Find the image of pt. c under an axial symmetry in line E.

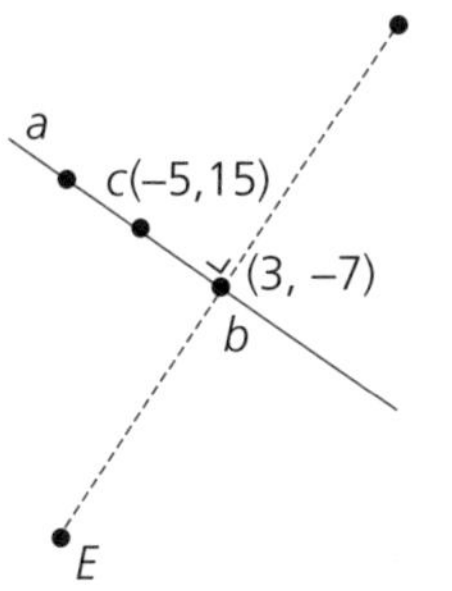

Therefore the image of pt. c under an axial symmetry in line E.

$\Downarrow$

Image of pt. c under a central symmetry in pt. b.

y down 22 each time

$c(-5,15) \rightarrow b\ (3,-7) \rightarrow (11,-29)$

x up 8 each time

Image $= (11, -29)$

> **(b)** Prove $2x - 5y + 1 = 0$ is perpendicular to $10x + 4y - 3 = 0$.

Slope of $2x - 5y + 1 = 0$ is $\boxed{\dfrac{2}{5}}$

Slope of $10x + 4y - 3 = 0$ is $\boxed{\dfrac{-10}{4}}$

$$\left(\frac{2}{5}\right)\left(\frac{-10}{4}\right) = \boxed{\frac{-20}{20}} = \boxed{-1}$$

As the product of their slopes is -1, the lines must be perpendicular.

Chapter 10

Constructions and Transformations

Construction

There are only 6 different constructions which we have to know.

They are quite easy but please remember:

① All construction lines should be drawn in pencil.

② Construction lines account for a lot of marks so show them clearly.

Construction 1

Construct the perpendicular bisector of the line $[ab]$.

① Place the compass on point a. Extend so that the compass is greater than half the length of $[ab]$.

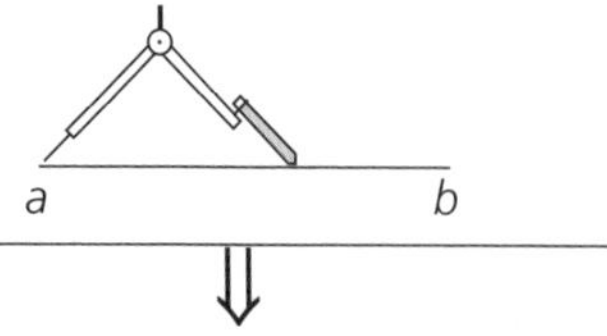

⇓

② With the compass on pt. a draw an arc above and below the line

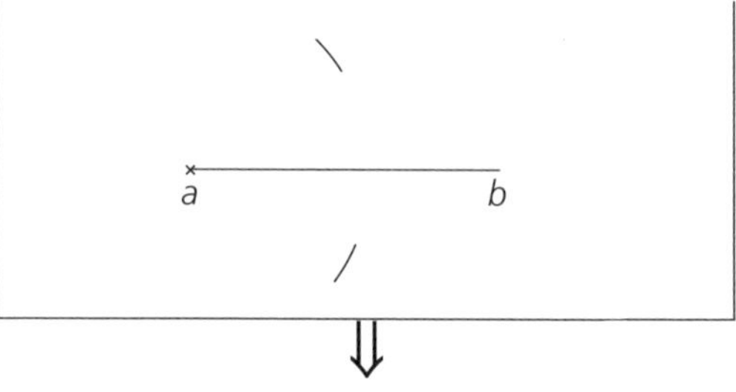

⇓

③ Place the compass on pt. b. Again, swing the same arc above and below the line.

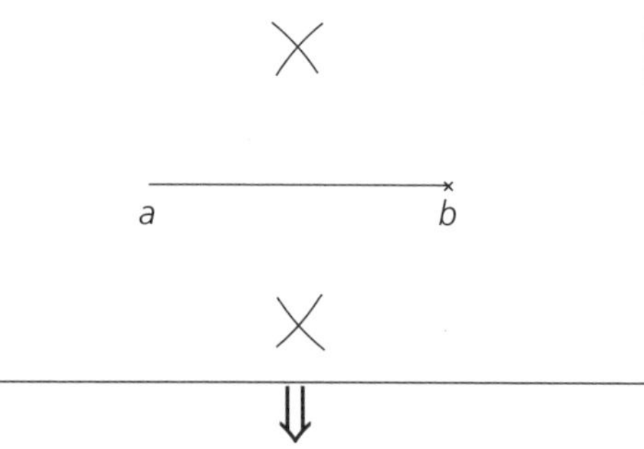

⇓

④ Draw a line joining the points where the arcs meet.

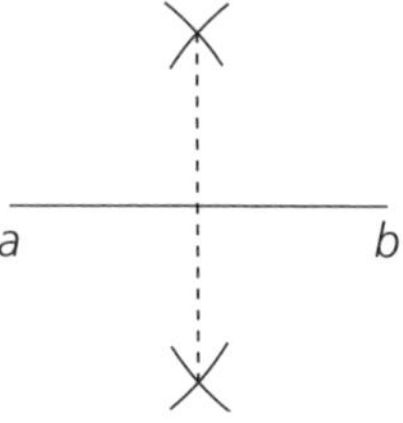

This line is the perpendicular bisector of $[ab]$.

Construction 2

Construct the circumcentre of the triangle *abc*.

① Construct line *M*, the perpendicular bisector of any side.

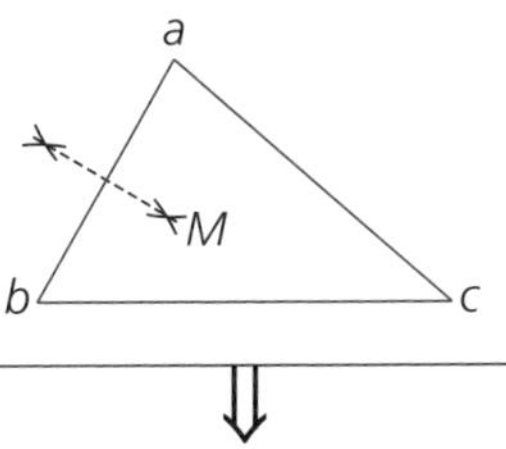

⇓

② Construct line *P*, the perpendicular bisector of a second side.

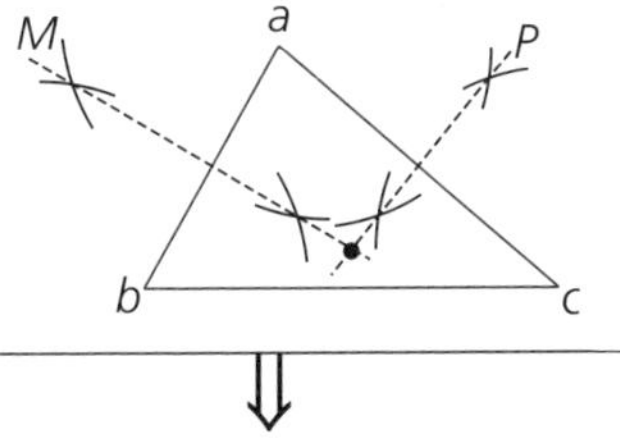

⇓

③ The point of intersection of line *M* and line *P* is the centre of the circumcircle.

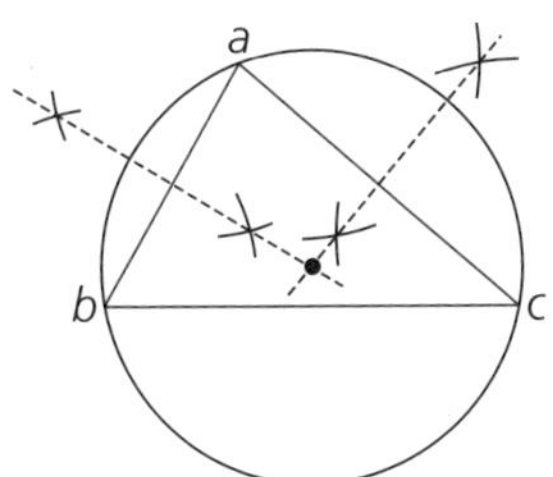

Draw the circumcircle through pt. *a*, pt. *b* and pt. *c*.

Construction 3

Construct the bisector of $\angle abc$.

① Place the compass at point *b*. Swing an arc as shown.

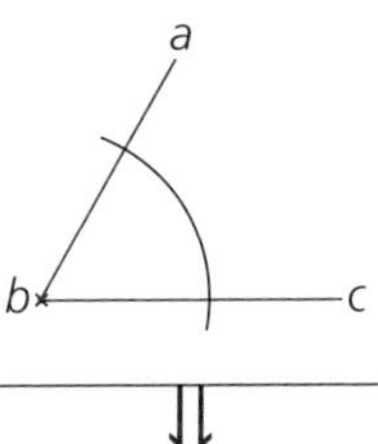

⇓

② Place the compass on point ① and swing an arc.

With the compass on point ② swing the same arc.

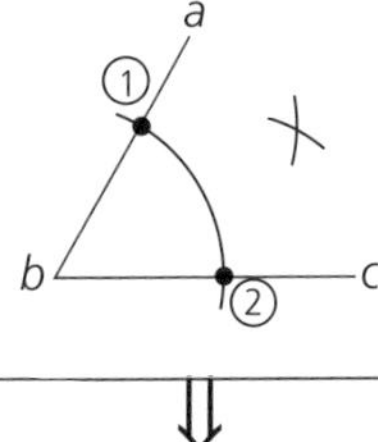

⇓

③ Join the point of intersection of both arcs to point *b*.

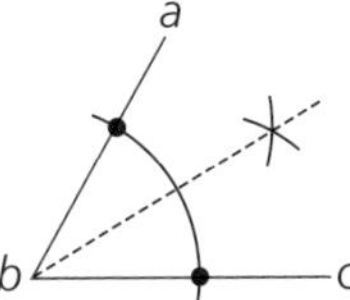

This line is the bisector of $\angle abc$.

Construction 4

Construct the incircle of $\triangle abc$.

① Construct line *M*, the bisector of any angle.

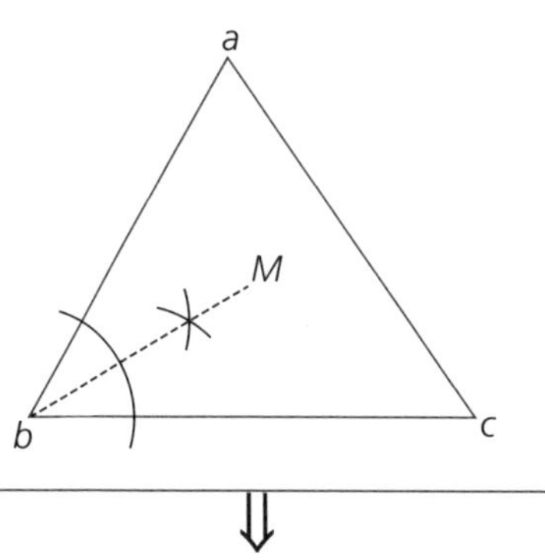

⇓

② Construct line *P*, the bisector of a second angle.

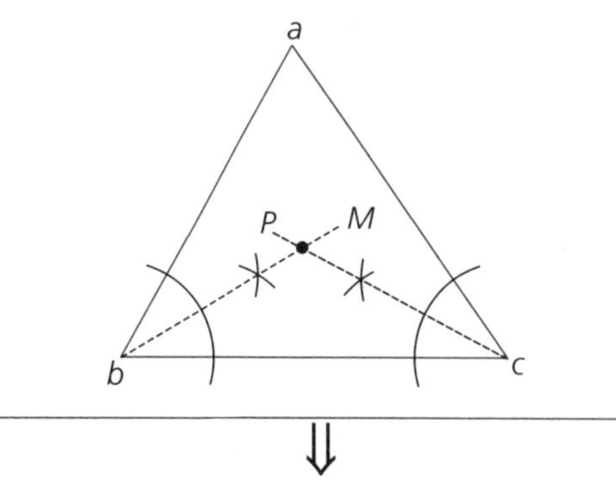

⇓

③ With pt. *k* as centre, draw the incircle of the triangle.
The incircle must touch all 3 sides at one point only.

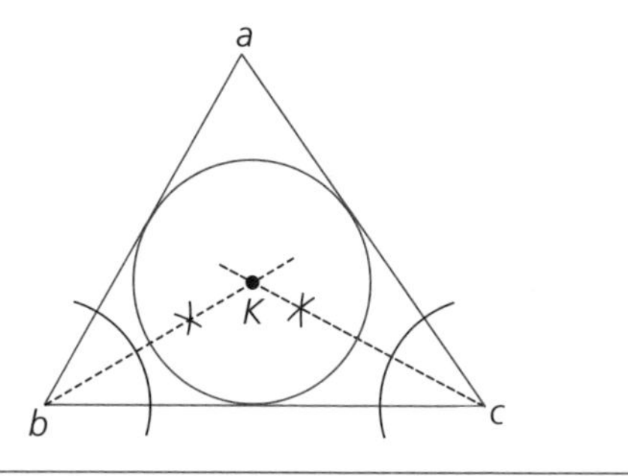

Construction 5

Divide [*ab*] into 4 equal parts.

① Draw a line from pt. *a* as shown:

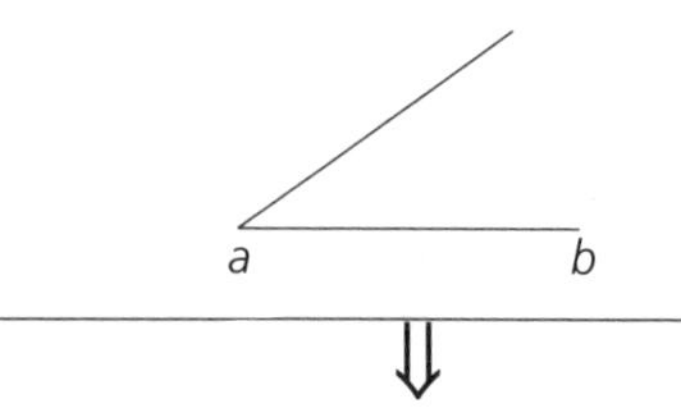

⇓

② Using the compass, draw 4 arcs along the line such that:

$$|ac| = |cd| = |de| = |ef|$$

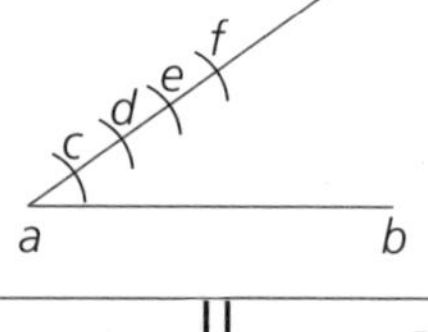

⇓

③ Join *f* to *b*. Draw parallel lines from pts *e*, *d* and *c*.

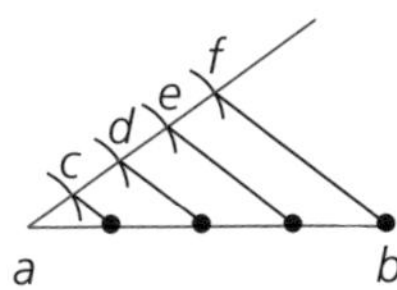

Hence $[ab]$ is divided into 4 equal parts.

Construction 6

Constructing triangles

There are two types of question which can be asked here. Please read through and understand the steps in each.

Type 1

Construct $\triangle abc$ such that $|ab| = 4$ cm, $|bc| = 6$ cm and $|ac| = 5$ cm.

① Draw a rough diagram of what $\triangle abc$ should look like.

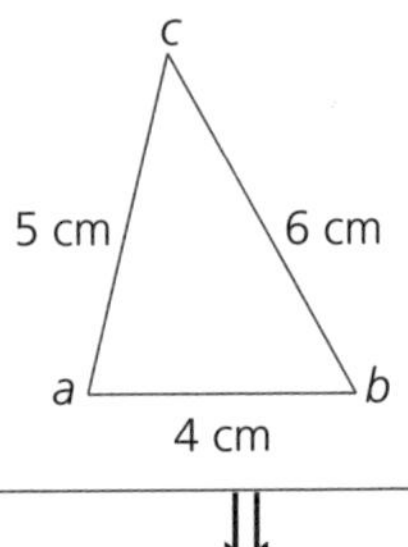

⇓

② Draw $[ab]$ 4 cm in length.

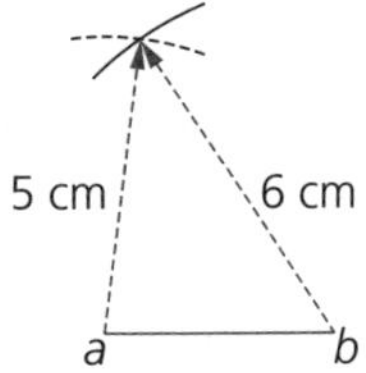

Put the compass on pt. a. Draw an arc 5 cm from a. Put the compass on pt. b. Draw an arc 6 cm from b.

③ Pt. c is the point where the arcs meet.

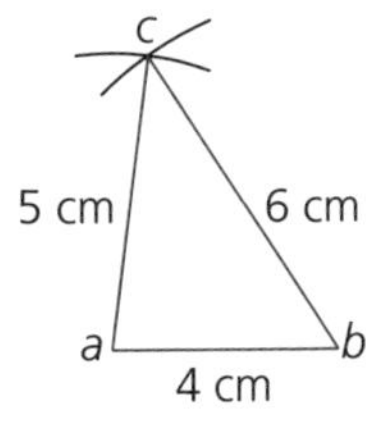

Type 2

Construct $\triangle mnp$ such that $|mn| = 6$ cm, $|mp| = 7$ cm and $|\angle mnp| = 72°$.

Important

Because n is the middle letter, $\angle mnp$ is at point n.

① Draw $[mn]$.

* We pick this line because it includes point n.

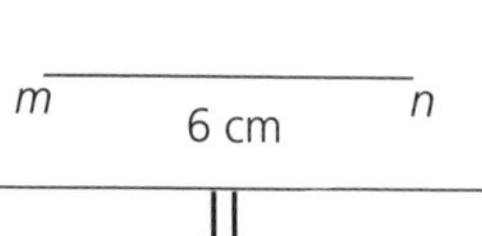

⇓

② At pt. n, use a protractor to measure an angle of 72°. Draw a line to show the angle.

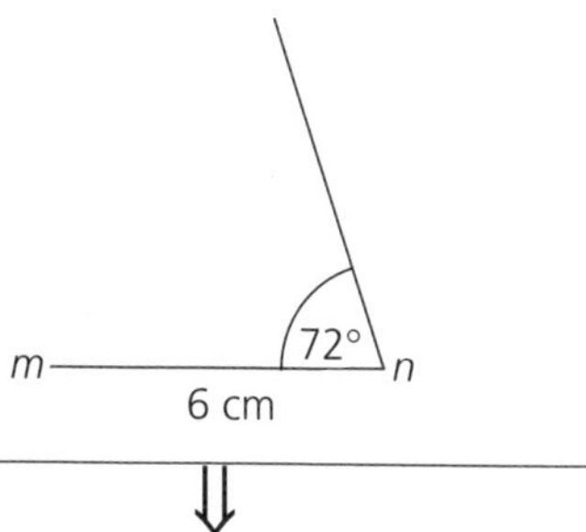

⇓

③ From pt. m draw an arc 7 cm from m.

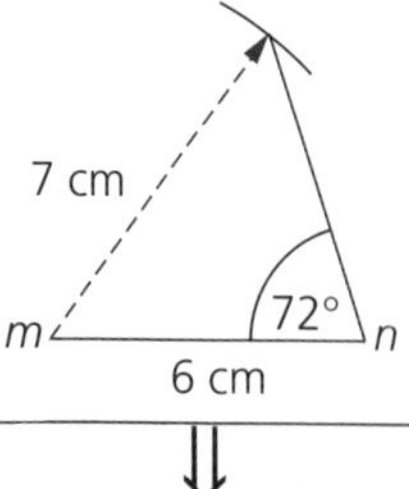

⇓

④ Point p is where the arc and the line meet.

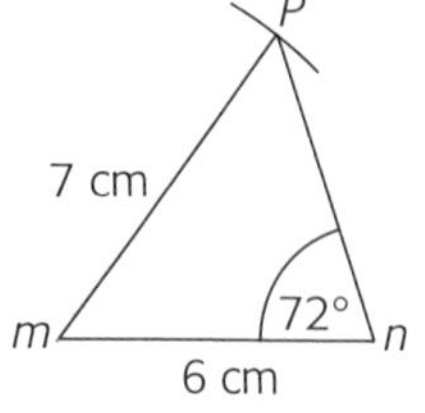

Transformations

A 'transformation' is the movement of an object from one position to another.

There are four transformations which we must know.

① Translation

Under a translation, the object moves along a given straight line.

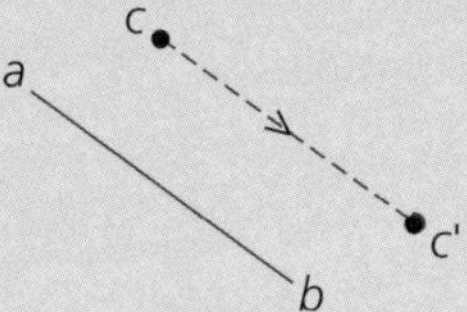

Here the image of pt. c under the translation $\overrightarrow{ab}$ is c'.

Note

c' is found by 'translating' point c

① In the same direction.

② The same distance as $\overrightarrow{ab}$.

Example 1

Find the image of M under the translation $\overrightarrow{cd}$.

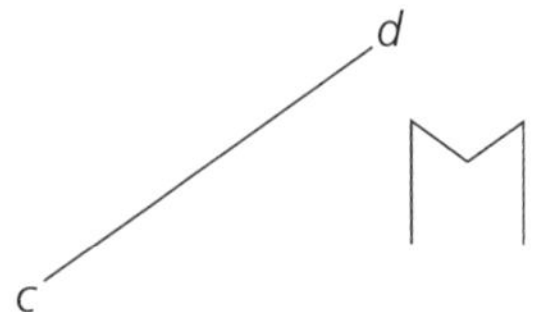

Solution

- Mark the five main points on M.
- Find the image of each pt. under $\overrightarrow{cd}$.

* The image of pt. a is called a' etc.

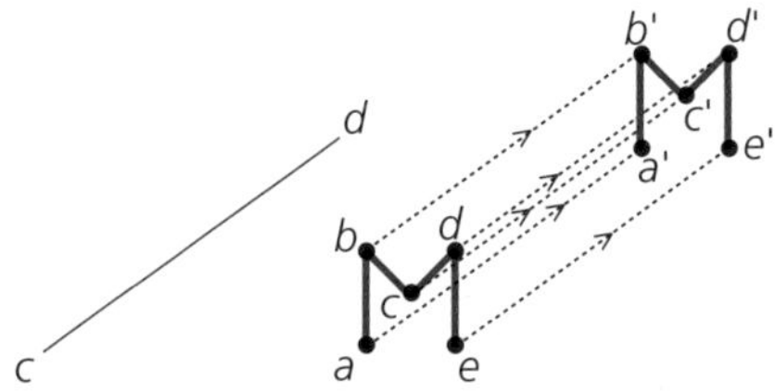

Example 2

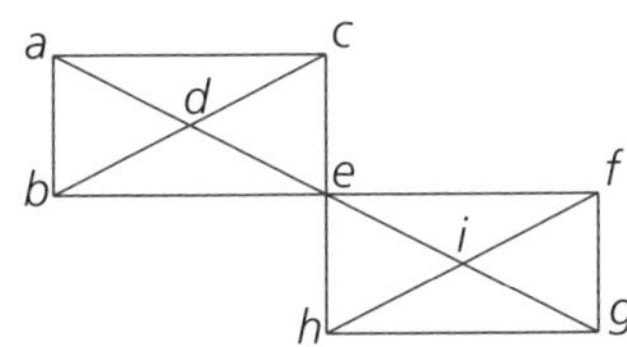

<u>Find the image of:</u>

① $[ab]$ under $\overrightarrow{hg}$.

$a \rightarrow c$
$b \rightarrow e$

Look at $\overrightarrow{hg}$. Bring both pt. a and pt. b in the same direction, and the same distance.

$\Rightarrow$ Image of $[ab]$ under $\overrightarrow{hg}$ is $[ce]$.

② $\triangle acd$ under $\overrightarrow{bh}$.

$a \rightarrow e$
$c \rightarrow f$
$d \rightarrow i$

$\Rightarrow$ Image of $\triangle acd$ under $\overrightarrow{bh}$ is $\triangle efi$.

③ $\triangle abd$ under $\overrightarrow{cf}$.

$a \rightarrow e$
$b \rightarrow h$
$d \rightarrow i$

$\Rightarrow$ Image of $\triangle abd$ under $\overrightarrow{cf}$ is $\triangle ehi$.

② Axial symmetry

Under axial symmetry, the object is reflected across a line.

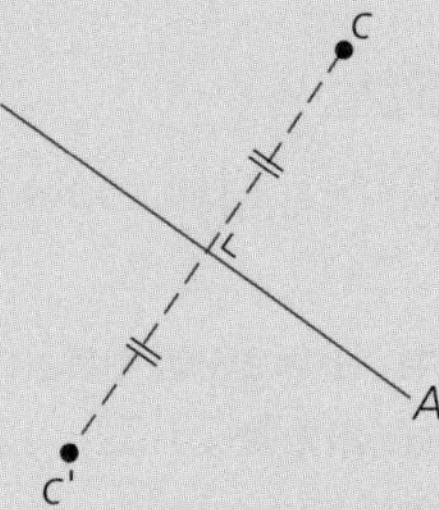

Here the image of pt. c under S_A is c'. To find c':

① From pt. c draw a perpendicular line onto A.

② Carry on the same distance the other side.

Example 1

Find the image of T under S_B, an axial symmetry in line B.

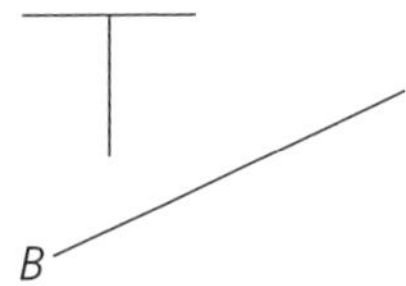

Solution

Again, we mark the four main pts. onto T and find the image of each.

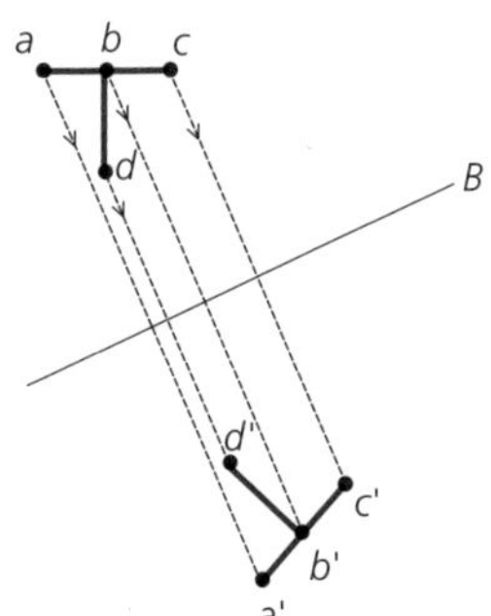

Example 2

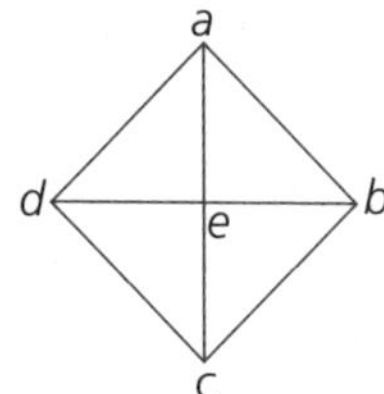

Find the image of:

(i) [*ad*] under S[*ac*], an axial symmetry in [*ac*].

$a \rightarrow a$ ⇒ Image of [*ad*] under S[*ac*] is [*ab*].

$d \rightarrow b$

* The image of pt. *a* under S[*ac*] is *a*. This is because pt. *a* is on the line [*ac*].

(ii) △*ebc* under S[*db*], an axial symmetry in [*db*].

$e \rightarrow e$ ⇒ The image of △*ebc*

$b \rightarrow b$ under S[*db*] is △*eba*.

$c \rightarrow a$

③ Central symmetry

Under central symmetry, the object is reflected through a fixed point.

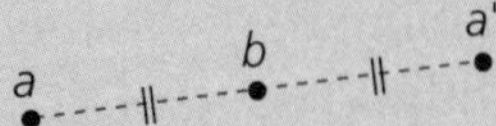

Here, the image of pt. *a* under S*b*, a central symmetry in pt. *b* is *a'*. To find *a'*:

① Draw a line from *a* to *b*.

② Carry on again the same distance the other side.

Example 1

Find the image of F under S_w, a central symmetry in pt. *w*.

Solution

Again, mark in the five main points onto F and find the image of each.

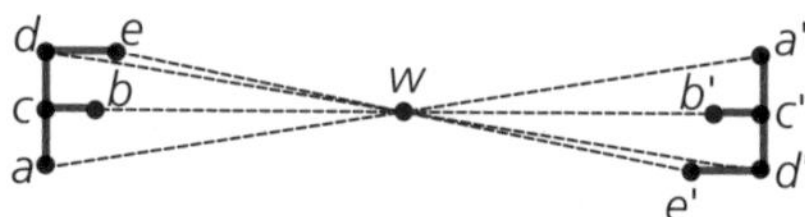

Example 2

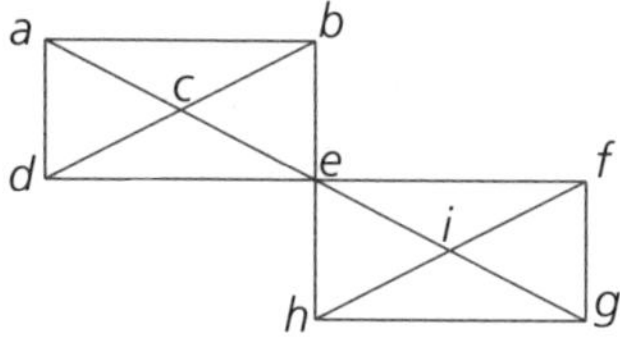

Find the image of:

(i) [*ad*] under S*c*, a central symmetry in pt. *c*.

$a \rightarrow e$ ⇒ Image of [*ad*] under

$d \rightarrow b$ S*c* is [*eb*].

(ii) △*dbe* under S*e*, a central symmetry in pt. *e*.

$d \rightarrow f$

$b \rightarrow h$

$e \rightarrow e$

* The image of pt. *e* under S*e* is itself.

⇒ Image of △*dbe* under S*e* is △*fhe*.

④ Rotation

A rotation is a 'circular movement through an angle about a fixed point'.

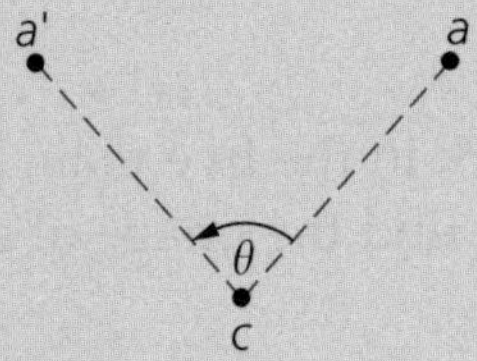

Here, a' is the image of pt. a under an anti-clockwise rotation around pt. c of $\theta°$.

Example

Find the image of the figure shown under a clockwise rotation of 120°.

Solution

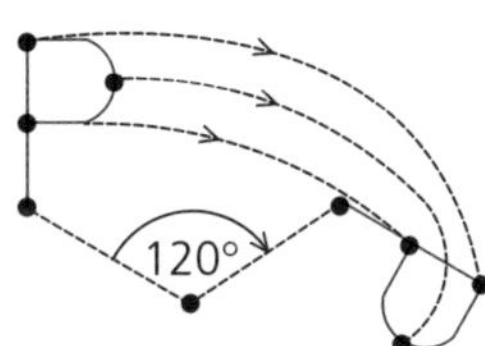

Characteristics of rotations, translations and symmetries

Rotations

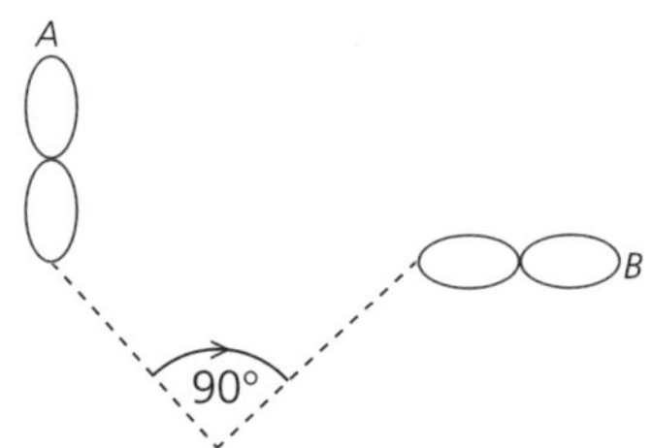

Here, figure B is the image of figure A under a clockwise rotation of 90°.

Such a rotation is quite easy to visualise. Take your time and you will find rotations very manageable.

Example

In the diagram below state whether or not figures A and B are images of the shaded figure under rotations.

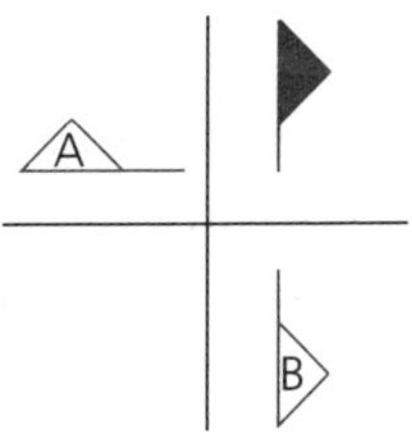

(i) Fig. A is the image of the shaded figure under an anti-clockwise rotation of 90°.

A 90°

(ii) Fig. B is not the image of the shaded figure under a rotation.

If we think about it, the image of the shaded figure under a rotation of 180° is slightly different to fig. B.

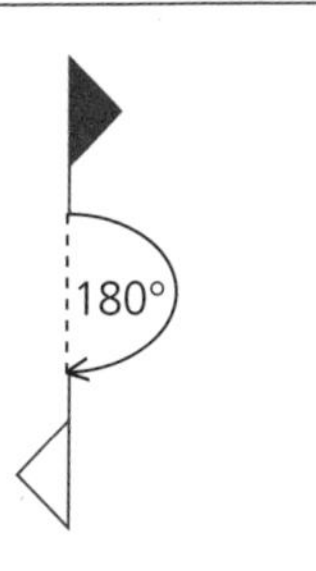

Central symmetries

Fig. A is the image of fig. B under a central symmetry.

How can we be so sure?

① Join the five main points in fig. A to the corresponding points in fig. B.

② If the image is a central symmetry, all the lines will intersect at the same point.

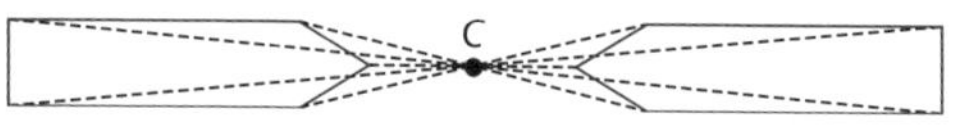

Pt. *c* is the centre of symmetry.

> **Very important**
> A central symmetry gives the same image as a rotation of 180°.

⇓

①

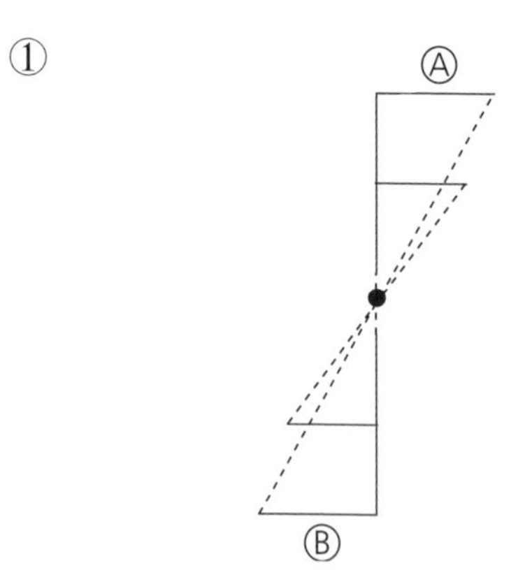

Here we prove that fig. B is the image of fig. A under a central symmetry.

②

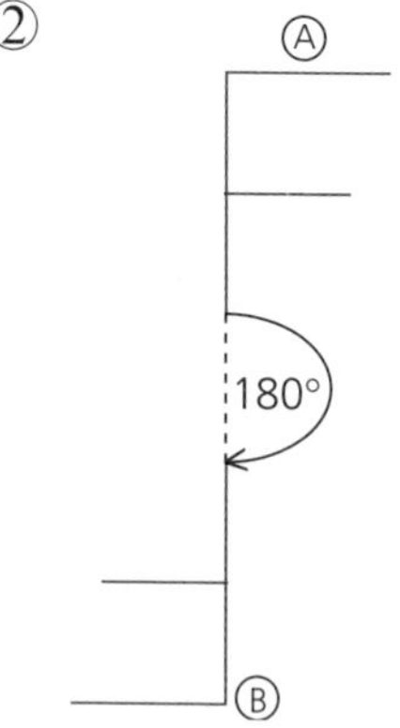

Here we see that under a rotation of 180°, fig. B is also the image of fig. A.

Axial symmetries

> If fig. A can fold exactly onto fig. B when folded over a straight line, it is the image of fig. B under an axial symmetry.

Example 1

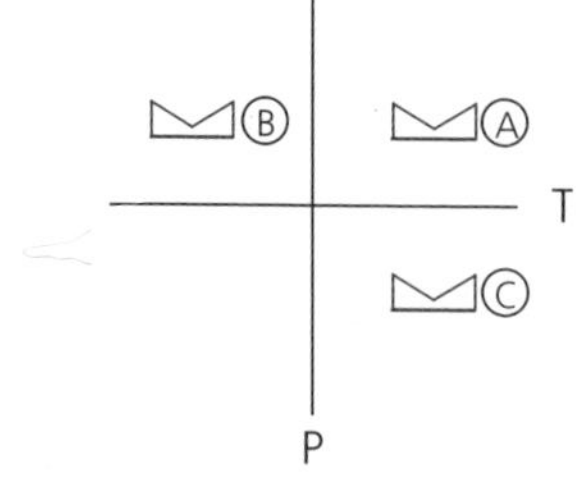

① Fig. B is the image of fig. A under axial symmetry in the line *P* (it folds exactly onto it).

⇒ Image of fig. A under S_P is fig. B.

② Fig. C is not the image of fig. A under axial symmetry in the line T. Please be clear fig. A does not fold onto fig. C.

Translations

Translations are by far the easiest transformation to recognise.

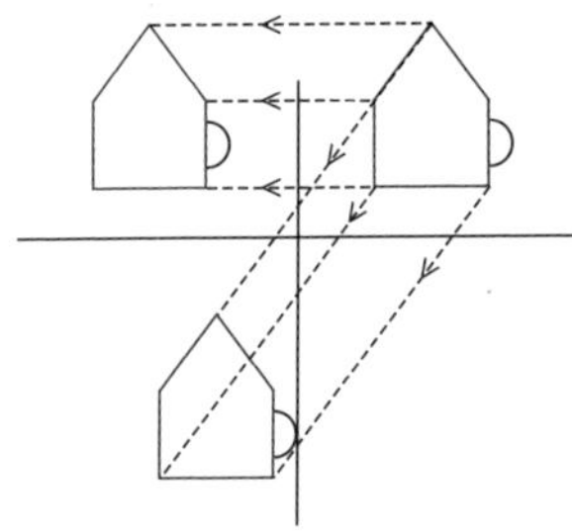

Characteristics of translations.
The image:

① Does not turn upside down.
② Does not turn 'inside out'.

Please recognise these characteristics in the diagram above.

Chapter 10 Sample questions for you to try

Question 1

(a) Shown is the incircle of $\triangle abd$ with centre c.

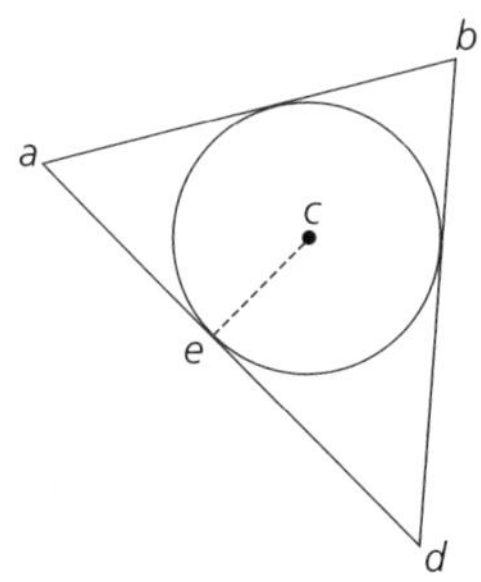

(i) If $|cd| = 8 \quad |ac| = 5 \quad |ce| = 4$

Calculate $|ad|$ correct to the nearest whole number.

(ii) Given $|ab| = 8$ and $|bd| = 9$ calculate the area of $\triangle abd$.

(iii) Express the area of the circle as a percentage of the area of $\triangle abd$.

(b)

Divide $[wr]$ into five equal parts without using a ruler.

Show all construction lines clearly.

Question 2

(a)

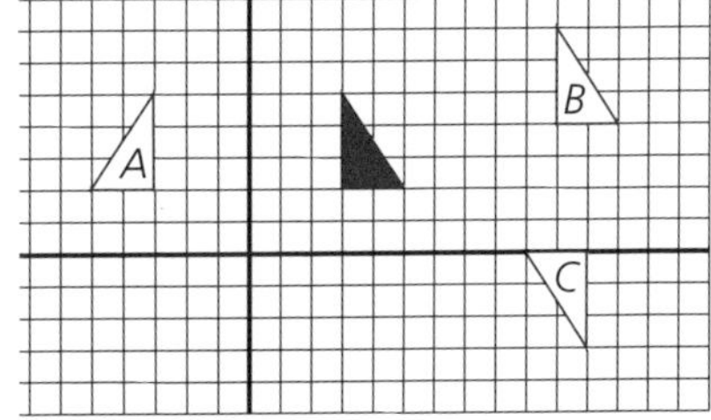

Which translation maps the shaded triangle onto:

(i) A **(ii)** B **(iii)** C

(b) In the given diagram $[ac]$ bisects $\angle bad$.

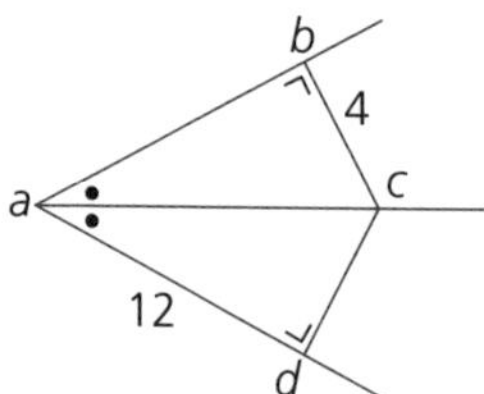

Calculate:

(i) $|ab|$ **(ii)** Area *abcd*

(c) Construct $\triangle mnp$ given $|mn| = 7$ cm, $|np| = 5$ cm and $|mp| = 4$ cm.

Hence construct the circumcircle of $\triangle mnp$.

Question 3

(a)

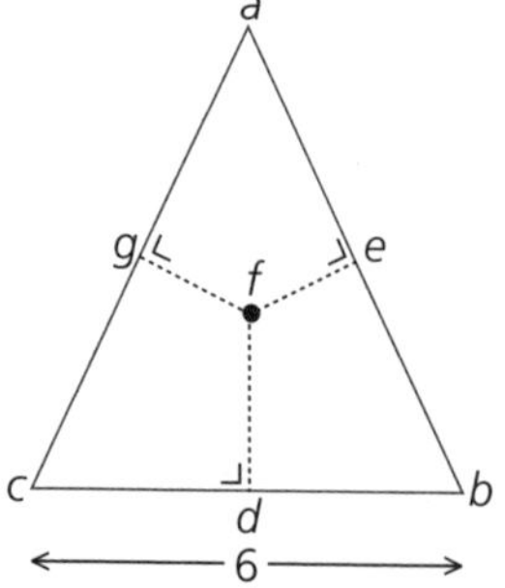

In the given diagram $[df]$ and $[fe]$ are the perpendicular bisectors of $[bc]$ and $[ab]$ respectively.

(i) Given $|df| = 4$ and $|bc| = 6$, find $|fb|$.

(ii) Calculate the area of $\triangle abc$ given $|ac| = 7$, $|gf| = 3$ and $|fe| = 2$.

(b)

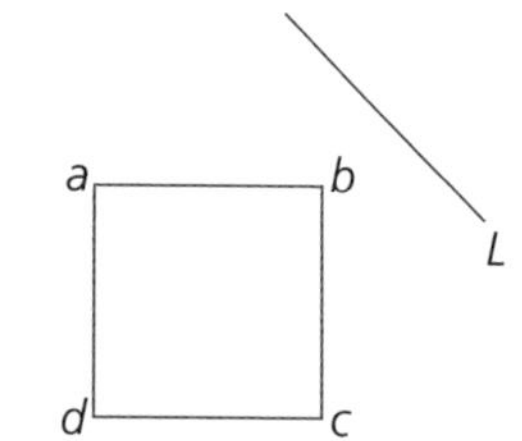

Construct the image of *abcd* under:

(i) A central symmetry in pt. *e*.

(ii) An axial symmetry in line *L*.

(iii) The translation $\overrightarrow{db}$.

(iv) An anti-clockwise rotation of 120° around pt. *c*.

(In each case show all construction lines clearly.)

Solution to question 1

(a)

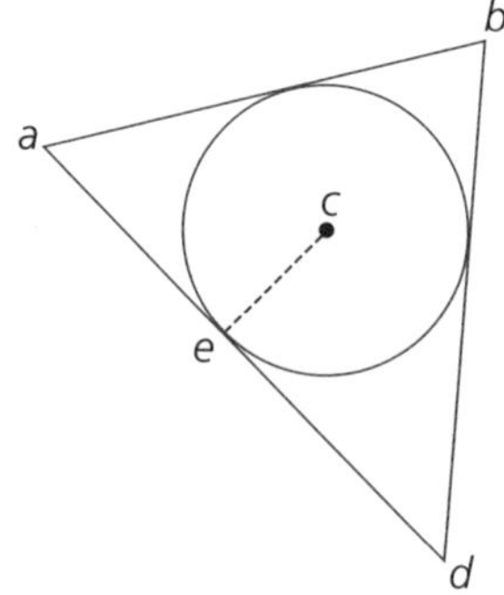

(i) If $|cd| = 8$, $|ac| = 5$ and $|ce| = 4$. Find $|ad|$.

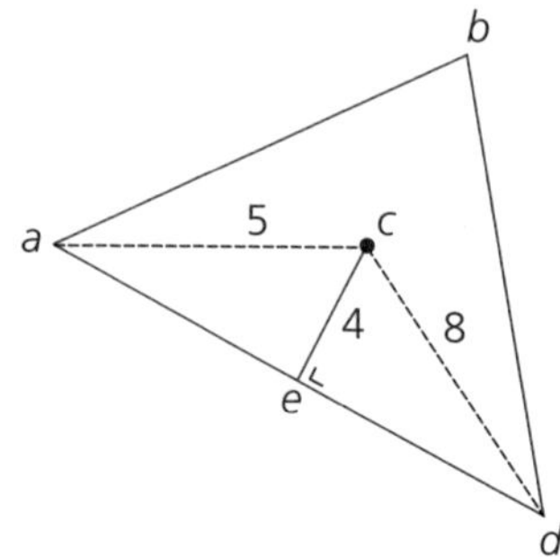

Find $|ae|$

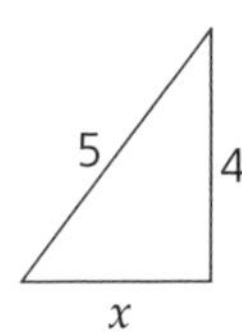

$5^2 = 4^2 + x^2$

$25 - 16 = x^2$

$9 = x^2$

$\Rightarrow \quad |ae| = 3$

Find $|ed|$

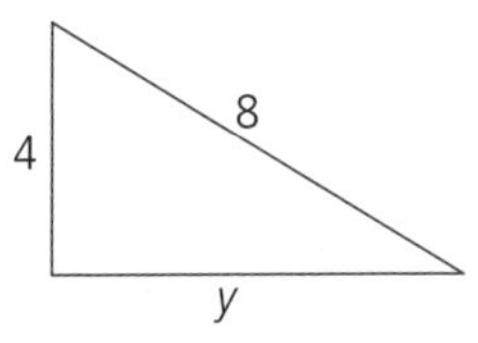

$8^2 = 4^2 + y^2$

$64 - 16 = y^2$

$48 = y^2$

$\sqrt{48} = y$

$\Rightarrow \quad |ed| = 7$

(nearest whole number)

$\Rightarrow \quad |ad| = 10$

(ii) Given $|ab| = 8$, and $|bd| = 9$. Calculate the area of $\triangle abd$.

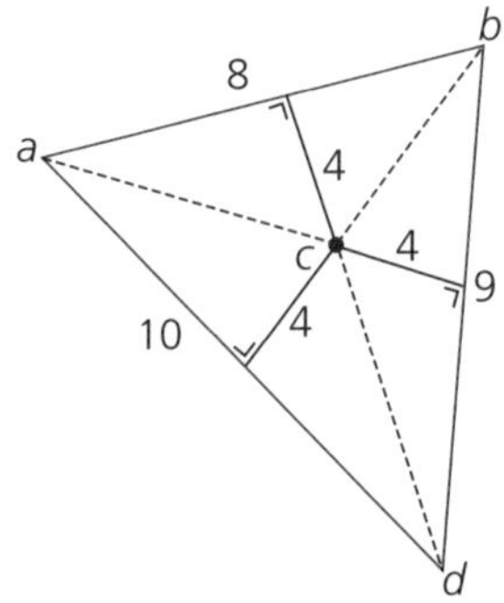

Important

Because pt. c is the incentre of $\triangle abd$, the perpendicular distances from pt. c to each side are equal (all = 4) as shown.

① Area $\triangle abc$

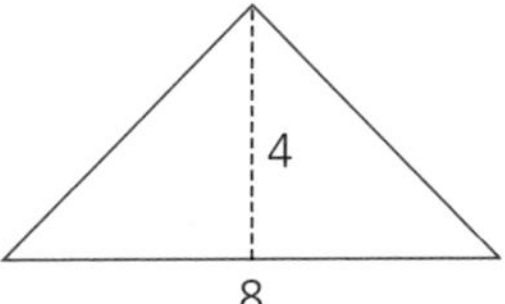

$= \frac{1}{2}$(base) × (perpendicular height)

$= \frac{1}{2}(8) \times 4 = \boxed{16}$

② Area $\triangle acd$

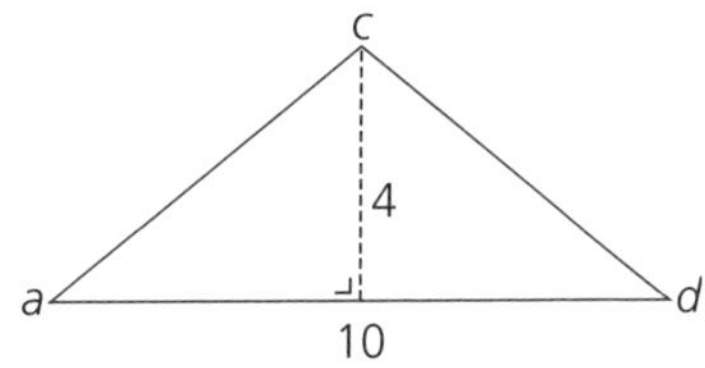

$Area = \frac{1}{2}(10) \times 4 = \boxed{20}$

③ Area $\triangle bcd$

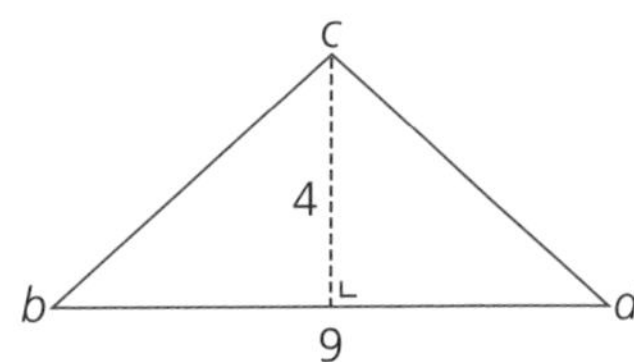

$\text{Area} = \frac{1}{2}(9) \times 4$

$= 18$

$\Rightarrow$ Area $\triangle abd = 16 + 20 + 18$

$= \boxed{54}$

(iii) Express the area of the circle as a percentage of the area of the triangle abd.

Area of circle $= \pi r^2$

$= \left(\frac{22}{7}\right) \times (4^2)$

$$= 50.29$$

$$\Rightarrow \frac{50.29}{54} \times \frac{100}{1} = 93.1\%$$

(b)

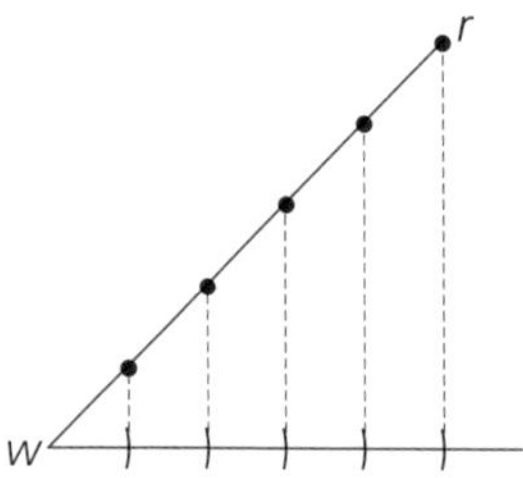

Solution to question 2

(a)

(i) The shaded triangle is mapped onto A under an axial symmetry in the y-axis.

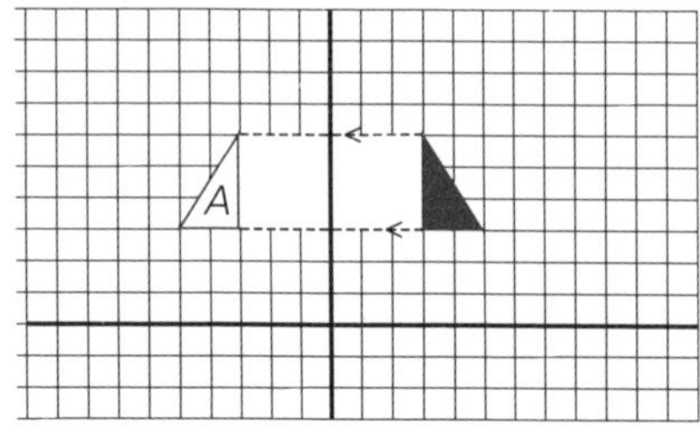

(ii) The shaded triangle is mapped onto B under the translation $(3, 2) \to (9, 4)$.

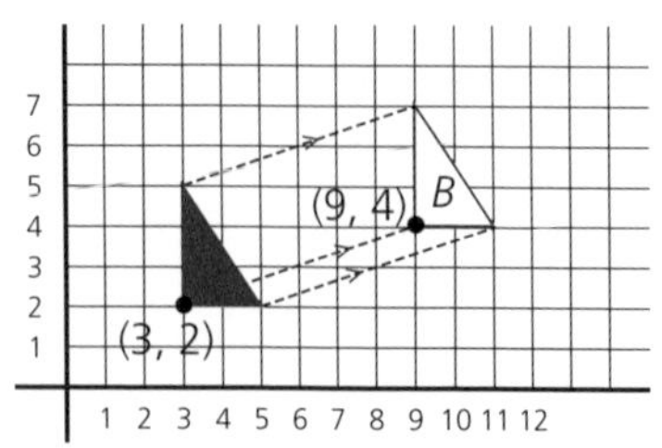

Note
From the diagram we see that the shaded triangle is also mapped onto B under the translation $(3, 5) \to (9, 7)$ and the translation

$$(5, 2) \to (11, 4).$$

(iii) The shaded triangle is mapped onto C under a rotation of 180°.

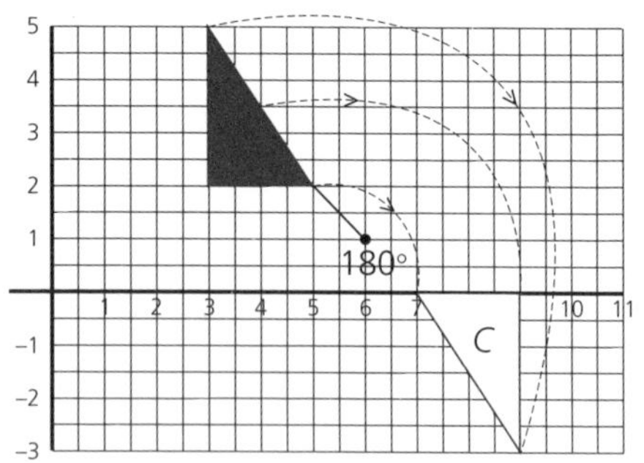

As we said, a central symmetry yields the same image as a rotation of 180°.

⇒ The shaded triangle is mapped onto C, also under a central symmetry in (6, 1).

(b)

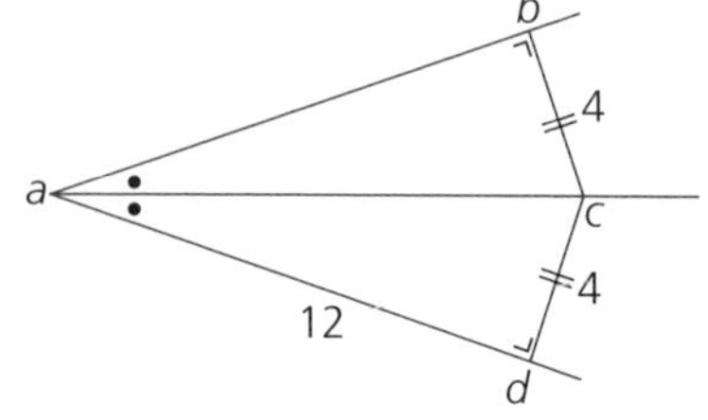

Note
Because $[ac]$ bisects $\angle bad$, $|bc| = |dc|$.

(i) Find $|ab|$.

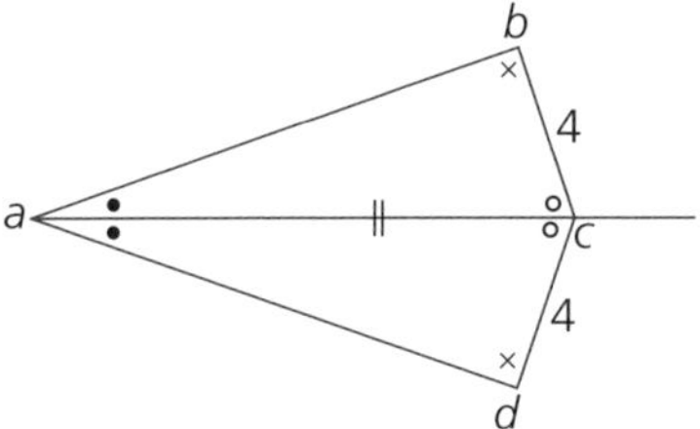

As we see, the triangles are congruent ... RHS.

$\Rightarrow |ab| = |ad|$

$\Rightarrow |ab| = 12$

(ii) Find area *abcd*.

Area $\triangle abc$

$= \frac{1}{2}(\text{base}) \times (\text{perpendicular height})$

$= \frac{1}{2}(12) \times 4 = \boxed{24}$

Area $\triangle abc = \frac{1}{2}(12) \times 4 = 24$ also

$\Rightarrow$ Area $abcd = 24 + 24 = \boxed{48}$

(c)

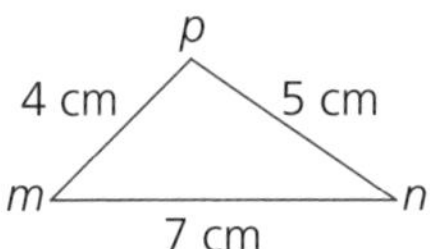

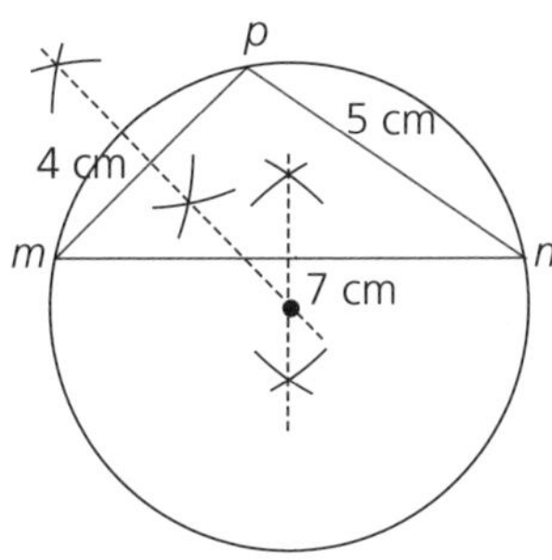

Solution to question 3

(a) (i) Find $|fb|$.

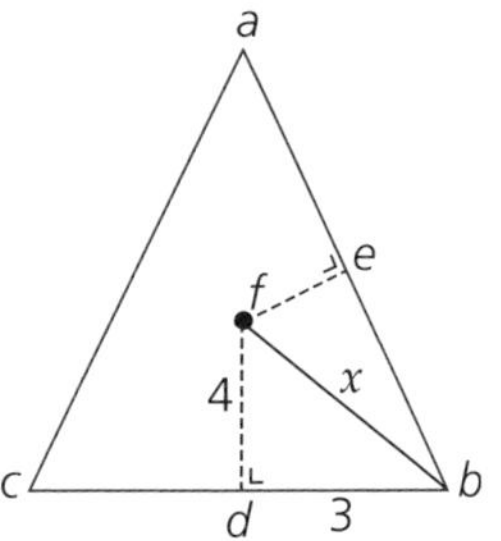

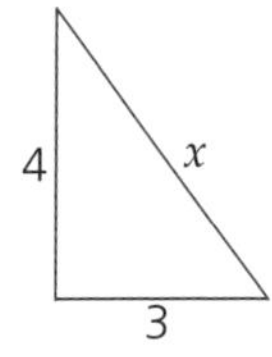

$x^2 = 4^2 + 3^2$

$x^2 = 25 \qquad \Rightarrow |fb| = 5$

(ii) Calculate area $\triangle abc$ given $|ac| = 7$, $|fa| = 3$ and $|fe| = 4$.

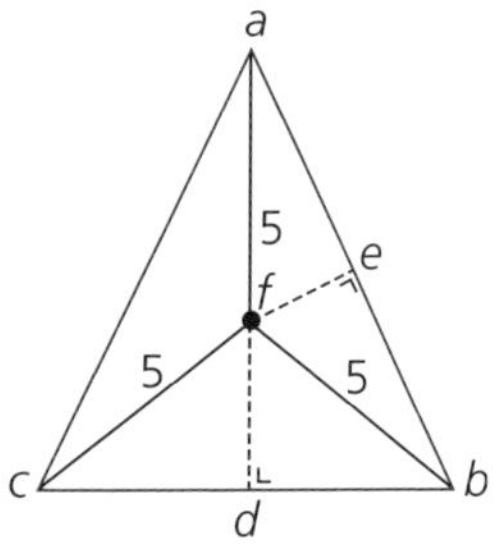

Important
Because $[fe]$ and $[fd]$ are perpendicular bisectors of $[ab]$ and $[bc]$:

$|fa| = |fb| = |fc| \quad$ (all 5)

① Area $\triangle cfb = \frac{1}{2}$(base) × (perpendicular height)

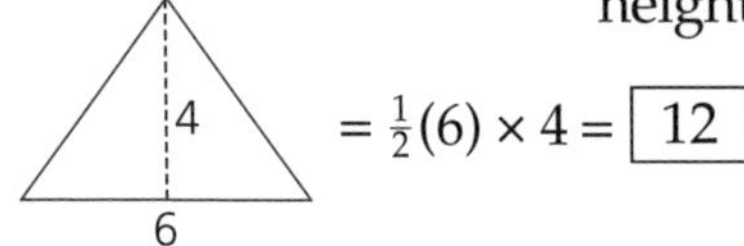

$= \frac{1}{2}(6) \times 4 = \boxed{12}$

② Area $\triangle acf$

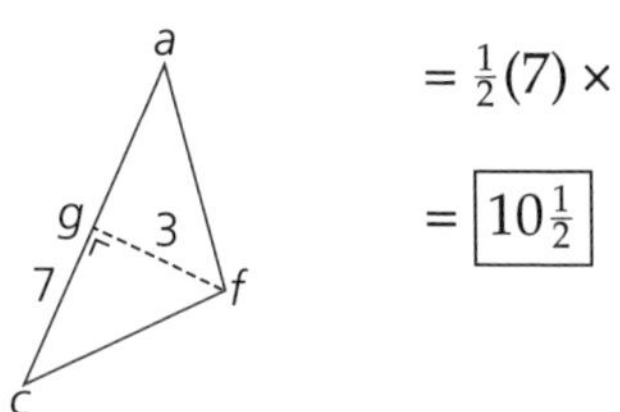

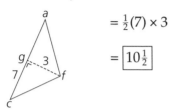

$= \frac{1}{2}(7) \times 3$

$= \boxed{10\frac{1}{2}}$

③ Area $\triangle afb$

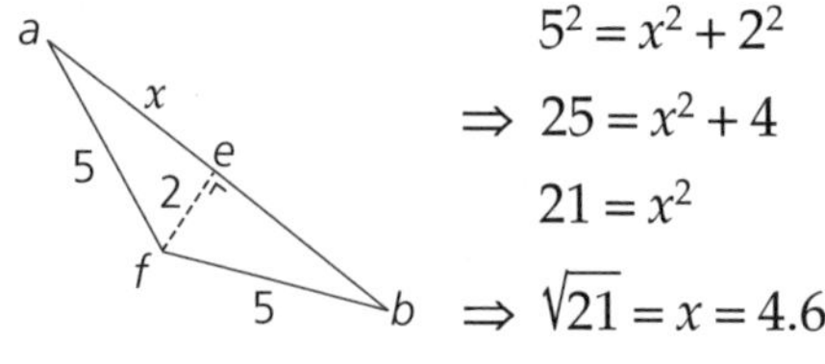

$5^2 = x^2 + 2^2$

$\Rightarrow 25 = x^2 + 4$

$21 = x^2$

$\Rightarrow \sqrt{21} = x = 4.6$

$\Rightarrow |ab| = 4.6 + 4.6 = 9.2$

$\Rightarrow$ Area $\triangle abf = \frac{1}{2}(9.2) \times 2$

$= \boxed{9.2}$

$\Rightarrow$ Area $\triangle abc = 12 + 10.5 + 9.2$

$= \boxed{31.7}$

(b)

(i) Construct the image of *abcd* under a central symmetry in pt. *e*.

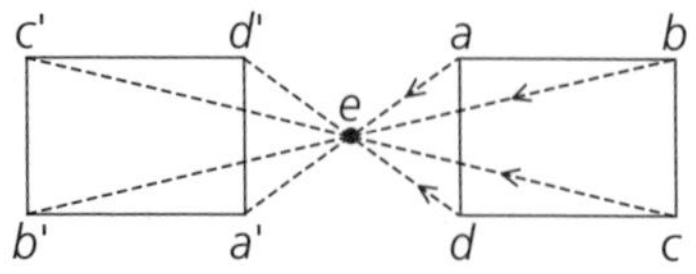

(ii) Construct the image of *abcd* under an axial symmetry in line *L*.

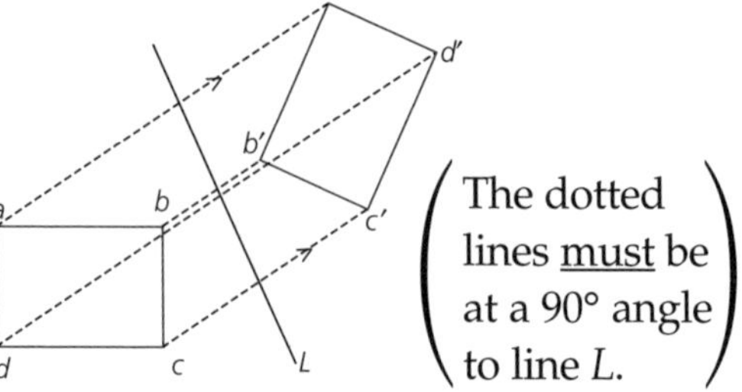

(The dotted lines must be at a 90° angle to line *L*.)

(iii) Construct the image of *abcd* under the translation $\overrightarrow{db}$.

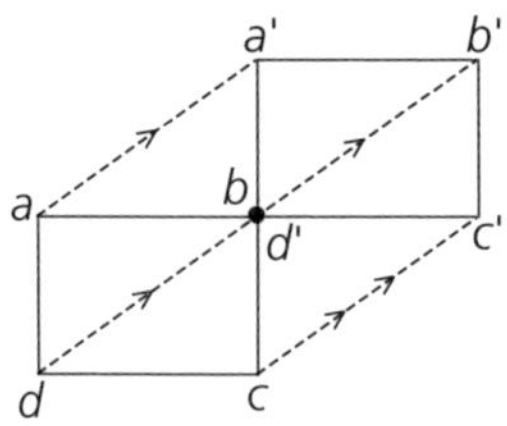

(iv) Construct the image of *abcd* under an anti-clockwise rotation of 120° around pt. *c*.

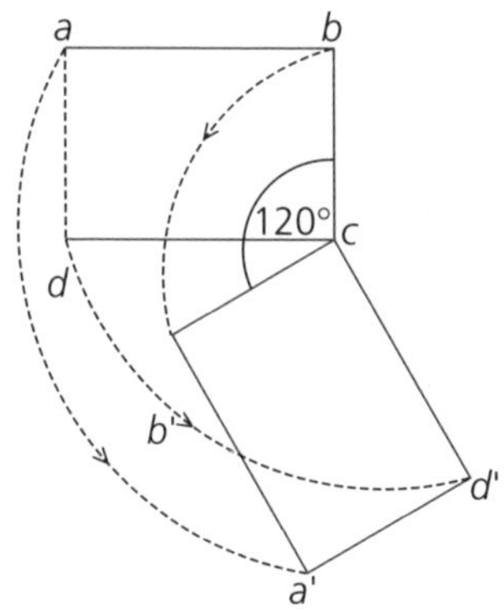

Chapter 11

Theorems One

Section A

This section contains five fairly basic theorems.

Theor. 1

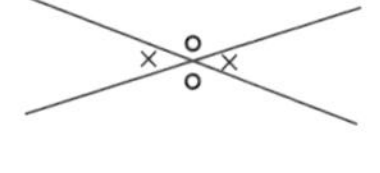

(×) = (×) (○) = (○)

'Vertically opposite angles are equal in measure.'

Theor. 2

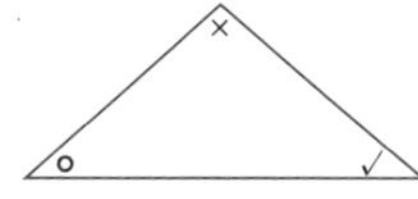

(○) + (×) + (✓) = 180°

'The measures of the three angles of a triangle sum to 180°.'

Theor. 3

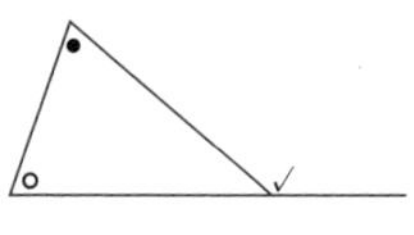

(✓) = (○) + (•)

'The exterior angle of a triangle is equal in measure to the sum of the two interior opposite angles.'

Theor. 4

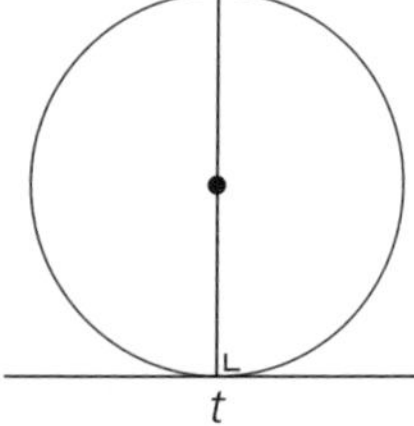

'If a line passes through a point t on a circle and is perpendicular to the diameter at t, then the line is a tangent to the circle at t.'

Theor. 5

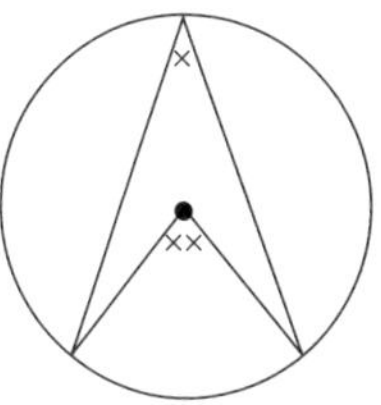

$(\times\times) = 2(\times)$

'The measure of the angle at the centre of a circle is twice the measure of the angle at the circumference standing on the same arc.'

This theorem has three important deductions, i.e. (i), (ii) and (iii).

(i) An angle subtended by a diameter at the circumference is a right angle.

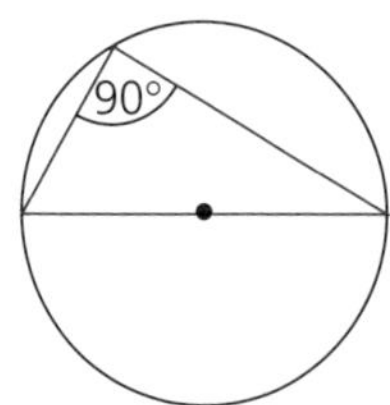

(ii) All angles at the circumference on the same arc are equal in measure.

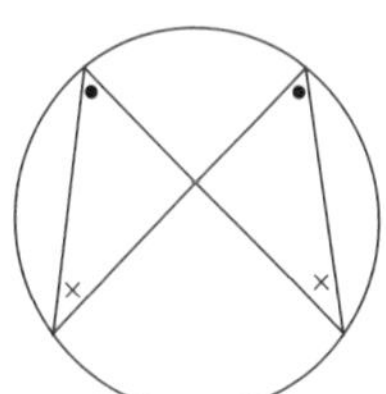

$(\bullet) = (\bullet)$

$(\times) = (\times)$

(iii) The sum of the opposite angles of a cyclic quadrilateral is 180°.

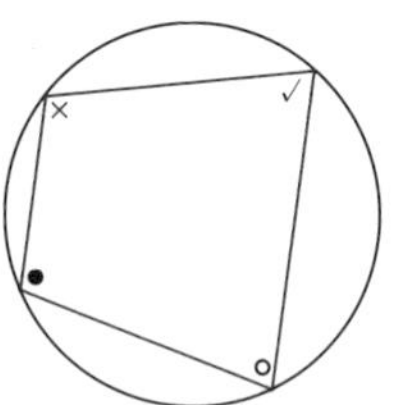

$(\times) + (\circ) = 180°$

$(\bullet) + (\checkmark) = 180°$

We will now prove these theorems:

① Vertically opposite angles are equal in measure.

Given Intersecting lines L and K with vertically opposite angles 1 and 3.

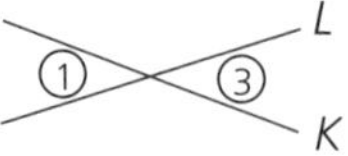

To prove ① = ③

Construction Label angle 2 as shown.

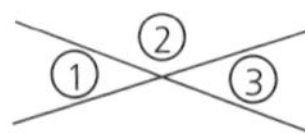

Proof

① + ② = 180° ... straight angle

② + ③ = 180° ... straight angle

⇒ ① + ② = ② + ③

Subtract ② from each side

⇒ ① = ③

② The measure of the three angles in a triangle sum to 180°.

Given $\triangle abc$ containing angles 1, 2 and 3.

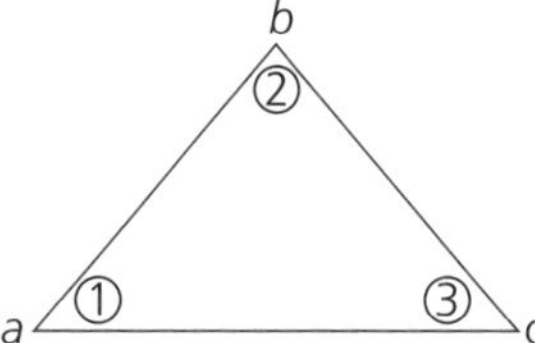

To prove ① + ② + ③ = 180°

Construction Draw a line through b parallel to $[ac]$.
Label angles ④ and ⑤.

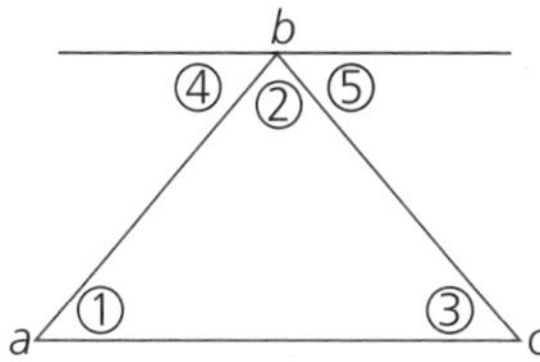

Proof

④ + ② + ⑤ = 180° ... straight angle

But ① = ④ and ③ = ⑤ ... alternate angles.

⇒ ① + ② + ③ is also equal to 180°

③ An exterior angle of a triangle equals the sum of the two interior opposite angles in measure.

Given $\triangle abc$ containing angles 1, 2 and 3. Base ac extended to d with exterior angle 4.

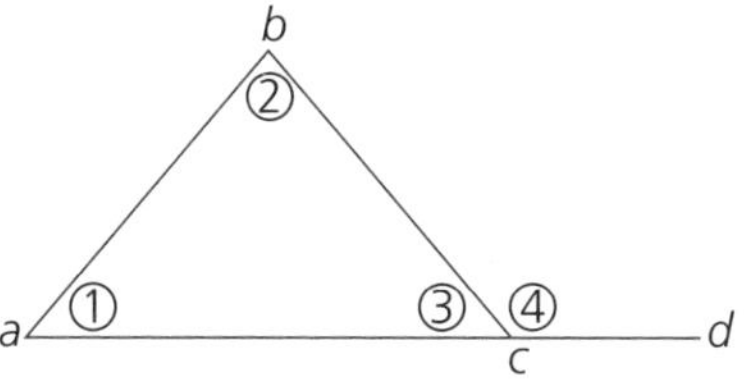

To prove ④ = ① + ②

Proof

① + ② + ③ = 180° ... 3 angles in a △

④ + ③ = 180°... straight angle

⇒ ① + ② + ③ = ④ + ③

Subtracting ③ from each side ...
① + ② = ④

④ If a line passes through a point t on a circle and is perpendicular to the diameter at t, then the line is a tangent to the circle at t.

Given A line L, perpendicular to the diameter act. L meets the diameter at point t.

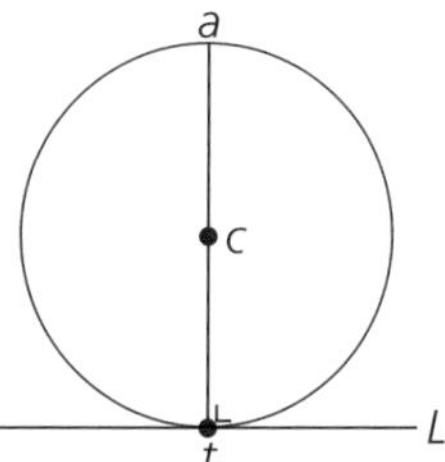

To prove That L is a tangent to the circle.

Construction Let x be any point on the line L. Join c to x.

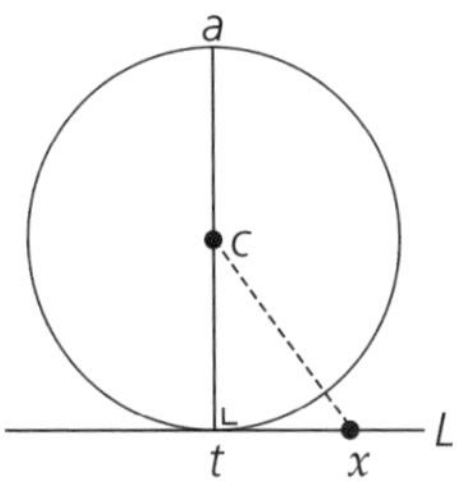

Proof

$[xc]$ is the hypotenuse of $\triangle ctx$ (as $|\angle ctx| = 90°$)

$\Rightarrow$ $[xc]$ is the longest side of $\triangle ctx$

$\Rightarrow$ $|xc| >$ radius $|ct|$

$\Rightarrow$ x must lie outside the circle.

Similarly, all other points, except t lie outside the circle.

$\Rightarrow$ L meets the circle at one point only.

$\Rightarrow$ L is tangent to the circle.

⑤ The measure of the angle at the centre of the circle is twice the measure of the angle at the circumference, standing on the same arc.

Given Circle with centre c, containing a, b and d.

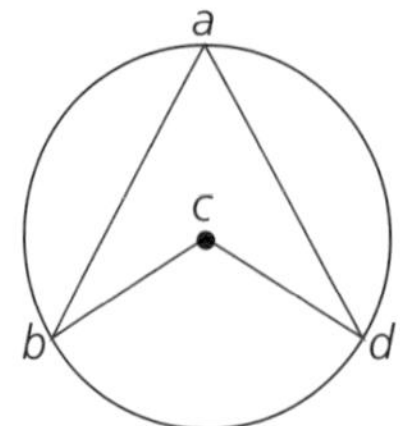

To prove $|\angle bcd| = 2|\angle bad|$

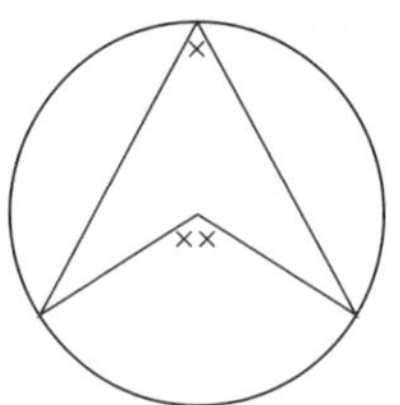

Construction Join a to c and extend to e.

Mark in angles 1, 2, 3, 4, 5 and 6.

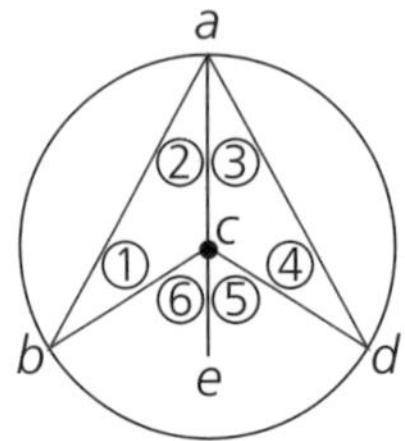

Proof

⑥ = ① + ② ... exterior angle

But ① = ② = ... $|ac| = |bc|$

$\Rightarrow$ ⑥ = 2 ② (i)

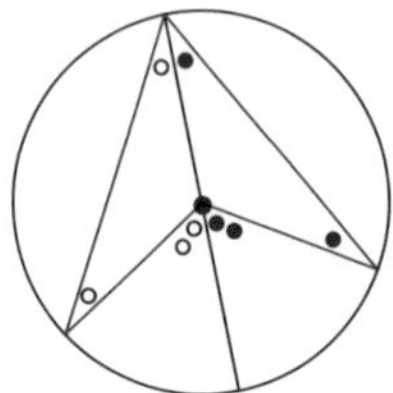

⑤ = ③ + ④ ... exterior angle

But ③ = ④ ... $|ac| = |cd|$

$\Rightarrow$ ⑤ = 2 ③ (ii)

Adding (i) and (ii):

⑥ + ⑤ = 2 ② + 2 ③

$\Rightarrow$ ⑥ + ⑤ = 2(② + ③)

$\Rightarrow$ $|\angle bcd| = 2|\angle bad|$

⑤ (a) Deduction 1 – All angles at the circumference on the same arc are equal in measure.

To prove ① = ②

Proof **(i)** Pt. e is centre of circle.

Angle 1 and angle 3 are both standing on arc bc.

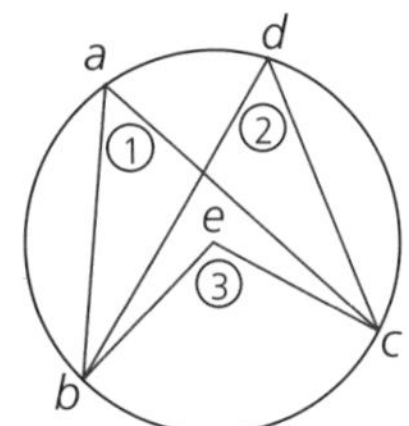

⇒ ③ = 2① ... from theorem

(ii) Pt. e is centre of circle.

Angle 2 and angle 3 are both standing on arc bc.

⇒ ③ = 2②

Therefore 2① = 2②

So ① = ②

⑤ (b) Deduction 2 – An angle subtended by a diameter at the circumference is a right-angle.

Given Circle with centre d. Pt. a and Pt. c end points of the diameter. Pt. b is on the circle.

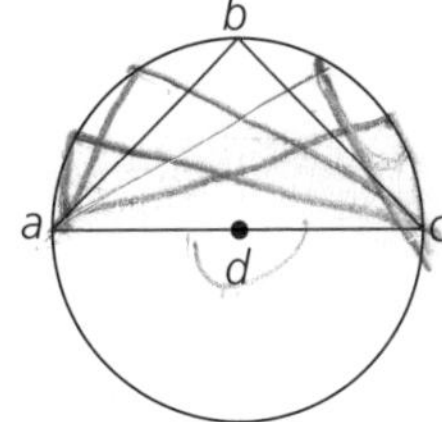

To prove $|\angle abc| = 90°$

Proof Pt. d is the centre of the circle.

Angle 1 and angle 2 are both standing on arc ac.

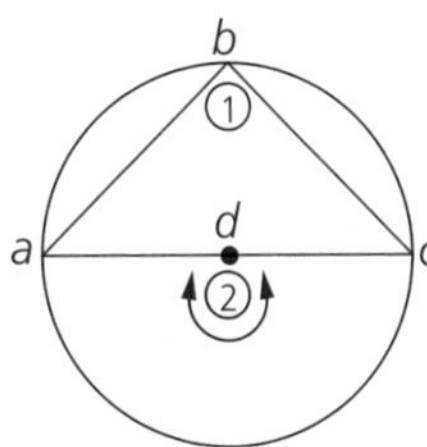

⇒ ② = 2①

But ② = 180° ⇒ ① = 90°

⑤ (c) Deduction 3 – The sum of opposite angles of a cyclic quadrilateral is 180°.

To prove $|\angle abc| + |\angle adc| = 180°$

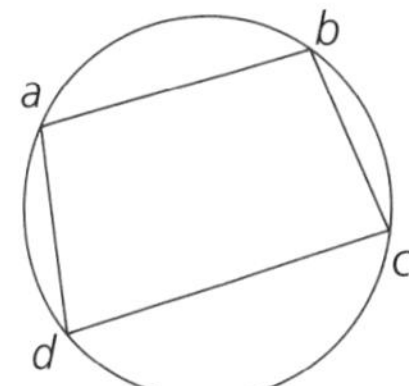

Proof **(i)** Angle 3 is at the centre of the circle. Angle 3 and angle 1 are both standing on the arc *ac*.

⇒ ③ = 2① (i)

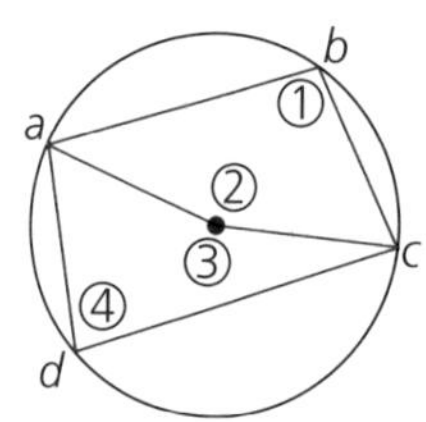

(ii) Angle 2 is at the centre of the circle. Angle 2 and angle 4 are both standing on the arc *ac*.

⇒ ② = 2④ (ii)

Adding (i) and (ii):

③ + ② = 2① + 2④

⇒ ③ + ② = 2(① + ④)

But ② + ③ = 360°

⇒ ① + ④ = 180°

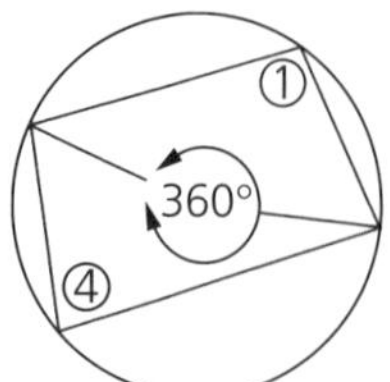

Section A
Important Questions

Note

'Standing on the same arc.'

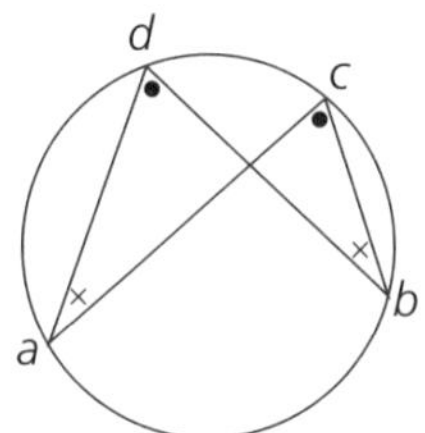

① (•) and (•) are said to be 'standing on the arc *ab*.'

If we look at both angles, they both start at pt. *a* touch the circle and finish at pt. *b*

Hence 'standing on the arc *ab*.'

② Similarly, (×) and (×) are 'standing on the arc *dc*.'

⇒ (•) = (•) and (×) = (×)

Question 1

Calculate *a* and *b*.

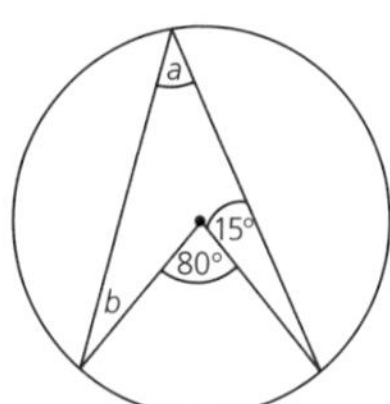

Very important

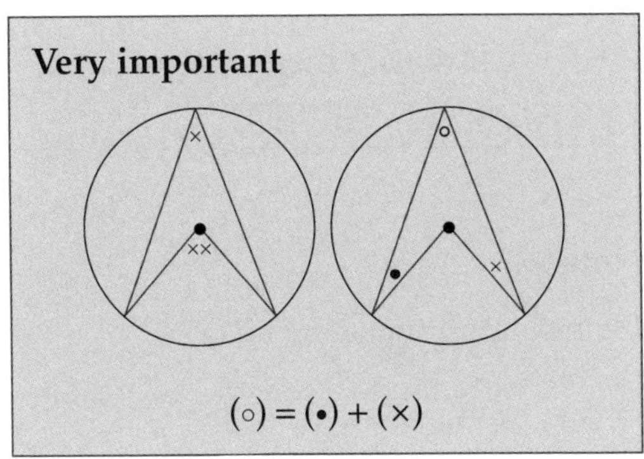

$(\circ) = (\bullet) + (\times)$

$80° = 2a$

$a = 40°$

$a = b + 15°$

$\Rightarrow 40° = b + 15°$

$\Rightarrow b = 25°$

Question 2

Calculate a, b, c.

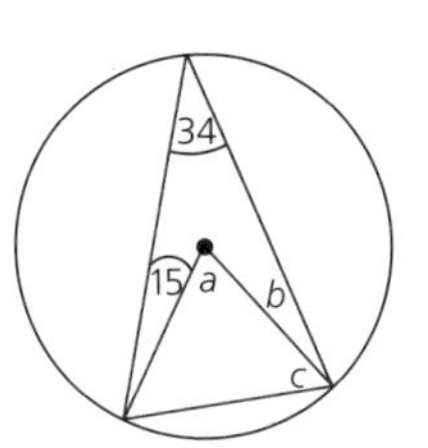

$a = 34 \times 2$

$\Rightarrow a = 68°$

$34° = b + 15°$

$\Rightarrow b = 19°$

Very important

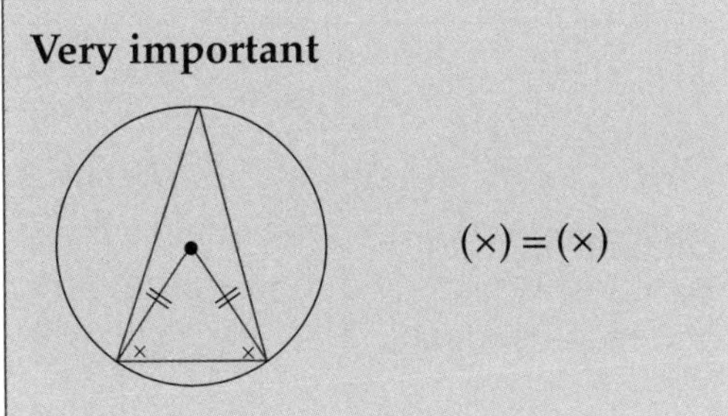

$(\times) = (\times)$

Find c.

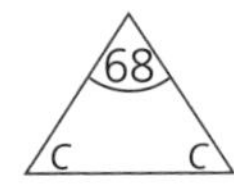

$180° - 68° = 112°$

$112° \div 2 = 56°$

$c = 56°$

Question 3

Calculate a.

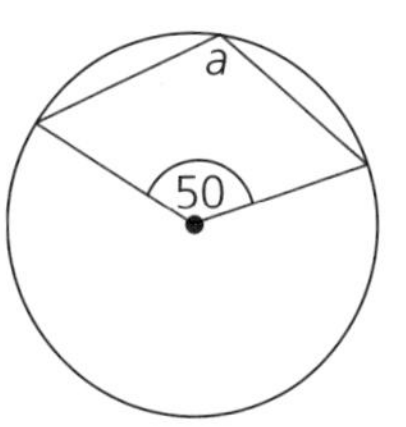

Very important

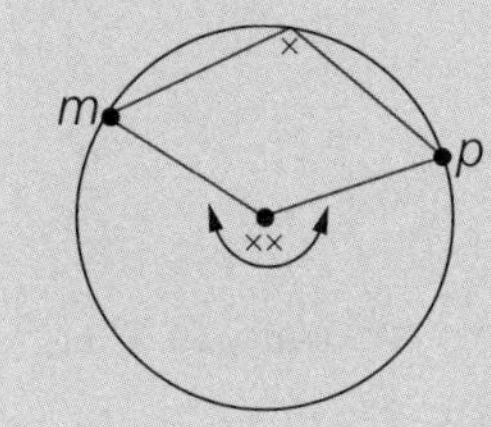

$(\times\times) = 2(\times)$

Both standing on arc mp.

$360° - 50° = 310°$

$\Rightarrow 310° = 2a$

$\Rightarrow 155° = a$

Question 4

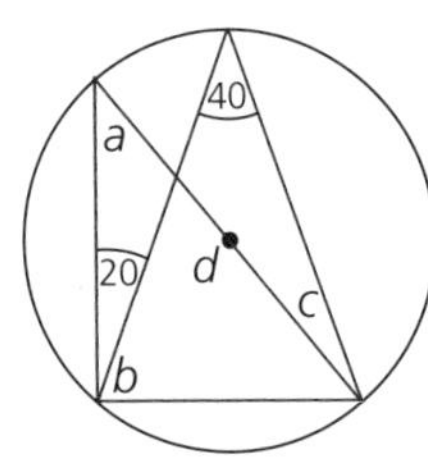

In the diagram d is the centre. Calculate a, b, c.

Very important

In the diag. above,

$(\bullet) = (\bullet)$ ... on same arc.

$(\times) = (\times)$ ... on same arc.

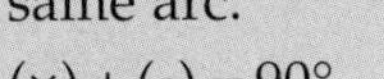

$(\times) + (\circ) = 90°$ ... standing on the diameter.

$\Rightarrow a = 40°$ and $c = 20°$

$b = 90° - 20° = 70°$

Question 5

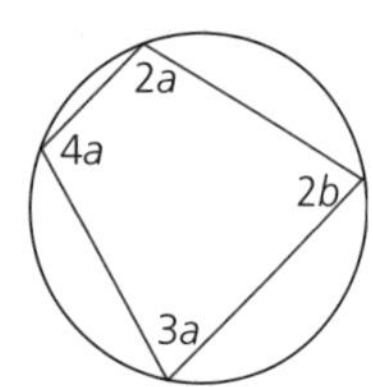

Calculate a and b.

Very important

$(\times) + (\circ) = 180°$

$(\bullet) + (\checkmark) = 180°$

$\Rightarrow\ 2a + 3a = 180°$

$5a = 180° \qquad \Rightarrow\ a = 36°$

$\Rightarrow\ 4a + 2b = 180°$

$4(36°) + 2b = 180°$

$2b = 180° - 144°$

$2b = 36° \qquad \Rightarrow\ b = 18°$

Section B – 'Congruent Triangles'

This section contains another four theorems. The proofs of these theorems involve congruent triangles.

It is extremely important that you understand:

(i) What it means if two triangles are congruent.

(ii) How to prove two triangles are congruent.

(i) What does it mean if two triangles are congruent?

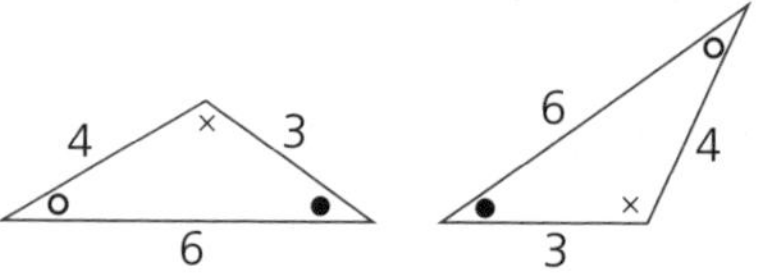

If two triangles are congruent...

The measure of all sides and angles in the first triangle are equal to the measure of all corresponding sides and angles in the second triangle.

The word 'corresponding' is very important in the above definition.

Two sides are corresponding if they are opposite the same angle.
We see this in the pair of congruent triangles above.

(ii) How can we prove two triangles are congruent?

① *SAS*

When 2 sides and the angle in between them in one triangle are equal to 2 sides and the angle in between them in the other triangle.

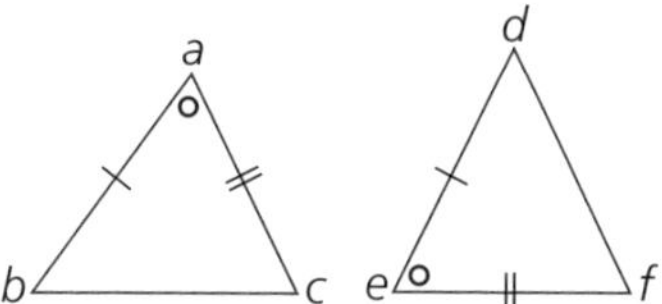

$\triangle abc$ and $\triangle def$ are congruent because of SAS.

② SSS

When the 3 sides in one triangle are equal in measure to the 3 sides in the other triangle.

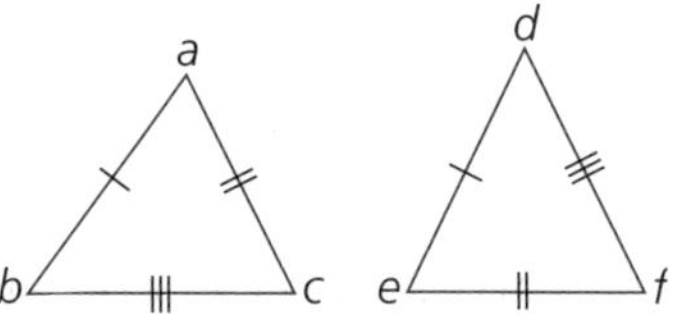

$\triangle abc$ and $\triangle def$ are congruent because of SSS.

③ RHS

When a right angle, hypotenuse and one other side are equal in both triangles.

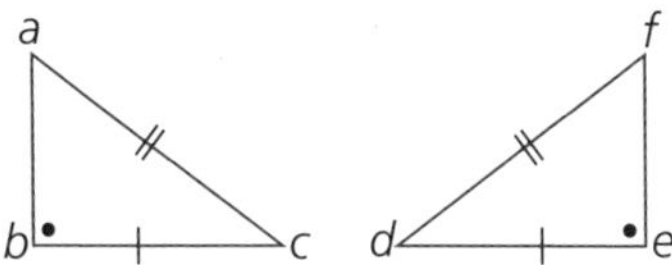

$\triangle abc$ and $\triangle def$ are congruent because of RHS.

④ ASA

When 2 angles and the side in between them in one triangle are equal to 2 angles and the side between them in the other triangle.

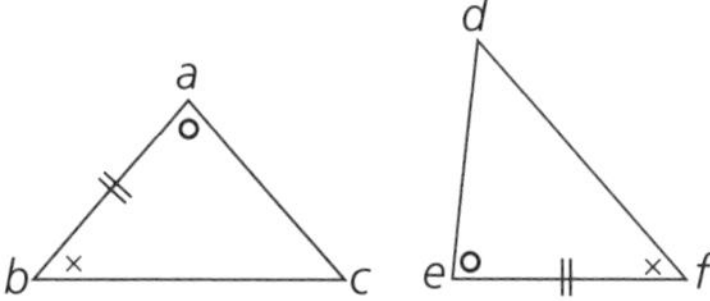

$\triangle abc$ and $\triangle def$ are congruent because of ASA.

We prove that two triangles are congruent therefore if we show any one of the following is true:

① SAS ③ RHS
② SSS ④ ASA

We will now go through a question asking us to prove two triangles are congruent.

Please study it closely and follow the three steps in all questions involving congruent triangles (including the proof of theorems).

Example

Investigate whether $\triangle mon$ and $\triangle por$ are congruent.

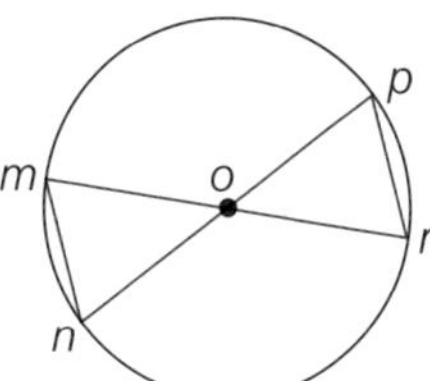

Step 1

① Investigate if any side in $\triangle mon$ is equal to a side in $\triangle por$ (you must be able to give a reason).

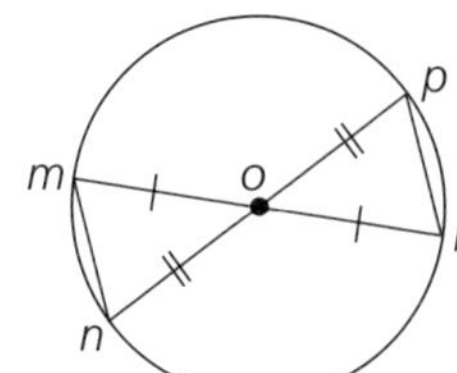

(i) $|mo| = |or|$ ... both radii

(ii) $|no| = |op|$ ... both radii

Step 2

② Investigate if any angle in $\triangle mon$ is equal to an angle in $\triangle por$ (again, you must be able to say why).

$|\angle mon| = |\angle por|$ ... vertically opposite

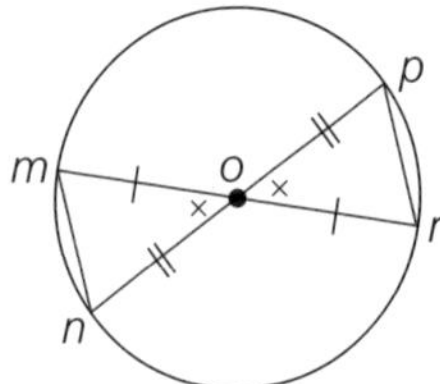

Step 3

③ Investigate if $\triangle mon$ is congruent to $\triangle pon$.

From the above diagram, we see that the triangles are congruent because of SAS.

The four theorems involving congruent triangles are:

Theor. 6

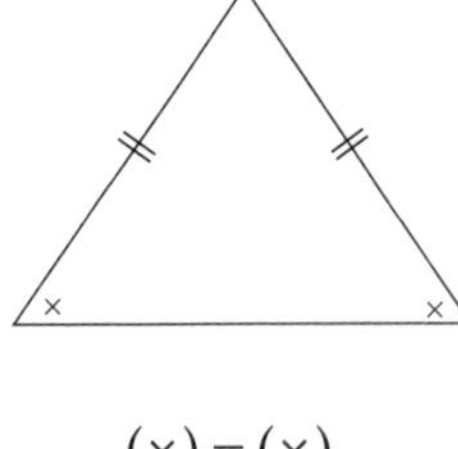

$(\times) = (\times)$

'If two sides of a triangle are equal in measure then the angles opposite these sides are equal in measure.'

Theor. 7

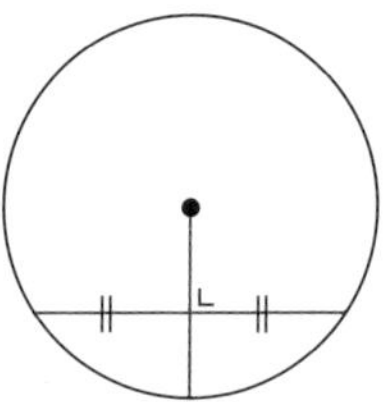

'A line through the centre of a circle perpendicular to a chord bisects the chord.'

Theor. 8

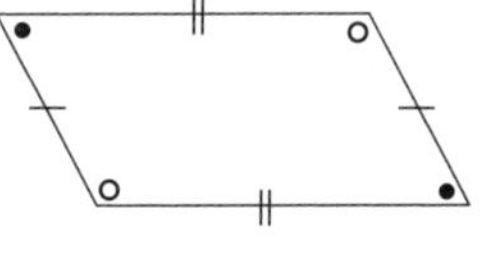

$(\bullet) = (\bullet)$

$(\circ) = (\circ)$

'The opposite sides and angles of a parallelogram are respectively equal in measure.'

Theor. 9

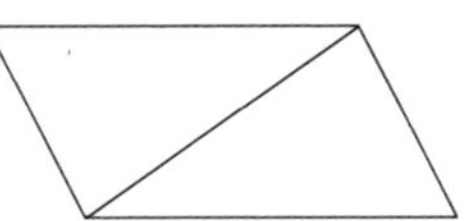

A diagonal bisects the area of a parallelogram.

We will now prove these theorems...

⑥ If two sides of a triangle are equal in measure then the angles opposite these sides are equal in measure.

Given $\triangle abc$ with $|ab| = |ac|$ and base angles 1 and 2.

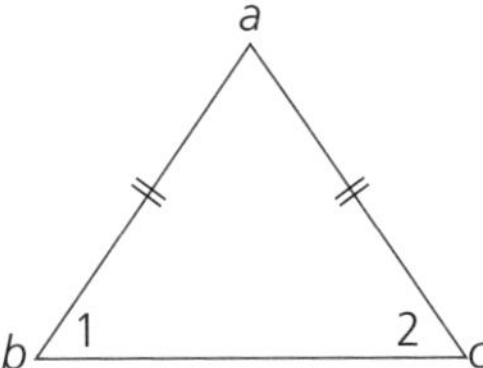

To prove $|\angle 1| = |\angle 2|$

Construction Draw $[ad]$ given pt. d is on $[bc]$ and $[ad]$ bisects $\angle bac$.

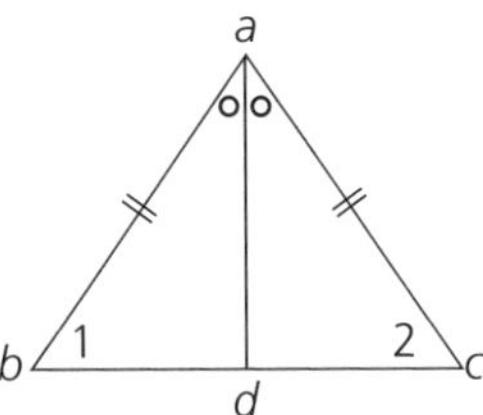

Proof Consider $\triangle abd$ and $\triangle adc$.

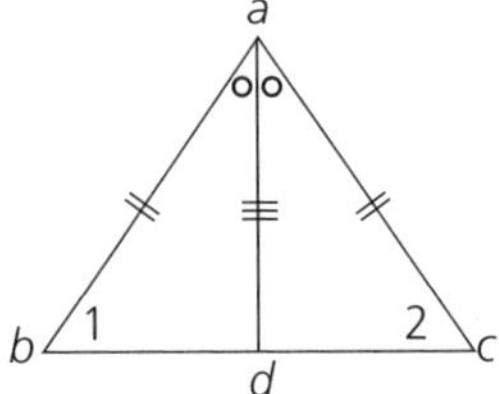

(i) $|ab| = |ac|$ ... given

$|ad| = |ad|$ ... common

(ii) $(\circ) = (\circ)$ ... $[ad]$ bisects $\angle bac$

(iii) Therefore $\triangle abd$ is congruent to $\triangle adc$ ... SAS.

$\Rightarrow$ $|\angle 1| = |\angle 2|$ ... corresponding angles

⑦ A line through the centre of a circle perpendicular to a chord bisects the chord.

Given Circle with centre c, line M through c.

Chord $[ab] \perp M$

$M \cap [ab] = d$

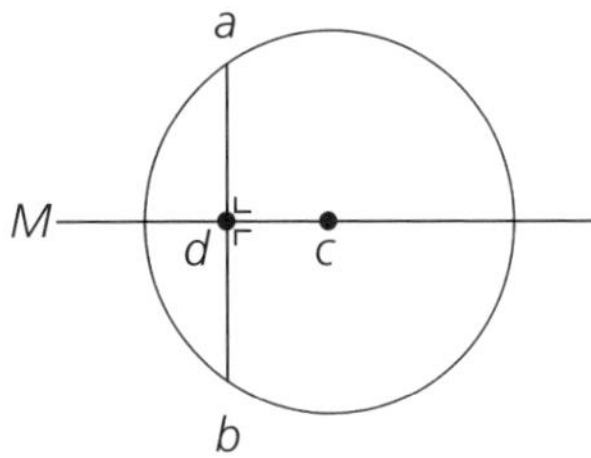

To prove $|ad| = |db|$

Construction Join a to c and also b to c.

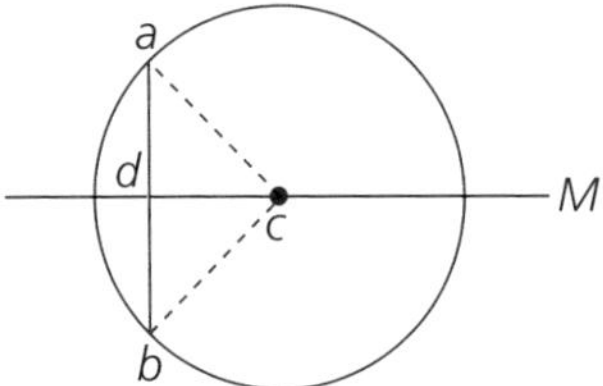

Proof Consider $\triangle adc$ and $\triangle bcd$.

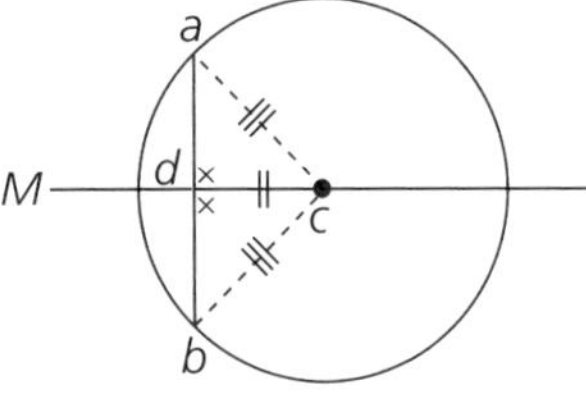

(i) $|dc| = |dc|$ ... common

$|ac| = |bc|$ ... both radii

(ii) $(\times) = (\times)$ ... both 90°

(iii) $\Rightarrow$ $\triangle adc$ is congruent to $\triangle bcd$ ... RHS.

$\Rightarrow$ $|ad| = |bd|$ ... corresponding sides

⑧ Opposite sides and opposite angles of a parallelogram are respectively equal in measure.

Given Parallelogram $abcd$.

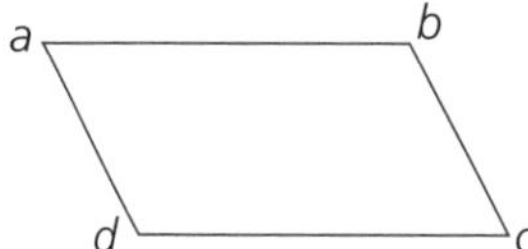

To prove $|ab| = |cd|$, $|ad| = |bc|$, $|\angle dab| = |\angle bcd|$, $|\angle adc| = |\angle abc|$

Construction Join a to c.

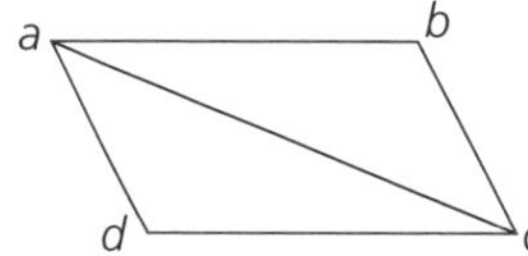

Proof Consider $\triangle abc$ and $\triangle adc$.

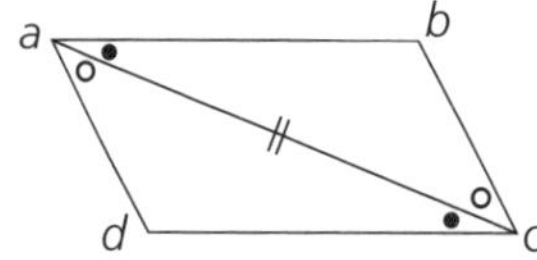

(i) $|ac| = |ac|$ ... common to both triangles.

(ii) $(\bullet) = (\bullet)$ ... alternate angles

$(\circ) = (\circ)$ ... alternate angles

(iii) $\triangle adc$ is congruent to $\triangle abc$ ... ASA.

$\Rightarrow$ $|ab| = |dc|$ and $|ad| = |bc|$ (corresponding sides)

$\angle bad| = |\angle dcb|$ (corresponding angles)

Similarly $|\angle adc| = |\angle abc|$

⑨ A diagonal bisects the area of a parallelogram.

Given Parallelogram $abcd$ with diagonal $[ac]$.

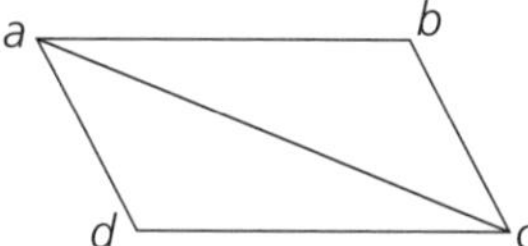

To prove Area $\triangle adc$ = Area $\triangle abc$

Proof Consider $\triangle adc$ and $\triangle abc$

$|ab| = |dc|$ ... opposite sides

$|ad| = |bc|$ ... opposite sides

$|ac| = |ac|$ ... common to both $\triangle$'s

$\Rightarrow$ $\triangle adc$ is congruent to $\triangle abc$ ... SSS.

$\Rightarrow$ Area $\triangle adc$ = area $\triangle abc$

Section B Important Questions

Question 1

In the diagram, $|ab| = 12$ and $|cd| = 4$. Calculate the area of the circle in terms of π.

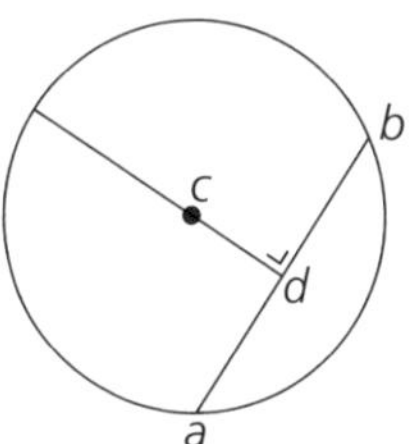

Important

① $|ad| = |db|$ [the chord is bisected]

② The radius $[ac]$ completes a right angled $\triangle adc$.

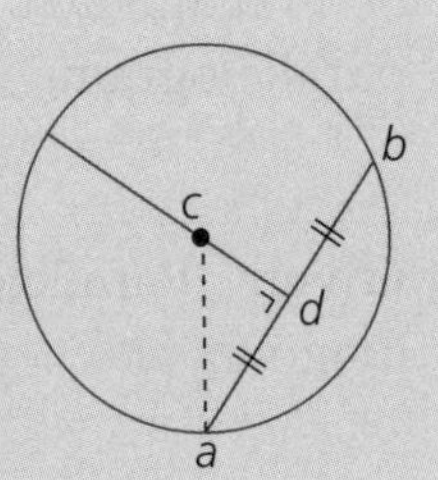

Find r.

$r^2 = 4^2 + 6^2$

$\Rightarrow\ r^2 = 52$

$\Rightarrow\ r = \sqrt{52}$

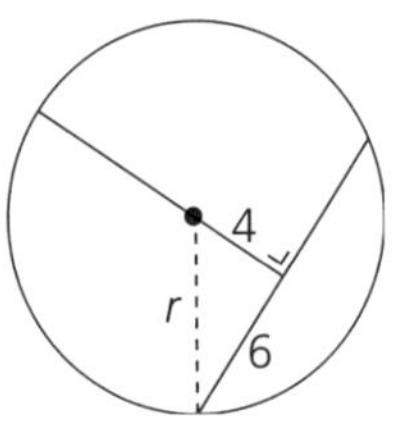

Find the area in terms of π.

Area $= \pi r^2$

$= \pi(\sqrt{52})(\sqrt{52})$

$= 52\pi$

Question 2

Prove that $y = 90°$.

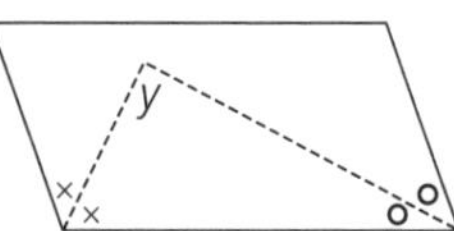

Important

① $(\bullet) = (\bullet)$ and $(\circ) = (\circ)$

② Because we can divide the parallelogram into two triangles:

$$(\bullet) + (\bullet) + (\circ) + (\circ) = 360°$$

$$\Rightarrow\ 2[(\bullet) + (\circ)] = 360°$$

$$\Rightarrow\ (\bullet) + (\circ) = 180°$$

③ $\Rightarrow$ The two angles along any side of a parallelogram add up to 180°.

$\Rightarrow\ (\times) + (\times) + (\circ) + (\circ) = 180°$

$\Rightarrow\ (\times) + (\circ) = 90°$

We know $(\times) + (\circ) + y = 180°$ (3 angles in a $\triangle$)

$\Rightarrow\ y = 90°$

Question 3

Pt. n is the centre of the circle. $|mp| = 8$

If area $\triangle mnp$ is 12 cm^2, find the radius of the circle.

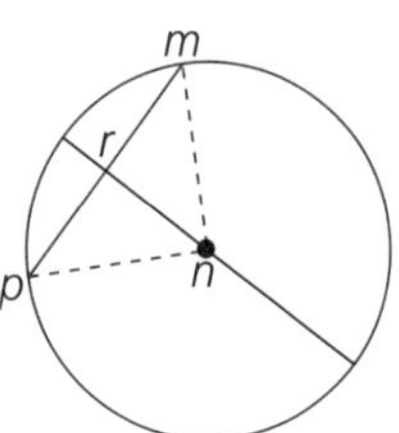

If area $\triangle mnp = 12$ and $|pm| = 8$.

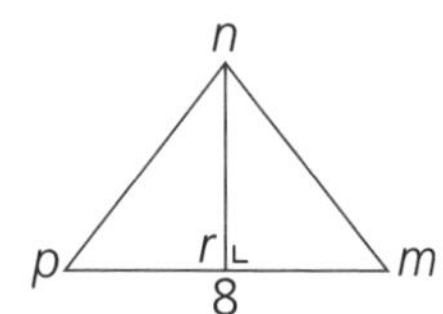

$\Rightarrow\ \frac{1}{2}(\text{base}) \times \text{perpendicular height} = 12$

$\Rightarrow\ \frac{1}{2}(8) \times |rn| = 12$

$\Rightarrow\ 4|rn| = 12$

$\Rightarrow\ |rn| = 3$

Calculate the radius.

$x^2 = 3^2 + 4^2$

$x^2 = 25$

$\Rightarrow\ |nm| = 5$

$\Rightarrow$ Radius $= 5$ cm

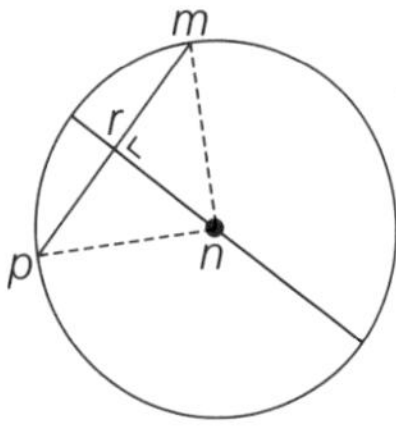

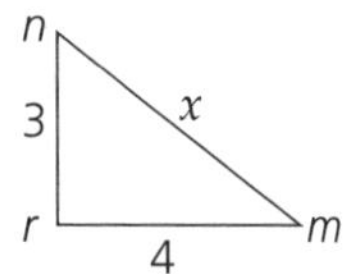

Chapter 11
Sample questions for you to try

Question 1

(a) Prove that the measure of an angle at the centre of a circle is twice the measure of the angle at the circumference standing on the same arc.

(b) Calculate w, t and p.

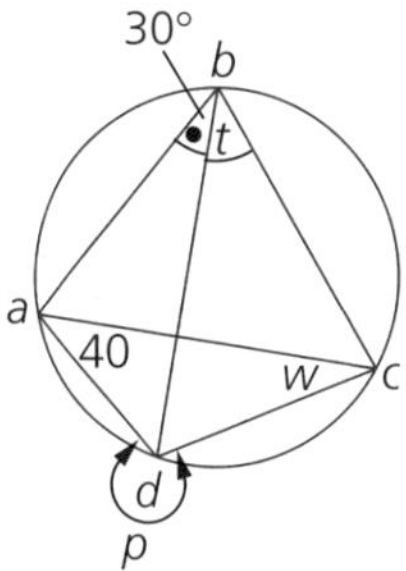

Question 2

(a) Prove that if a line passes through a point t on a circle and is perpendicular to the diameter at t, then the line is a tangent to the circle at t.

(b)

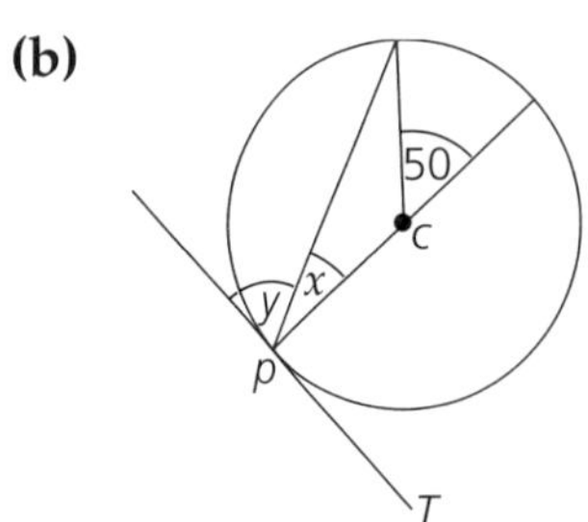

T is a tangent to the circle at pt. p. Calculate x and y.

(c) If $|ac| = \sqrt{80}$ and $|ab|$ is twice the length of $|bc|$, calculate the area of $\triangle abc$.

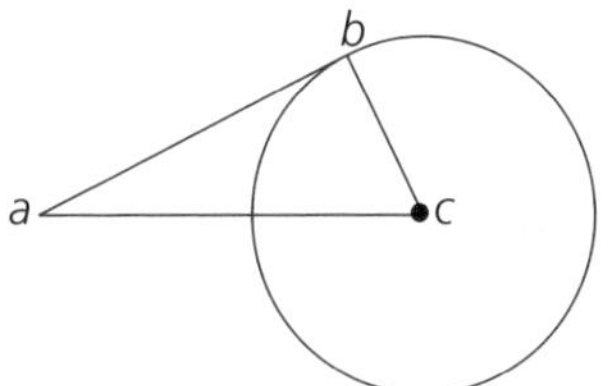

Question 3

(a) Prove that if two sides of a triangle are equal in measure, then the angles opposite them are equal in measure.

(b)

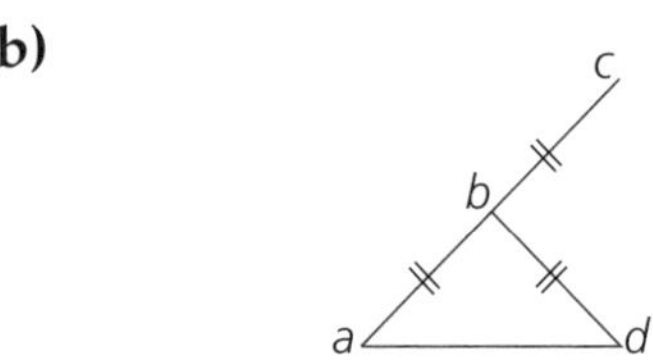

In the diagram, $|ab| = |bc| = |bd|$. By joining c to d, prove that $|\angle adc| = 90°$.

(c)

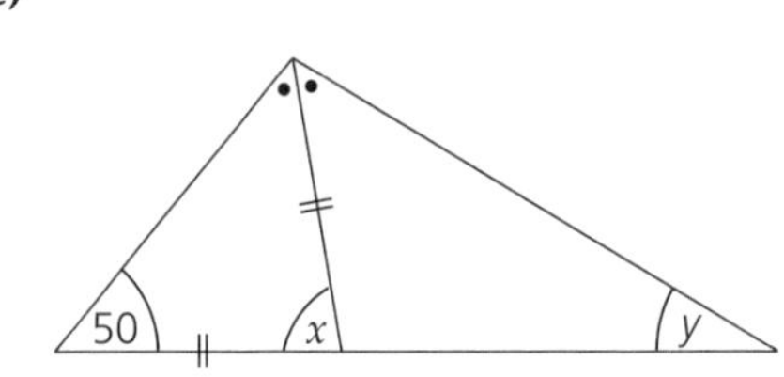

Evaluate x and y.

Solution to Question 1

(a) Please view the proof of theorem 5 earlier in the chapter.

(b)

Important

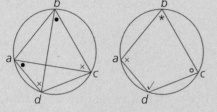

$(\bullet) = (\bullet)$ ... both standing on the arc *cd*.

$(\times) = (\times)$ ... both standing on the arc *ab*.

$(\times) + (\circ) = 180°$

$(\checkmark) + (*) = 180°$

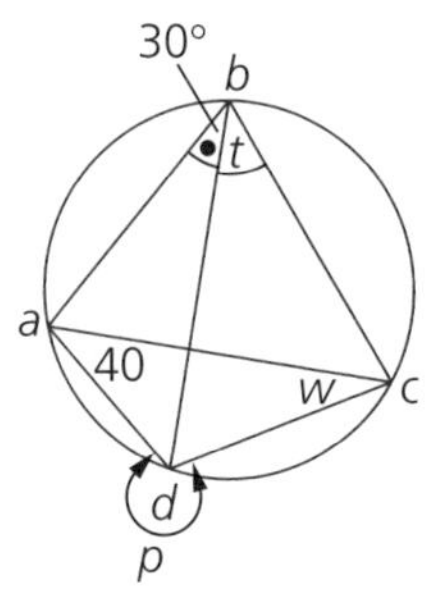

(b)

$\Rightarrow t = 40°$ (both standing on the arc *cd*)

$\Rightarrow w = 30°$ (both standing on the arc *ad*)

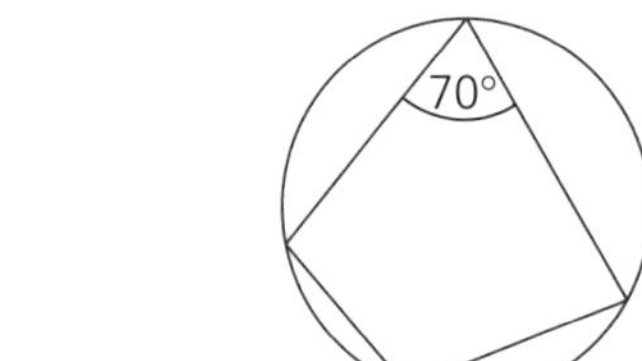

$\Rightarrow p = 360° - 110° = 250°$

Solution to question 2

(a) Please view the proof of theorem 4 earlier in the chapter.

(b)

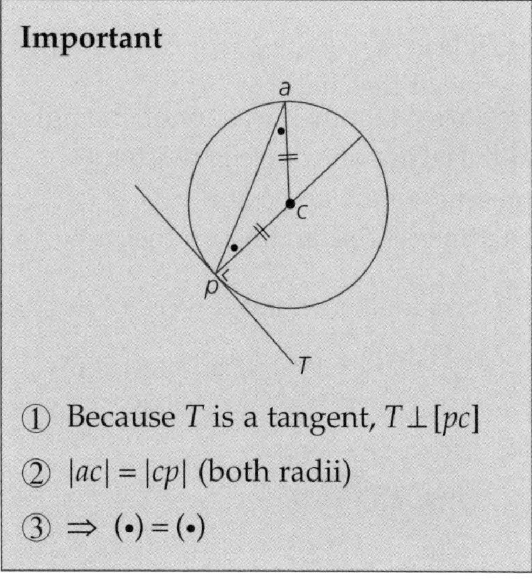

① Because T is a tangent, $T \perp [pc]$

② $|ac| = |cp|$ (both radii)

③ $\Rightarrow (\bullet) = (\bullet)$

Find x.

$$180° - 50° = 130°$$

$$130° \div 2 = 65°$$

$$\Rightarrow \quad x = 65°$$

Find y.

$$y = 90° - 65° = 25°$$

(c)

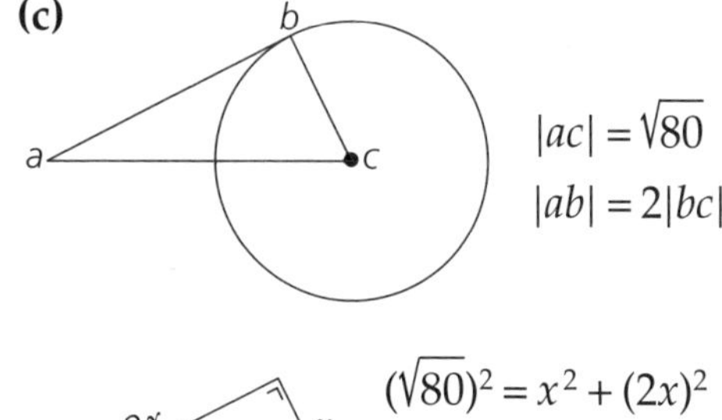

$|ac| = \sqrt{80}$

$|ab| = 2|bc|$

2x
x
√80

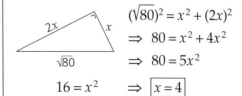

$(\sqrt{80})^2 = x^2 + (2x)^2$

$\Rightarrow 80 = x^2 + 4x^2$

$\Rightarrow 80 = 5x^2$

$16 = x^2 \quad \Rightarrow \boxed{x = 4}$

$$\text{Area} = \tfrac{1}{2}(\text{base}) \times (\text{perp. height})$$
$$= \tfrac{1}{2}(8) \times (4) = \boxed{16}$$

Solution to question 3

(a) Please view the proof of theorem 6 earlier in the chapter.

(b)

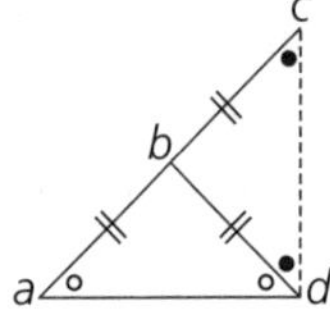

$(\bullet) + (\bullet) + (\circ) + (\circ) = 180°$ [3 angles in $\triangle acd$]

$\Rightarrow \quad 2(\bullet) + 2(\circ) = 180°$

$\Rightarrow \quad 2[(\bullet) + (\circ)] = 180°$

$\Rightarrow \quad (\bullet) + (\circ) = 90° \quad \Rightarrow \ |\angle adc| = 90°$

(c)

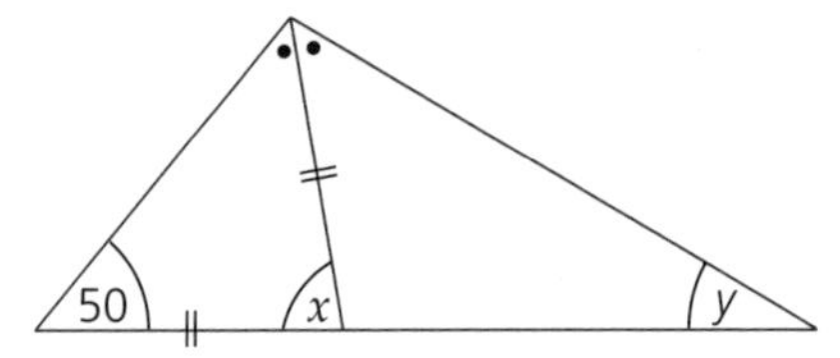

$(\bullet) = 50°$ (both opposite the equal sides)

$\Rightarrow \ x = 180° - (50° + 50°) \quad \Rightarrow \ x = 80°$

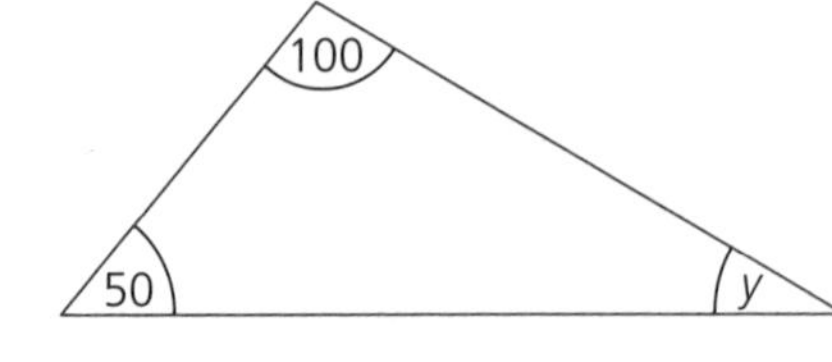

$\Rightarrow \ y = 180° - 150°$
$= 30°$

Chapter 11A

Theorems Two

This chapter covers the final two theorems. The proof of each involves similar triangles.

It is extremely important that you understand:

(i) What it means if two triangles are similar.

(ii) Once we know two triangles are similar, what statements can we make about them.

When are two triangles similar?

Two triangles are similar if they have equal angles.

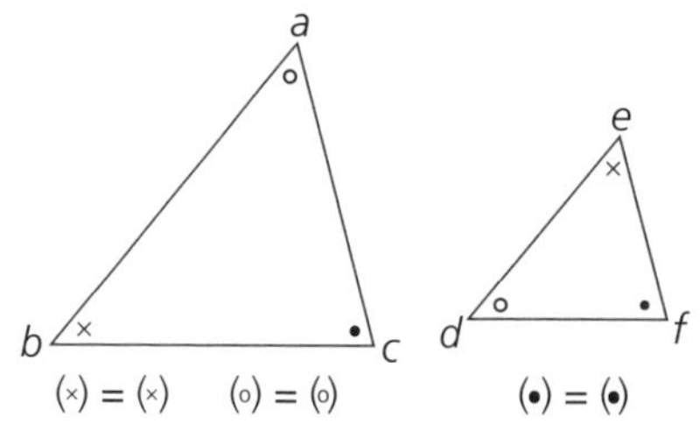

$\Rightarrow$ $\triangle abc$ is similar to $\triangle def$

What statements can we make as a result?

'When two triangles are similar, the lengths of the corresponding sides are proportional.'

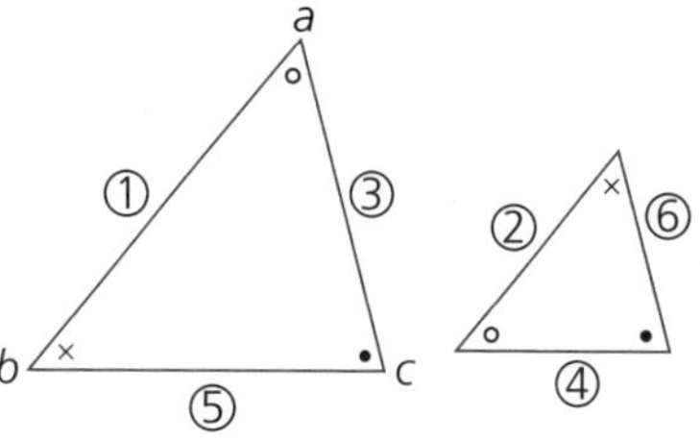

Note 1

① and ② are corresponding ... opposite (•)

③ and ④ are corresponding ... opposite (×)

⑤ and ⑥ are corresponding ... opposite (○)

Note 2

As the triangles are similar, the corresponding sides are proportional.

$\Rightarrow \frac{①}{②} = \frac{③}{④} = \frac{⑤}{⑥}$

Important

When proving two triangles are similar always state why two angles are equal.

Do not say two angles are equal if you can't explain why.

The two theorems involving similar triangles are:

Theor. 10

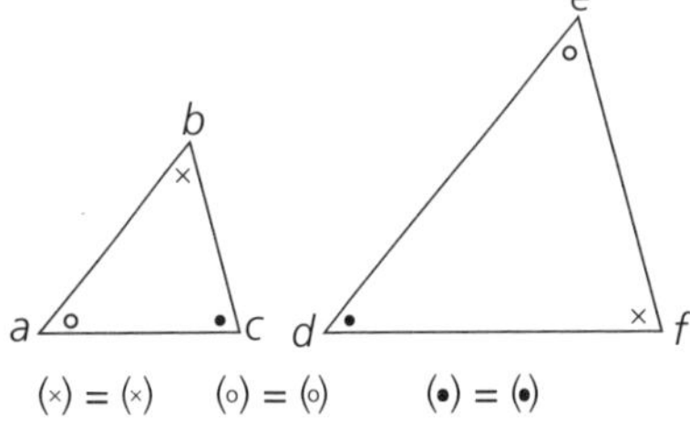

$$\Rightarrow \frac{|ab|}{|ef|} = \frac{|bc|}{|df|} = \frac{|ac|}{|ed|}$$

'If two triangles are equiangular, the lengths of corresponding sides are proportional.'

Closely associated with theorem 10 is the following deduction. It is very important that you understand and remember it.

'A line which is drawn parallel to one side of a triangle divides the other two sides in the same ratio.'

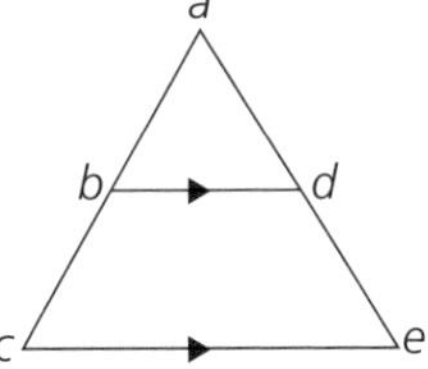

Here, $[bd]$ is parallel to $[ce]$.

$\Rightarrow$ $[ac]$ and $[ae]$ are divided in the same ratio

$$\Rightarrow \frac{|ab|}{|bc|} = \frac{|ad|}{|de|}$$

Theor. 11

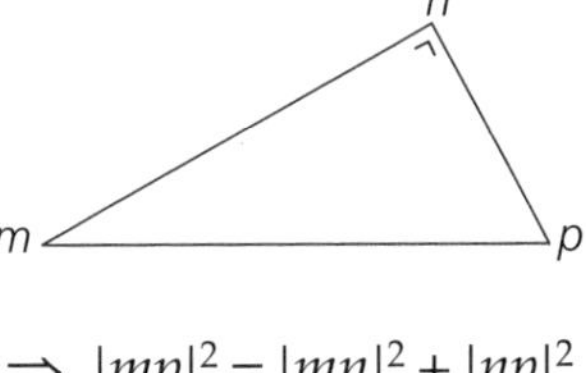

$$\Rightarrow |mp|^2 = |mn|^2 + |np|^2$$

'In a right-angled triangle, the square of the side opposite the right angle is equal to the sum of the squares of the lengths of the other two sides.'

⑩ If two triangles are equiangular, the lengths of corresponding sides are in proportion.

Given $\triangle abc$ and $\triangle def$ which are equiangular such that

$(\bullet) = (\bullet)$ $(\times) = (\times)$ and $|\angle 1| = |\angle 2|$

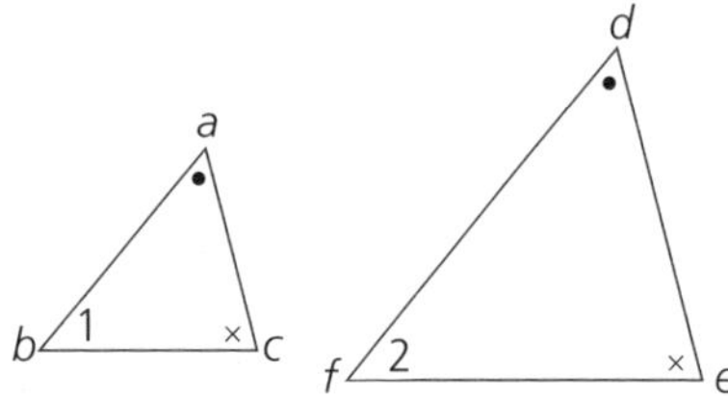

To prove $\dfrac{|ab|}{|df|} = \dfrac{|ac|}{|de|} = \dfrac{|bc|}{|fe|}$

Construction Mark pt. g on $[df]$ such that $|dg| = |ab|$. Mark pt. h on $[de]$ such that $|dh| = |ac|$.

Join g to h. Also mark in angle 3.

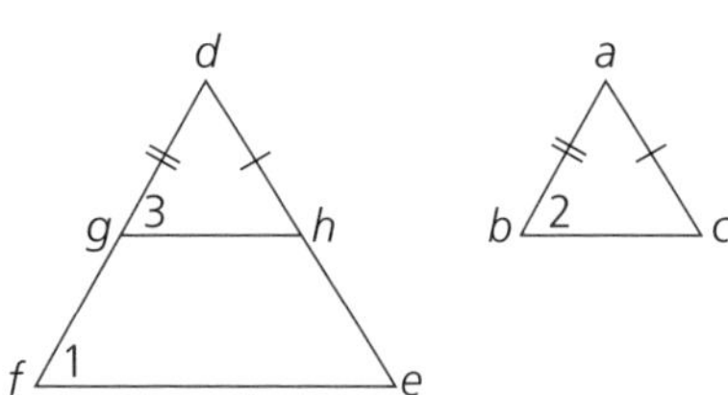

Proof

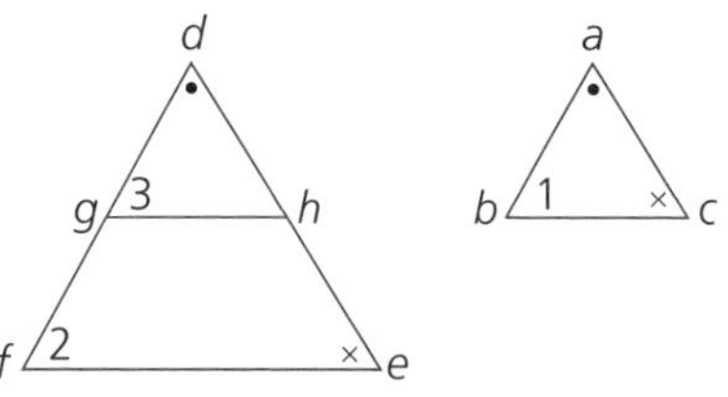

Consider $\triangle dgh$ and $\triangle abc$.

(i) $|dg| = |ab|$ ... given

$|dh| = |ac|$ ... given

(ii) $(\bullet) = (\bullet)$ ... given

(iii) $\Rightarrow$ $\triangle dgh$ is congruent to $\triangle abc$ ... SAS

Therefore $|\angle 3| = |\angle 2|$ ... corresponding.

But $|\angle 1| = |\angle 2|$

$\Rightarrow$ $|\angle 3| = |\angle 1|$

Therefore $[gh] \parallel [fe]$

A line drawn parallel to the base of a triangle divides the other two sides in the same ratio.

$$\Rightarrow \quad \frac{|dg|}{|gf|} = \frac{|dh|}{|he|}$$

So $\dfrac{|dg|}{|df|} = \dfrac{|dh|}{|de|}$

As $|dg|=|ab|$ and $|dh|=|ac|$

$$\frac{|ab|}{|df|} = \frac{|ac|}{|de|}$$

Similarly $\dfrac{|ab|}{|df|} = \dfrac{|bc|}{|fe|}$

$$\Rightarrow \quad \frac{|ab|}{|df|} = \frac{|ac|}{|de|} = \frac{|bc|}{|fe|}$$

Important Questions on Theorem 10

Question 1

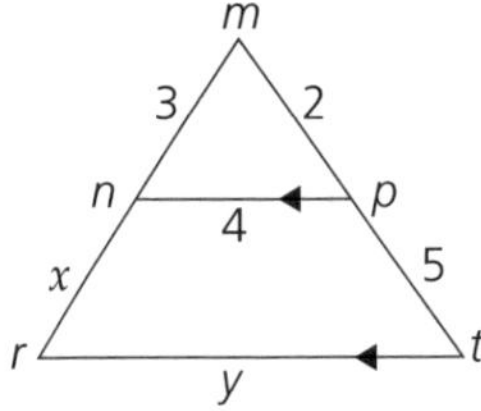

Evaluate x and y given $[np]$ // $[rt]$.

Find x.

> **Important**
>
> $[np]$ // $[rt]$
>
> $\Rightarrow$ $[mr]$ and $[mt]$ are divided in the same ratio.

$$\Rightarrow \frac{3}{x} = \frac{2}{5}$$

Cross-multiplying ... $(3)(5) = (2)(x)$

$15 = 2x \quad \Rightarrow \quad \boxed{x = 7\frac{1}{2}}$

Find y.

> **Important**
>
> In a question of this type, when we are asked to find the length of one of the horizontal sides:
>
> ① Draw each triangle separately.
>
> ② Write down the ratios involving the corresponding sides.

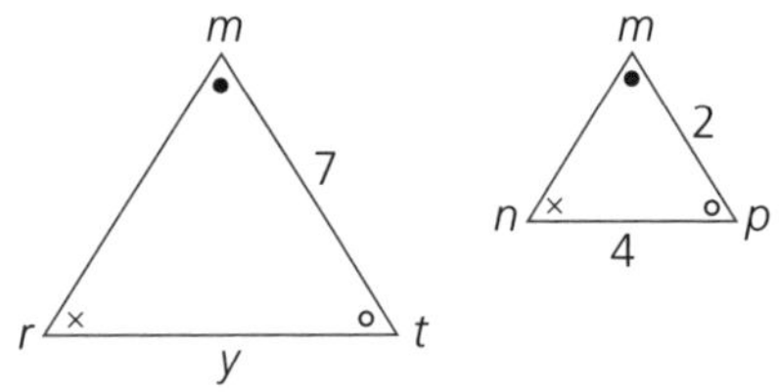

$$\Rightarrow \frac{7}{2} = \frac{y}{4} \quad 28 = 2y \quad \Rightarrow \boxed{14 = y}$$

Question 2

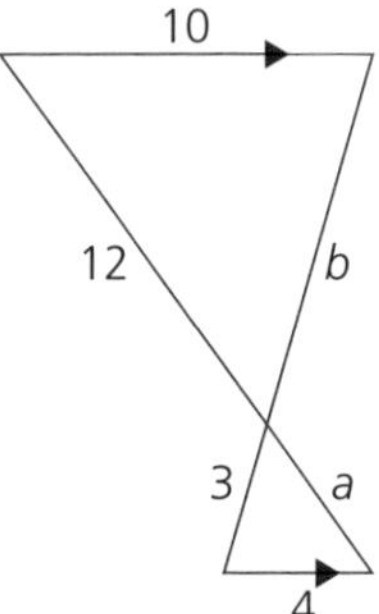

The arrows indicate that the lines are parallel. Evaluate a and b.

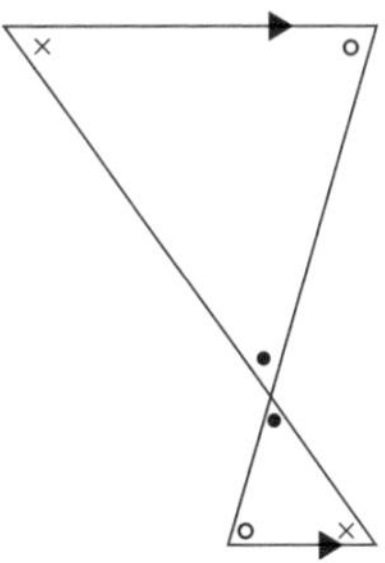

$(\times) = (\times)$ ... alternate angles

$(\circ) = (\circ)$ ... alternate angles

$(\bullet) = (\bullet)$ ... vertically opposite

> Before proceeding, be clear about which sides are corresponding.

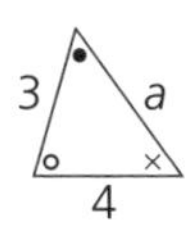

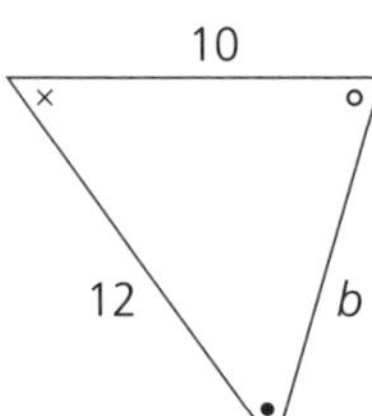

Find a.

$$\frac{10}{4} = \frac{12}{a}$$

$$48 = 10a$$

$$\Rightarrow 4.8 = a$$

Find b.

$$\frac{10}{4} = \frac{b}{3}$$

$$\Rightarrow 30 = 4b$$

$$7.5 = b$$

⑪ In a right-angled triangle, the square of the side opposite to the right angle is equal to the sum of the squares of the lengths of the other two sides.

Given $\triangle abc$ with $|\angle abc| = 90°$

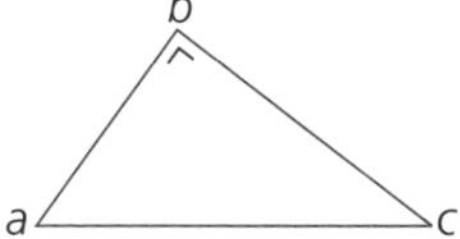

To prove $|ac|^2 = |ab|^2 + |bc|^2$

Construction Draw $[bd]$ such that $d \in [ac]$ and $[bd] \perp [ac]$.

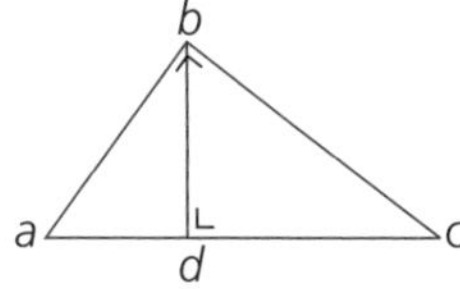

Proof

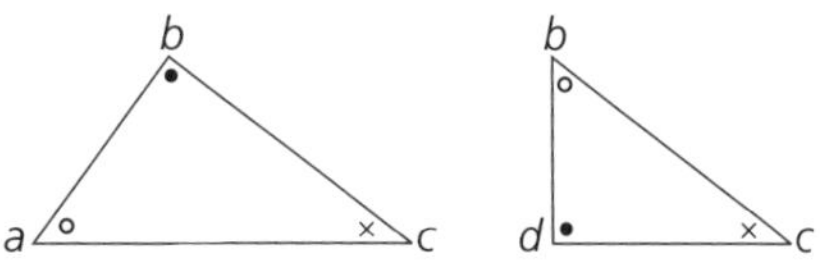

Consider $\triangle abc$ and $\triangle bdc$.

(•) = (•) ... both 90°

(×) = (×) ... same angle

(∘) = (∘) ... 3rd angle

$\Rightarrow$ $\triangle abc$ and $\triangle bcd$ are similar

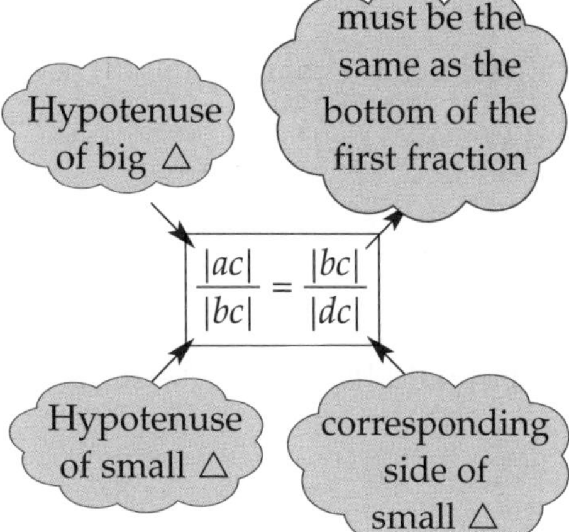

Cross-multiplying:

$|ac|.|dc| = |bc|^2$

Consider $\triangle abc$ and $\triangle abd$.

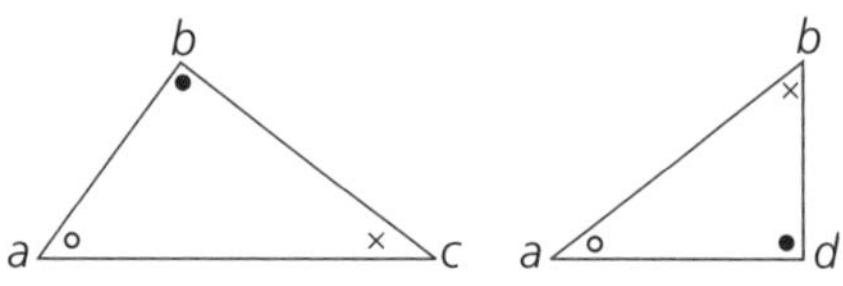

(•) = (•) ... both 90°

(∘) = (∘) ... same angle

(×) = (×) ... 3rd angle

① $|ac|$ over ② $|ab|$ = $|ab|$ ③ over $|ad|$ ④

$$\frac{|ac|}{|ab|} = \frac{|ab|}{|ad|}$$

① = Hyp. of big △
② = Hyp. of small △
③ Must be same as ②
④ Corresponding side on small △

Cross-multiplying: $|ac|.|ad| = |ab|^2$

Adding both results ...

$|bc|^2 + |ab|^2 = |ac|.|dc| + |ac|.|ad|$

$\Rightarrow\ |bc|^2 + |ab|^2 = |ac|(|dc| + |ad|)$

But from the diagram we see that

$|dc| + |ad| = |ac|$

$\Rightarrow |bc|^2 + |ab|^2 = |ac|.|ac|$

$\Rightarrow |bc|^2 + |ab|^2 = |ac|^2$

Important Questions on Theorem 11

Question 1

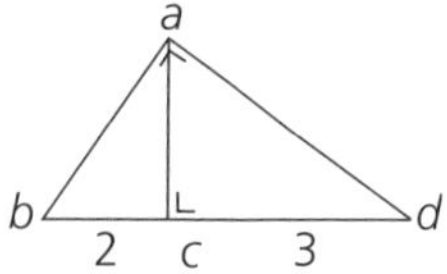

In the diagram, $|\angle bad| = 90°$, $|bc| = 2$ and $|cd| = 3$. If $[ac] \perp [bd]$ evaluate $|ab|$.

Important

$|ab|$ is on both $\triangle abc$ and $\triangle abd$. Therefore we:

① Draw each triangle separately.
② Prove they are similar.
③ Write the ratios involving corresponding sides.

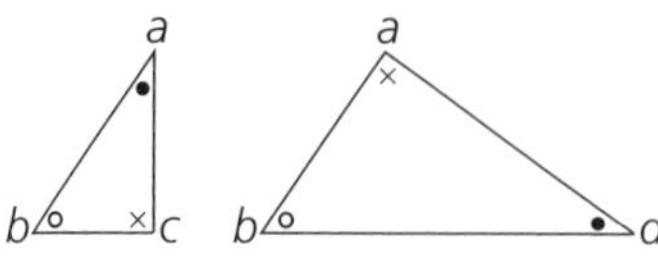

$(\times) = (\times)$ ... both 90°
$(\circ) = (\circ)$ ... same angle
$(\bullet) = (\bullet)$ ... 3rd angle

Find $|ab|$

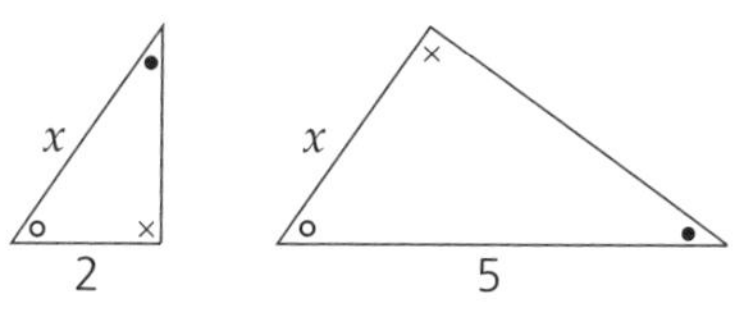

$$\Rightarrow \frac{x}{5} = \frac{2}{x} \quad 10 = x^2 \quad \Rightarrow \sqrt{10} = x$$

So, $|ab| = \sqrt{10}$

Question 2

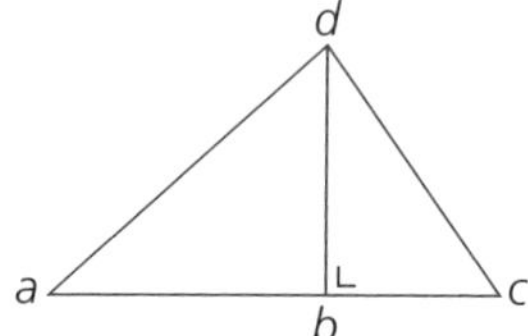

Prove $|dc|^2 + |ab|^2 = |ad|^2 + |bc|^2$

Solution

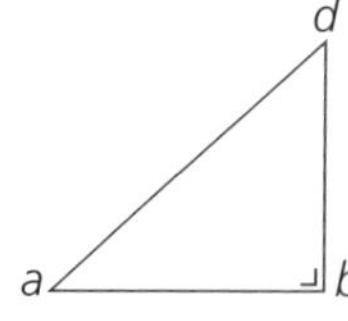

Draw each triangle separately.

$|ad|^2 = |ab|^2 + |bd|^2$

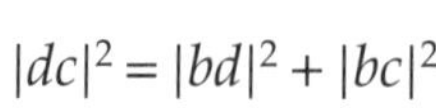

$|dc|^2 = |bd|^2 + |bc|^2$

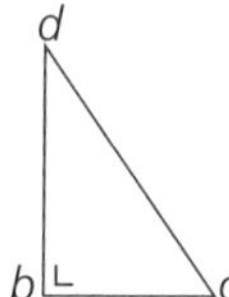

* The common side in both expressions is $[bd]$. So we write both in terms of $[bd]$.

$\lvert ad\rvert^2 = \lvert ab\rvert^2 + \lvert bd\rvert^2$	$\lvert dc\rvert^2 = \lvert bd\rvert^2 + \lvert bc\rvert^2$
⇓	⇓
$\lvert bd\rvert^2 = \lvert ad\rvert^2 - \lvert ab\rvert^2$	$\lvert bd\rvert^2 = \lvert dc\rvert^2 - \lvert bc\rvert^2$

$\Rightarrow\ |ad|^2 - |ab|^2 = |dc|^2 - |bc|^2$

$\Rightarrow\ |ad|^2 + |bc|^2 = |dc|^2 + |ab|^2$

Chapter 11A
Sample questions for you to try

Question 1

(a)

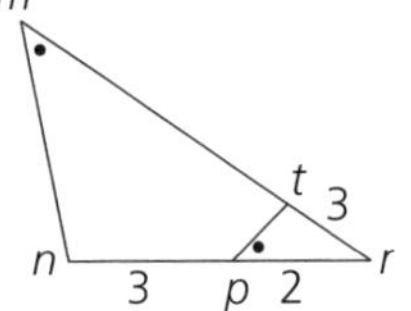

In the given diagram, $|\angle nmr| = |\angle tpr|$

(i) Prove $\triangle mnr$ and $\triangle tpr$ are similar.

(ii) Hence evaluate $|mr|$.

(b)

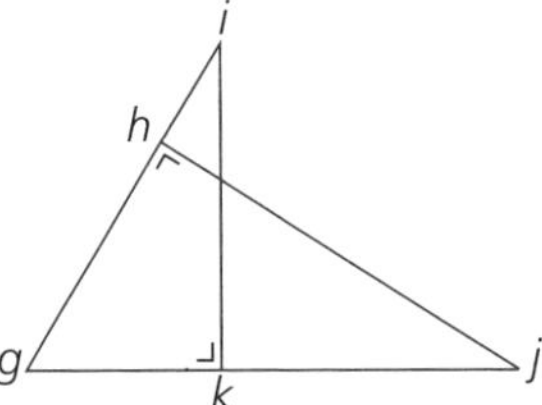

In the diagram, $[gj] \perp [ik]$ and $[gi] \perp [hj]$
$|ik| = |gh| = 6$

(i) Prove that $\triangle ghj$ and $\triangle gik$ are similar.

(ii) Hence evaluate $|hj| . |gk|$

Question 2

(a) Prove that in a right-angled triangle, the square of the side opposite the right angle is equal to the sum of the squares of the lengths of the other two sides.

(b)

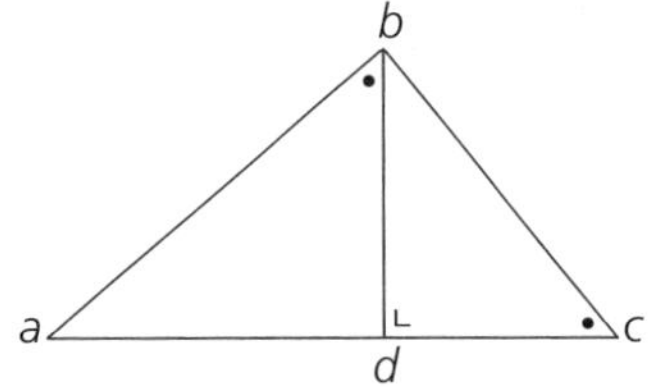

In the diagram, $|ab| = 4$, $|ad| = 3$ and $[ac] \perp [bd]$. Evaluate $|ac|$.

Question 3

(a) Prove that if two triangles are equiangular, the lengths of corresponding sides are proportional.

(b)

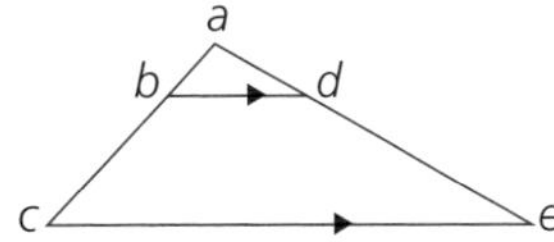

In the diagram, $|ab| = 2$
$|bc| = 5$, $|ae| = 10.5$ and $|bd| = 4$.

Calculate:

(i) $|ad|$ **(ii)** $|ce|$

Solution to question 1

(a)

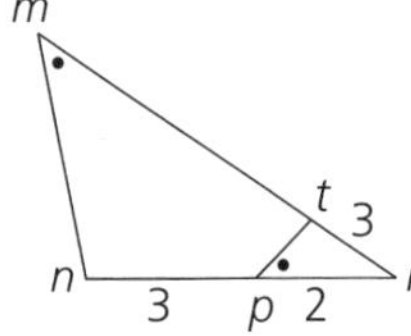

(i) Prove $\triangle mnr$ and $\triangle tpr$ are similar.

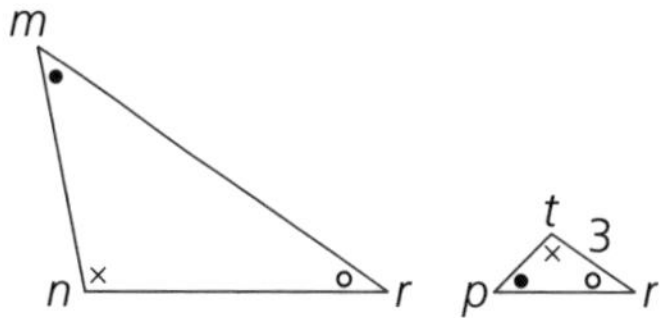

(•) = (•) ... given

(∘) = (∘) ... same angle

(×) = (×) ... third angle in the triangle

$\Rightarrow$ $\triangle mnr$ and $\triangle tpr$ are similar

(ii) Calculate $|mr|$.

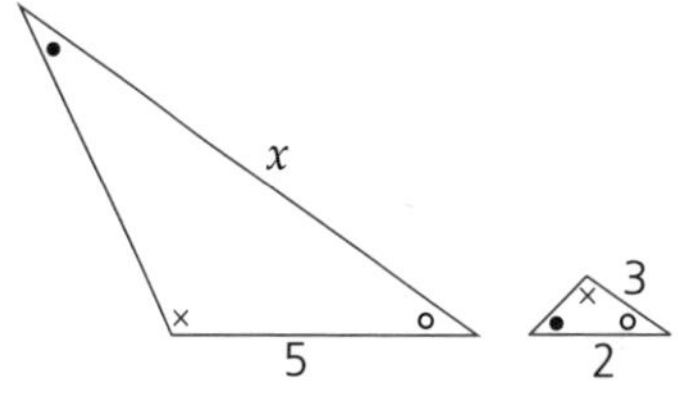

$\frac{5}{3} = \frac{x}{2}$ $10 = 3x$ $\Rightarrow 3\frac{1}{3} = x$

So $|mr| = 3\frac{1}{3}$

(b) $|ik| = |gh| = 6$

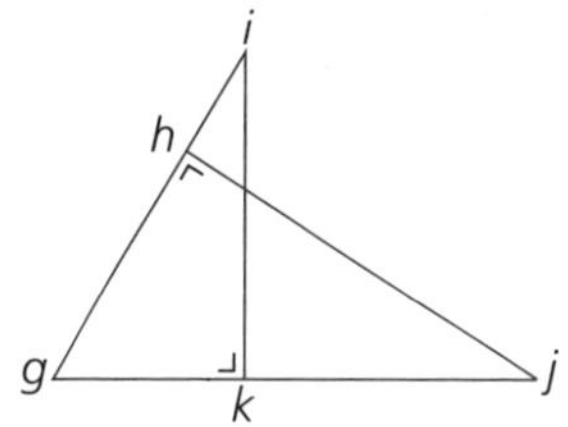

(i) Prove $\triangle gij$ and $\triangle gik$ are similar.

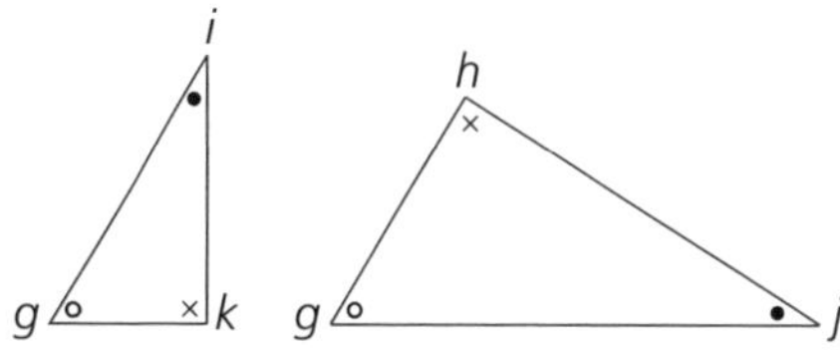

(×) = (×) ... both 90°

(∘) = (∘) ... same angle

(•) = (•) ... third angle

$\Rightarrow$ $\triangle ghj$ and $\triangle gik$ are similar

(ii) Evaluate $|hj| . |gk|$

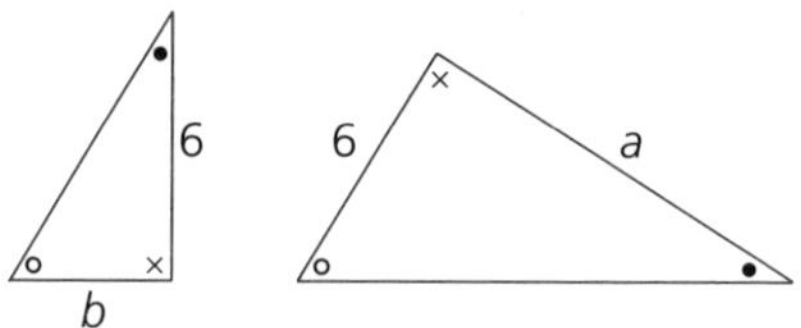

$\Rightarrow \frac{b}{6} = \frac{6}{a}$ $\Rightarrow ab = 36$

So $|hj| . |gk| = 36$

Solution to question 2

(a) Please view the proof of theorem 11 earlier in this chapter.

(b)

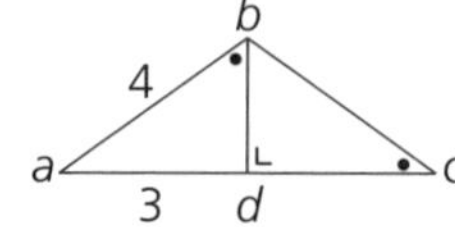

Calculate $|ac|$.

Important

We have the measure of two sides of $\triangle adb$. We are asked to evaluate $|ac|$ which is on the $\triangle abc$.

Therefore, we draw these two triangles separately.

$(\bullet) = (\bullet)$ ... given

$(\times) = (\times)$ ... same angle

$(\circ) = (\circ)$ ... third angle

$\Rightarrow \dfrac{4}{x} = \dfrac{3}{4} \qquad \Rightarrow 16 = 3x$

$$5\frac{1}{3} = x$$

$$\boxed{\text{So } |ac| = 5\frac{1}{3}}$$

Solution to question 3

(a) Please view the proof of theorem 10 earlier in this chapter.

(b)

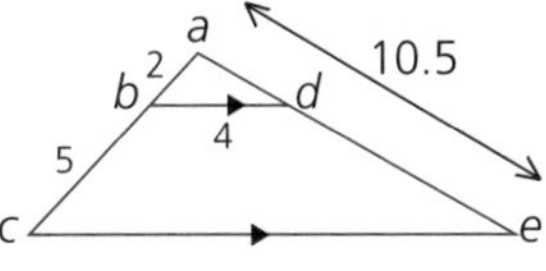

(i) Calculate $|ad|$.

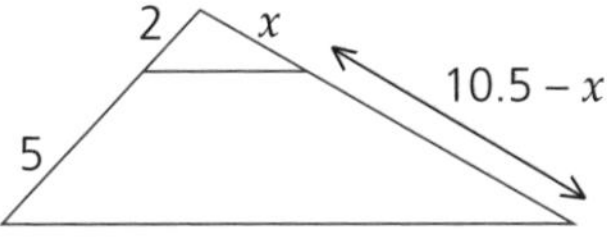

$$\frac{2}{5} = \frac{x}{10.5 - x}$$

$$\Rightarrow (2)(10.5 - x) = 5x$$

$$21 - 2x = 5x$$

$$\Rightarrow 21 = 7x$$

$$\boxed{\text{So } |ad| = 3}$$

(ii) Calculate $|ce|$.

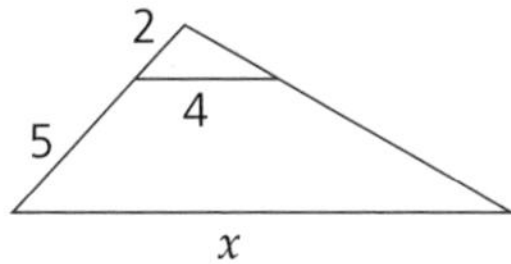

> Again, because we are asked to evaluate one of the horizontal lines, we draw the two triangles separately.

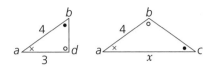

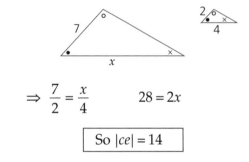

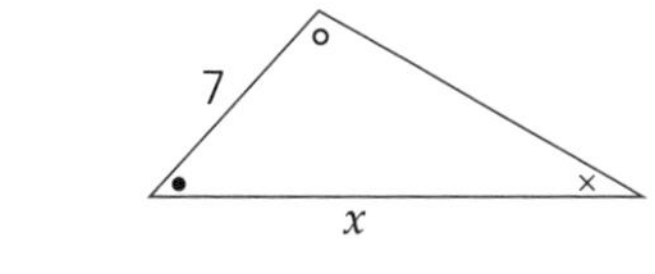

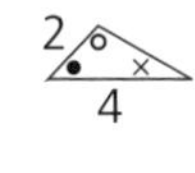

$\Rightarrow \dfrac{7}{2} = \dfrac{x}{4} \qquad 28 = 2x$

$$\boxed{\text{So } |ce| = 14}$$

Chapter 12
Trigonometry

Using your calculator

Sharp calculator	Casio calculator
DMS	° ′ ″
2nd F	Shift

* It is very important to check that your calculator is in 'Deg' mode before you use it.

Sharp → 'Deg' must be on screen. If 'Grad' or 'Rad' is on the screen, use the DRG button to change this.

Casio → 'D' must be on screen. If 'G' or 'R' is on the screen, use the MODE button to change this.

(i) Evaluate Cos 78°19′.

Cos 78 DMS 19 DMS = 0.2025

(ii) Evaluate angle A if Tan $A = 0.247$

2nd F Tan 0.247 = 13.874

2nd F DMS 13°52′

With the older type of Sharp scientific calculator, it is not necessary to press the 2nd F button here.

(iii) Evaluate angle B such that:

$$\text{Cos } B = \frac{2}{7}$$

2nd F Cos (2 ÷ 7) = 73.398

2nd F DMS 73°23′

Obviously we must always write our answer in degrees and minutes.

Notice that when changing from a decimal answer we do not press the = button.

Section A

The unit circle

Type 1

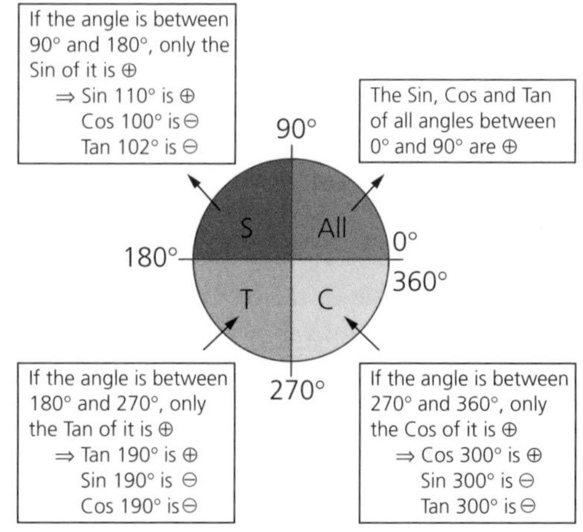

If the angle is between 90° and 180°, only the Sin of it is ⊕
⇒ Sin 110° is ⊕
Cos 100° is ⊖
Tan 102° is ⊖
The Sin, Cos and Tan of all angles between 0° and 90° are ⊕
90°
S
All
180°
0°
360°
T
C
270°
If the angle is between 180° and 270°, only the Tan of it is ⊕
⇒ Tan 190° is ⊕
Sin 190° is ⊖
Cos 190° is ⊖
If the angle is between 270° and 360°, only the Cos of it is ⊕
⇒ Cos 300° is ⊕
Sin 300° is ⊖
Tan 300° is ⊖

Example 1

Evaluate angle A such that $\text{Cos } A = \frac{2}{3}$.

> Here the Cos of angle A is positive. We see from the unit circle that angle A is in the 'All' quadrant and also in the 'C' quadrant.

'All' quadrant

[2nd F] [Cos] $(2 \div 3) = 48.189$

[2nd F] [DMS] $48°11'$

We must now find our value of A in the 'C' quadrant.

> **Important**
>
> When evaluating, angles in the 'S', 'T' or 'C' quadrants, add or subtract to/from 180° or 360°.
>
> * Never add or subtract to or from 90° or 270°.

'C' quadrant

$$A = 360° - 48°11'$$
$$= 311°49'$$

$\Rightarrow$ $\underline{\underline{A = 48°11'}}$ and also $\underline{\underline{311°49'}}$

Example 2

Evaluate angle B if $\text{Sin } B = -0.241$

> Because the Sin of this angle is negative, angle B cannot be in the 'All' or 'S' quadrants. Therefore angle B can only be in the 'T' or 'C' quadrants.

$\text{Sin } B = -0.241$

Evaluate the angle whose Sin is $+0.241$

If $\text{Sin } C = +0.241 \quad C = 13°56'$

'T' quadrant

$$B = 180° + 13°56' = \underline{\underline{193°56'}}$$

'C' quadrant

$$B = 360° - 13°56' = \underline{\underline{346°4'}}$$

Example 3

Evaluate angle C such that

$\text{Tan } C = -0.4$ and $90° \leqslant C \leqslant 270°$

> The Tan of angle C is ⊖. Therefore C would normally be in the 'S' and 'C' quadrants.
>
> But we are told angle C must be between 90° and 270°.
>
> $\Rightarrow$ Angle C can only be in the 'S' quadrant.

(i) Again, evaluate the angle whose Tan is $+0.4$

If $\text{Tan } D = +0.4 \quad D = 21°48'$

(ii) Evaluate angle C.

'S' Quadrant

$$C = 180° - 21°48' = \underline{\underline{158°12'}}$$

Unit circle

Type 2

Sin and Cos of 90°, 180°, 270° and 360°.

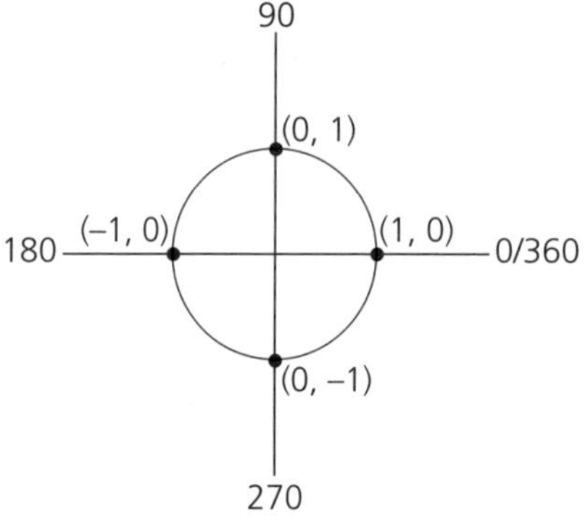

Note 1

This circle is called a 'unit' circle because it has a radius of one unit. Therefore we find the given points [(−1, 0) etc.] by going up and down 1 unit on both the 'x' and 'y' axes.

Note 2

The coordinates of any point on the unit circle are (Cos θ, Sin θ).

$\Rightarrow$ From the diagram we see

Cos 270° = 0   Sin 270° = −1

Cos 180° = −1   Sin 180° = 0 etc.

Example 1

Evaluate angle A such that:

$$\text{Sin } A = 0$$

Because each point on the unit circle can be written as (Cos θ, Sin θ), we look for the point whose second coordinate is 0.

(−1, 0) is at 180°

$\Rightarrow$ Sin 180° = 0

(1, 0) is at 0°/360°

$\Rightarrow$ Sin 0° = 0

$\Rightarrow$ $A = 0°$ and also 180°

Section B

Page 9 of the Mathematical (Log) Tables.

On page 9 of the 'Log' tables we are given the Sin, Cos and Tan of specific angles with the results expressed in surd ($\sqrt{\ }$) form or as a fraction or whole number.

Important

In this table, $\boxed{\pi = 180°}$

$$\Rightarrow \frac{\pi}{2} = 90° \quad \frac{\pi}{3} = 60° \quad \frac{\pi}{4} = 45° \text{ etc.}$$

From the table we see that:

$$\text{Sin } 60° = \text{Sin } \frac{\pi}{3} = \frac{\sqrt{3}}{2}$$

$$\text{Cos } 45° = \text{Cos } \frac{\pi}{4} = \frac{1}{\sqrt{2}}$$

$$\text{Tan } 30° = \text{Tan } \frac{\pi}{6} = \frac{1}{\sqrt{3}} \quad \text{etc.}$$

A	0	π	$\frac{\pi}{2}$	$\frac{\pi}{3}$	$\frac{\pi}{4}$	$\frac{\pi}{6}$
Cos A	1	-1	0	$\frac{1}{2}$	$\frac{1}{\sqrt{2}}$	$\frac{\sqrt{3}}{2}$
Sin A	0	0	1	$\frac{\sqrt{3}}{2}$	$\frac{1}{\sqrt{2}}$	$\frac{1}{2}$
Tan A	0	0	gan sainmhíniú not defined	$\sqrt{3}$	1	$\frac{1}{\sqrt{3}}$

Example 1

Without using a calculator, write each of the following in surd form:

(i) $\text{Sin}^2 30° \times \text{Cos}^2 45°$

(ii) $\text{Cos}^2 30° + \text{Sin}^2 45°$

> **Note 1** – 'In surd form' means leave the answer as a $\sqrt{\ }$.
> **Note 2** – $\text{Sin}^2 60° = (\text{Sin } 60°)^2$ etc.

(i) $\text{Sin}^2 30° \times \text{Cos}^2 45°$

$$\Downarrow$$

$$(\text{Sin } 30°)^2 \times (\text{Cos } 45°)^2$$

$$\Downarrow$$

$$\left(\text{Sin } \frac{\pi}{6}\right)^2 \times \left(\text{Cos } \frac{\pi}{4}\right)^2$$

$$\downarrow \qquad \downarrow$$

$$\left(\frac{1}{2}\right)^2 \times \left(\frac{1}{\sqrt{2}}\right)^2$$

$$\downarrow \qquad \downarrow$$

$$\left(\frac{1}{2}\right)\left(\frac{1}{2}\right) \times \left(\frac{1}{\sqrt{2}}\right)\left(\frac{1}{\sqrt{2}}\right)$$

$$\downarrow \qquad \downarrow$$

$$\frac{1}{4} \times \frac{1}{2}$$

$$\Rightarrow \text{Sin}^2 30° \times \text{Cos}^2 45° = \boxed{\frac{1}{8}}$$

(ii) $\text{Cos}^2 30° + \text{Sin}^2 45°$

$$\Downarrow$$

$$(\text{Cos } 30°)^2 + (\text{Sin } 45°)^2$$

$$\Downarrow$$

$$\left(\text{Cos } \frac{\pi}{6}\right)^2 + \left(\text{Sin } \frac{\pi}{4}\right)^2$$

$$\downarrow \qquad \downarrow$$

$$\left(\frac{\sqrt{3}}{2}\right)^2 + \left(\frac{1}{\sqrt{2}}\right)^2$$

$$\downarrow \qquad \downarrow$$

$$\left(\frac{\sqrt{3}}{2}\right)\left(\frac{\sqrt{3}}{2}\right) + \left(\frac{1}{\sqrt{2}}\right)\left(\frac{1}{\sqrt{2}}\right)$$

$$\downarrow \qquad \downarrow$$

$$\frac{3}{4} + \frac{1}{2}$$

$$\Rightarrow \text{Cos}^2 30° + \text{Sin}^2 45° = \frac{3}{4} + \frac{1}{2} = \boxed{1\frac{1}{4}}$$

Example 2

Without using the calculator, evaluate a and b.

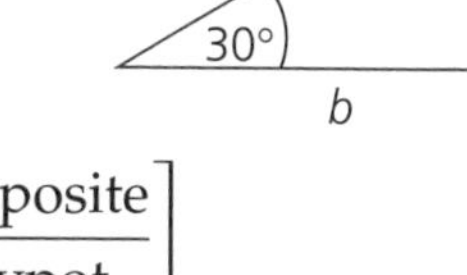

Find a.

$$\text{Sin } 30° = \frac{a}{6} \quad \left[\frac{\text{Opposite}}{\text{Hypot.}}\right]$$

From page 9 of the log tables

we see that $\text{Sin } \frac{\pi}{6} = \frac{1}{2}$

$$\Rightarrow \frac{a}{6} = \frac{1}{2}$$

Cross-multiplying: $2a = 6$

$$\boxed{a = 3}$$

Find b.

$\text{Cos } 30° = \frac{b}{6}$ $\left[\frac{\text{Adjacent}}{\text{Hypot.}}\right]$

$\Rightarrow$ As $\text{Cos } \frac{\pi}{6} = \frac{\sqrt{3}}{2}$

$\frac{\sqrt{3}}{2} = \frac{b}{6}$ $\Rightarrow (6)(\sqrt{3}) = 2b$

$\Rightarrow \frac{6\sqrt{3}}{2} = b$ $\Rightarrow$ $\boxed{3\sqrt{3} = b}$

Section C

Constructing angles

Example 1

Construct angle B if $\text{Sin } B = \frac{3}{5}$. Hence express Tan B in the form $\frac{a}{b}$ where $a, b \in Z$.

① Draw a rough diagram.

Silly **O**ld **H**arry $\Rightarrow \text{Sin} = \left[\frac{\text{Opposite}}{\text{Hypot.}}\right]$

Caught **A** **H**erring $\Rightarrow \text{Cos} = \left[\frac{\text{Adjacent}}{\text{Hypot.}}\right]$

Trawling **O**ff **A**merica $\Rightarrow \text{Tan} = \left[\frac{\text{Opposite}}{\text{Adjacent}}\right]$

$\text{Sin } B = \frac{3}{5} = \left[\frac{\text{Opposite}}{\text{Hypot.}}\right]$

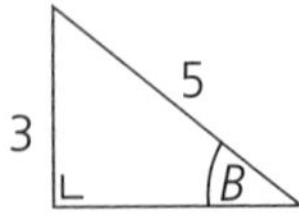

② Draw an exact diagram.

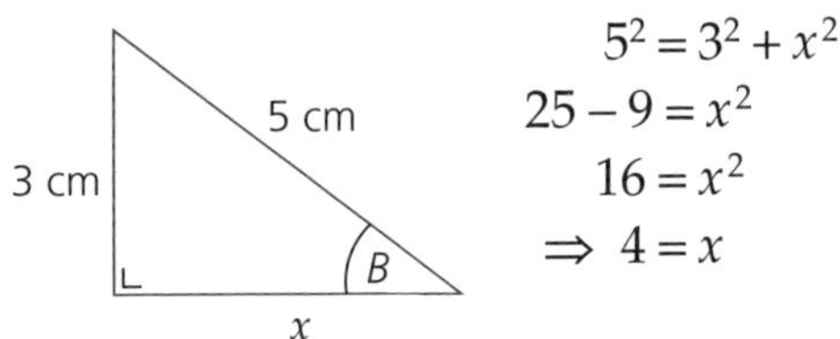

$5^2 = 3^2 + x^2$

$25 - 9 = x^2$

$16 = x^2$

$\Rightarrow 4 = x$

$\text{Tan } B = \left[\frac{\text{Opposite}}{\text{Adjacent}}\right] = \boxed{\frac{3}{4}}$

Example 2

Given 3 Cos $A = 2$, construct angle A. Hence, without using a calculator, evaluate 2 Tan A. Leave your answer in surd form.

> In order to construct any angle, the Sin, Cos or Tan must be written as a fraction.
>
> $3 \text{ Cos } A = 2 \qquad \Rightarrow \text{Cos } A = \frac{2}{3}$

$\text{Cos } A = \frac{2}{3} = \frac{\text{Adjacent}}{\text{Hypot.}}$

Rough diagram

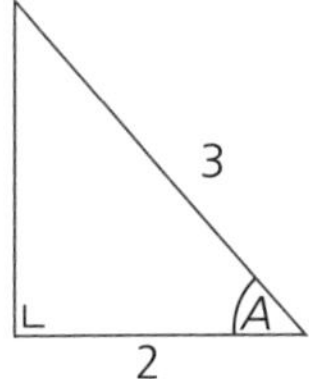

Correct diagram

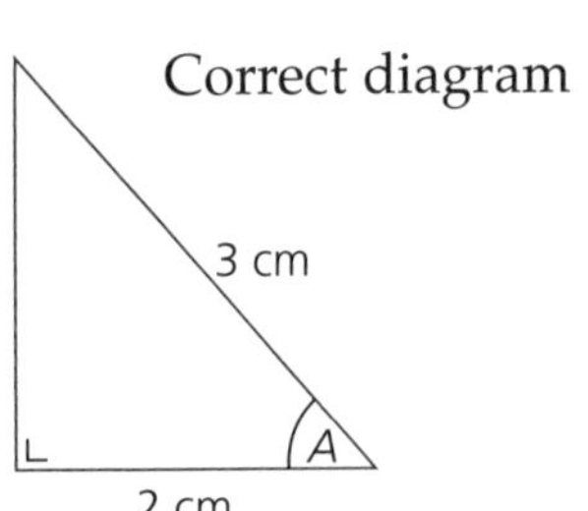

Evaluate Tan A

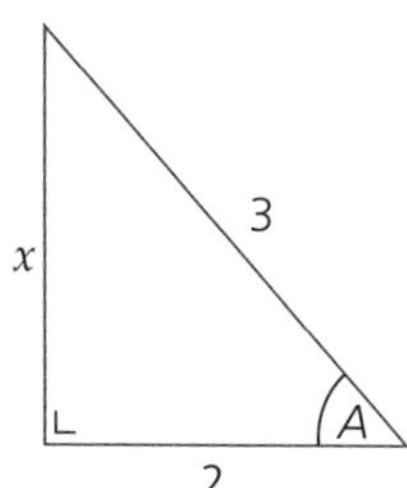

$$3^2 = x^2 + 2^2$$
$$9 - 4 = x^2$$
$$\boxed{\sqrt{5} = x}$$

$$\Rightarrow \text{Tan } A = \frac{\text{Opposite}}{\text{Adjacent}} = \frac{\sqrt{5}}{2}$$

$$\Rightarrow 2 \text{ Tan } A = 2\left(\frac{\sqrt{5}}{2}\right) = \boxed{\sqrt{5}}$$

Section D

Area of a triangle

$$\text{Area} = \tfrac{1}{2}ab \text{ Sin } C$$

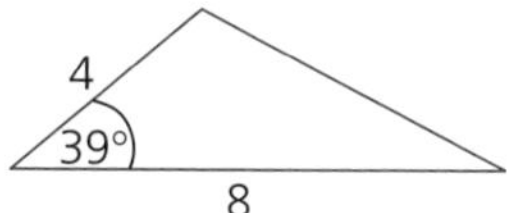

'Half the product of any two sides multiplied by the Sin of the angle between them.'

$\Rightarrow$ Area $= \frac{1}{2}(4)(8)(\text{Sin } 39°)$

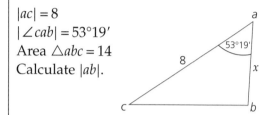

Example 1

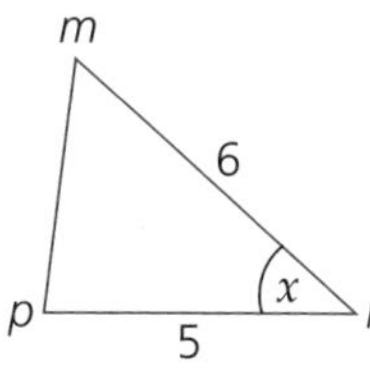

Area $\triangle mnp = 10$
$|mn| = 6 \quad |pn| = 5$
Calculate $|\angle mnp|$.

$\Rightarrow \frac{1}{2}(5)(6)(\text{Sin } x) = 10$

* Isolate Sin x...

$15 \text{ Sin } x = 10 \quad \Rightarrow \text{Sin } x = \dfrac{10}{15}$

[2nd F] [Sin] [(] 10 ÷ 15 [)] = 41.81°

[2nd F] [DMS] 41°48′

Example 2

$|ac| = 8$
$|\angle cab| = 53°19'$
Area $\triangle abc = 14$
Calculate $|ab|$.

$\Rightarrow \frac{1}{2}(8)(x)(\text{Sin } 53°19') = 14$

$\Rightarrow (0.5)(8)(x)(0.802) = 14$

$\Rightarrow (3.2)(x) = 14$

$\Rightarrow x = \dfrac{14}{3.2}$

$\Rightarrow |ab| = 4.375$

Example 3

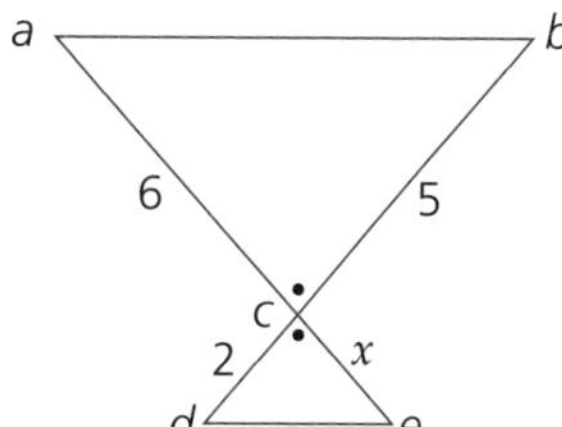

In the given diagram the area $\triangle abc$ is 5 times the area $\triangle cde$. Evaluate x.

Note

(•) = (•) ... vertically opposite

Area $\triangle abc = 5(\text{Area } \triangle cde)$

$$\Rightarrow \quad \frac{1}{2}(6)(5)(\text{Sin}\,\cdot) = 5\left(\frac{1}{2}\right)(2)(x)(\text{Sin}\,\cdot)$$

$$\Rightarrow \left(\cancel{\frac{1}{2}}\right)(6)(5)\cancel{(\text{Sin}\,\cdot)} = 5\left(\cancel{\frac{1}{2}}\right)(2)(x)\cancel{(\text{Sin}\,\cdot)}$$

$$\Rightarrow \quad (6)(5) = (5)(2)(x)$$

$$30 = 10x$$

$$\Rightarrow \quad \boxed{3 = x} \quad \Rightarrow \ |ce| = 3$$

Section E

The Sine Rule

Note 1

To use the Sine Rule we need the measure of a side, its opposite angle and one other piece of information (either a side or an angle).

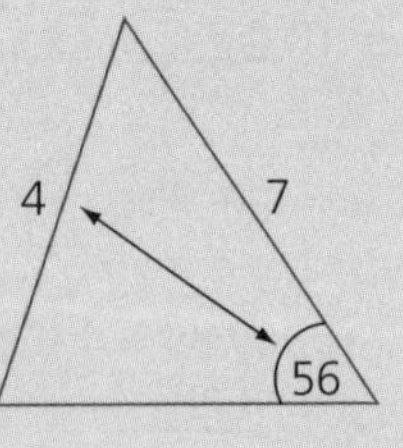

Note 2

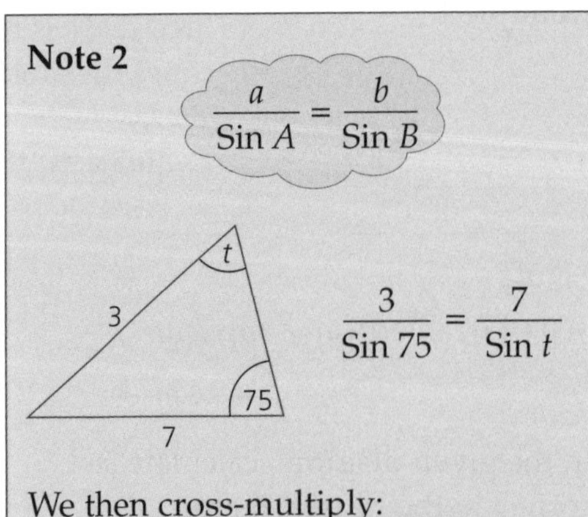

$$\frac{a}{\text{Sin } A} = \frac{b}{\text{Sin } B}$$

$$\frac{3}{\text{Sin } 75} = \frac{7}{\text{Sin } t}$$

We then cross-multiply:

$3(\text{Sin } t) = 7(\text{Sin } 75)$.....

Note 3

Important

If we are asked to find X, we can't make the statement below:

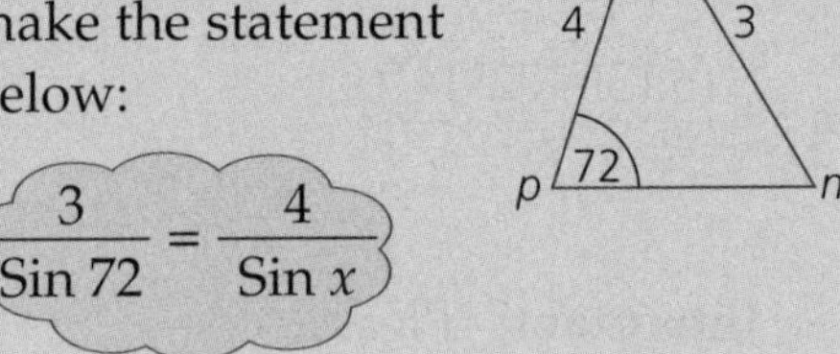

$$\frac{3}{\text{Sin } 72} = \frac{4}{\text{Sin } x}$$

because 4 and x are not opposite each other:

Solution

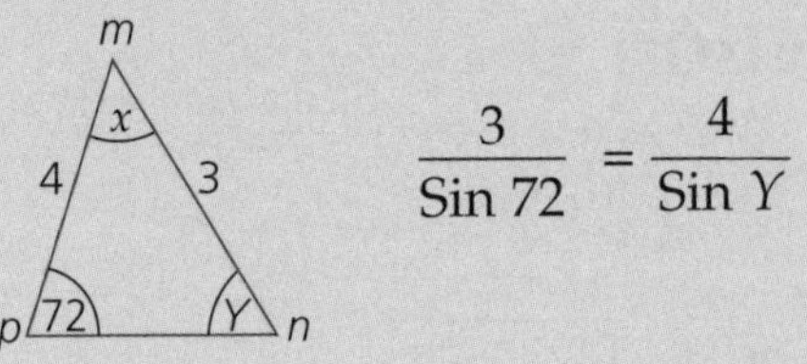

$$\frac{3}{\text{Sin } 72} = \frac{4}{\text{Sin } Y}$$

* This is correct because angle Y is opposite 4.
* When we find angle Y, we can then calculate angle x (the 3 angles add up to 180°).

Example 1

Calculate X.

Again we can't find X directly as we don't know the opposite side.

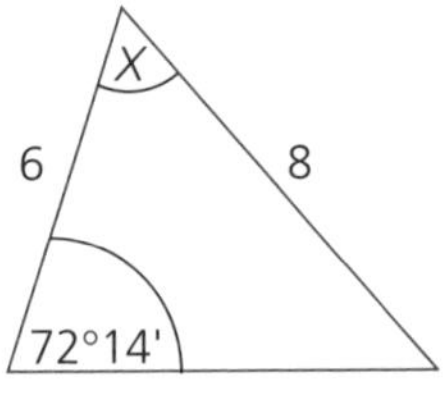

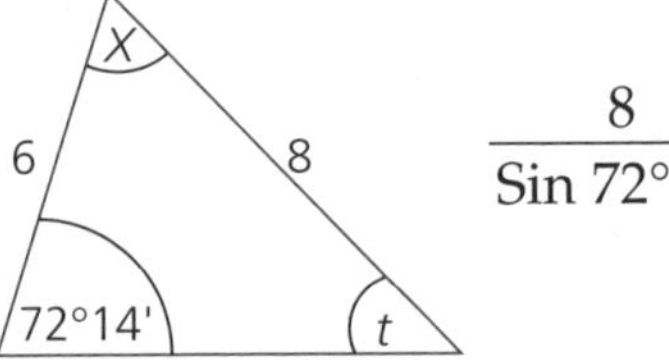

$$\frac{8}{\text{Sin } 72°14'} = \frac{6}{\text{Sin } t}$$

Cross-multiplying:
$(8)(\text{Sin } t) = (6)\ (\text{Sin } 72°14')$

$\Rightarrow$

> Sin 72°14′ = 0.952 (make this statement)
> (Showing you can calculate this correctly.)

$$\text{Sin } t = \frac{(6)(\text{Sin } 72°14')}{8}$$

> **Important** Please type Sin 72°14′ again when calculating Sin t.
>
> $\frac{6(0.952)}{8}$ → Will not give an exact answer.
>
> Will give an exact answer. ← $\frac{6(\text{Sin } 72°14')}{8}$

Sin t = 0.714230308

$\Rightarrow$ $t = 45°34'$

Evaluate X.

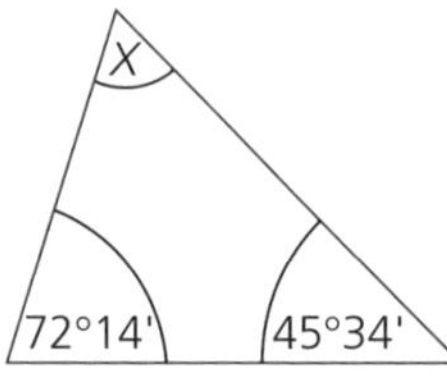

$X = 180° - (72°14' + 45°34')$

$X = 62°12'$

> Please remember to press DMS after the amount of minutes as well as the amount of degrees:
>
> $\Rightarrow$ 72°14′ + 45°34′
>
> = 72 DMS 14 DMS
>
> + 45 DMS 34 DMS

Example 2

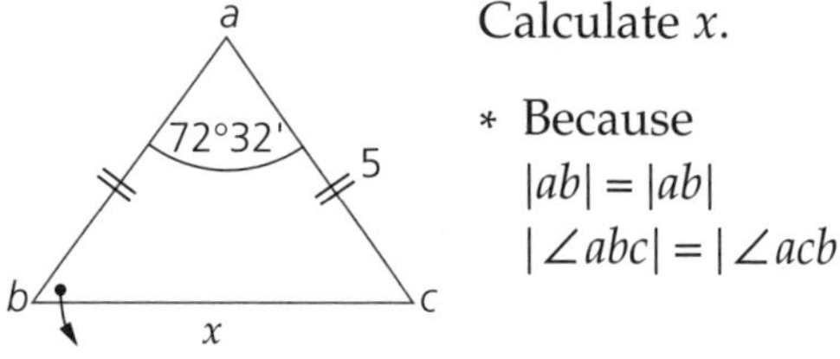

Calculate x.

* Because
$|ab| = |ab|$
$|\angle abc| = |\angle acb|$

> 180° − 72°32′ = 107°28′
> 107°28′ ÷ 2 = 53°44′

$$\frac{5}{\text{Sin } 53°44'} = \frac{x}{\text{Sin } 72°32}$$

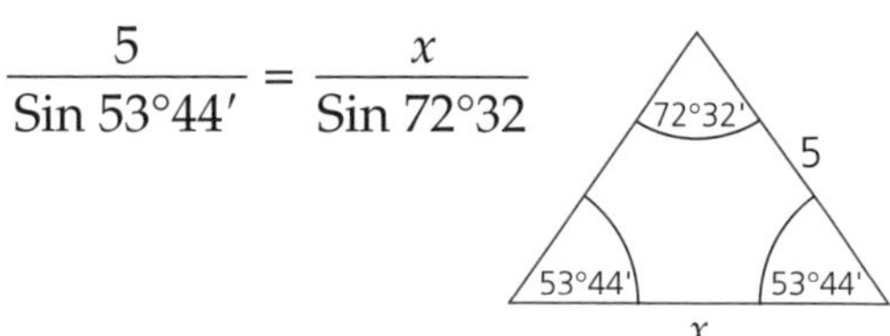

> Sin 53°44′ = 0.8063
> Sin 72°32′ = 0.954

(5)(Sin 72°32′) = (x)(Sin 53°44′)

$$\Rightarrow \frac{(5)(\text{Sin } 72°32')}{\text{Sin } 53°44'} = x$$

$\Rightarrow |bc| = 5.915$

Example 3

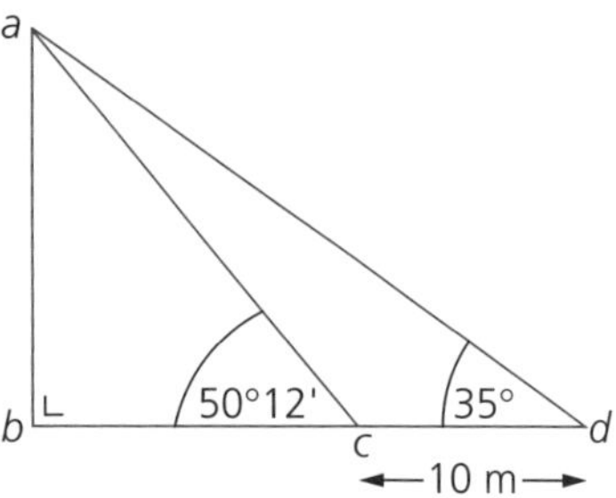

In the given diagram, calculate $|ab|$ correct to the nearest metre.

Step 1
Before starting, always find as many of the unknown angles as possible.

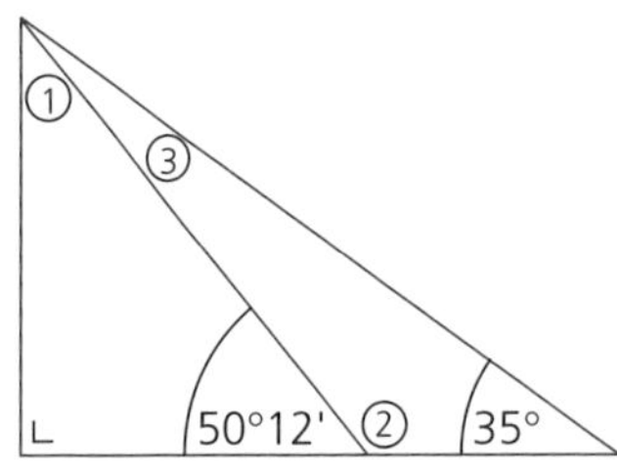

Angle ① $= 180° - (90° + 50°12')$
$= 39°48'$

Angle ② $= 180° - 50°12'$
$= 129°48'$

Angle ③ $= 180° - (35° + 129°48')$
$= 15°12'$

Step 2
We can't find $|ab|$ straight away (understand why). Therefore we first find $|ac|$.

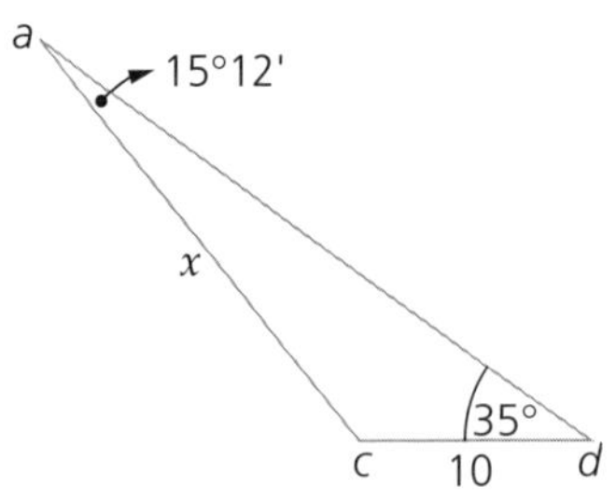

$$\frac{10}{\text{Sin } 15°12'} = \frac{x}{\text{Sin } 35°}$$

$\Rightarrow$ $10(\text{Sin } 35°) = x(\text{Sin } 15°12')$

$$\frac{10(\text{Sin } 35°)}{\text{Sin } 15°12'} = x$$

Sin 35° = 0.57357
Sin 15°12′ = 0.2621

$\Rightarrow$ $x = 21.876$

Step 3
We can now find $|ab|$.

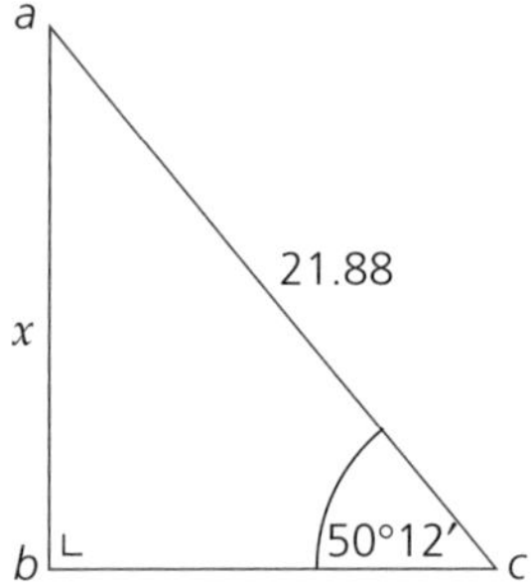

$$\frac{21.88}{\text{Sin } 90°} = \frac{x}{\text{Sin } 50°12'}$$

$\Rightarrow$ $(21.88)(\text{Sin } 50°12') = (\text{Sin } 90°)(x)$

$$\frac{(21.88)(\text{Sin } 50°12')}{\text{Sin } 90°} = x$$

Sin 90° = 1
Sin 50°12′ = 0.768

$\Rightarrow$ $x = 16.81$

$\Rightarrow$ $|ab| = 17$ m

Chapter 12
Sample questions for you to try

Question 1

(a) Construct angle A such that $4 \text{ Cos } A = 3$.
Hence evaluate Sin A, without using a calculator.

(b) In the given diagram $|pn| = |rp|$.

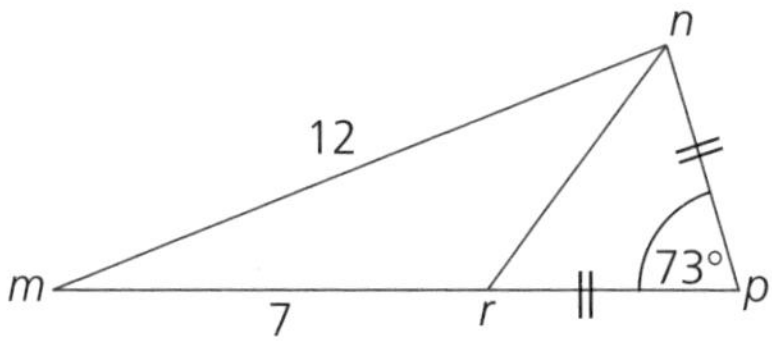

$|\angle nrp| = 73°$ $\quad |mr| = 7$ and $|mn| = 12$

If area $\triangle rnp = 7.65$, find:

(i) $|rp|$ **(ii)** $|\angle nrp|$ **(iii)** $|\angle mnr|$

(c) Given Tan $B = -1.88$, calculate two possible values of B.

Question 2

(a) In $\triangle abc$, $|ab| = 8$, $|bc| = 6$ and area of $\triangle abc = 14.1$. Find two possible values of $|\angle abc|$.

(b) In the given triangle, $|tr| = 2$, $|pr| = 2\sqrt{3}$.

Evaluate:

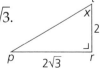

(i) $|\angle ptr|$ **(ii)** Area $\triangle ptr$ **(iii)** $|pt|$

(c) **(i)** Given $\text{Sin } A = \frac{-3}{4}$ evaluate angle A if $A > 270°$.

(ii) Hence investigate whether

$$\text{Cos } \frac{A}{2} = \frac{\text{Cos } A}{2}$$

Question 3

(a) **(i)** Construct angle A such that $\text{Sin } A = 0.4$

(ii) Evaluate $3 \text{ Cos } A$ leaving your answer in surd form.

(b) In the diagram

$|ad| = 13$, $\quad |ab| = 5$ and $|\angle bdc| = 52°$

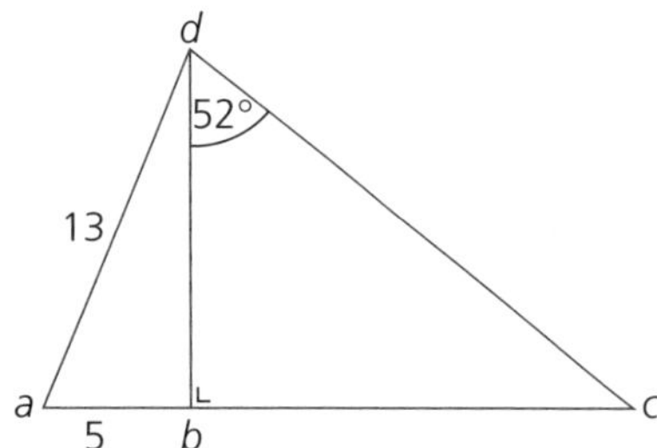

Evaluate **(i)** $|\angle dab|$ **(ii)** $|bd|$

(iii) $|bc|$ **(iv)** Area $\triangle adc$

(c)

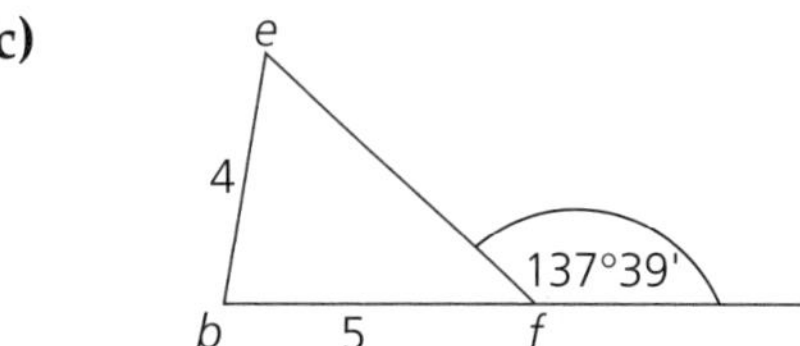

In the given diagram $|be| = 4$ $|bf| = 5$.
Calculate:

(i) $|\angle bef|$ **(ii)** $|ef|$

Solution to question 1

(a) Construct angle A such that 4 Cos $A = 3$.

4 Cos $A = 3$

$\Rightarrow$ Cos $A = \dfrac{3}{4}$

$$\text{Cos} = \frac{\text{Adj.}}{\text{Hypot.}}$$

Hence evaluate Sin A.

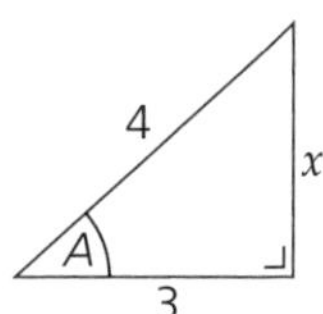

$$4^2 = x^2 + 3^2$$

$$16 - 9 = x^2$$

$$7 = x^2 \qquad \boxed{x = \sqrt{7}}$$

$$\text{Sin} = \frac{\text{Opp.}}{\text{Hypot.}} \qquad \Rightarrow \text{Sin } A = \frac{\sqrt{7}}{4}$$

(b)

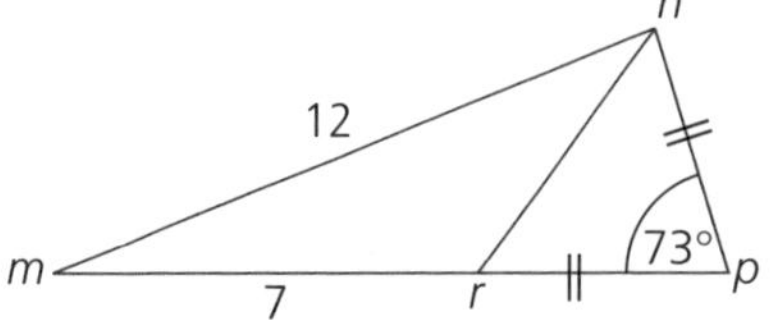

Important

When attempting a question such as this, it is important you:

① Calculate as many unkown angles as is possible before you start.

② Draw a separate diagram for each part. State what you are looking for 'Calculate $|rt|$' and call that side/angle x in the diagram.

(i) Area $\triangle rnp = 7.65$, calculate $|rp|$.

Find $|rp|$.

∗ Because both sides are equal, call both x.

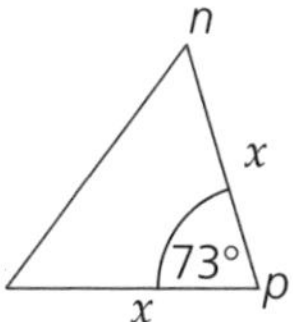

Area of a $\triangle = \frac{1}{2}ab$ Sin C

$\Rightarrow \quad \frac{1}{2}(x)(x)(\text{Sin } 73°) = 7.65$

$\Rightarrow \quad (0.5)(x^2)(0.9563) = 7.65$

$\Rightarrow \quad (0.478)(x^2) = 7.65$

$$x^2 = \frac{7.65}{0.478} = 16$$

$\Rightarrow \quad x = 4$

$$\boxed{|rp| = 4}$$

(ii) Calculate $|\angle nrp|$.

∗ Because $|np| = |rp|$
$|\angle prn| = |\angle pnr|$.

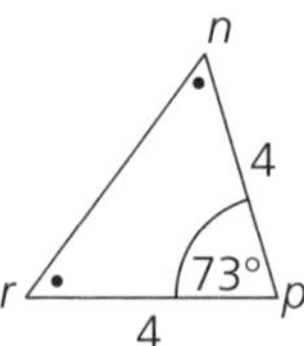

Find $|\angle nrp|$.

∗ $180° - 73° = 107°$

$$\frac{107°}{2} = 53°30'$$

$\Rightarrow \boxed{|\angle nrp| = 53°30'}$

> **(iii)** Calculate $|\angle mnr|$.

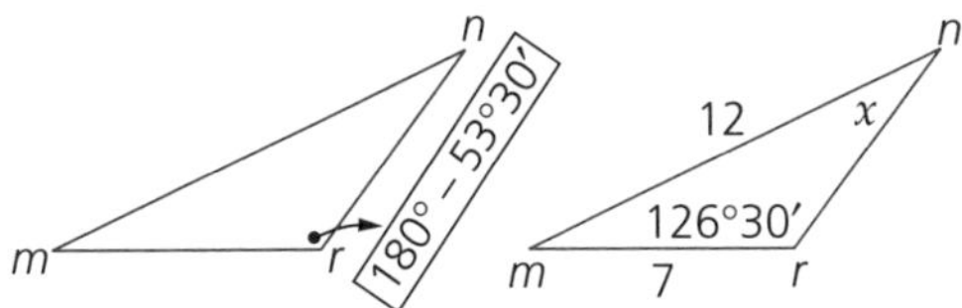

$$\frac{12}{\text{Sin } 126°30'} = \frac{7}{\text{Sin } x}$$

$\Rightarrow \quad (12) \text{ Sin } x = (7)(\text{Sin } 126°30')$

> $\text{Sin } 126°30' = 0.8038$

$$\text{Sin } x = \frac{7(\text{Sin } 126°30')}{12}$$

$$\text{Sin } x = 0.4689$$

$\Rightarrow \quad |\angle mnr| = 27°57'$

(c)

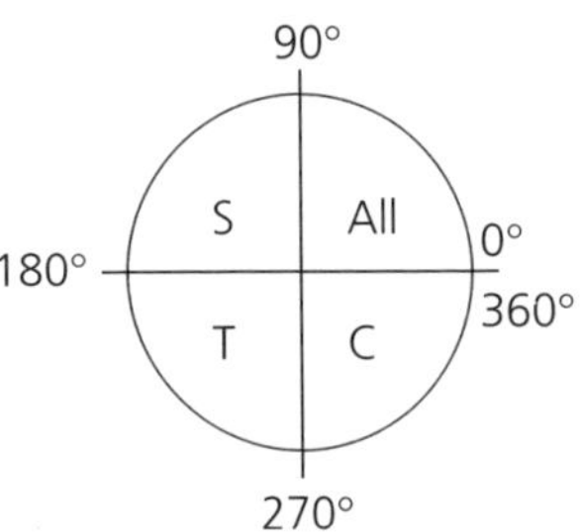

Here, the Tan of angle B is ⊖. Therefore angle B may be in the 'S' and 'C' quadrants.

> If Tan $C = +1.88$, $C = 61°59'$

(i) 'S' quadrant

$B = 180° - 61°59'$

$= 118°1'$

(ii) 'C' quadrant

$B = 360° - 61°59'$

$= 258°1'$

Solution to question 2

> **(a)** In $\triangle abc$, $|ab| = 8$, $|bc| = 6$ and area $\triangle abc = 14.1$. Find two possible values of $|\angle abc|$.

Possible diagram 1

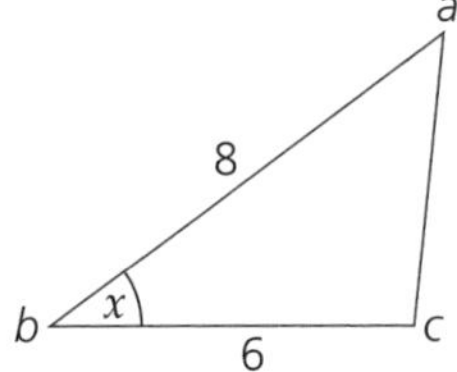

$$\text{Area} = 14.1$$

$\Rightarrow \quad \frac{1}{2}ab \text{ Sin } C = 14.1$

$\Rightarrow \quad \frac{1}{2}(8)(6)(\text{Sin } x) = 14.1$

$\Rightarrow \quad 24 \text{ Sin } x = 14.1$

$\Rightarrow \quad \text{Sin } x = \frac{14.1}{24}$

$\Rightarrow \quad x = 35°58'$

> **Important**
>
> $$\text{Sin } x = \frac{14.1}{24}$$
>
> $\Rightarrow$ Sin x is (+)
>
> 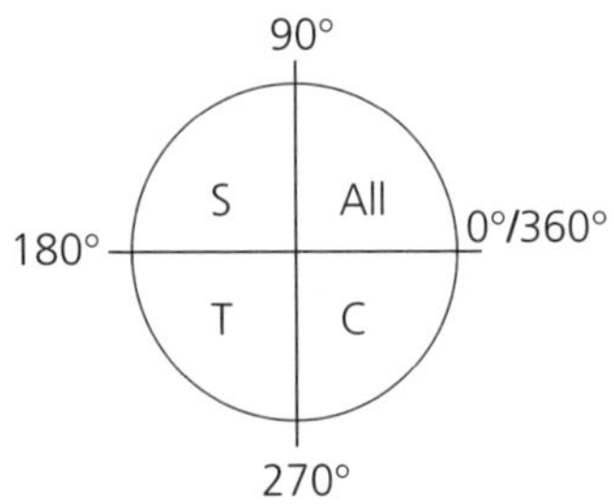
>
>
> From the unit circle we see that Sin is (+) in the 'All' and 'S' quadrants.

'All' quadrant $\rightarrow$ 35°58′

'S' quadrant $180° - 35°58'$

$= 144°2'$

Possible diagram 2

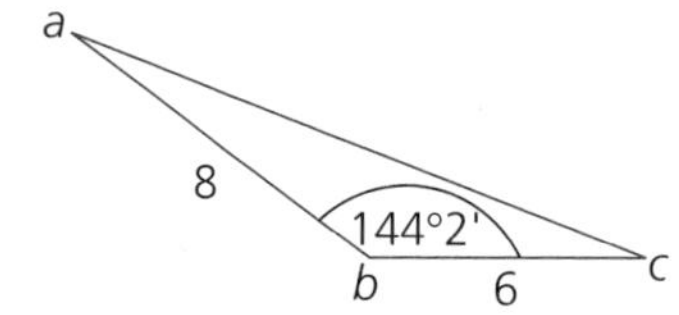

Therefore $|\angle abc|$ could be either 35°58′ or 144°2′.

(b)

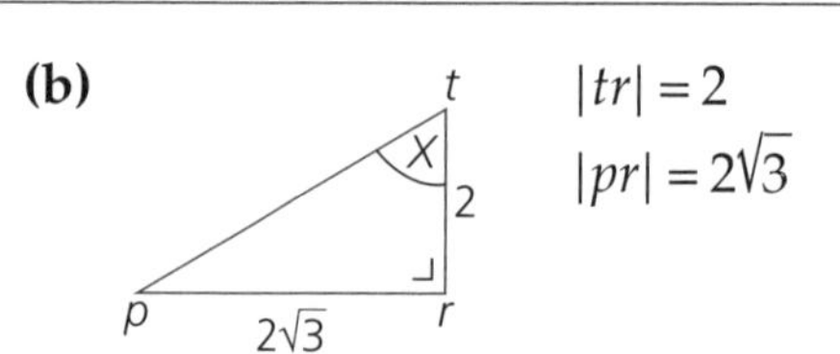

$|tr| = 2$

$|pr| = 2\sqrt{3}$

Find:

① $|\angle ptr|$

② Area $\triangle ptr$

③ $|pt|$

(i) Calculate $|\angle ptr|$.

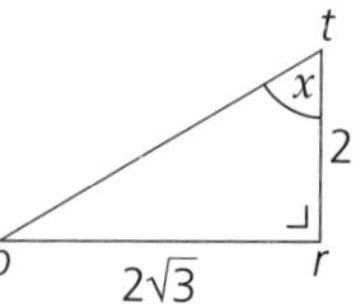

$2\sqrt{3} =$ Opposite

$2 =$ Adjacent

SOH CAH TOA

$$\text{Tan} = \frac{\text{Opp.}}{\text{Adj.}}$$

$\Rightarrow \text{Tan } X = \dfrac{2\sqrt{3}}{2} \quad \Rightarrow \text{Tan } X = \sqrt{3}$

2nd F Tan $(\sqrt{3}) = 60°$

$\Rightarrow \quad |\angle ptr| = 60°$

(ii) Calculate area $\triangle ptr$.

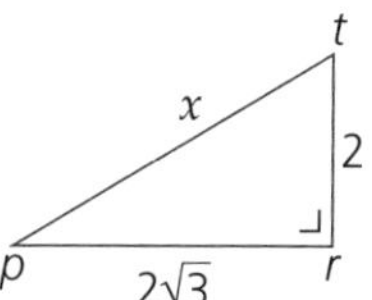

$\text{Area} = \frac{1}{2}ab \text{ Sin C}$

$= \frac{1}{2}(2)(2\sqrt{3})(\text{Sin } 90°)$

$= 3.464$

$\Rightarrow$ Area $\triangle ptr = 3.464$

(iii) Evaluate $|pt|$.

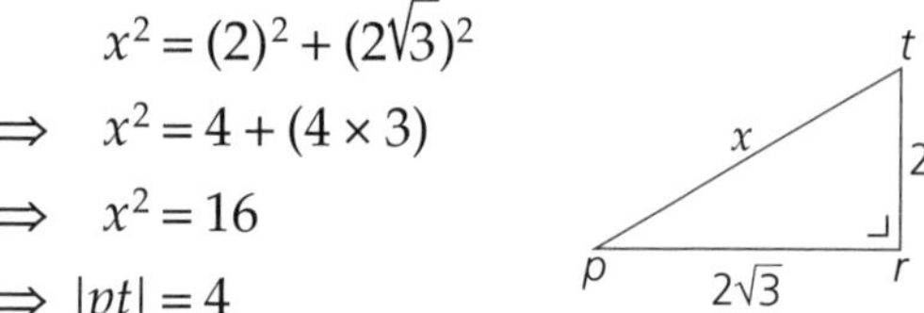

$x^2 = (2)^2 + (2\sqrt{3})^2$

$\Rightarrow \quad x^2 = 4 + (4 \times 3)$

$\Rightarrow \quad x^2 = 16$

$\Rightarrow \quad |pt| = 4$

(c)

(i) Given $\text{Sin } A = -\dfrac{3}{4}$ evaluate angle A if $A > 270°$.

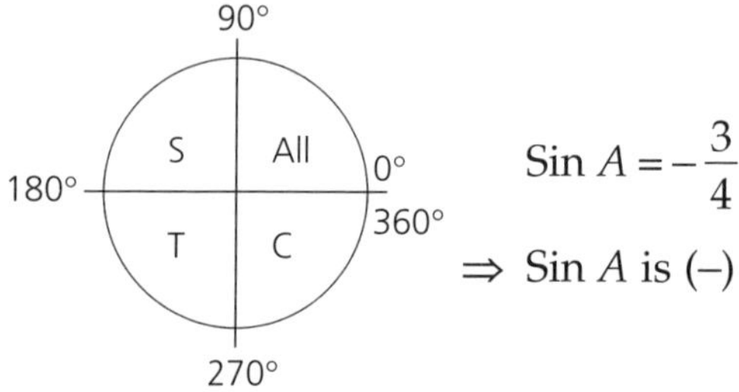

$\text{Sin } A = -\dfrac{3}{4}$

$\Rightarrow$ Sin A is (–)

As we can see from the unit circle, Sin is (–) in the 'T' and 'C' quadrants.

* But we are told $A > 270°$. Therefore angle A can only be in the 'C' quadrant.

If $\text{Sin } B = +\frac{3}{4}$

$B = 48°35'$

$\Rightarrow$ 'C' quadrant

$A = 360° - 48°35'$

$= 311°25'$

(ii) Hence investigate whether

$$\text{Cos } \frac{A}{2} = \frac{\text{Cos } A}{2}$$

$$\text{Is Cos}\left(\frac{A}{2}\right) = \frac{\text{Cos } A}{2} \ ?$$

$$\Rightarrow \text{Is Cos}\left(\frac{311°25'}{2}\right) = \frac{\text{Cos } 311°25'}{2} \ ?$$

$$\text{Is Cos } 155°12' = \frac{0.6615}{2}$$

$$\Rightarrow \quad \text{Is } -0.911 = 0.33 \qquad \text{No}$$

$$\Rightarrow \quad \text{Cos } \frac{A}{2} \neq \frac{\text{Cos } A}{2}$$

Solution to question 3

(a)

(i) Construct angle A if $\text{Sin } A = 0.4$

Again, because we are asked to construct angle A, we express Sin A as a fraction.

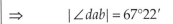

$\text{Sin } A = 0.4$

$\Rightarrow \text{Sin } A = \frac{2}{5}$

SOH $\Rightarrow \text{Sin} = \frac{\text{Opp.}}{\text{Hypot.}}$

(ii) Hence evaluate 3 Cos A.

① Evaluate Cos A.

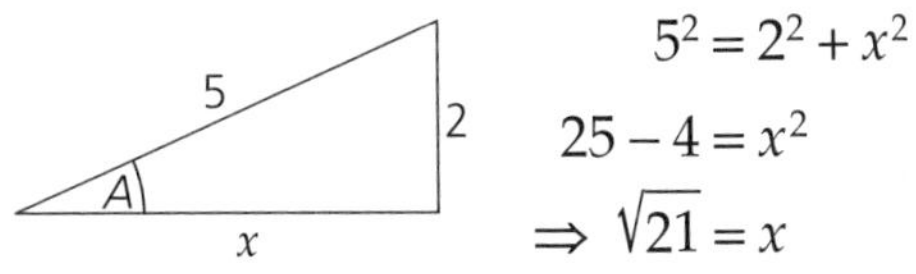

$5^2 = 2^2 + x^2$

$25 - 4 = x^2$

$\Rightarrow \sqrt{21} = x$

CAH $\Rightarrow \text{Cos} = \frac{\text{Adj.}}{\text{Hypot.}}$

$$\Rightarrow \quad \text{Cos } A = \frac{\sqrt{21}}{5}$$

$$\Rightarrow \quad 3(\text{Cos } A) = 3\left(\frac{\sqrt{21}}{5}\right) = \boxed{\frac{3\sqrt{21}}{5}}$$

(b)

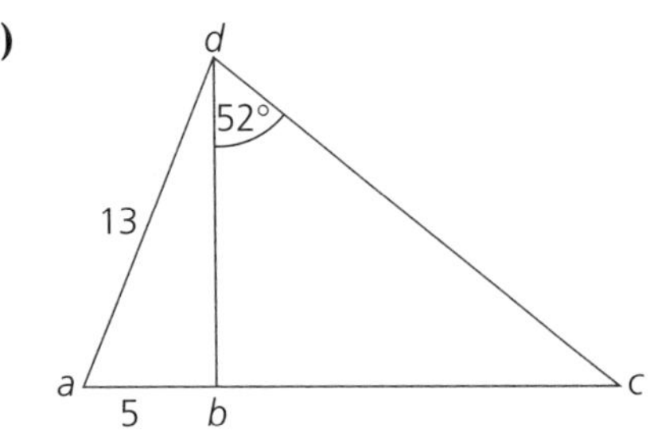

(i) Evaluate $|\angle dab|$.

Again, we draw a separate diagram for each part, state what we are looking for and call it X.

$5 = \text{Adj.} \qquad 13 = \text{Hypot.}$

CAH $\Rightarrow \text{Cos} = \frac{\text{Adj.}}{\text{Hypot.}}$

$$\Rightarrow \quad \text{Cos } X = \frac{5}{13}$$

$$\Rightarrow \quad |\angle dab| = 67°22'$$

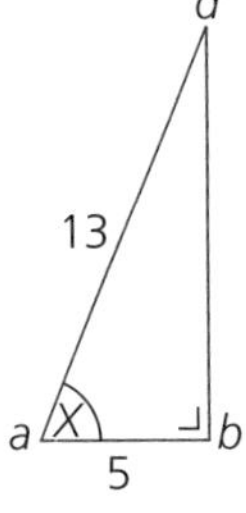

(ii) Evaluate $|bd|$.

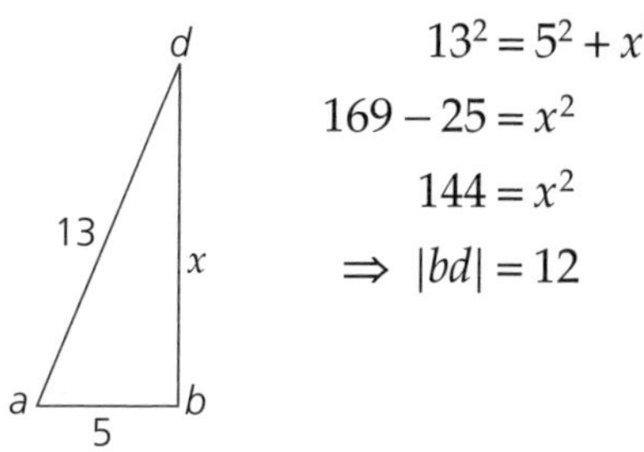

$$13^2 = 5^2 + x^2$$
$$169 - 25 = x^2$$
$$144 = x^2$$
$$\Rightarrow \; |bd| = 12$$

(iii) Evaluate $|bc|$.

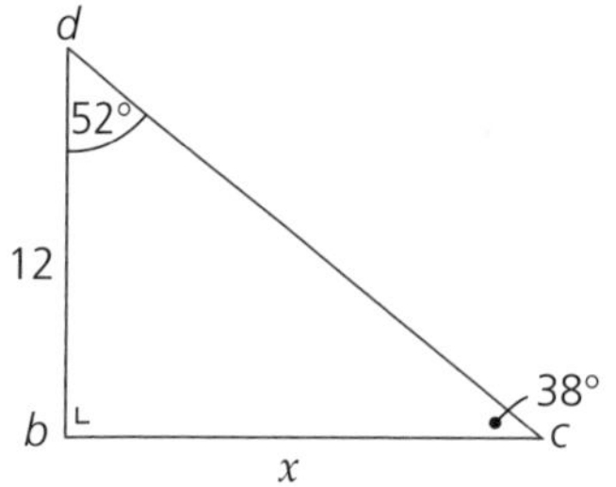

$$\frac{12}{\text{Sin } 38°} = \frac{x}{\text{Sin } 52°}$$

Sin 38° = 0.6157
Sin 52° = 0.788

$$\Rightarrow \; 12(\text{Sin } 52) = x(\text{Sin } 38)$$

$$\Rightarrow \; \frac{12(\text{Sin } 52)}{\text{Sin } 38} = x$$

$$\Rightarrow \; |bc| = 15.36$$

(iv) Area $\triangle adc$.

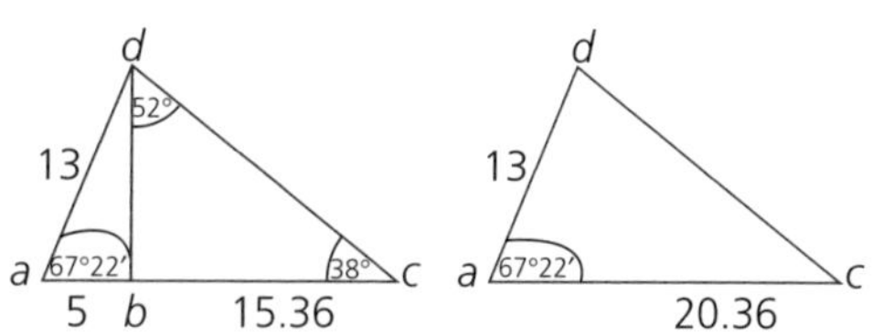

$$\text{Area} = \tfrac{1}{2}ab \text{ Sin C}$$

$$\Rightarrow \; \text{Area} = \tfrac{1}{2}(13)(20.36)(\text{Sin } 67°22') = \boxed{122}$$

(c)

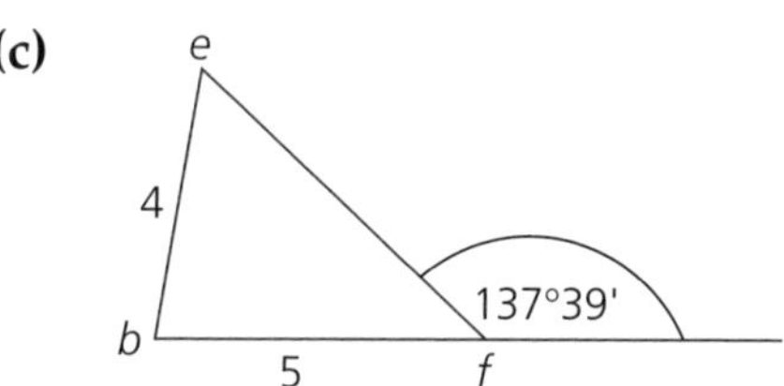

Calculate:

(i) $|\angle bef|$ **(ii)** $|ef|$

(i) Calculate $|\angle bef|$.

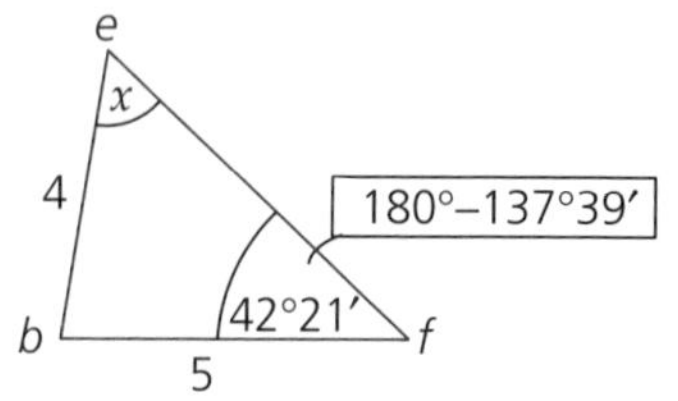

$$\frac{4}{\text{Sin } 42°21'} = \frac{5}{\text{Sin } x}$$

Sin 42°21′ = 0.6736

$$4(\text{Sin } x) = (5)(\text{Sin } 42°21')$$

$$\text{Sin } x = \frac{(5)(\text{Sin } 42°21')}{4}$$

$$\Rightarrow \; |\angle bef| = 57°21'$$

(ii) Evaluate $|ef|$.

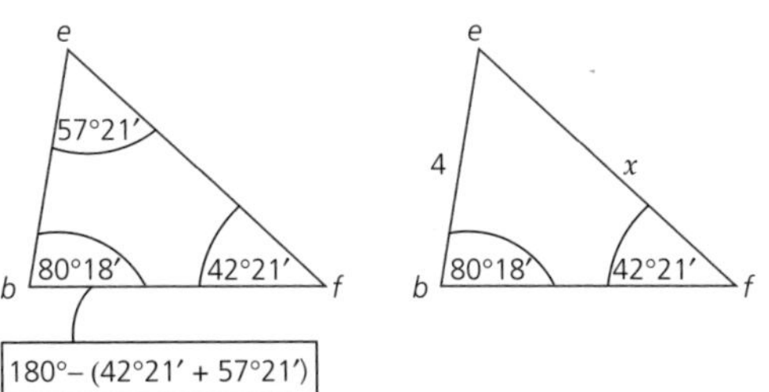

$$\frac{4}{\text{Sin } 42°21'} = \frac{x}{\text{Sin } 80°18'}$$

$\Rightarrow$ $(4)(\text{Sin } 80°18') = x(\text{Sin } 42°21')$

$\boxed{\text{Sin } 80°18' = 0.9857}$

$$\frac{(4)(\text{Sin } 80°18')}{\text{Sin } 42°21'} = x$$

$\Rightarrow$ $\boxed{|ef| = 5.85}$

Chapter 13

Statistics

Questions involving mean

Type 1

Find the mean, mode and median of 3, 2, 4, 6, 2, 5, 2, 8.

$$\text{Mean} = \frac{3+2+4+6+2+5+2+8}{8} = \boxed{4}$$

Mode = the term which occurs most often

$\Rightarrow$ mode = $\boxed{2}$

Median

① Arrange the list in numerical order

2, 2, 2, 3, 4, 5, 6, 8

② The median is the middle number

2, 2, 2, 3, 4, 5, 6, 8

Here we have two middle numbers

$$\Rightarrow \text{Median} = \frac{3+4}{2} = \boxed{3\frac{1}{2}}$$

Type 2

Find the mean and mode of:

Marks	10	15	20	25
No. of pupils	4	7	8	12

$$\text{Mean} = \frac{(10 \times 4) + (15 \times 7) + (20 \times 8) + (25 \times 12)}{4+7+8+12}$$

and evaluate to calculate the mean mark.

Mode – This is the number which occurs most often (has the highest frequency).

$\Rightarrow$ mode is 25.

Type 3

Find the mean of:

Marks	0–10	10–24	24–30	30–40
No. of pupils	5	6	8	10

* This is a grouped frequency table. To calculate the mean mark here, first evalute the **mid-interval values**.

We find the mid-interval value of the 0–10 group first:

$$\frac{0+10}{2} = \boxed{5} \qquad \frac{24+30}{2} = \boxed{27}$$

$$\frac{10+24}{2} = \boxed{17} \qquad \frac{30+40}{2} = \boxed{35}$$

Now replace the groups with the mid-interval values.

Marks	5	17	27	35
No. of pupils	5	6	8	10

Therefore mean =

$$\frac{(5 \times 5) + (17 \times 6) + (27 \times 8) + (35 \times 10)}{5 + 6 + 8 + 10}$$

Type 4

Find x if the mean of 3, 4, 5 and x is 5.

> **Important**
> If the mean of a list containing 'a' numbers is 'b', they add up to (ab).

Here 4 numbers have a mean of 5, they add up to 20 (4×5).

$\Rightarrow 3 + 4 + 5 + x = 20$

$\Rightarrow x = 20 - 3 - 4 - 5 \quad \Rightarrow \boxed{x = 8}$

Type 5

8 pupils have an average (mean) of €52 saved. If John is excluded from the group the mean drops to €50. How much has John in his savings?

① 8 pupils ⇔ mean = €52

⇒ Total saved by the 8 is

(8 × €52) = €416

② 7 pupils ⇔ mean = €50

⇒ Total saved by the 7 is

(7 × €50) = €350

⇒ John had €66 (€416 – €350) saved.

Type 6

The mean of the frequency table below is 13. Calculate m. Find also the modal group.

Marks	1–3	3–13	13–23	23–41
Number	3	8	m	2

* Work away as if the value of m is known.

Mid-interval values:

$$\frac{1+3}{2} = \boxed{2} \qquad \frac{3+13}{2} = \boxed{8}$$

$$\frac{13+23}{2} = \boxed{18} \qquad \frac{23+41}{2} = \boxed{32}$$

Marks	2	8	18	32
Number	3	8	m	2

$$\text{Mean} = \frac{(2\times3)+(8\times8)+(18\times m)+(32\times2)}{3+8+m+2}$$

$$= \frac{6+64+18m+64}{13+m} = \frac{134+18m}{13+m}$$

$$\Rightarrow \quad \frac{134+18m}{13+m} = \frac{13}{1} \leftarrow \text{(given as the mean)}$$

Cross-multiplying:

$(134 + 18m)(1) = (13)(13 + m)$

$134 + 18m = 169 + 13m$

$\Rightarrow 18m - 13m = 169 - 134$

$\Rightarrow 5m = 35 \quad \Rightarrow m = 7$

The modal group.

The modal group is the group which occurs most often.

⇒ Modal group = (3–13)

(it has the highest frequency)

Questions involving pie charts

Type 1

The pie chart shows the favourite sports of 72 pupils. Calculate how many like each sport.

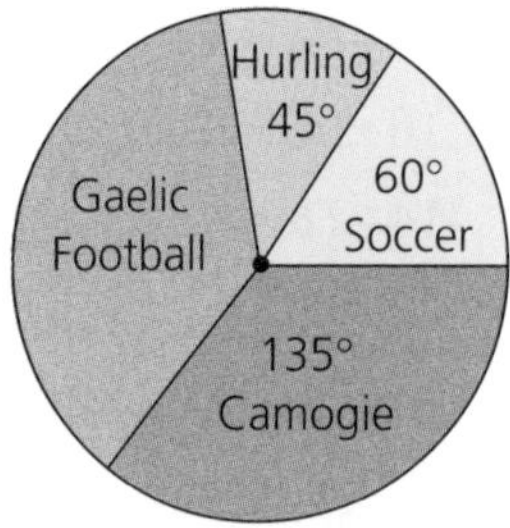

Number who prefer Soccer

$$\frac{60°}{\text{Total degrees}} \times \text{Total no. of people}$$

$$\Rightarrow \frac{60}{360} \times 72 = 12 \text{ people}$$

$$\Rightarrow \text{Hurling} = \frac{45}{360} \times 72 = 9 \text{ people}$$

$$\Rightarrow \text{Camogie} = \frac{135}{360} \times 72 = 27 \text{ people}$$

Number who prefer Gaelic Football:

① Calculate the angle representing Gaelic Football.

$$360° - (135° + 60° + 45°) = 120°$$

② $\Rightarrow$ Gaelic Football $= \frac{120}{360} \times 72$

$= 24$ people

We know we are correct because $12 + 9 + 27 + 24 = 72$ ✓

Type 2

The table shows the TV channels watched by 45 houses. Represent the information on a Pie Chart.

Channel	RTE 1	RTE 2	TV 3	Sky 1
Number	10	12	8	15

Angle representing RTE 1

$$\frac{10}{\text{Total number}} \times \text{Total amount of degrees}$$

$$\Rightarrow \frac{10}{45} \times 360° \quad \Rightarrow 80°$$

$$\text{RTE 2} = \frac{12}{45} \times 360° = 96°$$

$$\text{TV 3} = \frac{8}{45} \times 360° = 64°$$

$$\text{Sky 1} = \frac{15}{45} \times 360° = 120°$$

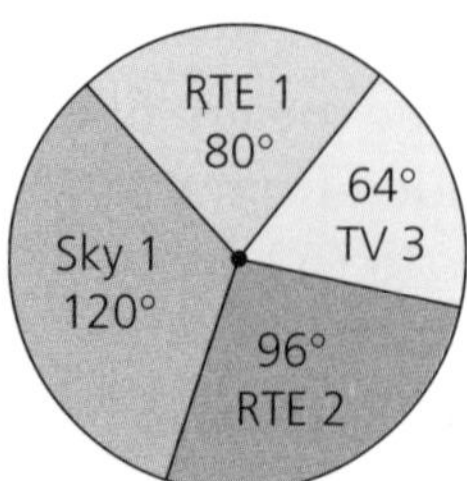

Again, we know we are correct because $80° + 64° + 96° + 120° = 360°$ ✓

Type 3

The pie chart shows the favourite subjects of a group of students. If 9 pupils prefer Science how many like each of the other subjects?

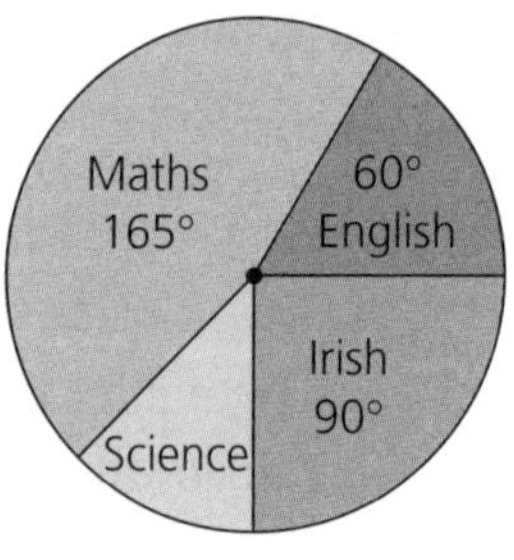

Angle representing Science

$= 360° - (165° + 60° + 90°)$

$= 45°$

9 pupils = 45°

⇒ 1 pupil = 5°

Maths

$165° \div 5° = 33$

⇒ 33 pupils prefer maths.

English

$60° \div 5° = 12$

⇒ 12 pupils prefer English.

Irish

$90° \div 5° = 18$

⇒ 18 pupils prefer Irish.

Questions involving histograms

Type 1

From this frequency table, draw a histogram:

Age in years	4–10	10–14	14–22	22–32
No. of people	9	8	6	25

Always let the group with the smallest width have a width of 1. From that, find the other widths.

It is very important you can find each width.

⇓

Group	Amount of numbers	Width
4–10	6	$1.5 (6 \div 4)$
10–14	4	smallest ⇒ 1
14–22	8	$2 (8 \div 4)$
22–32	10	$2.5 (10 \div 4)$

The height of each group is found by dividing the frequency of the group by its width.

Age in years	4–10	10–14	14–22	22–32
No. of people	9	8	6	25
Width	1.5	1	2	2.5
Height	6	8	3	10
	↑ $(9 \div 1.5)$	↑ $(8 \div 1)$	↑ $(6 \div 2)$	↑ $(25 \div 2.5)$

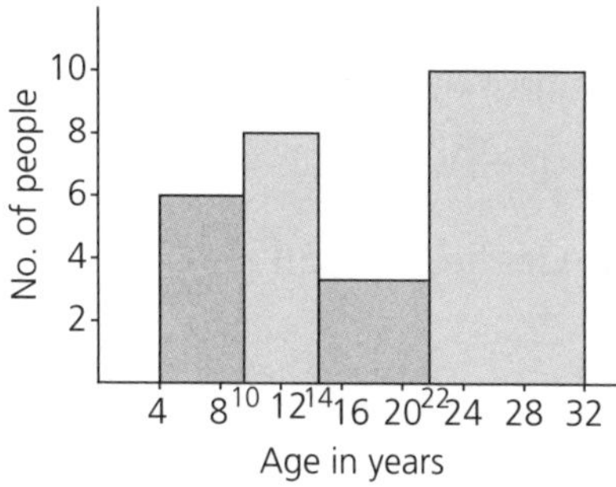

Type 2

From the histogram below, draw a frequency distribution table:

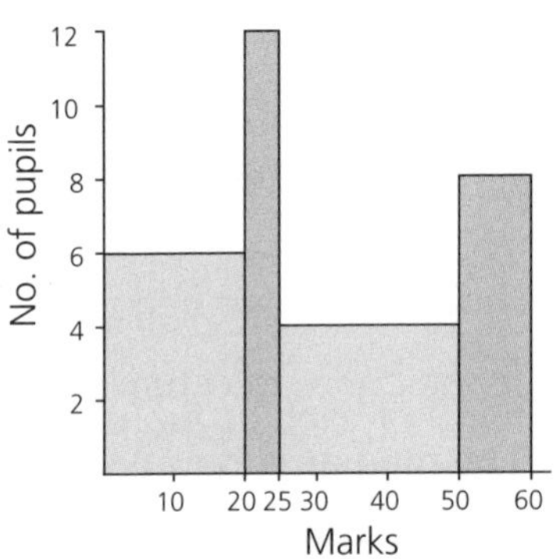

Important
When we are given a histogram, we find the frequency of each group by finding the area (length × width) of each rectangle.

① Find the width of each group.
(Again, the smallest width = 1.)

⇓

Group	Amount of numbers	Width
0–20	20	4
20–25	5	1
25–50	25	5
50–60	10	2

② Find the area of each rectangle.

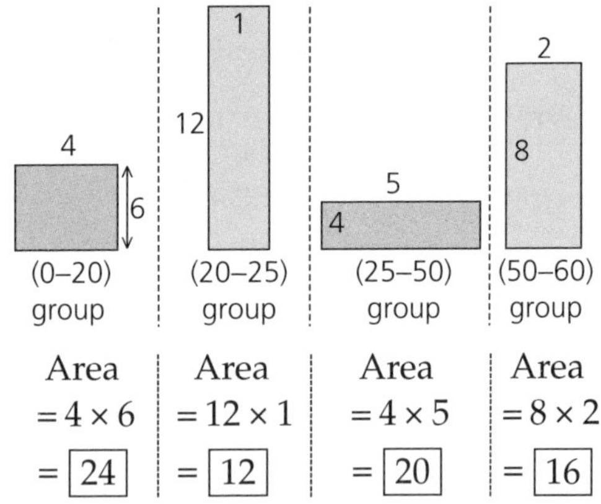

Area $= 4 \times 6 = \boxed{24}$	Area $= 12 \times 1 = \boxed{12}$	Area $= 4 \times 5 = \boxed{20}$	Area $= 8 \times 2 = \boxed{16}$

The height of each group can be seen in the histogram.

Marks	0–20	20–25	25–50	50–60
No. of pupils	24	12	20	16

Type 3

Given the histogram below, complete the frequency table.

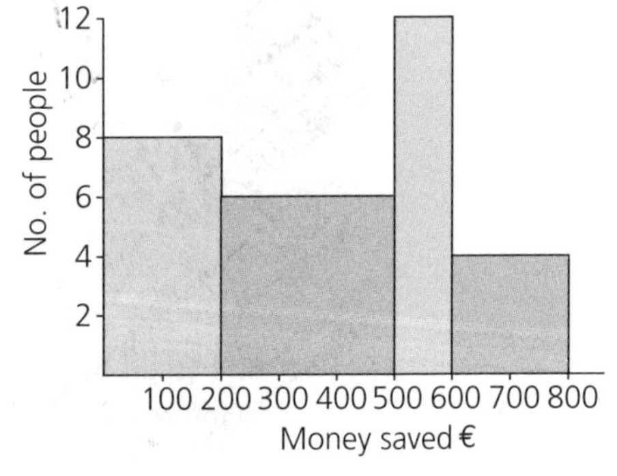

Money saved	0–200	200–500	500–600	600–800
No. of people		36		

① Find the width of each rectangle.

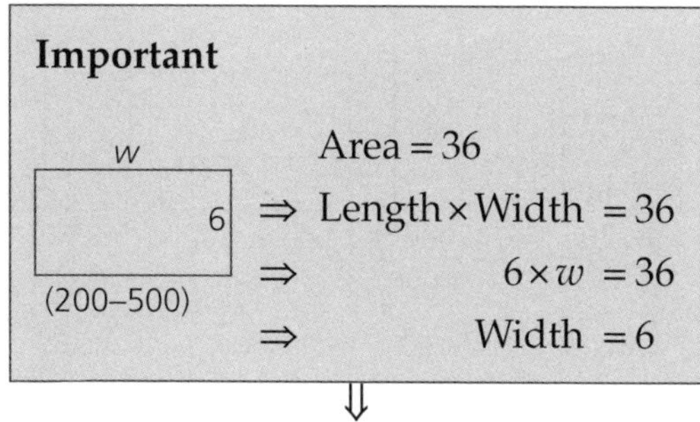

Area = 36

$\Rightarrow$ Length × Width = 36

$\Rightarrow$ $6 \times w = 36$

$\Rightarrow$ Width = 6

⇓

* 200–500 group → 300 numbers → Width = 6

⇒ Any group → 50 numbers → Width = 1

⇓

Group	Amount of numbers	Width
Any	50	1
0–200	200	4
500–600	100	2
600–800	200	4

② Find the area of each rectangle.

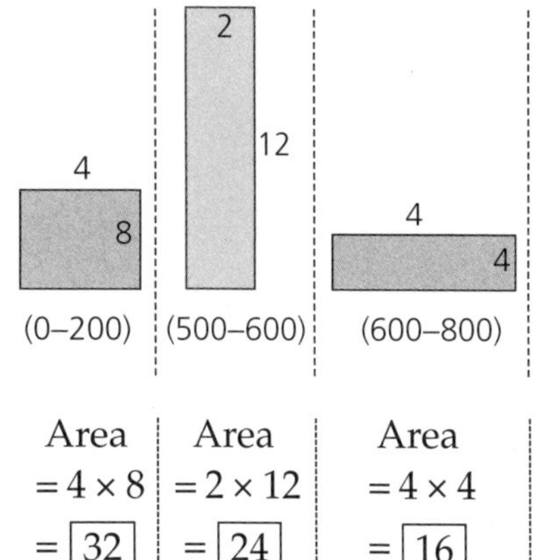

Area = 4 × 8 = 32	Area = 2 × 12 = 24	Area = 4 × 4 = 16

Money	0–200	200–500	500–600	600–800
No.	32	36	24	16

Questions involving cumulative frequency curves (ogives)

From the frequency distribution table below:

(i) Construct a cumulative frequency table.

(ii) Draw a cumulative frequency curve.

(iii) Use the curve to estimate:

- The median amount saved.
- The interquartile range.

Money €	0–50	50–150	150–250	250–400
No. of people	15	25	18	22

Cumulative frequency table

Money	< 50	< 150	< 250	< 400
Number	15	(15+25) 40	(40+18) 58	(58+22) 80

Cumulative frequency curve

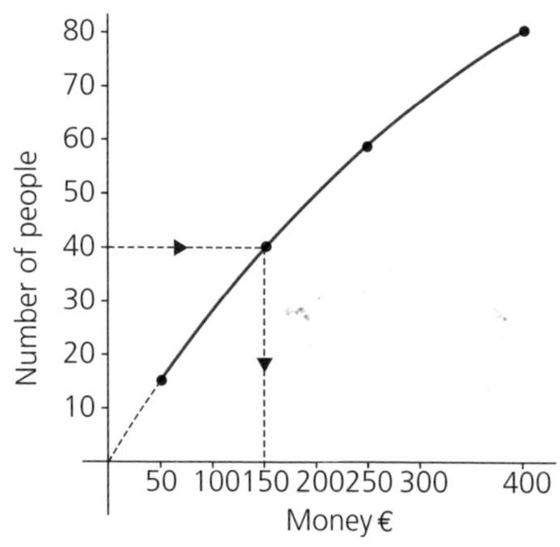

(i) Median Go from halfway on the vertical axis. Find the corresponding value on the horizontal axis.

$\Rightarrow$ Median = €150

(ii) Interquartile range Go from $\frac{1}{4}$ and from $\frac{3}{4}$ on the vertical axis.

$$\tfrac{1}{4} \text{ of } 80 = 20$$

$$\tfrac{3}{4} \text{ of } 80 = 60$$

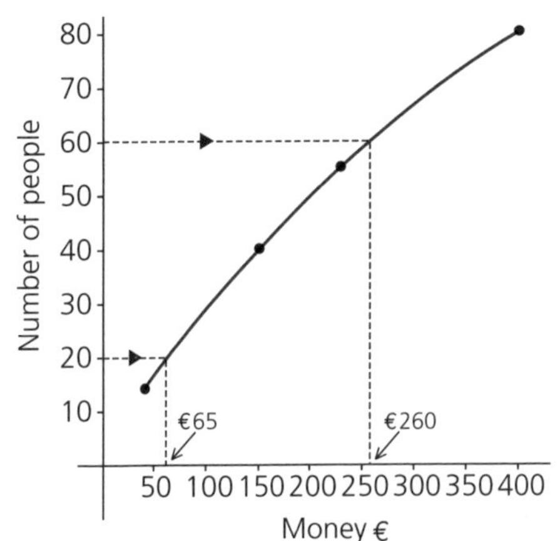

Lower quartile = €65

Upper quartile = €260

$\Rightarrow$ Interquartile range = €260 − €65

= €195

(iii) How much did the 'richest' 10 people save?

The 'richest' ten people are represented at the top of the vertical axis [70–80].

We must therefore find which area on the horizontal axis corresponds to that area.

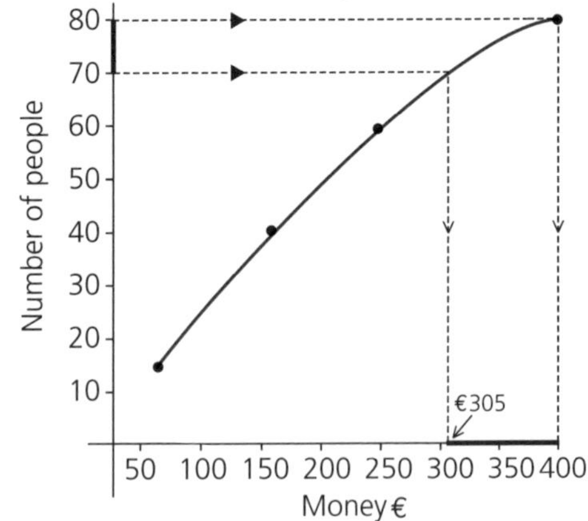

We see that the richest 10 people saved €305–€400.

(iv) What percentage of people saved between €100 and €200?

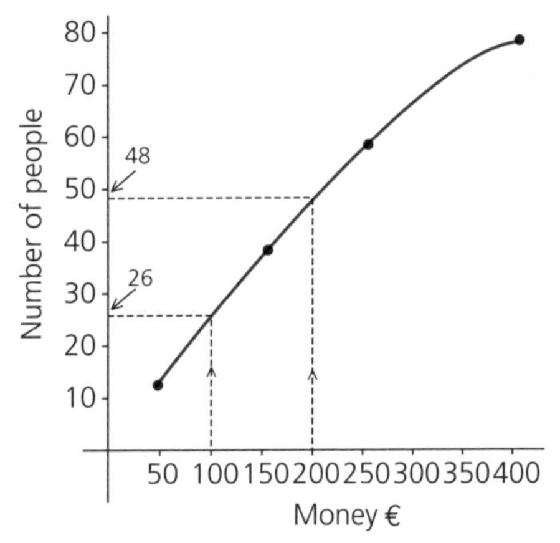

From the diagram we see that 22 [48–26] people saved between €100 and €200.

% who saved €100 – €200 $= \dfrac{22}{\text{Total number}} \times \dfrac{100}{1}$

$= \dfrac{22}{80} \times \dfrac{100}{1} = 27.5\%$

Chapter 13
Sample questions for you to try

Question 1

(a) Draw a pie chart to illustrate the following frequency table which

Bar	Mars	Twix	Moro	Yorkie	Snickers
Number	18	12	23	9	10

shows the favourite chocolate bar of a group of children.

(b) Illustrate the following grouped frequency table by means of a histogram.

Interval	0–10	10–15	15–30	30–50	50–60
No. of pupils	12	7	12	20	18

(c) **(i)** Mary is 17 yrs 8 months of age, John is 16 yrs 7 months and Seán is 15 yrs 3 months. Calculate their mean age.

(ii) Sheila joins the group and the mean age of the four teenagers is then 15 yrs 9 months. Find Sheila's age.

Question 2

(a) **(i)** Illustrate the following histogram using a grouped frequency table:

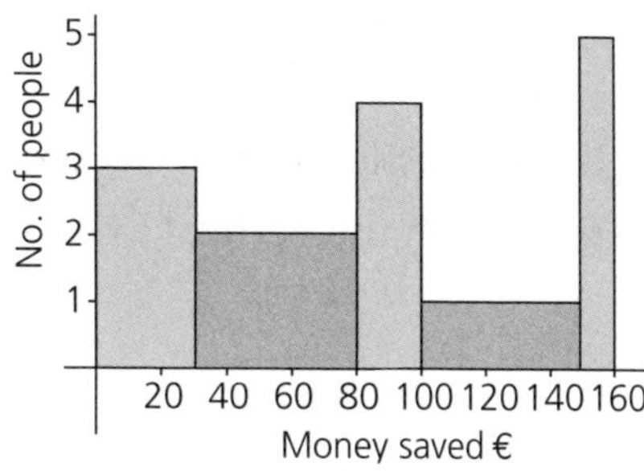

(ii) From your answer in part (**i**) use mid-interval values to calculate the mean amount of money saved.

(b) From the following grouped frequency table, construct a cumulative frequency table and cumulative frequency curve (ogive).

Marks in exam	0–10	10–25	25–50	50–70	70–100
No. of pupils	8	10	16	12	18

From the ogive, calculate:

(i) The median mark.

(ii) The interquartile mark.

(iii) How many pupils received a grade B (70%–85%) in the exam.

(iv) What mark did the 'best' 20 students receive?

Question 3

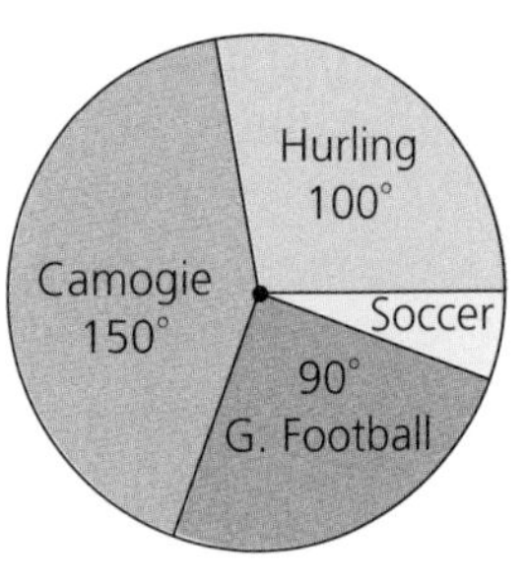

(a) The pie chart shows the proportion of students who prefer various sports at a particular school.

Calculate:

(i) The number of pupils who like each sport if 2 kids prefer soccer.

(ii) The percentage of pupils who prefer camogie.

(b) From this histogram, complete the given frequency table:

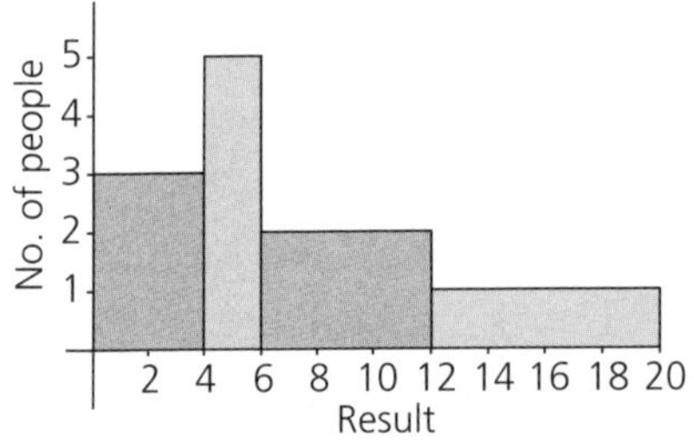

Result	0–4	4–6	6–12	12–20
No. of people				4

(c) **(i)** The mean of the following frequency table is 6. Calculate t.

Pocket money (€)	2–4	4–6	6–10
No. of kids	3	t	7

(ii) Find the modal group.

(iii) What is:

(a) the greatest number.

(b) The smallest number of kids who could have got less than €4.50 pocket money.

Solution to question 1

(a)

Bar	Mars	Twix	Moro	Yorkie	Snickers
Number	18	12	23	9	10

Illustrate the table using a pie chart.

$18 + 12 + 23 + 9 + 10 = 72$

$$\text{Mars} = \frac{18}{72} \times 360° = 90°$$

$$\text{Twix} = \frac{12}{72} \times 360° = 60°$$

$$\text{Moro} = \frac{23}{72} \times 360° = 115°$$

$$\text{Yorkie} = \frac{9}{72} \times 360° = 45°$$

$$\text{Snickers} = \frac{10}{72} \times 360° = 50°$$

Total (just to check) 360° ✓

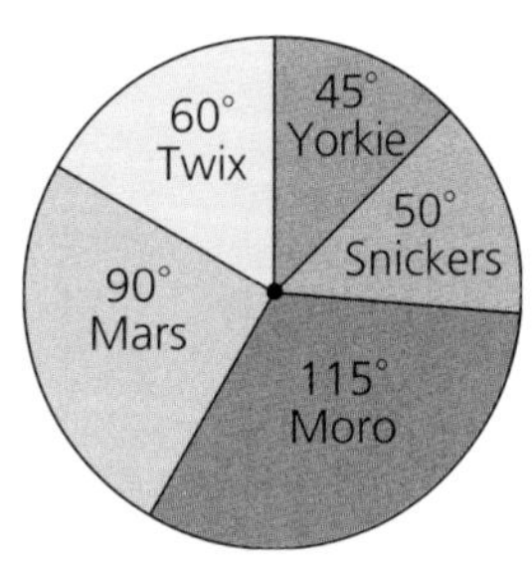

(b) Illustrate this frequency table by means of a histogram.

Interval	0–10	10–15	15–30	30–50	50–60
No. of pupils	12	7	12	20	18

① Find the width of each group.

Group	Amount of numbers	Width
0–10	10	2
10–15	5	1 (smallest)
15–30	15	3
30–50	20	4
50–60	10	2

② Find the height of each group.

(frequency ÷ width)

⇓

Interval	0–10	10–15	15–30	30–50	50–60
No. of pupils	12	7	12	20	18
Width	2	1	3	4	2
Height	6	7	4	5	9

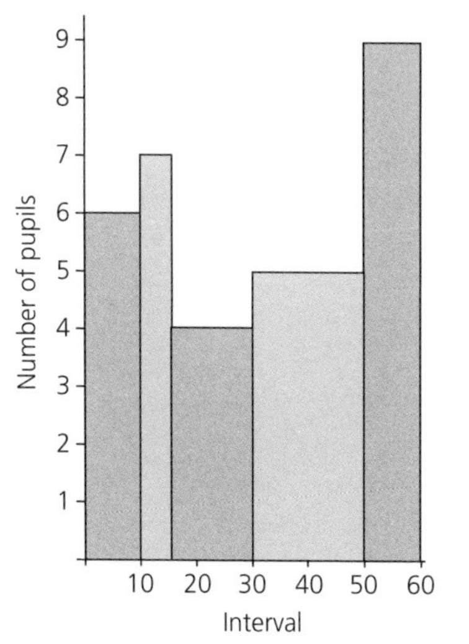

(c)

(i) Mary is 17 yrs 8 months old. John is 16 yrs 7 months old and Seán is 15 yrs 3 months. Find their mean age.

17 yrs 8 months
16 yrs 7 months
+ 15 yrs 3 months

48 yrs 18 months

3 | 48 yrs 18 months

16 yrs 6 months

⇓

Mean = 16 yrs 6 months

(ii) Sheila joins the group and the mean age is 15 yrs 9 months. Find Sheila's age.

Mean age of Mary, John and Seán is 16 yrs 6 months.

⇒ Their ages add up to 49 yrs 6 months (16 yrs 6 months × 3).

When Sheila is added, the mean ages is 15 yrs 9 months.

⇒ The group's ages then add up to 63 years (15 yrs 9 months × 4).

⇒ Sheila is 13 yrs 6 months.

(63 yrs – 49 yrs 6 months)

Solution to question 2

(a)

(i) Illustrate the histogram below on a frequency distribution table:

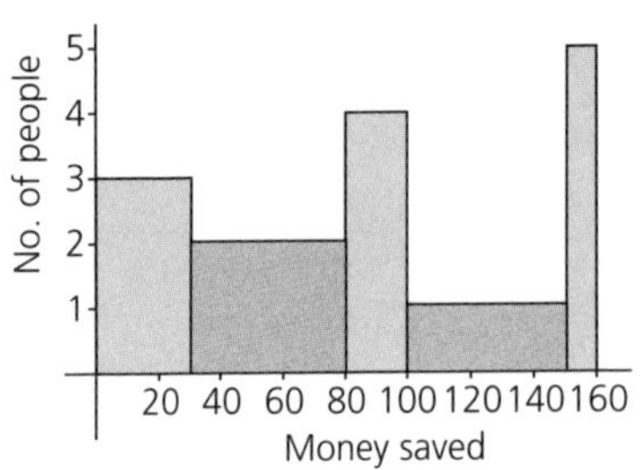

① Evaluate the width of each group.

Group	Amount of numbers	Width
0–30	30	3
30–80	50	5
80–100	20	2
100–150	50	5
150–160	10	1

② Find the area of each rectangle.

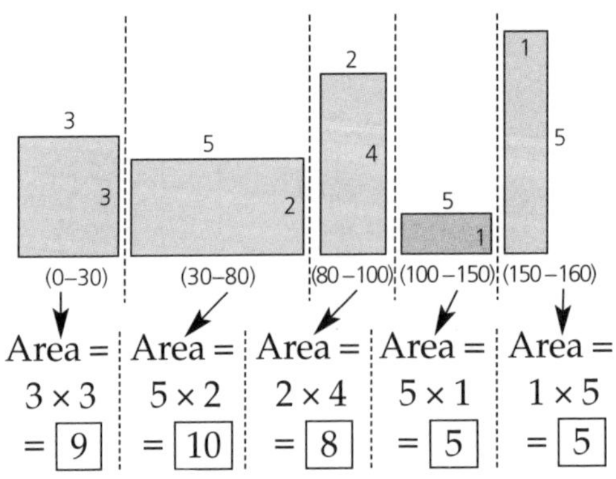

Money saved	0–30	30–80	80–100	100–150	150–160
No. of people	9	10	8	5	5

(ii) Use the answer above to calculate the mean amount of money saved.

Money	0–30	30–80	80–100	100–150	150–160
Number	9	10	8	5	5

① Calculate the mid-interval values.

$$\frac{0+30}{2} = \boxed{15} \qquad \frac{30+80}{2} = \boxed{55}$$

$$\frac{80+100}{2} = \boxed{90} \qquad \frac{100+150}{2} = \boxed{125}$$

$$\frac{150+160}{2} = \boxed{155}$$

Money	15	55	90	125	155
Number	9	10	8	5	5

Mean =

$$\frac{(15\times9)+(55\times10)+(90\times8)+(125\times5)+(155\times5)}{9+10+8+5+5}$$

$\Rightarrow$ Mean amount of savings = €75.81

(b)

Marks	0–10	10–25	25–50	50–70	70–100
Number	8	10	16	12	18

Cumulative frequency table

Marks	< 10	< 25	< 50	< 70	< 100
Number	8	18	34	46	64

Cumulative frequency curve (ogive)

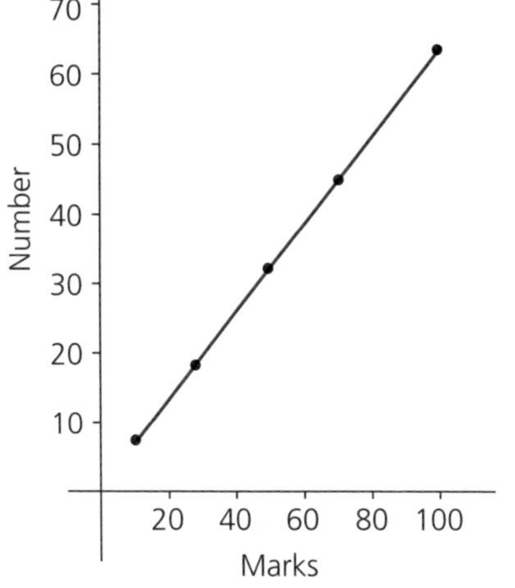

> **(i)** Calculate the median mark.
>
> **(ii)** Find also, the interquartile range.

(i) Median Mark

Go to halfway on the vertical axis. Find the corresponding mark. Therefore the median mark is 48.

(ii) Interquartile range

Go to $\frac{1}{4}$ and $\frac{3}{4}$ on the vertical axis.

$\Rightarrow$ Lower quartile = 24 marks

Upper quartile = 72 marks

$\Rightarrow$ Interquartile range
= (72 – 24) marks = 48 marks

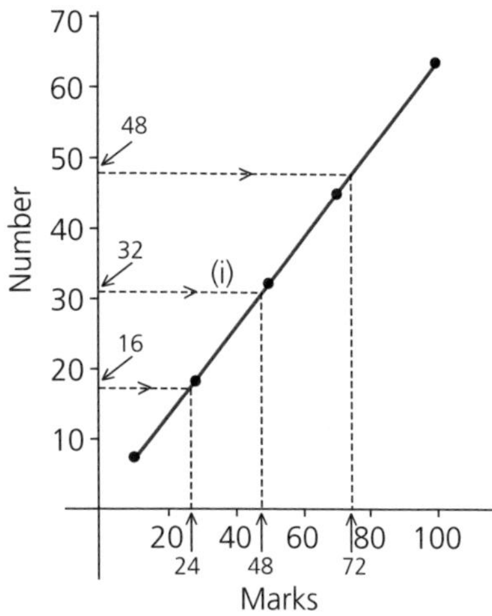

> **(iii)** How many pupils received 70%–85% in the exam?
>
> **(iv)** What mark did the 'worst' 20 students receive?

(iii) How many got 70%–85%?

From the graph below we see that ten [56 – 46] pupils got 70%–85%.

(iv) What mark did the worst 20 get?

Again, we see from the graph that the worst 20 received 0%–28%.

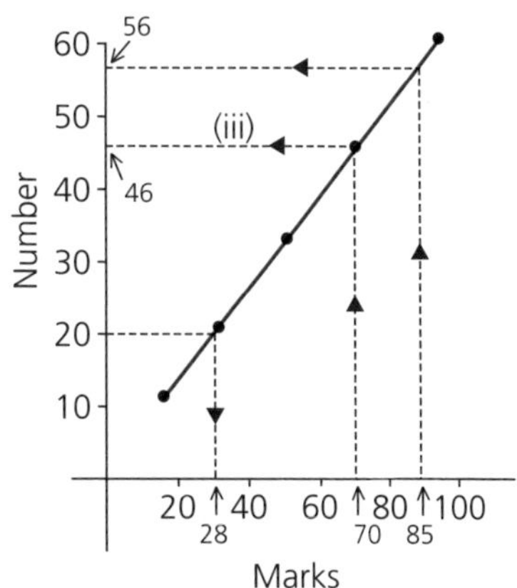

Solution to question 3

(a)

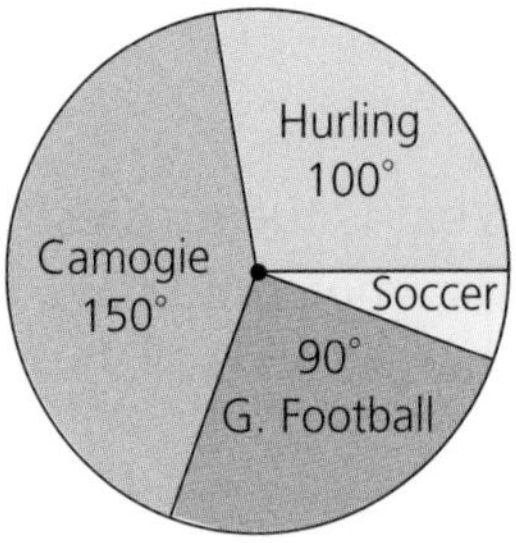

Angle representing soccer $360° - (100° + 150° + 90°) = 20°$

(i) Calculate the number who like each sport.

Soccer $\Leftrightarrow$ $20°$ $\Leftrightarrow$ 2 pupils

$\Rightarrow$ $10°$ $\Leftrightarrow$ 1 pupil

Hurling $= 100°$

$= 10$ pupils $(100 \div 10)$

G. football $= 90°$

$= 9$ pupils $(90 \div 10)$

Camogie $= 150°$

$= 15$ pupils $(150 \div 10)$

(ii) What percentage of pupils prefer camogie?

Total number $= 2 + 10 + 9 + 15$

$= 36$ pupils

Camogie $= 15$ pupils

$\Rightarrow$ Percentage $= \dfrac{15}{36} \times \dfrac{100}{1} = 41.7\%$

who prefer camogie.

(b)

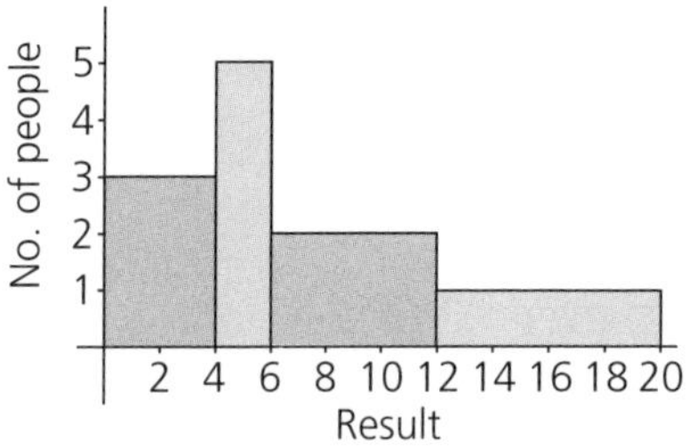

Complete the frequency distribution table.

Result	0–4	4–6	6–12	12–20
No. of pupils				4

Area of rectangle =

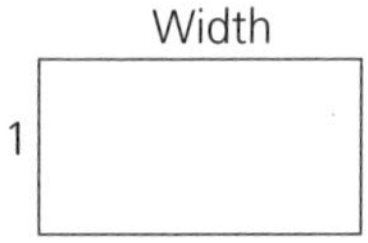

$\Rightarrow$ height × width = 4

$\Rightarrow$ 1 × width = 4 $\Rightarrow$ width = 4

(12–20) group $\rightarrow$ 8 numbers $\rightarrow$ width = 4

$\Rightarrow$ Any group $\rightarrow$ 2 numbers $\rightarrow$ width = 1

Calculate the remaining widths.

Group	a/m of numbers	Width
Any	2	1
0–4	4	2
4–6	2	1
6–12	6	3

Calculate the frequency of each group.

(0–4) group

Frequency = height × width

$= 3 \times 2 = \boxed{6}$

(4–6) group

Frequency $= 5 \times 1$

$= \boxed{5}$

(6–12) group

Frequency $= 2 \times 3$

$= \boxed{6}$

Result	0–4	4–6	6–12	12–20
No. of people	6	5	6	4

(c)

Pocket money	2–4	4–6	6–10
No. of kids	3	t	7

(i) The mean is 6. Calculate t.

Mid-interval values

$\frac{2+4}{2} = \boxed{3}$ $\frac{4+6}{2} = \boxed{5}$ $\frac{6+10}{2} = \boxed{8}$

Pocket money	3	5	8
No. of kids	3	t	7

$$\text{Mean} = \frac{(3 \times 3) + (5 \times t) + (8 \times 7)}{3 + 7 + t}$$

$$\frac{9 + 5t + 56}{10 + t} = 6$$

$$\Rightarrow \frac{65 + 5t}{10 + t} = \frac{6}{1}$$

Cross-multiplying:

$(65 + 5t)(1) = (6)(10 + t)$

$\Rightarrow 65 + 5t = 60 + 6t \quad \Rightarrow 65 - 60 = t$

$\Rightarrow t = 5$

(ii) Find the modal group.

The modal group is (6–10) because it has the highest frequency.

(iii)

(a) What is the greatest number of kids who could have received less than €4.50 pocket money?

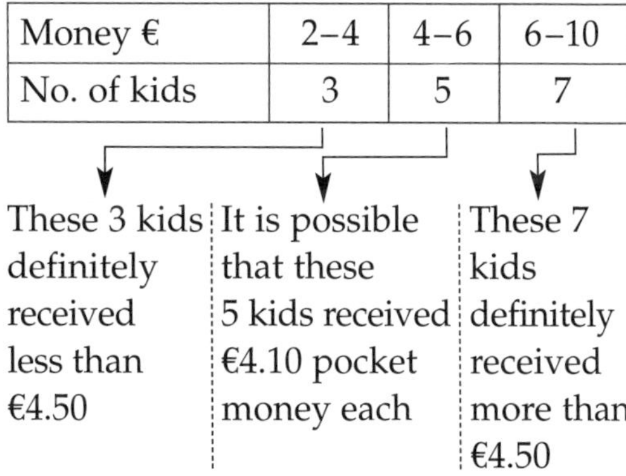

Money €	2–4	4–6	6–10
No. of kids	3	5	7

These 3 kids definitely received less than €4.50
It is possible that these 5 kids received €4.10 pocket money each
These 7 kids definitely received more than €4.50

$\Rightarrow$ It is possible that 8 kids received less than € 4.50

(b) The smallest number of kids who could have received less than €4.50

Money €	2–4	4–6	6–10
No. of kids	3	5	7

These 3 kids definitely received less than €4.50

It is possible that each of these 5 kids received €5.20 pocket money

These 7 kids definitely received more than €4.50

$\Rightarrow$ It is possible that only 3 kids received less than €4.50

Chapter 14

Sample Paper Two with Solutions

Please revise chapters 7–12 before attempting this paper. Detailed solutions are given.

Question 1

(a)
(i)

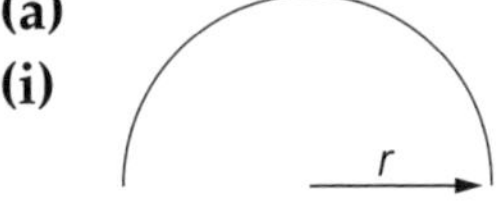

The length of this semicircle is 9.42 cm. Calculate its radius.

(ii) A triangle is inscribed in a semi-circle as shown. Calculate the area enclosed between them.

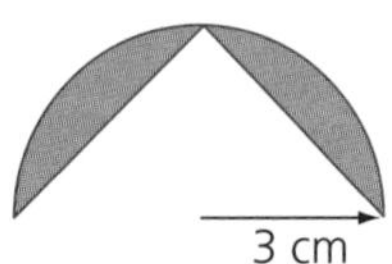

(b)

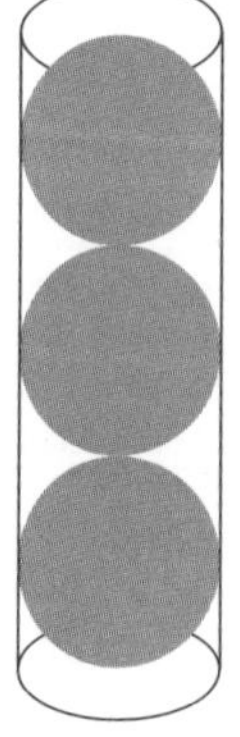

(i) Calculate the volume, in terms of π, of a sphere of radius 3 cm.

(ii) Three such spheres are packed into a cylindrical container as shown. Calculate the volume of the cylinder in terms of π.

(iii) Calculate the % of space in the cylinder taken up by the spheres.

(c) The diagram shows a cylinder surmounted by a hemisphere. Prove that if the cylinder's height is 6 times greater than its radius, its volume would be 9 times that of the hemisphere.

Question 2

Given $L: 2x - y + 1 = 0$ and
$K: x + 2y - 7 = 0$

(a) **(i)** Find pt. b, the point of intersection of L and K.

(ii) L intersects the x-axis at pt. n. K intersects the x-axis at pt. p. Find pt. n and pt. p and hence draw a rough sketch of line L and line K.

(iii) Calculate the area of the triangle enclosed by L, K and the x-axis.

(iv) Prove that the triangle bpn is right-angled.

(b) **(i)** Find pt. d, the image of $(3, -2)$ under a central symmetry in $(-1, 4)$.

(ii) Show that the image of $(-3, 4)$ under the translation $(-2, -1) \rightarrow (-4, 5)$ is also d.

Question 3

(a) Construct $\triangle npr$ given $|np| = 5$ cm, $|nr| = 7$ cm and $|\angle nrp| = 50°$. Hence, construct the incircle of $\triangle npr$.

(b)

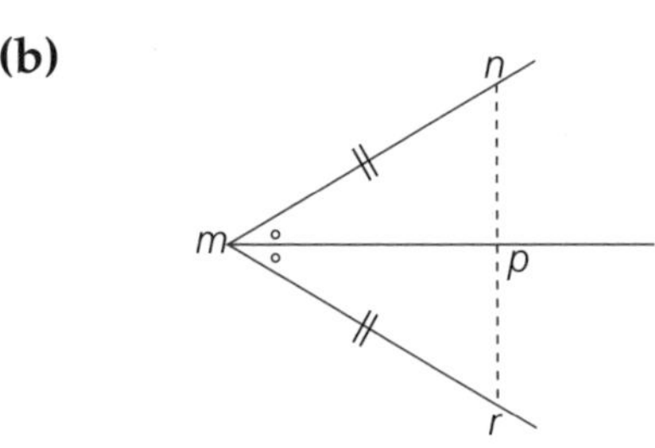

$[mr]$ is the bisector of $\angle nmr$. If $|mn| = |mr|$ prove that $|np| = |pr|$.

(c)

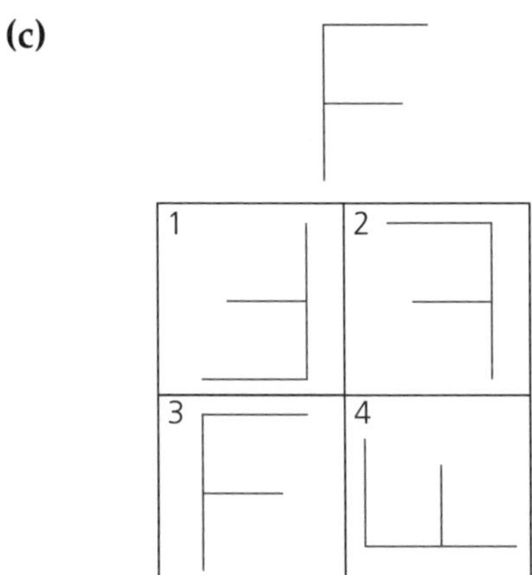

Each of the four shapes here is the image of the top 'F'. State (in each case) whether the shape is the image under an axial symmetry, a central symmetry, a translation or a rotation.

Question 4

(a)

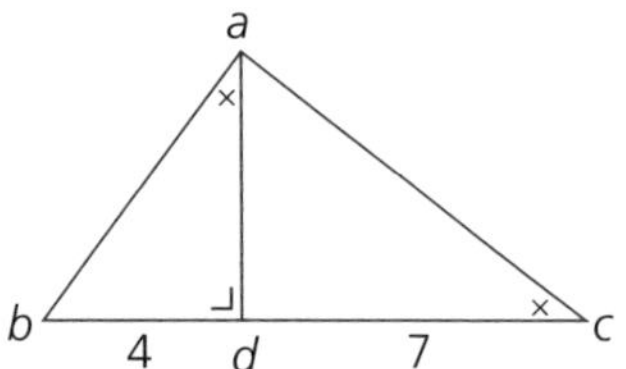

In the diagram given $|bd| = 4$, $|dc| = 7$, $|\angle acd| = |\angle bad|$, $[ab] \perp [ac]$ and $[ad] \perp [bc]$.

Calculate $|ad|$.

(b)

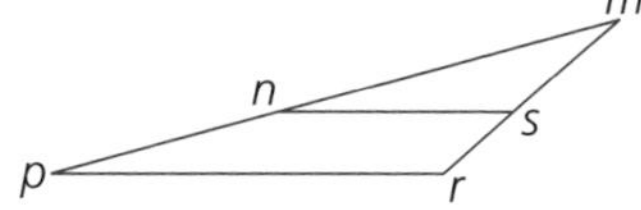

In the diagram above $|mp| = 25$, $|ms| = 6$, $|sr| = 4$ and $|ns| = 5$.

Calculate:

(i) $|pn|$ **(ii)** $|pr|$

Question 5

(a)

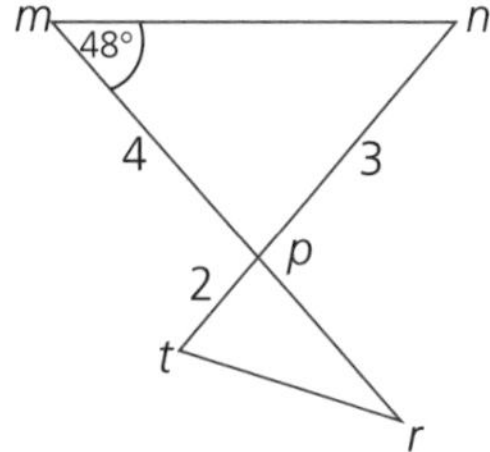

In the given diagram, the area $\triangle mnp$ is 3 times bigger than the area of $\triangle ptr$. $|tp| = 2$, $|pn| = 3$, $|mp| = 4$, $|\angle pmn| = 48°$.

Calculate:

(i) $|pr|$ **(ii)** $|\angle mnp|$ **(iii)** $|mn|$

(iv) the area $\triangle tpr$

(b) Evaluate angle B if Sin $B = 0.829$ and Cos $B = -0.5592$

(c)

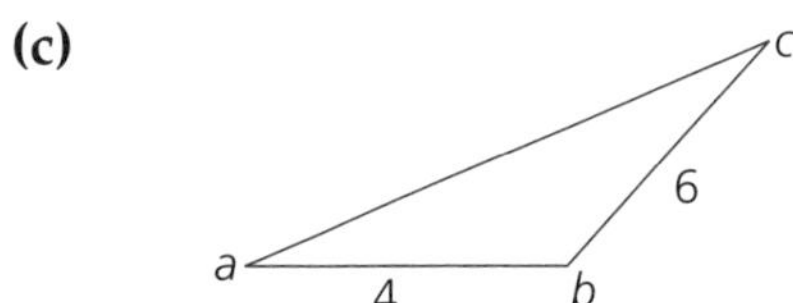

In the diagram $|ab| = 4$, $|bc| = 6$ and area $\triangle abc = 10$.

Calculate $|\angle abc|$.

Question 6

(a) The table shows the age of children in a creche. The mean age is 4 yrs.

(i) Calculate p.

(ii) What is the mode age?

(iii) Illustrate the table on a pie chart.

Age in years	1	2	3	4	5
No. of children	1	0	p	2	5

(b) The frequency table shows the ages of 100 people.

Age in yrs	0–20	20–50	50–55	55–70	70–90
No. of people	16	24	12	24	24

(i) Illustrate the data on a histogram.

(ii) From the table above, construct a cumulative frequency table and a cumulative frequency curve (ogive).

(iii) Use your ogive to find:

(a) The median age.

(b) The interquartile range.

(c) The age of the oldest 30 people.

(d) How many people were less than 40 years old?

(c) **(i)** The mean of 3, 4, 6, x, 8 is 5. Find x.

(ii) Find the median and mode.

Detailed Solutions to Paper Two

Solution to question 1

(a)

(i)

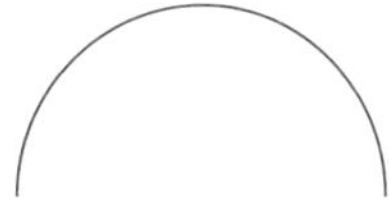

9.42 cm = circumference of semicircle

$\Rightarrow$ Let 9.42 = formula

$$9.42 = \tfrac{1}{2}(2\pi r)$$

$$9.42 = (0.5)(2)(3.14)r$$

$$\Rightarrow \quad 9.42 = (3.14)r$$

$$\Rightarrow \quad \frac{9.42}{3.14} = r \qquad \Rightarrow \text{Radius} = 3 \text{ cm}$$

(ii) 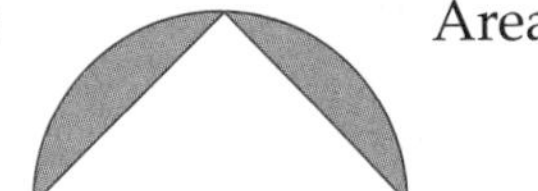 Area of semicircle

$\frac{1}{2}\pi r^2 = \left(\frac{1}{2}\right)(3.14)(3)(3)$

$= 14.13 \text{ cm}^2$

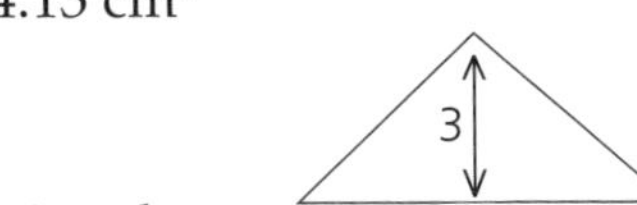

Area of triangle

$\frac{1}{2}(\text{base}) \times \text{perp. height}$

$= \frac{1}{2}(6) \times (3) = 9 \text{ cm}^2$

$\Rightarrow$ Shaded area $= 14.3 \text{ cm}^2 - 9 \text{ cm}^2$
$= 5.13 \text{ cm}^2$

(b)

(i) Volume of sphere $= \frac{4}{3}\pi r^3$

$= \frac{4}{3} \times \pi \times 3 \times 3 \times 3 = 36\pi$

(ii)

Vol. of cylinder

$= \pi r^2 h$

$= \pi \times 3^2 \times 18$

$= 162\pi$

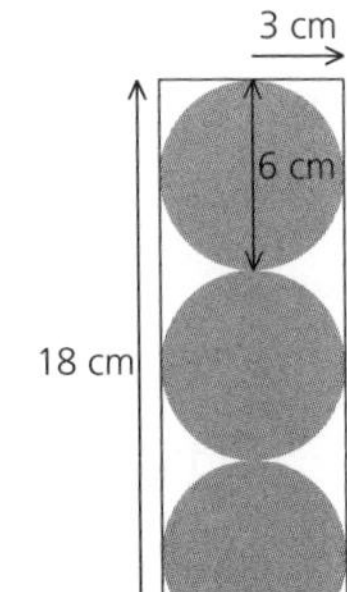

(iii) The spheres take up

$36\pi \times 3 = 108\pi$

$\Rightarrow$ % taken up $= \dfrac{108\pi}{162\pi} \times \dfrac{100}{1}$

$= 66.67\%$

(c)

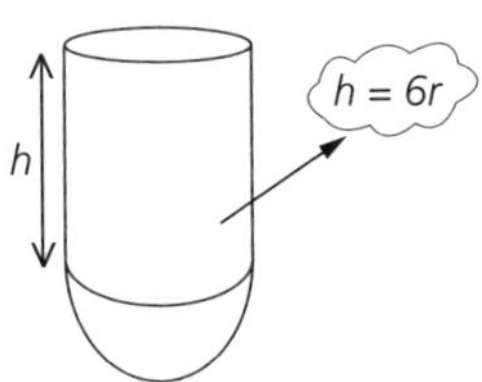

Volume of cylinder $= \pi r^2 h$

$= \pi \times r^2 \times 6r$

$= 6r^3\pi$

Volume of hemisphere $= \frac{2}{3}\pi r^3$

$\Rightarrow$ Vol. of cylinder : Vol. of hemisphere

$= 6r^3\not{\pi} : \frac{2}{3}r^3\not{\pi}$

$= 6 : \frac{2}{3}$

$= \dfrac{18}{3} : \dfrac{2}{3}$

$= 18 : 2$

$= 9 : 1$

> We can cancel the r^3 on both sides because we see from the diagram that the radius of the cylinder is equal to the radius of the hemisphere.

Solution to question 2

(a) $L: 2x - y + 1 = 0$
$K: x + 2y - 7 = 0$

(i) $L \cap K = b$, find b.
Solving simultaneously $b(1, 3)$

(ii) L cuts x-axis at pt. n
$2x - y + 1 = 0$
Let $y = 0 \quad \Rightarrow 2x + 1 = 0$

$\Rightarrow x = -\frac{1}{2} \quad \Rightarrow n\left(-\frac{1}{2}, 0\right)$

K cuts the x-axis at pt. p
$x + 2y - 7 = 0$
let $y = 0 \quad \Rightarrow x - 7 = 0$
$x = 7 \quad \Rightarrow p(7, 0)$

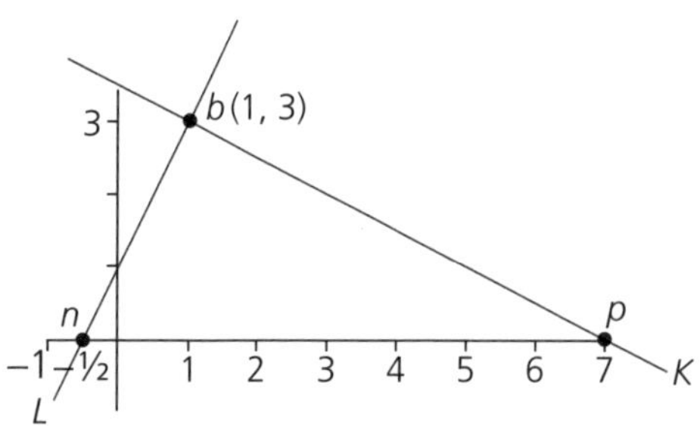

(iii) Calculate the area of $\triangle nbp$.

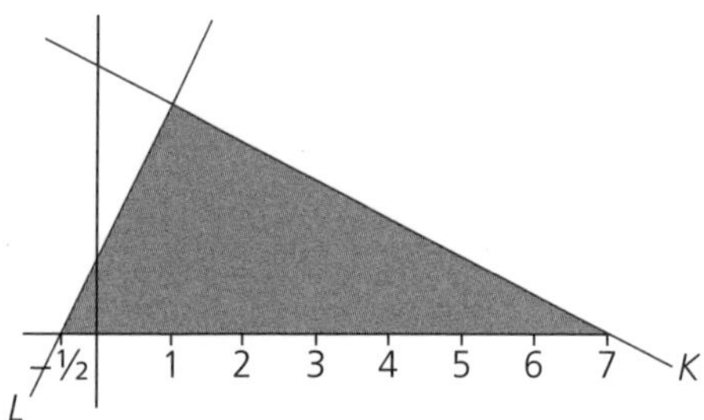

$$\text{Area } \triangle bpn = \tfrac{1}{2}(\text{base}) \times (\text{perp. height})$$
$$= \tfrac{1}{2}(7.5) \times (3)$$
$$= 11.25 \text{ square units}$$

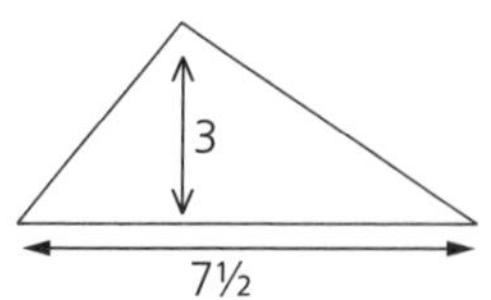

(iv) Prove $\triangle nbp$ is right-angled.

If we prove two of the sides are perpendicular, the triangle is right-angled.
Remember...
if (slope of A) × (slope of B) = −1 then $A \perp B$.

Slope of [*bn*]

$b(1,\ 3)\ \ n(-\tfrac{1}{2},\ 0)$

$x_1\ y_1 \qquad x_2\ y_2$

$$\text{Slope} = \frac{y_2 - y_1}{x_2 - x_1}$$
$$= \frac{0-3}{-\frac{1}{2}-1} = \frac{-3}{-1.5}$$
$$= \boxed{2}$$

Slope of [*bp*]

$b(1,\ 3)\ \ p(7,\ 0)$

$x_1\ y_1 \quad x_2\ y_2$

$$\text{Slope} = \frac{0-3}{7-1} = \frac{-3}{6} = \boxed{-\frac{1}{2}}$$

$$\text{As } (2) \times \left(-\frac{1}{2}\right) = -1$$

$\Rightarrow\ [bn] \perp [bp]$

$\Rightarrow\ \triangle pbn$ *is* right-angled.

(b)

(i) Image of (3, −2) under a central symmetry in (−1, 4).

$(3, -2) \rightarrow (-1, 4) \rightarrow d(-5, 10)$

$\begin{pmatrix} x \text{ value goes down 4} \\ y \text{ value goes up 6} \end{pmatrix}$ each time

(ii) Image of (−3, 4) under the translation $(-2,\ -1) \rightarrow (-4, 5)$.

$(-2,\ -1) \rightarrow (-4, 5)$ $\quad$ x down 2, y up 6

$(-3, 4) \rightarrow d(-5, 10)$ $\quad$ $\left.\begin{matrix} x \text{ down 2} \\ y \text{ up 6} \end{matrix}\right\}$ also

Solution to question 3

(a) Rough

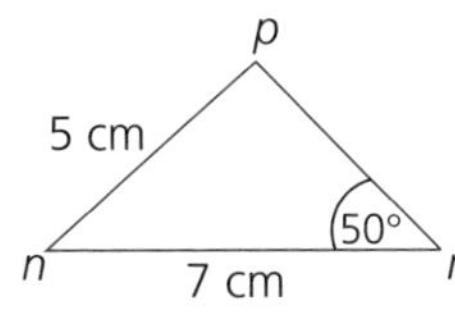

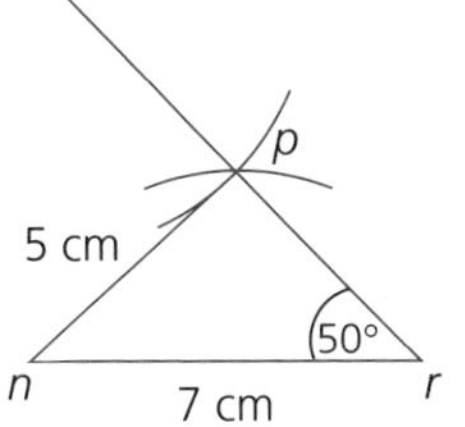

Construct the incircle of $\triangle npr$.

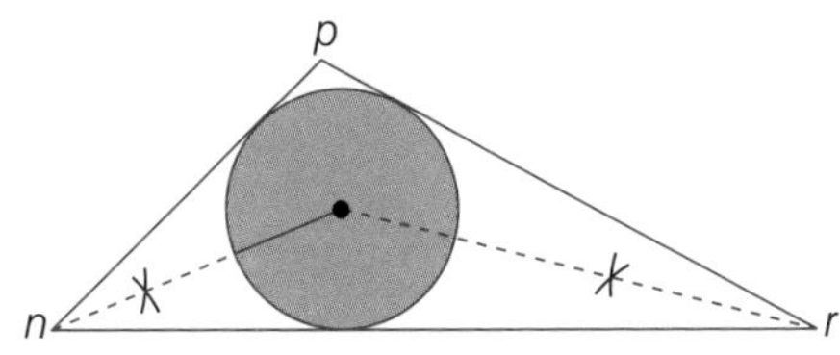

(b)

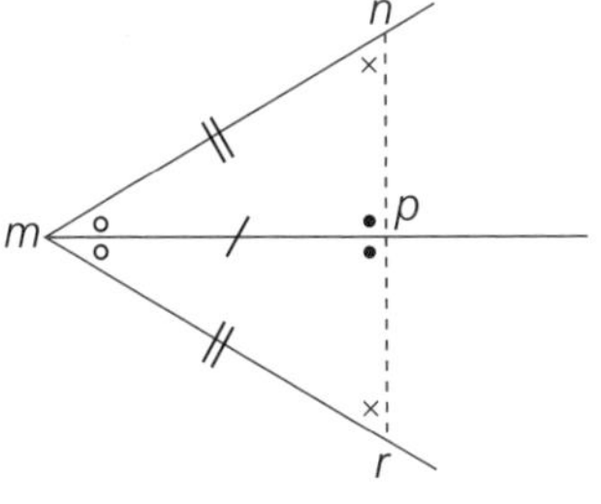

Prove $|np| = |pr|$.

$(\circ) = (\circ)$ ... given
$(\times) = (\times)$ ... because $|mn| = |mr|$
$(\bullet) = (\bullet)$ ... third angle
$|mp| = |mp|$ ... common

$\Rightarrow$ $\triangle mnp$ is congruent to $\triangle mpr$... SAS
$\Rightarrow$ $|pn| = |pr|$... corresponding sides

(c)

① is the image of F under a central symmetry.

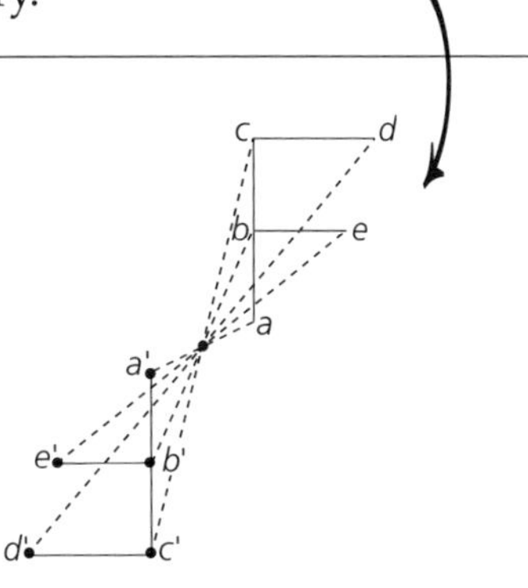

① is the image of F under a rotation of 180° also.

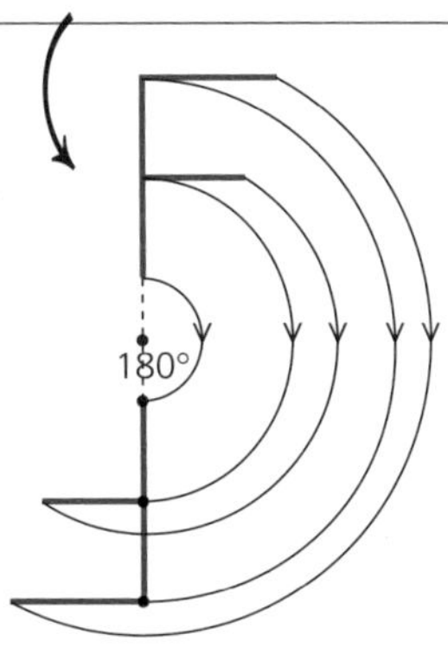

② is the image of F under an axial symmetry.

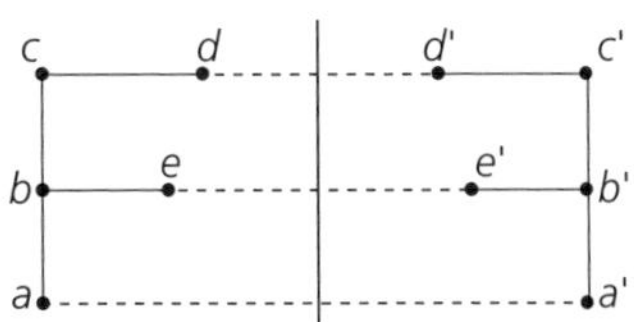

③ is the image of F under a translation.

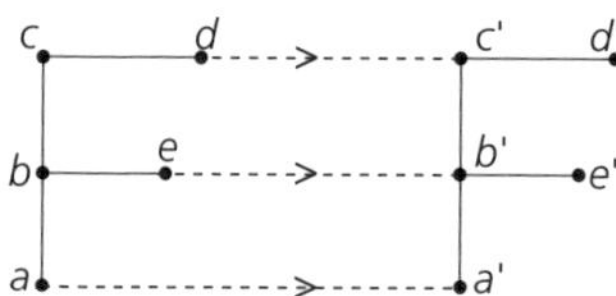

④ is the image of F under a rotation of 90° in an anti-clockwise direction.

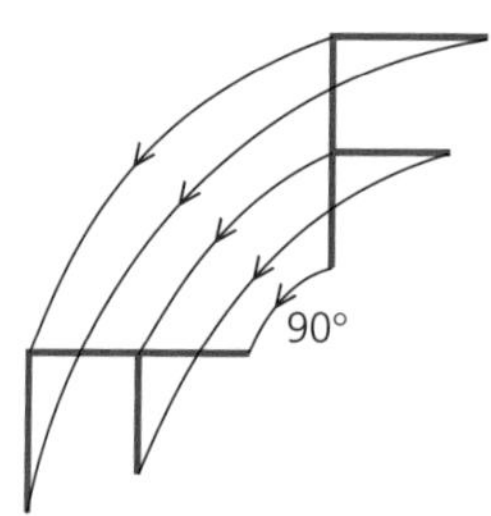

Solution to question 4

(a)

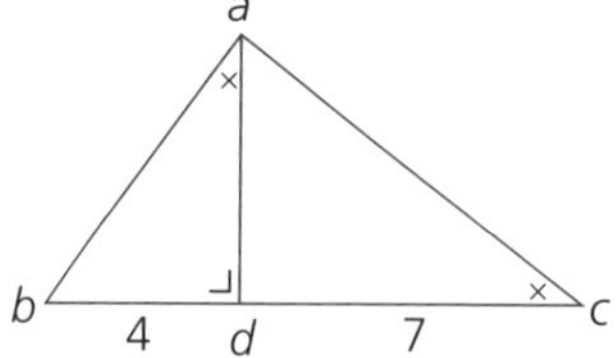

We are trying to find $|ad|$.

> **Important**
>
> $|ad|$ is a side on both $\triangle abd$ and $\triangle adc$. To find $|ad|$ therefore, we compare $\triangle abd$ and $\triangle adc$.

① Show the triangles are similar.

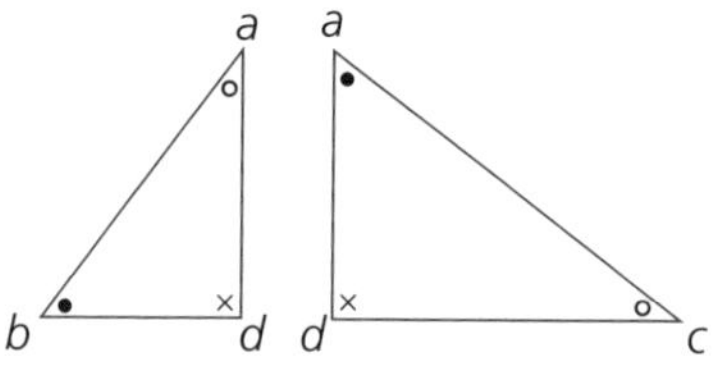

(×) = (×) ... both 90°
(•) = (•) ... 3rd angle
(○) = (○) ... given

As $\triangle abd$ and $\triangle adc$ are similar, the lengths of the corresponding sides are proportional.

② Be clear on which sides are proportional.

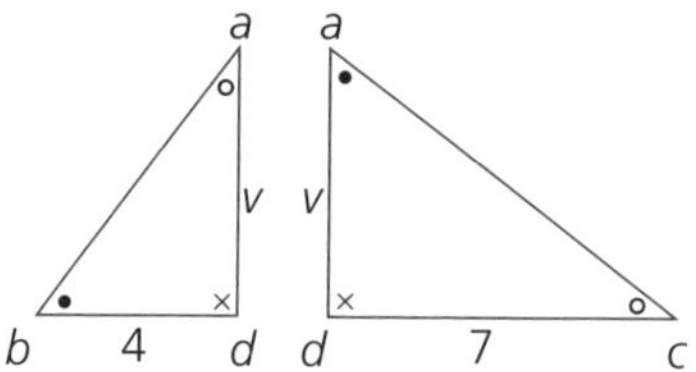

'4' corresponds with 'v' (on $\triangle adc$) ... both opposite (○)
'v' (on left $\triangle$) corresponds with '7'... both opposite (•)

③ Calculate $|ad|$.

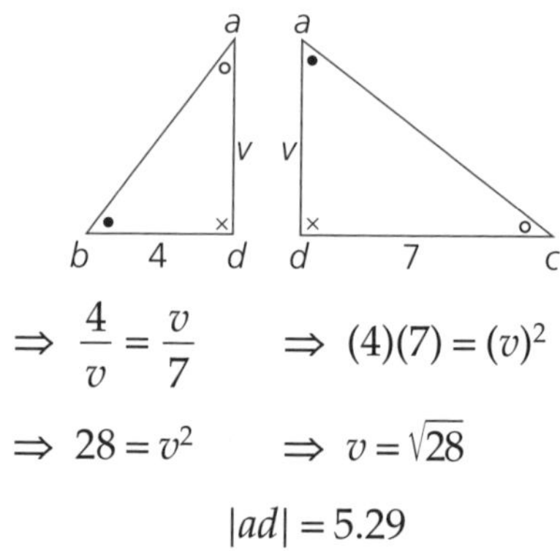

$\Rightarrow \dfrac{4}{v} = \dfrac{v}{7} \qquad \Rightarrow (4)(7) = (v)^2$

$\Rightarrow 28 = v^2 \qquad \Rightarrow v = \sqrt{28}$

$|ad| = 5.29$

(b)

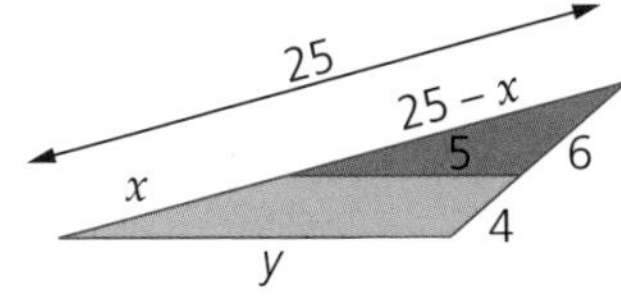

(i) Calculate $|pn|$ (call it x).

$$\frac{6}{4} = \frac{25 - x}{x}$$

$$\Rightarrow \quad (6)(x) = (25 - x)(4)$$

$$\Rightarrow \quad 6x = 100 - 4x$$

$$10x = 100 \quad \Rightarrow x = 10$$

$$\Rightarrow \quad |pn| = 10$$

(ii) Calculate $|pr|$ (call it y).

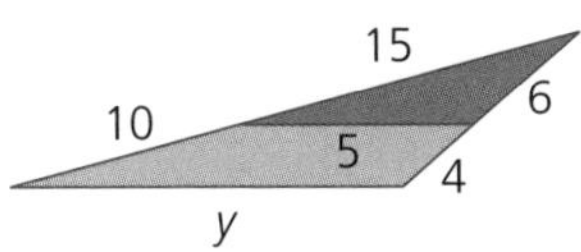

Because we are finding one of the horizontal lines, it is easier to draw both triangles separately.

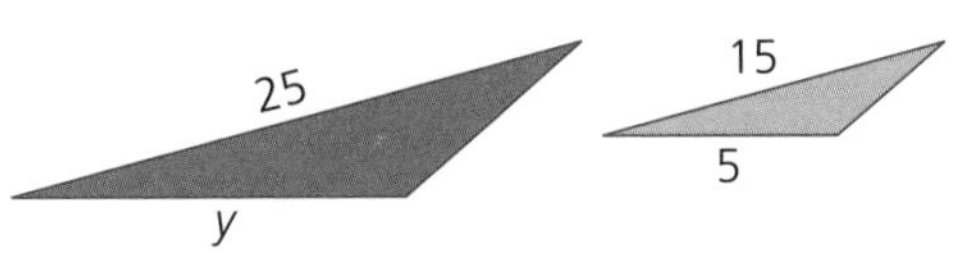

$$\frac{25}{15} = \frac{y}{5}$$

$$\Rightarrow \quad (15)(y) = (25)(5)$$

$$\Rightarrow \quad 15y = 125$$

$$\Rightarrow \quad y = \frac{125}{15} = 8.33$$

$$\Rightarrow \quad |pr| = 8.33$$

Solution to question 5

(a)

Area $\triangle mnp$ is 3 times area $\triangle tpr$.

(i) Calculate $|pr|$.

$*$ $|\angle mpn| = |\angle tpr|$ because they are vertically opposite.

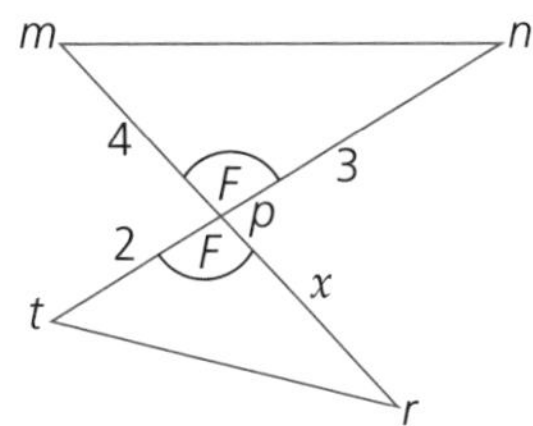

Area $\triangle mnp = 3(\text{area } \triangle ptr)$

$$\Rightarrow \frac{1}{2}(4)(3)(\cancel{\text{Sin} f}) = 3\left(\frac{1}{2}\right)(2)(x)(\cancel{\text{Sin} f})$$

$$\Rightarrow 6 = 3x \qquad \Rightarrow |pr| = 2$$

(ii) Calculate $|\angle mnp|$.

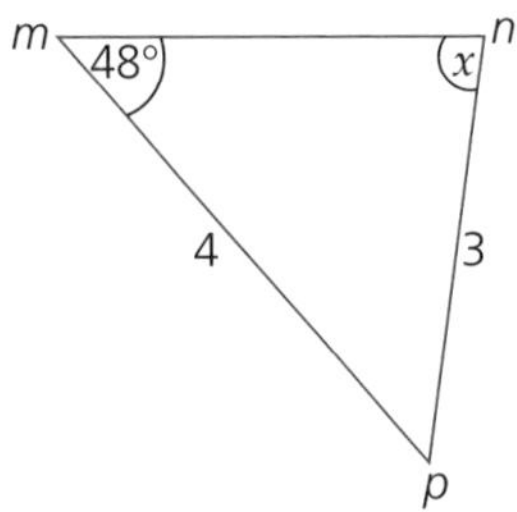

$$\frac{3}{\text{Sin } 48°} = \frac{4}{\text{Sin } x}$$

$\text{Sin } 48° = 0{\cdot}743$

$$3(\text{Sin } x) = 4(\text{Sin } 48)$$

$$\text{Sin } x = \frac{4(\text{Sin } 48)}{3}$$

$$x = 82°14'$$

$$\Rightarrow |\angle mnp| = 82°14'$$

(iii) Calculate $|mn|$.

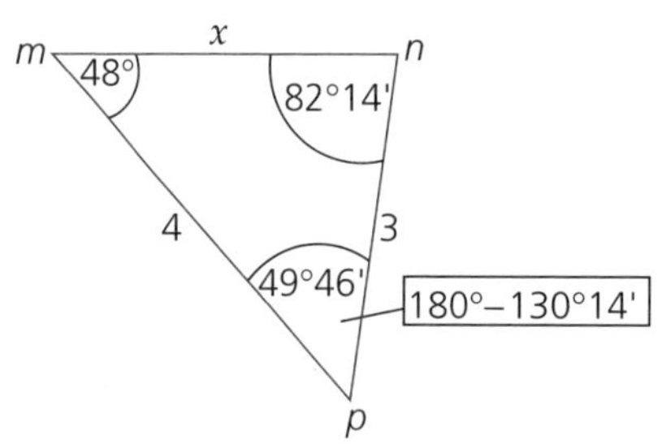

$$\frac{4}{\text{Sin } 82°14'} = \frac{x}{\text{Sin } 49°46'}$$

$$(4)(\text{Sin } 49°46') = (x)(\text{Sin } 82°14')$$

$\text{Sin } 49°46' = 0.7634$

$\text{Sin } 82°14' = 0.99$

$$\frac{(4)(\text{Sin } 49°46')}{\text{Sin } 82°14'} = x$$

$$\Rightarrow |mn| = 3.08$$

(iv) Find area $\triangle tpr$.

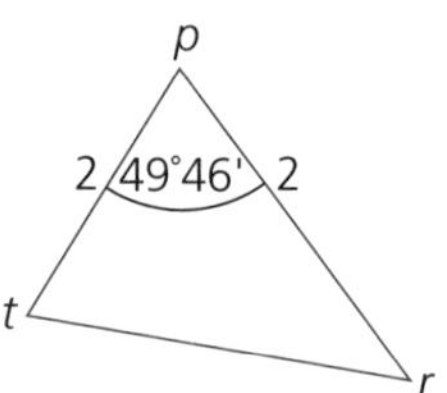

$$\text{Area} = \tfrac{1}{2}ab \text{ Sin } C$$

$$= \left(\tfrac{1}{2}\right)(2)(2)(\text{Sin } 49°46')$$

$$\Rightarrow \text{Area } \triangle tpr = 1.53$$

(b) Evaluate angle B if $\text{Sin } B = 0.829$ and $\text{Cos } B = -0.5592$

Here, Sin B is (+) and Cos B is (–).

* This only occurs in the 'S' quadrant.

90°
S All
180° 0°
360°
T C
270°

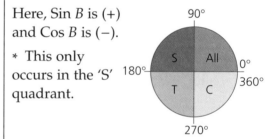

If $\text{Sin C} = 0.829 \quad C = 60°$

'S' quadrant $\rightarrow$ $B = 180° - 60°$

$B = 120°$

(c)

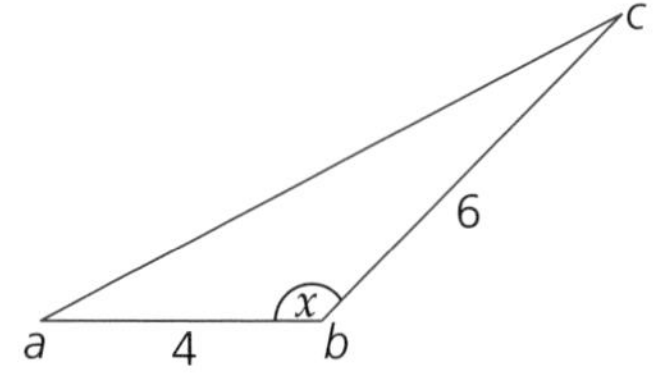

Area $\triangle abc = 10$. Find $|\angle abc|$.

Area $= \frac{1}{2}ab \text{ Sin } C$

$$\Rightarrow \left(\tfrac{1}{2}\right)(4)(6)(\text{Sin } x) = 10$$

$$\Rightarrow 12 \text{ Sin } x = 10$$

$$\Rightarrow \text{Sin } x = \frac{10}{12}$$

$$\Rightarrow x = 56°26'$$

Important

But from the diagram, we see that $|\angle abc| > 90°$.

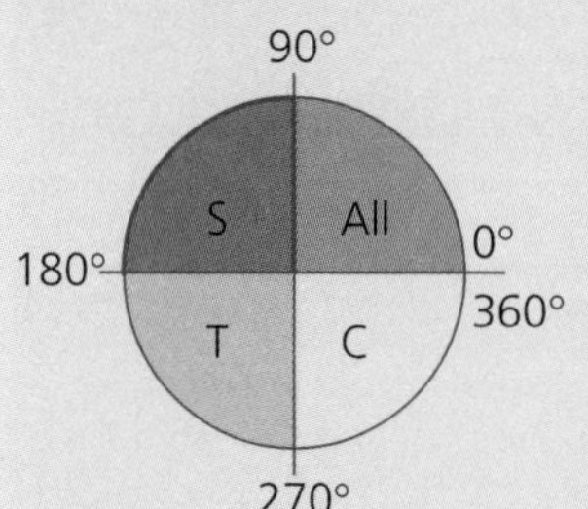

We see from the unit circle that Sin x is (+) in the 'All' and 'S' quadrants.

$\Rightarrow$ As $|abc| > 90°$, it must be in the 'S' quadrant.

'S' quadrant $\rightarrow$ $|\angle abc| = 180° - 56°26'$

$\Rightarrow |\angle abc| = 123°34'$

Solution to question 6

(a)

Age in years	1	2	3	4	5
No. of children	1	0	p	2	5

(i) The mean age is 4 yrs. Calculate p.

$$\text{Mean} = \frac{(1\times1)+(2\times0)+(3\times p)+(4\times2)+(5\times5)}{1+0+p+2+5}$$

$$= 4$$

$$\Rightarrow \frac{1+0+3p+8+25}{1+0+p+2+5} = 4$$

$$\Rightarrow \frac{3p+34}{p+8} = \frac{4}{1}$$

Cross-multiplying:

$(3p+34)(1) = (p+8)(4)$

$\Rightarrow 3p + 34 = 4p + 32 \quad \Rightarrow p = 2$

(ii) What is the mode age?

The mode age is 5 years because it has the highest frequency (of 5).

(iii) Illustrate the data on a pie chart.

Age in yrs	1	2	3	4	5
No. of children	1	0	2	2	5

Total number of children = 10
(1 + 0 + 2 + 2 + 5)

$$1 \text{ year old} = \frac{1}{10} \times \frac{360°}{1} = 36°$$

$$2 \text{ years old} = \frac{0}{10} \times \frac{360°}{1} = 0°$$

$$3 \text{ years old} = \frac{2}{10} \times \frac{360°}{1} = 72°$$

$$4 \text{ years old} = \frac{2}{10} \times \frac{360°}{1} = 72°$$

$$5 \text{ years old} = \frac{5}{10} \times \frac{360°}{1} = 180°$$

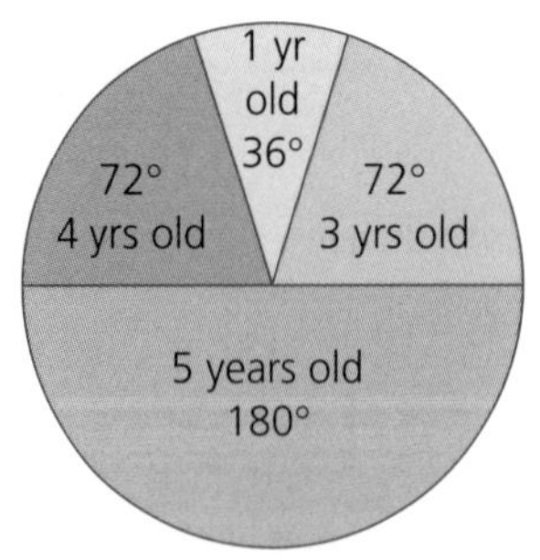

(b)

Age in yrs	0–20	20–50	50–55	55–70	70–90
No. of people	16	24	12	24	24

(i) Illustrate the data on a histogram.

Calculate the width of each group.

Group	Amount of numbers	Width
0–20	20	4
20–50	30	6
50–55	5	1 (smallest)
55–70	15	3
70–90	20	4

⇓

Age in years	0–20	20–50	50–55	55–70	70–90
No. of people	16	24	12	24	24
Width	4	6	1	3	4
Height	4	4	12	8	6
	(16 ÷ 4)	(24 ÷ 6)	(12 ÷ 1)	(24 ÷ 3)	(24 ÷ 4)

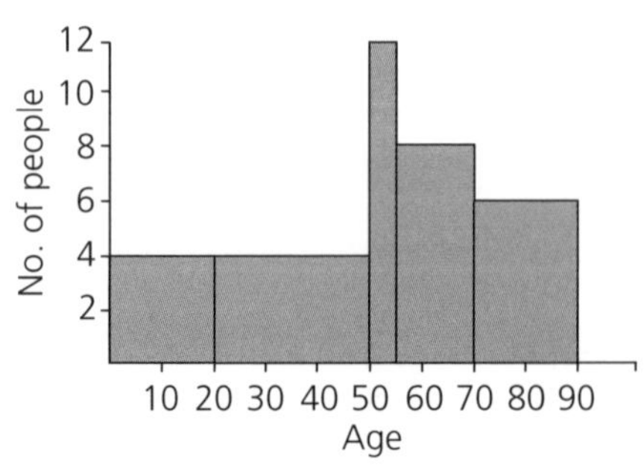

(ii) From the table, construct a cumulative frequency curve.

Age in yrs	0–20	20–50	50–55	55–70	70–90
No. of people	16	24	12	24	24

⇓

Age in yrs	< 20	< 50	< 55	< 70	< 90
No. of people	16	40	52	76	100

Cumulative Frequency Curve (ogive)

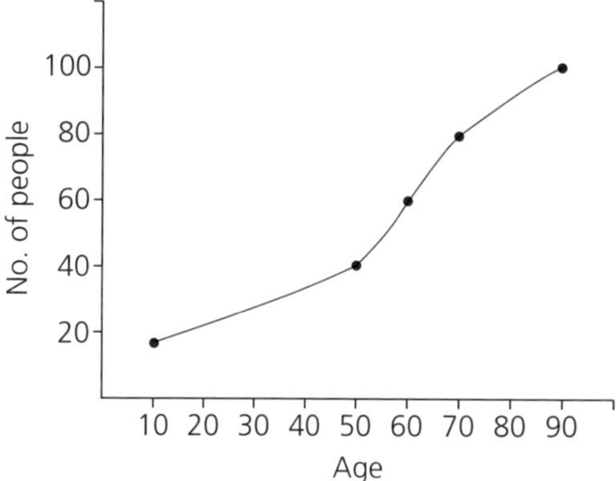

(iii)

(a) Calculate the median.

(b) Calculate the interquartile range.

(a) Median

Go to 50 on the vertical axis $\left(\frac{1}{2}\text{ way}\right)$.

The corresponding age is 54 years.

⇒ The Median age is 54 yrs old.

(b) Interquartile range

Go to $25\left(\frac{1}{4}\right)$ and $75\left(\frac{3}{4}\right)$ on the vertical axis.

⇒ Lower quartile = 33 years

Upper quartile = 69 years

⇒ Interquartile range = 36 yrs (69 – 33)

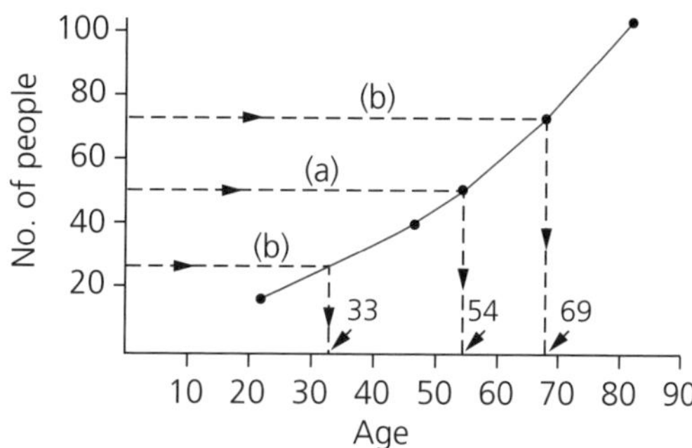

(c) Find the age of the eldest 30 people.

(d) Find how many people were less than 40 yrs old.

(c) What age were the eldest 30 people?

Go to 70 on the vertical axis.

From the graph below we find that the eldest 30 people were 63–90 years old.

(d) How many were less than 40 yrs old?

Go to 40 on the horizontal axis. From the graph below we find that 28 people were less than 40 years old.

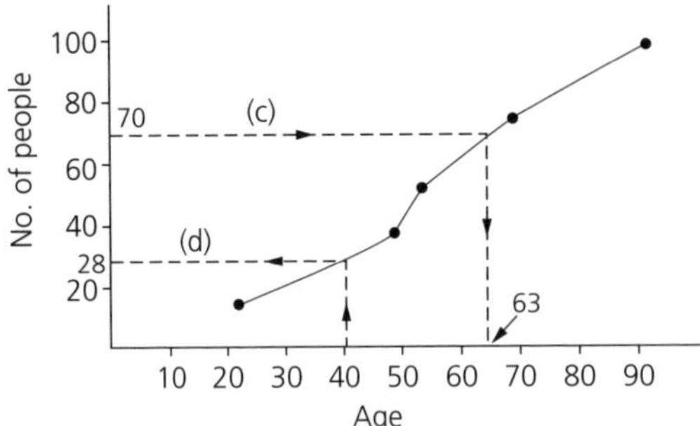

(c)

(i) The mean of 3, 4, 6, x and 8 is 5. Calculate x.

The 5 numbers have a mean of 5.

$\Rightarrow$ They add up to 25 (5×5).

$\Rightarrow 3+4+6+x+8=25 \Rightarrow x=4$

(ii) Find the median and mode.

Mode – The mode is 4 because it occurs most often.

Rearrange in order $\rightarrow$ 3, 4, 4, 6, 8

Median – The median is 4 as it is the middle number.